# THE RAILWAY CLOSURE

# CONTROVERSY

by

**E.A. Gibbins** M.C.I.T., M.I.L.T.

Published by:-


Leisure Products
11 Bedford Grove
Alsager
Stoke on Trent  ST7  2SR

ISBN 0-9521039-4-X

This branch line will be needed in the next war
*....but railways were screwed by Government in two Wars*

The Council says the line will be needed.......
*....if new industries come to the area*

Agriculture, industry and buses are subsidised in this area .....
*....but railways should be able to run at a profit*

As taxpayers, we are entitled to keep our loss making line ........
*.....but Ministers say no line will be subsidised*

This line is very busy on August Bank Holiday Monday ........
*.....but dead for most of the year*

Branch line trains are useful .........
*....when the car breaks down or the bus is cancelled*
*....if the roads are flooded*
*....in a bad winter*

Although this line lost money competing with horses ............
*....it only requires huge capital and imagination to pay its way*

Borrow a diesel from "elsewhere"
*.....they can revert to steam*

An anonymous expert says the line could be made to pay....
*.....unfortunately, he is not a railway expert*

The line would pay if it was modernised **and** fares were reduced
*.....higher costs, more passengers, but less revenue*

Rail fares are too high ............
*.....it will cost more by bus & take longer*

1,400 people sign a petition to keep the line .....
*.....fourteen times the level of usage*

This line was reprieved and equipped with modern diesels.....
*.....but user declined*

BR figures should be proved in a court of law.....
*......but objectors will still advance uncosted generalisations*

Dedicated to Irene with all my love and gratitude
for her continued encouragement in my research

The author wishes to thank those who assisted his research:

Public Record Office, House of Lords Record Office,
Chartered Institute of Transport Library, Keele University,
National Railway Museum, British Library & Newspaper Library,
London Metropolitan Archives, Isle of Wight Record Office,

Alsager, Birmingham, Crewe, Ellesmere Port,
Hanley, Liverpool, Manchester, Norwich, Somerset, Widnes libraries;

Rail Users Consultative Committees
(formerly known as Transport Users Consultative Committees - TUCC's)
for the
Eastern, Midlands, North Eastern, North Western, Southern & Western Areas

and many others.

Written in memory of
the many BR & BTC managers who tried to make railways viable,
despite inequitable Government policies and a scale of
unwarranted interference never experienced in any other industry.

Cover illustration by D.N. Moreton, B.A.

# CONTENTS

# INTRODUCTION

The UK has seen its' manufacturing industry, which was a world leader, virtually vanish. The consequential effect on railways is overlooked. Some of the residual rump of industry shows no regard for the welfare of the community, in their disposal of waste by-products. In contrast, BR was criticised for not immediately clearing rubbish thrown over fences onto railway land. Town centres decimated by shop closures attracted graffiti and vandalism, but no criticism. Comparable activity at closed stations led to bitter criticism of BR. We hear in radio and TV business programmes that: "there is not much activity in the City because *they* are down at Wimbledon, The Oval, Ascot, Henley, Wembley, etc.".

The historic principle of trade, commerce and industry: "the customer is always right" has almost disappeared. One is far more likely to be told: "you haven't maintained it properly" (without a scrap of evidence), that "you have misused it" or "it is not covered by the guarantee", after 12 months plus five minutes. Your guarantee lasts for about 10% of the life that you hope to get from your purchase. By analogy, if British Railways had guaranteed the punctuality of their trains to the same standard, they would have guaranteed them for the first 10% of a journey.

Recall Notices continue to appear in newspapers every week. Most are couched in similar language, usually referring to defects discovered in a "*small number*" of items during "*on-going quality assurance checks*". They do not explain why management systems failed to discover defects *before* goods found their way into consumer's hands. Invariably, these Notices attract little or no criticism. In marked contrast, all failures on railways received full criticism, frequently couched in sarcastic language. This is illogical, given the long time lapse between factory production and consumption, compared to minutes for a train between depot and station. Railway accidents incurring single fatalities, or even no fatalities, attracted several hundred times as much coverage as road accidents with greater fatality rates. The former are invariably described as disasters, the latter as tragic accidents.

Educational standards fell. The importance of the three R's, which are required for most jobs, was neglected in many schools. In the mid 1970's, a careers teacher, visiting industry and BR stations and depots was surprised to learn that even recruits to non clerical jobs on BR had to be able to read, write and use figures. (See also page 215).

Some critical letters to the media on railway subjects, can be disproved by research and statistics - or had they been written in a less emotive form, would have led to different conclusions. If a response based on research from another reader is not given equal space, the public will be less well informed. Radio personalities, who frequently got the time wrong, mixed up tapes and names, were unrelenting in criticism of any BR failing.

It was arrogant, for those in other professions to claim they had the expertise to proffer unsolicited advice to railway professionals. Their own industries were going down the drain, or given their policies, would eventually do so. A lack of skill in preserving or expanding their own business, in which, one assumes, they had been trained, did not prevent many from believing they could resolve the problems of others. Such worthies were not slow to quote media reports of railway complaints' statistics, without, of course, relating them to total user.  In contrast, their own industries published no data.  Anyone who believed that was because those industries are totally complaint free was very naive.

No other profession has been on the receiving end of so much gratuitous, ill qualified advice, as British Railways' managers.  Given that those in other professions could not solve their own problems and effectively compete with foreign companies, whence did they believe their railway expertise derived?  Explaining the economics of branch line working to one  businessman, he told me he knew what the customer wanted, because he travelled by train - how frequently, he did not say.  My journeys, had by then, aggregated to the million miles' level.  Moreover, when hearing uniformed nonsense, I was not slow to deliver the facts, backed by experience and market research.  He was informed that I knew how to drive a car, and maintain it, but it didn't qualify me to run General Motors.  To another who asked why BR did not run more trains from the Hope Valley to Sheffield, I pointed out that passengers would have to bear the cost.  He suggested that we run extra trains only in the peak.  He was graceful in admitting that he hadn't realised that the Hope Valley "peak" is the same period, albeit vastly less in volume, than anywhere in the country and there were already thousands of coaches standing idle outside the peak.

I have concluded that critics' advice can only stem from the playroom floor.  The belief that full size railways should be able to operate with similar ease was amply demonstrated by the bus company manager who would not disclose the basis of bus schedules.  He said that it was different for railways - they had their own track.  It was different in only one respect.  When the lines are blocked by causes which affect both rail and road - weather, accidents (involving road vehicles in both cases), vandalism, equipment breakdowns, etc. - rail, obliged to fund its own infrastructure, often has no convenient alternative route, unlike buses that have 220,000 miles available!  It is noticeable that the new franchisees have wasted no time in excluding from their rail performance statistics: "circumstances beyond our control" - an exclusion never conceded to BR but consistently accepted in respect of the bus, sea and air industries, as well as the rest of industry and commerce.

No other industry, in the private or public sector, has been subject to as much interference in day to day decisions as British Railways.   Interference did not begin after years of nationalisation, but began from Day One.  BR could not decide its own prices, which were held for 34 consecutive years by a Court of Law and Ministerial intervention, below the rate of inflation, which without dispute, the rest of industry was handsomely exceeding.  Ministers interfered in wages' negotiations, forcing wages *up* to levels BR had already declined to concede.  British Railways were denied a fair share of essential materials for ten years after the war, whilst competitors exceeded Government "limits". [See "*Blueprints for Bankruptcy*", Page 83 and "*Square Deal Denied*", Chapter 16].

BR began life virtually bankrupt due to Government's iniquitous and inequitable pre-war and wartime policies. [See "*Square Deal Denied*"].  They were nationalised on the cheap.  Government claimed to be buying railways from their owners, but instead required the industry to buy itself out of revenue, to purchase half a million life expired wagons for £43m from non railway companies (collieries & traders), to run the business so as to break even, and donate the assets to the State free of charge!  BR's entire capital was redeemable interest bearing loans.  No other industry was, or is, expected to redeem its *entire* capital.

BR was prevented from achieving profits by external interference, consequently redemption of capital and fixed interest payments thereon, became a crushing burden.

No other industry had so many customers on the "factory floor". I told a branch of the British Institute of Management visiting London Midland Region offices at Crewe in February 1979, that my job of Operations Officer was similar to a factory Production Manager. However, my "factory" was 3,000 miles long, had no roof, no heating and customers at the elbow of the staff. I invited them to try operating in *that* environment. They readily admitted that they hadn't realised that. Neither had several million others!

All other businesses facing a demand in excess of supply, increase prices to capitalise thereon. British Railways was urged to meet peak commuter demand by increasing supply - run even more trains - increasing costs to achieve the same income. Inevitably, losses would have increased. Naturally, these "experts", including, notably, Rail Users Watchdogs, did not, of course, expect fares to rise - rather they urged fare reductions.

Branch lines attracted an undue share of unsolicited advice which was especially flawed and came only *after* closure was proposed. Criticism of closures often bordered on paranoia. BR's attempts to rid themselves of dead wood were delayed by objectors - most of whom, by definition, were *not* using the line in question. In all cases - not one person, company, nor local authority *promised* to make increased use of the threatened railway. There were hints that if charges were reduced there may be more traffic. However, the lines were losing money at existing prices! All wanted it to be there - losing money, subsidised by others - as a standby to be used when other means of transport failed. No local authority bought a line to demonstrate the expertise they professed to have.

My research reveals many instances of counter criticism to objections and significant responses by British Railways to objectors' views which were not picked up by critical authors and others, who concentrated purely on points made by objectors, as if to imply that managers had no effective answer. Whilst BR figures were criticised, objectors' figures (which were few), and statements have not been subject to analysis - until now.

Inferences by Ministers that uneconomic lines had been kept open by management decision were wide of the mark. Many loss making lines were kept open by the Direction of the MoT and his agents. Where closed lines have been taken over by preservation groups, they are heavily dependent on free labour, do not operate year round services, often secure Grants or other help from local authorities and other bodies, and charge fares which exceed those charged on BR. [See "*Blueprints for Bankruptcy*", Page 205].

Whenever railway closures are mentioned, there is an automatic assumption that one is speaking of Beeching closures. Pre-war privately owned railways closed lines and stations, and so did BR long before Beeching became its Chairman. Some closures which had been rejected by Watchdogs and Ministers appeared in Beeching's list. which also included closures which had already been approved or were in hand. Closures accelerated under Beeching partly due to the continued expansion of private motoring, but also because a change in the law reduced the role of Consultative Committees whose Public Hearings had created mind boggling delays. Papers at the Public Record Office relating to Beeching era closures are still not available to public access under the thirty year rule.

The ten lines examined in this book had a number of features in common :-

1. All were proposed before the Beeching Reshaping Report was published.
2. Most were built, amalgamated or expanded in the 1860-1880 period - "railway mania" - when insufficient attention was paid to potential viability, and constructional standards slipped. [See Smiles, Page 441 et seq.]
3. Those which were independent were constantly in financial difficulties, even when competing with the horse. Those which were part of an existing company had the effect of worsening the company's finances. Most of the ten were saved from the receivers in the last century by being taken over, one tried to get itself taken over.
4. Most were in areas where agriculture, fishing and even manufacturing industry was subsidised. They couldn't see why BR could not operate profitably in these areas, but were expected to survive on interest bearing loans.
5. The basis of objection to closure mostly followed similar lines:-
   - Industrial development was just around the corner, if BR would carry on making losses for just a year or two longer. In two cases which were reprieved, each for ten years, there was no improvement, but local authorities were still hoping.
   - Diesels would eliminate losses, or, at worst, reduce them to a level which BR should subsidise from "elsewhere". In two closure cases, reviewed in this book, which were reprieved, diesels were introduced but losses increased.
   - In most cases, no prior suggestion had been made that services needed improving.
   - Fares, already below the inflation rate, should be reduced to some unspecified level, unlike prices outside BR, which rose unrelentingly, driving up BR costs.
   - Costs could be cut, by vague unquantified measures, so that losses would be less.
   - The line was needed in severe winters, (which come every 7-8 years), when even bread came by train, Spring and bad memories ended gratitude and usage.
   - Local authorities and commerce having failed to attract tourists, blamed BR for not abstracting them from other routes and resorts, which would have made another line, instead of the one proposed for closure, or, possibly both, unprofitable.
   - Experts were found who *knew* the solution. Most had no railway experience. Some wisely remained anonymous.
6. Apart from a short section of line purchased by preservation groups in three cases, the objectors who were convinced a line would be viable, refrained from buying a line and operating a service. The three instances concerned do not operate a daily service throughout the year and enjoy some free labour.

There can be no doubt that, if railways had not been nationalised, the owners of the Big Four would have wasted no time in closing lines which were unprofitable, and high on their list would have been those covered in this book. Indeed, they would have been obliged to do so, because of their responsibility to shareholders. There would have been no circus of hearings. Of course, Government may have stepped in to subsidise these lines, had they considered them as vital as many locals and their MP's have since claimed. Since Government was happily handing out taxpayers' money to subsidise agriculture, fishing and industry, often, in the same areas, that would have been appropriate.

# ABBREVIATIONS

| | | | |
|---|---|---|---|
| AA | Automobile Association | MP | Member of Parliament |
| AGM | Annual General Meeting | MS&LR | Manchester, Sheffield & Lincolnshire |
| BR | British Railways (BTC subsidiary) | | Railway |
| BRB | British Railways Board | NBPI | National Board for Prices & Incomes |
| BTC | British Transport Commission | NER | North Eastern Railway |
| col | column in Hansard | NFU | National Farmers Union |
| CSO | Central Statistical Office | NRM | National Railway Museum Library |
| CTCC | Central Transport Consultative | NUR | National Union of Railwaymen |
| | Committee | OPCS | Office for Population Censuses & |
| cwt | hundredweight (5% of a ton) | | Surveys |
| DMU | Diesel multiple unit | OPRAF | Office of Passenger Rail Franchising |
| DoT | Department of Transport | pa | per annum |
| ECITO | European Central Inland Transport | PRO | Public Record Office |
| | Organisation | PSO | Public Service Obligation (Grant to |
| ECMT | European Conference of MoT's | | BR after 1974 for uneconomic lines) |
| EEC | European Economic Community | PSV | Public Service Vehicle |
| EMU | Electric multiple unit | QC | Queens Counsel |
| GER | Great Eastern Railway | RAC | Royal Automobile Club |
| GNR | Great Northern Railway | RDA | Railway Development Association |
| GWR | Great Western Railway | RDS | Railway Development Society |
| HGV | Heavy goods vehicle | RDC | Rural District Council |
| IoW | Isle of Wight | Rly | Railway |
| LB&SCR | London, Brighton & South Coast Rly | RPI | Retail Price Index |
| LCC | London County Council | S&DR | Somerset & Dorset Railway |
| LMR | London Midland Region (of BR) | SER | South Eastern Railway |
| LMS | London, Midland & Scottish Rly | SRUBLUK | Society for the Re-Invigoration of |
| LNER | London & North Eastern Railway | | Unremunerative Branch Lines in the UK |
| L&NWR | London & North Western Railway | TUCC | Transport Users Consultative |
| LPTB | London Passenger Transport Board | | Committee |
| L&SWR | London & South Western Railway | UDC | Urban District Council |
| M&GN | Midland & Great Northern | UIC | International Union of Railways |
| min | minute | UN | United Nations |
| MoT | Minister of Transport | vol | volume |

## NOTES

Before 1971, there were 240 pence or 20 shillings to the £. Six pence was shown as 6d which equalled 2.5p. One shilling was shown as 1/- which equalled 5p. One shilling and sixpence was shown as 1/6, or 1s.6d. One pound, ten shillings and six pence was shown as £1.10.6.

[..........] Used, following text, to indicate the source.

(..........) Text enclosed thus, was not part of the quoted text, but is included for clarification.

Italics used throughout are the author's.

**P**age is used when the Page number is that of the source

**p**age is used when referring to another page in this book.

Maps are not to scale.

# Chapter 1                             The Background

Before a public railway in Great Britain can be constructed, it is necessary to obtain an Act of Parliament, (usually called an Enabling Act). Before a Bill is read, the route must be surveyed, plans deposited with local authorities concerned, notice of intention to apply for a Bill advertised, and notice served on each owner or occupier of property which it is proposed to take compulsorily. The Bill, plans, estimates and details of the proposals must be deposited with the Parliamentary examiners of Private Bills and a deposit of 5% of the estimated cost of the railway is required to be made as security for its completion. When the Bill becomes an Act, the promoters are incorporated into a Statutory Company and the Act takes the place of an ordinary Company's Memorandum and Articles of Association. The Act authorises the Company to acquire by compulsion, if the price is not agreed, the lands, way-leaves and other rights described, to raise capital and to work the railway. The Company is placed under a number of obligations. It must not undertake businesses beyond the scope of its authority from Parliament, and it must satisfy the MoT on matters connected with public safety, such as signalling arrangements and the suitability of bridges, tunnels and other works. The chief obligations after the initial stages are in relation to rates and fares chargeable to its users, and the compiling and publishing of accounts and statistics of its working. [Wood & Stamp, Page 26]

## Inflated Costs of Railways

Claims for compensation were made by landowners, clergy and farmers, for the purchase of land, and, if a railway passed close by, progressively increased on the most fantastic grounds. [Rogers, Page 97].

A Bill is remitted to a Committee of Members and many have a right to appear as objectors to the Bill as a whole or seek the deletion or modification of powers sought, or have clauses inserted for their protection. Land owners whose property is to be acquired or who fear a railway will harm the amenities of their property, local authorities, trade associations, and persons with whom the railway may compete are entitled to be heard. Contested proceedings before a Parliamentary Committee are expensive, it has frequently happened that "ransom" terms have been given to objectors rather than that the promoters should stand the racket of a prolonged fight in Committee. [Wood & Stamp, Page 28].

Heavy expense was incurred in the acquisition of land and compensation for loss of profits to other interests including existing transport agencies. The early railways were strenuously opposed by the land owning interest who generally supported the proprietors of canals and turnpike roads. The great land-owners who then largely controlled the affairs of Parliament, not only retarded railway construction but placed many burdens on the authorised railways, which are still borne by them. Land had to be fenced off and station accommodation built in towns where land value had a high cost. More expense was caused when increased traffic necessitated widening. [Wood & Stamp, Pages 29 & 31]

Opponents to the London & Birmingham Railway Bill were 'conciliated' by paying them £0.75m - treble the original estimate of the land cost. Parliamentary costs were £72,868. Another line, "like most others, was greatly fleeced by landowners who sought to extort the most exorbitant prices for their land". "Landowners discovered that railways were a golden mine to them". [Smiles, Pages 328, 418 & 431].

The GNR had spent £0.5m - on Parliamentary and legal costs - and not lifted one sod. During 1847, nearly 1,200 contracts with landowners had to be arranged and of some of these gentry, their acuteness as to the means of wringing out money from a railway company was beyond anything which he - Baxter, GNR solicitor - or any other individual could have conceived. Baxter said the cost of railway construction in the Metropolis is exceptionally great and suburban traffic, though expansive is not very remunerative. [Grinling, Pages 62, 70 & 443].

Among professions which gained hugely from railway mania, the legal profession ranks high. It is ironic that 19th century lawyers made huge profits by *opposing* Parliamentary Bills for the construction and *opening* of railways, whereas their 20th century counterparts profited by *opposing* line *closures*!

Brassey built 60 miles of a difficult railway line in Italy for the same sum - £430,000 - as it cost to put through the Bill for the Lancashire & Yorkshire Railway. [Faith, Page 22].

In June 1920, the MoT told Parliament that the cost of building railways per mile, was - UK: £34,000, France: £31,000, Prussia: £26,000, USA: £14,000. [Hansard vol. 130, col. 2453].

In 1930, the Royal Commission on Transport stated: British railways suffered as pioneers - due to heavy capital expenditure, extremely high prices for land and compensation in respect of depreciation - real or fancied. [Cmd 3751, Page 16].

## Overbuilding

Branch lines were often built by local groups who saw that some railways were making, or promising, good profits. Many were promoted by 'trunk' railway companies to block an approach route of a competitor into an industrial area. Some branches, having run into financial troubles, were absorbed by 'big brothers', as blocking tactics, picking up a route and assets at knock down prices. It was *possible* that an insolvent rural route may later spawn new industry. Unfortunately, that did not happen too often. These scenarios meant that the branches concerned were then subsidised by trunk route traffic. Some companies having sought an Act to construct a railway, as a blocking tactic, took no action to build it, therefore Parliament took steps to restrict the practice in the Railway Consolidated Clauses Act 1863, and the Abandonment of Railways Acts 1850 & 1869.

Most of the unprofitable lines which the BTC is now closing were uneconomic to build in the first place, other lines have failed to survive competition with road transport. [Economist, 24.1.59, Page 335].

Great Britain had a multiplicity of railway lines, rarely over the most direct routes, and competing with each other. In contrast, the French "planned a coherent system before a single mile of main line track had been laid". They were not State owned: "French railways were privately owned until just before World War II". [Faith, Pages 72 & 73]. Had the UK Government paused, after the first tranche had been authorised, and done likewise, there would have been fewer uneconomic lines a century later. Certainly, they would have done well to reflect on the prospects of so many lines in rural areas. Given that our Government was lacking in foresight, there was no valid reason to block mergers and local monopolies since the 1844 Act limited profits to 10%, a principle which never applied to shipping, waterways, canals or turnpikes, nor to motor transport.

"Once the major British lines had been built, a mere 25 years after opening the Liverpool & Manchester Railway, contractors had to go abroad or conjure up new lines in Britain, usually unnecessary and uneconomic lines. Contractors' Lines soon, and rightly, got a bad name. Promoters and contractors desperately needed new schemes, but all the most viable had already been constructed. So they were left with a rag bag of inevitably unsound projects - including contractors lines". [Faith, Page 92/93].

Many branch lines literally served the same villages along parallel routes, albeit, often some distance away from villages they served. Low traffic potential meant that services were invariably infrequent, which as, originally, there was no real alternative, was not a handicap. However, the advent of motor transport changed that. If they were economic in the earlier years, the combined effects of extraction of traffic to road and attempts to retain rail traffic by operating more frequent services would inevitably widen the gap between income and expenditure. The closure of branch lines generally created no heavy burden for bus services, and many replacement bus services ceased operation in their turn.

Governments failed to give adequate direction on route selection. Hence, the UK ended up with many railways laid over some disadvantageous routes. Other countries saw the long term advantages of railways and avoided that problem. It is usually pleaded that this happened because the UK was first in the field, but the policies continued in respect of subsequent railways even after other countries had initiated wiser policies. Moreover, even self educated George Stephenson saw the longer term possibilities, because he insisted that all railways with which he was associated were laid to a standard gauge, even when they were being built far apart. ["*Square Deal Denied*", Page 13]. "Time and time again, Parliament blocked proposed direct routes". [Grinling, Page 215].

*"Too many branch lines* - In Reports of all our railways for last year, we read the same tale - bad times and increased competition. It was equally certain that all our companies running out innumerable branch lines into others' districts would run down one another and would do so all the more desperately in bad times. How can it pay if a train carries ten passengers. We could be proud of the marvels, but they did not pay". [Times 17.8.1858].

Early railway development led to "a dense network to minimise horse transport; even then there was excessive construction and many services did not pay. Stations were serving a radius of $2^1/_2$ miles". [BTC 1961 Report, Paras 13 & 14].

In 1930, the Royal Commission on Transport stated: Stations often had to be constructed at inconvenient places remote from the centre of towns, (due to local opposition). The consequences were either capital is unremunerative or higher charges ensue. Excessive wasteful competition was fostered by Government. [Cmd 3751, Page 17].

## Legislation

Under an 1832 Act, railway companies had to pay a discriminatory tax - the Railway Passenger Duty. No similar tax was imposed on competing trams or buses when they appeared, hence rail fares were inflated by Government policy. This tax was not removed until 1929, after nearly sixty years of complaint by railways and users. Even then, companies had to use the capitalised value of the abolished tax to help to create employment in a period of depression to help UK industry which couldn't compete with imports in the home market or in foreign markets. ["*Square Deal Denied*", Page 18].

The **Construction of Future Railways Act 1844**, Sec.6: directed railways to run trains, calling at every station at cheap fares. Had these "Parliamentary Trains" been of commercial value, railways would have introduced them of their own initiative. They were operated by BR, despite very poor loadings, until the provision was repealed in 1962.

Acts were passed to restrict attempts to abandon or delay projected lines :-

**Abandonment of Railways Act 1850**

Sec.1 Where it has been found that such railways cannot be carried on with advantage ...... and it is expedient that facilities be given for the abandonment of such railway or part of railway. A company whose railway or part of railway has not been commenced, may with the consent of three-fifths of the shareholders apply to the Railway Commissioners setting out details or grounds for abandonment.

**Railway Consolidated Clauses Act 1863**

Sec.20 Required railways to seek approval if they wished to delay construction.

**Railway Companies Act 1867**

Sec.31 The Abandonment of Railways Act, 1850, shall extend to all companies authorised to make railways by an Act of Parliament passed before the present session. The Board of Trade is not obliged to authorise abandonment.

**Railway (Extension of Time) Act 1868**

Allows a company to apply to the Board of Trade for time extension to build a railway.

**Abandonment of Railways Act 1869**

Doubts have arisen as to whether a company may be wound up on the petition of a creditor. It is expedient to remove such doubts.

Sec.4 Where a Warrant - authorising abandonment - has been granted under the principal Acts (1850 and 1867), a petition for winding up such company may be presented under the Companies Acts 1862 and 1867.

"The 1867 Act applies only to Railways authorised before 1867, of which construction has not been completed". "Jurisdiction rests with the Railway & Canal Commission, if railways withdraw reasonable facilities, the Commission can require reinstatement". [DoT Memos 19.7.29 & 30.7.29, PRO: MT6/3465]. They did not have that power. (See page 17).

"Abandonment of Railways is dealt with mainly by the Acts of 1850 & 1869, but it appears that this legislation applies to incorporations previous to 1867. The **Land Clauses Act 1845** required railways to offer surplus land, which was not in towns or had not been built upon, back to original owners, and if they refused, to adjoining owners. It is the obligations of railway companies - such as fencing, bridges, tunnels and works - which have to be got rid of, before a line can be abandoned. Until legal sanction is obtained, those obligations continue". [Railway Gazette, 9.8.29]

The question of the MoT's power to authorise abandonment was put to Law Officers in 1922 - their opinion was that the MoT had no powers. [DoT Memo 4.7.29, PRO: MT6/3465].

Under the **Regulation of Forces Act, 1871**, railways were taken over by Government for the duration of the 1914-18 war. This iniquitous sequestration was, later, to prove the origin of ruin for many rural lines. No other industry was subject to such penal terms. Rolling stock was sent abroad to war zones by Government, some never returned, whilst most was held abroad for years after the war, and most required substantial expenditure to restore it to operational condition. Branch line tracks were lifted by Government decree and sent to war zones to be relaid for military use by British railwaymen sent for the purpose. It took railways ten years to recover from the excessive wear and tear. This iniquitous policy was to be repeated in the 1939-45 war. [See "*Square Deal Denied*"].

Prior to the 1914-18 war, Government began overtly to subsidise the sale of motor vehicles to the public as well as making purchases for war use. Immediately the war ended, the country was flooded with surplus ex-military motor transport - lorries, buses, cars, motor cycles, sold at knock down prices, some in mint condition. This abundance of transport was used without having to contribute to road costs, and without regulation or control such as applied to railways. Road transport drivers could, and did, work hours without limit, whilst the Government imposed an eight hour day on all railway staff, not merely drivers. This increased railway costs, at a time when traffic was standing waiting for wagons, when thousands were still held abroad by the military. It opened the door for the infant road transport industry. Branch lines, many dependent on being subsidised by trunk routes, were bound to suffer first and hardest as their wages costs rocketed. Buses on rural routes had a big impact on branch lines. [See also "*Square Deal Denied*"].

**Companies Consolidation Act 1908**, Sec. 267 provided for winding up unregulated companies which would include companies incorporated by Act of Parliament and in fact tramway and waterworks companies have been wound up under the Companies Act. Sec. 267 does not exclude Railway Companies incorporated by Act of Parliament from the definition of unregulated companies, which seems to date back to the Companies Act 1862. Under the Abandonment of Railways Act 1869, petition for winding up may be presented under the Companies Act if a warrant has been granted for abandonment. [PRO: MT6/3465 1929-30].

**Ministry of Transport Act, 1919,** Sec 20: "The Minister may hold such inquiries as he considers necessary for the purposes of this Act". This section was referred to in Sec. 90 of the 1962 Transport Act, which was prayed in aid by objectors to the S&DR closure. (See page 178). There was no reference to closures in the 1919 Act, which was passed to set up the Ministry and give it powers which placed it in a position to merge railways. The 1919 Act refers only to Inquiries and not Public Inquiries. The first such Inquiry was not in public and concerned the payment of compensation to railways sequestrated in 1914 for the duration of the war. There was no need for it, as the 1871 Act precisely specified the extent of compensation. It was a scandalous ploy to enable the Government to escape its legal obligations. (See "*Square Deal Denied*"). In all probability, the clause was inserted with that specific objective in mind.

10

**Railways Act 1921** established a court of law to determine freight charges. The imposed rate structure facilitated creaming-off of profitable traffic by hauliers. Coupled with unregulated road transport whose infrastructure was subsidised by municipal rates, and through them by railways, it led inevitably to a steady decline in freight traffic which was subsidising branch line operations. The Act imposed Standard Revenue limitation - i.e. the 1913 profits - on profits in perpetuity putting branch lines at greater risk. The level of Standard Revenue was not inflation linked. [See *"Square Deal Denied"*].

During the past 100 years, there have been 200 public Acts dealing with the regulation of railways. [1930 Royal Commission on Transport, Cmd 3751, Page 18].

"At present, railways are obliged to keep all lines running and maintain services. They cannot abandon lines without the approval of the Railway & Canal Commission". [DoT Memo 7.12.38 - PRO: MT6/2876]. They were not obliged to do so. (See page 17).

**Transport Act 1947** specified procedures for closure of road, but not rail services.

Sec.2 (2) The BTC may do anything which, in their opinion, is necessary to facilitate the proper conduct of their business.

Sec.2 (7) The BTC may dispose of any part of the undertaking, which in their opinion, is not required for the discharge of their duties.

Sec.3 (1) The BTC's duty is to provide ....... an economical, integrated system of transport. (This was bound to lead to proposals to close lightly used lines).

Sec.3 (3) The BTC must give not less than one month's notice before discontinuing any regular road goods service.

Sec.3 (4) All parts shall form one undertaking. The BTC must pay its way, *taking one year with another*. (This encouraged users to delay closures and fare increases).

Sec.6 (7) Set up Consultative Committees with powers "to consider any matter".

Sec.6 (8) Gave power to the Minister to give such Directions to the BTC as he thinks fit as to the recommendations of the CTCC & TUCC's.

The Act did not provide for public hearings by TUCC's. If they opposed closure, the MoT decided whether to overrule BR, and usually did. What began by a response to a CTCC request to consider one closure, expanded to cover all closures with costly consequences.

**Transport Act 1953** was intended to "give BR freedom", but did not address costly delays in closing lines. The DoT file on the Draft Bill for the 1953 Act reveals that "The main principle is that road haulage should be allowed to expand to the extent that may be justified by demand and BR should effect economies to offset the loss of traffic". [PRO: MT62/138]. (This was only valid if Government foresaw that BR could not avoid traffic loss, due to statutory rates control). The file refers to an Economist article criticising the retention of BR's common carrier obligations, and reveals that Ministers and Civil Servants could not see how *"these obligations bear so hardly upon railways, which would not turn away traffic, just as hauliers do not, although they have no common carrier obligation"*. (Hauliers refused empty crates, and traffic to remote areas. BR could not refuse nor price up to cover costs. Cabinet Minutes on 14th

December 1938, reveal that they were given evidence of this). The MoT wrote to the Prime Minister: "*Had talked to Economist, who said the Bill was unjustifiable unless we were prepared to relieve BR of all obligations: common carrier, prohibition of undue preference, and so see out-and-out competition. This would lead to outlying and sparsely populated districts paying more for railway services than towns*". (Only true if hauliers rejected traffic, leaving BR with no competition because traffic was uneconomic. It is only one example of Government's role in BR's financial demise).

## Transport Act 1962

Sec.22 The MoT may make Grants up to £450m to BR to meet any deficit for a period of five years. The Board shall conduct their business so as to place themselves in a position that revenue will be sufficient to meet charges taking one year with another.

Sec.56 (7) Where it is intended to discontinue all passenger services from any station or line, BR must give six weeks notice and inform a TUCC.

Sec.56 (8) If anyone objects, a closure must not proceed until the TUCC has reported to the MoT.

Sec.56 (9) The TUCC will report to the MoT on possible hardship.

Sec.56 (13) Oral objections to be held in public. (These were not "*Public Inquiries*", but committee meetings held in public. They were often called Inquiries or Hearings).

Sec.90 The MoT may hold Inquiries for purposes of powers under this Act, as if they were purposes of the 1919 Act, Sec.20. (Such Inquiries are usually conducted by a QC)

Whilst, not admitted, Sec.22 had to be inserted because their policy had ensured that BR had already lost £643m from control of charges alone. [See "*Blueprints for Bankruptcy*", Page 192]

This Act ended the closure role of the CTCC and limited the TUCC's role in closures to reporting on hardship to the Minister. Hitherto, TUCC's made recommendations to the CTCC, to review and pass to the MoT, or refer back to the TUCC. The procedure seemed the most convoluted system a bureaucrat could devise - but they made it worse. In 1965, "two steps were added : the MoT scrutinises all proposals before statutory announcement to the public and all proposals are referred to new Regional Economic Planning Councils and Boards, adding to the time before a decision is made". [BRB 1965 Report, Para. 16].

The **1968 Transport Act** provided for the first time, Grants or Subsidies for loss making lines retained for social or other reasons. The **1974 Railways Act** endorsed the arrangement but modified the methodology. (See pages 195 & 196).

## The Rural Transport Bill - 1955
[Hansard vol. 547, cols. 699-779]

Some ideas to prevent or delay closures defy belief. A classic was this private member's Bill tabled by Archer Baldwin. Implementation would have increased losses.

- Clause 2 was a gem : "*It enables a local authority to request the Transport Tribunal to ask the BTC to show cause why a railway service should be discontinued. If the local authority is slow to move and there is any other body of railway users who want to prevent a railway being closed, they can do so*".

- Clause 4 "*Requires the Transport Tribunal to hold a public local inquiry*". (The Tribunal was a court of law. Other industries serving the public were not required to go before a court to request permission to close. It was fully committed in hearing BTC applications to increase fares and charges which were trailing inflation indices by up to 41 points, and delayed increases by an aggregate $12^3/_4$ years in 20 years! They envisaged one overworked Tribunal replacing nine TUCC's which were already delaying unavoidable closures for an average of 2-3 years. MP's were told by a Minister that the Tribunal President said they could not possibly take on the task).
- Clause 5 related to Light Railways "*enabling traffic to be carried without applying out of date regulations relating to signalling, level crossings etc. It should be possible to operate with traffic lights at 60-70 mph particularly with light vehicles which can be more easily stopped*". (Signalling regulations were not regarded as 'out of date' or irrelevant by MoT Inspectors when there was an accident, if they had not been fully applied. I am unaware of any evidence that steel wheels on steel rails can be brought to a stand when a 'traffic light' changes 240 metres ahead, which is the safe braking distance of a rubber tyred vehicle at 60 mph).

Asked about children getting to school, the promoter said the trains could stop nearer to schools (climbing down into the cess and trooping miles over fields!). He envisaged trains would stop where there is a road or footpath - about every mile and claimed that light weight vehicles would cost £9,000, or £5-6,000 if ordered in batches of six! (No motor nor rolling stock manufacturer could have kept solvent tooling up to supply in sixes. Stops placed a mile apart would not compete with bus stops. He identified no supplier).

Other comments by MP's included:
- Have always been in favour of closing unremunerative lines. When we say that branch lines should be closed, we are thinking of those in other people's constituencies, but take a very different view when the closure is in our own constituency.
- BR should not be allowed to close a line until they have proved it in the normal British way, with the calling of evidence, cross examination and with reasons given for decisions at a proper public inquiry held by people qualified to hold it. (It would apply abnormally and uniquely to BR, the only UK industry prevented from adjusting its own prices to reflect rising materials and other costs. No business serving the public was required to prove that it had cause to cease to provide a product or facility)
- The Tribunal should decide on reasonable facilities under the 1854 Act. (That Act did not prevent the withdrawal of rail services - see page 17).
- Light Railways needed no signals. (The MoT later stated that this was not the case).
- Many mourners of deceased lines had not been near them for years.
- BR should substantiate its figures. (But not, of course, the objectors!).
- Some rural buses have too few passengers to maintain a service but are able to cross subsidise from profitable services. This produced the response that the "Regional Traffic Commissioners seem to allow increases in fares whenever a bus company

makes an application". (Unlike BR which had to ask the Tribunal and wait many months to be told they could only raise fares by less than they sought).

Mr. Champion said the Bill does not seem to make one single sensible provision for the improvement of rural transport. A better title might be: *A Bill to make it more difficult to close a branch line, no matter how little used, to give power to a Tribunal never designed for that purpose, to give Directions without making provision for the finance to enable it to ensure the carrying out of that Direction.* TUCC's are far more representative of people in the area than the remote Transport Tribunal. He had worked on a light railway in 1918, collecting fares on trains. It was later closed due to loss of traffic to more convenient buses. The Bill is completely meaningless. Cmd 8538 ["Transport Policy"] envisaged competition. If competition is allowed, the loser must be allowed to succumb. If not the resulting charge should be on the public purse, not the BTC. The Post Office can only deliver a letter to the Isle of Wight at the same rate, because it has a monopoly. Retaining unremunerative services would be unfair to other transport users, employees and the BTC.

The sponsor made the mistake of moving off the popular ground of trying to block railway closures to tackling privately owned bus companies, who did not pay for the infrastructure, but may withdraw buses: *"Hopes that Licensing Authorities will consider getting big companies to run light vehicles to outlying districts".* He was asked : "Does he want to compel bus companies to introduce these services? Is he aware that many were cut out because they are unremunerative? Does he intend to compel private companies to run unremunerative services?" He replied: "The Bill does not try to compel people to do anything*. The Licensing Authority should make it plain to a bus company, that if they are not prepared to do so, they will find other operators who are". (If it was profitable, there would be no problem, and services would not be withdrawn). He continued : "In some areas, a shooting brake might do the job". (If a shooting brake would do, surely taxis would cope). "The Tribunal should have powers to recommend to the Licensing Authority that a bus service should be operated if anyone makes an application".

* *Except, of course, British Railways.*

Casting a spanner in the utopian works, another MP said :"Over recent years, small bus operators have found that there are not enough passengers to maintain a service". Another pointed out that the BTC had attempted to institute Area passenger schemes - co-ordinated rail & road - in the North East, but it had been blocked by MP's opposition.

The Parliamentary Secretary to the MoT said: The requirements for Light Railways depend on the number of trains. There is no substantial economy from Light railways in respect of signals. I have consulted with the President of the Tribunal who considers it would be quite an inappropriate task for them. On the proposal to sell a line - provided we have adequate safeguards about the price paid to BR, I see no objection in principle. Rails have been left in the Isle of Wight for two years waiting for some enterprising speculator to start running a service, so far no one has been willing to do so. These branch lines were built in an orgy of speculation in the 1840's. Large numbers of lines were built in rural districts which were not even likely to be profitable. But at the time, railways enjoyed a monopoly. Parliament imposed a limit on fares and profits, but did not go so far as to oblige them to operate at a loss. *They were free to close lines if they wished to do so.* Road transport took away traffic in the 20th century. Nationalisation has not altered the problem. Now the BTC loan carries a Treasury guarantee, Government and Parliament are concerned to see that the revenue will pay the interest on the loan.* West Cumberland operating costs are down from £150,000 to £80,000, receipts are up from £45,000 to £70,000 pa. It has not resulted in receipts covering outgoings although the gap has diminished. Lightweight diesels such as St. Albans-Watford cost £22,000 as compared to DMU of two cars £26,000. they are cheaper, but not much so. Steel tyres wear out after 10,000 miles compared to 60,000 on DMU's. They do not have great advantages. Battery car trains - a 25 ton vehicle requires 10 tons of batteries, but cost several times as much as a bus. He expressed doubts they could be made or run at the price suggested. He decried the concept of request stops and people going over farmer's fields. Parliament imposed a duty on the BTC to pay its way under Sec 3 (4). It is unworkable to take from TUCC's the role in closing rural lines and leave urban to them. Indeed it is difficult to define the boundary between them. On further reflection, I think Members will agree, the onus of proof should lie with objectors. He said that the Isle of Wight MP had referred to the road cost of £15,000, when railway closure produces £30,000, which was a clear indication of ample justification. The MP replied, I accept that if the MoT will find the £15,000.

*They had gone about it in a strange way, by holding down revenue and increasing costs.
(See "*Blueprints for Bankruptcy*").

The concept of passengers laden with heavy luggage, prams, bikes and babies in arms - which had all been prayed in aid at every closure hearing - would be a sight to behold as they descended to track level and climbed over a stile to follow a footpath. Trains stopping on a level crossing would go down like a lead balloon with motorists, who would soon be complaining to MP's and demanding an end to the practice. If they descended on a level crossing - the gates being across the road for the train to approach - they would have an interesting time manoeuvring to keep out of the way as gates closed against the railway after the train departed and avoid being knocked down by road vehicles.

BR's critics who saw this Bill as the Holy Grail, neglect to mention the weaknesses highlighted in the Commons Debate, nor to give space to criticisms by other MP's and responses by the Minister that totally undermine the concept.

"The aim of Archer Baldwin and the Railway Development Association was to force the BTC to downgrade branch lines, both in terms of manpower and operating expenses, until they could pay their way. If a line was subsequently put up for closure, the Commission would be forced to give evidence in public detailing economy measures that had been attempted. The procedure would be held before the Transport Tribunal, a truly independent body, rather than the TUCC's". [Henshaw, Pages 89-90]. It was claimed that the latter were not independent because they were funded by the BTC - so was the Tribunal. It implied an unjustified assumption that all branch lines could pay their way.

Ministry of Transport "Requirements for Passenger Lines" includes standards for Light Railways, and the standards are more stringent than disciples of that method appear to believe. Whilst distant signals are not necessary, stop signals are still required. [Para 65].

Dispensing with distant signals would mean a speed reduction. Protection on gradients would still be appropriate. Whereas on gradients of more than 1 in 260, double lines must have self acting trailing catch points, on single lines *worked* catch points are required in running lines. On long gradients additional points may be required. [Para 37]. (Worked points are more costly and require manpower). A "prescribed method of railway signalling" on single lines was still required. Level crossing arrangements "are for consideration in each case" - hence, it could not be assumed that requirements would be as cheap as hoped.

### Rural Transport Debated Again - 1956
[Hansard vol. 551, cols. 1621-1682].

The opening speaker said that few people expect BR to keep all branch lines, as the number of passengers in rural areas is less than it used to be. He was concerned at the price of buses, which was too high. Other MP's views or comments included :-

- When a bus company with a local monopoly asked a Licensing Authority to approve fares increases, they did so, despite objections "to meet mounting costs". (*BR attempts to do likewise were turned down on virtually every occasion by the Tribunal*).
- "Double diesels" cost one third of steam, so it should not be beyond the wit of man to design a light single diesel which cost one third that of a double diesel. (*UK industry did not seem to find anyone with the wit to do so*. BTC Accounts show a two car unit cost the same as a loco and two coaches. The real comparison was of a *new* diesel unit and an *old* steam loco and *old* coaches).
- Crossing lights could be brought on by the approach of a railbus. (Their light weight made them unreliable in the operation of devices which could trigger lights. Some MP's would be on their feet after the first car was written off in a collision).
- BR's diesels cost £25,000, what we want is something costing £2-3,000, which he was convinced could be provided. (No company came forward offering to do so - an opportunity missed by the private sector, which BR was supposed to emulate. The first 22 railbuses were built by the private sector in 1958 at an average £12,500 each).
- Rural public transport will not pay. BR has saved £1m by closing lines, by enterprise they could have saved £0.5m and kept lines open. If the Treasury provided the other £0.5m, it would be money well spent. The MoT said that there would be no subsidy. (*No proof was advanced that BR could have saved £0.5m*).
- BR costs should be cut by ending the statutory duty to fence off the railway and for station shelters to be financed by taxpayers or ratepayers, as applies with bus shelters

### Rural Transport Debated Yet Again - 1961
[Hansard, vol. 651, cols. 48-98]

The debate was more concerned with helping rural bus services, than railways, although attention was drawn to the Select Committee's recommendation that loss making lines be funded by Government. Of course, no action was taken. The use of diesels was reiterated, and one MP suggested that a coach could be attached to a freight train "which stops at all stations". *They stop to attach and detach wagons - not a five minute job.*

## Judicial Rulings

It was ruled on 10th September 1925 in Darlaston Local Board v L&NWR in 1894, that the Railway & Canal Commission would not normally require a Company to restore expensive equipment to restore a line which did not pay. A Company would be fairly safe discontinuing permanently, without statutory authority, services on a branch line that did not pay. If a Company desired to make discontinuance permanently effective and dispose of land, it would be necessary to obtain an Act. One of the objects of Grouping was for Companies to provide reasonable service. The burden of non paying portions should be borne by higher receipts secured by more profitable portions. [MT6/3464 Closed to 1956].

This case, reported in The Law Report Digest, [1891-1900, II, col. 1666], under a heading "Closing of stations for passenger traffic - Reasonable Facilities Jurisdiction, 1854 Act", states that it was held by the Railway & Canal Commission that where a railway company close a station for passenger traffic at which there is a substantial amount of traffic without providing an equivalent, they commit a breach of their obligation "to afford all reasonable facilities for receiving, forwarding and delivering of traffic" pursuant to Sec.2 of the 1854 Act. The Commission ordered the company to afford reasonable facilities for traffic from the said railway. This Order was reversed by the Court of Appeal on the grounds that the Commission had no jurisdiction to make the Order, on the grounds that the Act does not compel a railway company to maintain and use its railway stations.

At a Hearing into the application to appoint a Receiver of the derelict Halesworth-Southwold railway, neither the court nor anybody else could order a winding up of a company incorporated by Act of Parliament. Acts which apply to abandonment do not help the situation. Under the Grouping, power was given to wind up a subsidiary company. But the company in the present case was not included in Grouping. There are similar railways which would need to be dealt with as the severity of road competition increased. Individual Bills to wind up such companies are expensive and some General Act ought to be passed enabling the court to deal promptly with such a situation as the present for which there is no remedy. He hoped the attention of the Board of Trade would be called to the matter so that steps might be taken by Parliament to pass an Act. He made an Order for the Receiver but thought he could do very little. He could not dispose of the undertaking nor sell the rolling stock, nor part with the permanent way. [Times 26.6.29].

## Railway Powers

Until the development of motor vehicles, railways had a near monopoly, but lost it over the last half century. Flexible road transport was the key factor. Although former railway companies obtained powers to construct and operate lines, except in a very few instances, there was no statutory obligation to keep them open for traffic. Acts requiring the BTC, as successors to the former companies, to afford reasonable facilities, do not compel them to keep open any railway line or station. The BTC is, therefore, entitled to close any part of the railway system which is operated at a loss. [BR Memo to TUCC, March 1956, PRO: AN103/3].

# Chapter 2                    Closures Before Nationalisation

Most branch lines were initiated during the Railway Mania periods, when investors were conned into funding impractical proposals, and Parliament approved lines which had no economic justification: "The previous lack of foresight by Parliament in dealing with sound schemes was equalled by a fatal abandon to approve projects based on the wildest speculation". [Smiles, Page 434].

Closures are not a phenomenon of nationalised railways. In 1916-17, Government closed 400 passenger stations. In 1917, to release rolling stock, locos and drivers to France, passenger trains were withdrawn, lines closed or singled, speeds reduced (permitting heavier trains) and Sunday trains cut. In addition, some lines were closed to release rails to send to France to enable military railways to be laid. In 1918, more stations were closed, and trains withdrawn to further reduce civilian travel. [Pratt, Pages 145 &.154].

In 1916, the GNR closed its Nottingham suburban service and Peterborough - Leicester service. In 1917, some stations closed, never to re-open. [Grinling, Page 470]. At the end of the 1914-18 war railways faced increased competition from motor transport which benefited from surplus army vehicles and demobilised manpower. [See page 10 & "*Square Deal Denied*"].

When railways began to face real competition from road transport, it was inevitable that branch lines which had struggled to achieve profitability when competing with the horse, would succumb. The advent of the motor vehicle was bound to make inroads into railway business, and that on branch lines was especially vulnerable.

A problem of great difficulty remains - cutting expenditure of branch lines which carry little traffic. The problem is due to the advent of road competition. It is hard to see how it can be met by railway management. Bus services enjoy advantages of smaller units, are able to pick up people at their doors, and are easy to divert. [Sherrington, Pages 168 & 289].

Motor cars have penetrated into regions where the railway could not economically go and have created a large amount of new traffic, apart from short distance and light traffic previously carried by rail. [Wood & Stamp, Page 25]

'Creaming-off' profitable freight and passenger traffic from railways by unregulated road transport was at the root of the decline of railways, and the impact was felt first of all by branch lines and rural railways. [See "*Square Deal Denied*"].

In 1930, the Royal Commission on Transport stated: "There is much to commend the closing of branch lines. To ensure the public have other facilities in place of these discontinued railways, the companies should be required to inform the appropriate Licensing Authority of their intention to close any station or branch. and to inform them when actually closing". [Cmd 3751, Paras. 144 & 145].

Railways were criticised for investing in buses instead of branch lines. "They invested £9m in buses, the return on investment was very satisfactory - the LNER received over 9% in 1936". [Sherrington, Page 294]. Compared to 3.3% return on railways. Railways' wartime earnings were restricted by Government's inequitable "Control". [See "*Square Deal Denied*"].

Critics of BR's closures have said that post-war light traffic on branch lines was due to privately owned railways not modernising. The Big Four could not progress electrification in Greater London without approval of the Joint Committee, set up under the

LPTB Act 1933. [Cabinet minutes, 27.6.33]. Railways were praised for being equipped for war needs, so they could not have been backward. They carried 50% more traffic in the war, free of charge, due to Government's seizure of railways. In the immediate post war period loads were still heavy but resources depleted by the war. [See "*Square Deal Denied*" Page 141].

A DoT Paper dated 21st November 1938 stated: "Small sections may be closed if running at a loss, but they are few. The moral effect may well be bad and the loss of efficiency in wartime might be serious". A major war being foreseen, Government's real concern was to preserve the network at no cost to the State. [See "*Square Deal Denied*", Page 98].

During discussions on the railways demand for a "Square Deal" in 1938/39, Government papers show that they foresaw that the privately owned railway companies may resort to closures if demands for legal and commercial equality with road transport were denied. To avoid this and avoid conceding their demand, which would precipitate the need for Government, instead of railways, to subsidise inefficient industry, Government prevaricated until war broke out. Contrary to the impression fostered by Government, the war did *not* block the conceding of the Square Deal - Government papers reveal that they never had any intention of implementing change. [See "*Square Deal Denied*"].

Some minor closures were progressed. The Southern Railway announced the Devil's Dyke line in Sussex would close on 31st December 1938. There were no public hearings, but people complained that when it snowed the line was used! As usual on the last day, many who never used the line, made a "nostalgic" journey. The line opened in 1877. "It was not successful in earning an adequate return on capital". [Railway Gazette, 6.1.39, Page 2].

On 14th June 1939, Sir William Wood, LMS Vice President told the Railway Rates Tribunal that "In eleven years, 235 miles of track and 223 stations were closed to all traffic and 951 miles and 412 stations to passenger traffic only".

The proposed post-war Transport Corporation should be self supporting. Uneconomic requirements imposed by the State should be paid for by the Government. It must have financial independence and the freedom to fix tariffs. [DoT Memo, 15.10.40 - PRO: MT47/275]. *None* of these requirements were enacted.

Before the war, the Big Four correctly forecast that reduced fuel supplies and attacks on coastwise shipping would transfer huge volumes of traffic to rail. This, together with a vast increase in industrial production for military purposes created a 50% increase in rail traffic. Trunk and branch lines were busier, but profits were capped. [see "*Square Deal Denied*"]

An estimated 1,400 miles of track needed immediate replacement and considerable mileage was in need of urgent repair Railways needed five years of sustained investment, but as a result of impending nationalisation, management lost interest and the system stagnated. The immediate post war years should have seen frantic reconstruction and forward planning, but they were largely wasted. [Henshaw, Page 37].

Directors did not lose interest. Railways were under Government control up to the eve of nationalisation, and they controlled the purse strings, the raw materials and resources, whilst railway workshops had to convert back from armaments production to rolling stock. Motor car factories had no major delay in returning to civilian production. A lorry type which served the military could serve civilians equally well. Railway workshops produced tanks, aircraft and armaments. Government said railways would need 8-10 years to recover. [PRO: MT47/275]. The Big Four had begun forward planning *during the war*.

The LNER Chairman told shareholders in 1946 that work on Shenfield electrification was suspended in 1939. "If the necessary priorities for labour and materials are received, the Scheme will be operating in two years". He said that the MoT had publicly stated that wartime achievements proved how well railways were maintained in a state of readiness in the interlude between the two wars. They were also told that the British Iron & Steel Federation had "Appreciated the manner in which traffic was handled during the war. No steel works had to shut down or seriously curtail output through lack of transport of raw materials. Home produced ore was up from 120,000 to 250,000 tons, imported steel was up and steel works output had increased". (Home produced ore was of poorer quality, and hence needed more trains for the same steel output).

The LNER Chairman stated that passenger journeys were 20% above pre-war, journey lengths much greater, but train miles were 22.5% below pre-war, no coaches were built in the war, whilst the combined effects of wartime damage and lack of materials for repairs had reduced availability by 27%. Freight was still at peak war levels - 2,000 specials per week were being run on Government account (effectively free of charge, due to the iniquitous wartime sequestration terms, which continued until Nationalisation). Track arrears amounted to eighteen months of normal maintenance. Freight was still at wartime levels with 150,000 wagons awaiting repairs - equal to a 600 mile queue. Wagon shops were still in the hands of the Ministry of Aircraft Production. [Times, 25.2.46, 5f].

Later, he replied to Ministerial criticism about the condition of assets, saying: that but for the war, suburban routes would have been electrified, indeed, orders had been placed with manufacturers for new electric trains before the war. [Railway Gazette, 3.1.47, Page 5]:

Responding to Dr Hugh Dalton, who had said the railways and their assets were a national disgrace, the LNER Chairman said that if the railways were a disgrace, it was nothing to do with railway management. He pointed out that there were huge sums for deferred maintenance and abnormal wear and tear which they had at their disposal to spend when the Cabinet permits. [Railway Gazette, 10.1.47, Page 58]. These sums were held by Government in a Trust Fund, and when released, were hit by inflation.

The LNER Chairman told the 1947 AGM: "Ministers have forbidden or made it impossible for railways to restore assets to the same good condition they were in at the start of the war". He said that compensation terms for nationalisation arbitrarily decided by Government would "bring a blush of shame to the leathery cheek of a Barbary pirate".

In 1947, the Southern Railway Chairman told shareholders that the MoT was still in complete control of railways. The Southern Railway had plans for more electrification, new ships, improved docks and stations. They had been *allowed* to approve a £1.2m signalling scheme on the London-Brighton line. [Railway Gazette, 29.11.46, Page 605].

The Association of British Chambers of Commerce said that railways should be relieved of maintaining and operating lines of strategic or social importance, but which are uneconomic from a transport point of view, which should be the responsibility of the State or local authorities. [Ian Allan : Modern Transport, 18.5.46].

Post-war opposition to closures of irretrievable loss making lines received the support of politicians at national and local level, causing costly delays to essential rationalisation.

## Root Causes of Closures

"The Big Four closed 1,000 miles to passengers. A far higher mileage was closed in the first six years of Nationalisation than the previous 24 years of private ownership". [Henshaw, Page 84]. Acceleration is unsurprising given the growth of unfettered competition, and rolling stock again detained abroad by the military after the war, whilst railways were tied by legislation. Nothing would be closed 1939-47 except due to bombing, as railways were controlled by Government who were paying the owners a pittance out of their revenue to use the entire system. Even a reference to 16 years would be meaningless, as competition was progressive. In the first years of Grouping, no closures would appear necessary, later, they became inescapable. Perpetuation of Joint Railways delayed closure of some less essential routes. This political error had an adverse effect on profitability. Had railways been built from the beginning by one company or the State, thousands of miles built to compete with other railways, or block competitors' expansionist plans, would not have been built. Towns with two or more stations would have had one station. Branch and secondary lines were the most vulnerable to 'creaming-off' by unfettered road transport. Moreover, in the post war period, railways were denied a fair share of raw materials to restore the system to its pre-war condition. [See "*Square Deal Denied*", Page 178]

In March 1947, Government announced a 10% cut in passenger transport and summer services delayed until 1st June instead of 1st May. They confirmed serious arrears of maintenance due to the wartime workload. Coal and industry will take priority over passengers this year especially next winter. [Hansard vol. 434, col. 964]. Of course, they were focusing solely on railways. No reduction was enforced on passenger road transport.

In 1948, when railways were vested in the BTC, they were badly run down by wartime use, modernisation was overdue, routine replacement and repair having been kept to a minimum during the war. Reserves were inadequate to meet all these arrears or provide any cushion to tide them over the period of rehabilitation and re-organisation that was bound to adversely affect the revenue position. [DoT Memo, May 1956 - PRO: MT132/32].

Nationalised railways were placed in an organisation (BTC) with the statutory remit to integrate and make best use of alternative forms of transport. The opportunity to eliminate much dead wood emerged for the first time and closures became more compelling due to:-

- BTC's remit to pay its way. (Albeit, it was undermined by Government policies).
- Materials & labour costs increasing, despite substantial manpower cuts. Wages were *increased* by Government interference! [See "*Blueprints for Bankruptcy*", Pages 38-40].
- Denial of a fair share of resources and materials, prevented clearance of wartime arrears for ten years, thus delaying modernisation. [See "*Square Deal Denied*", Page 179].
- A court of law held fares below inflation and delayed increases, essential to close up on inflation, for an aggregate $12^3/_4$ years. The most regular objectors to increases were Councils, who objected to closing loss making lines. [See "*Blueprints for Bankruptcy*"].

- The resumption of road haulage's privileged position with the 1953 change of law which reverted rail and road to the iniquitous pre-war relationship - rail tied hand and foot, and road completely free, leading to continued transfer of traffic to road.
- The collapse of mismanaged and inefficient UK industry which lost a world lead in so many fields, and caused a loss of heavy freight which railways had, by legislation, been compelled to convey at low rates, leaving them with worthless assets.

"Post war material rationing provided a breathing space by holding road transport in check". [Henshaw, Page 86]. The reverse was the case. BR was directed by Government only to overtake arrears of track renewal necessary for safety, continuing speed limits which would increase losses, and were denied materials to replace 3,000 coaches short on pre-war. In 1947, Government stated "the overtaking of arrears of maintenance and production will have to be gradual. A programme for carriage replacement will have to proceed slowly". In 1950, they stated : "Restrictions on railways will be severe. Since the war, maintenance expenditure on BR has been severely limited. It has not been possible to overtake wartime arrears". In 1951: "BR will have substantial cuts in the programme for replacement of rolling stock & locos; work on stations, bridges, tunnels must be severely restricted and track renewal curtailed". By 1947, car sales to the home market rose from zero at the end of the war to 75% of pre-war; lorry and PSV sales to the home market were allowed to exceed Government's economic policy limits. By 1948, the PSV fleet was 29% up on pre-war. By 1950, the fleet had almost doubled. In those three years, they had obtained 30% more than Government's own limit. These were generally larger capacity vehicles than pre-war. Within two years of the end of the war, the road haulage fleet was a third greater than pre-war. [Government Economic Surveys - See "Square Deal Denied", Page 83].

Due to steel shortages, BR operated the 1949 service with 3,000 fewer coaches than pre-war. [BTC 1949 Report, Para. 278]. Government allocation of steel to BR was 20% below needs. [BTC 1952 Report, Para. 1]. BR will fulfil only 65% of normal wagon construction due to steel shortages, and it is unlikely that a single coach of its 1952 programme will be built. The fleet of coaches is adequate in number but has a high percentage which are obsolete, and uneconomical to repair. Due to steel and labour shortages it would be necessary to impose speed restrictions, preventing trains being accelerated. Development schemes, including the introduction of diesel and electric power were seriously delayed due to investment restrictions. [Times, 13.3.52, 2d]. Virtually a complete post war re-equipment of road fleets, passenger and freight, but on BR even arrears of maintenance due to intensive use made of railways in the war have hardly been made good. [BTC 1953 Report, Para. 125].

"Development of an integrated transport system requires that services which no longer effectively answer a public need should be withdrawn and replaced by other suitable facilities. Very careful consideration is given to the closure of lines because of the abandonment of a costly investment". [BTC 1951 Para. 30]. In many rural areas the traffic needed to make a reasonable train service pay is non existent. [CTCC 1951 Report, Para. 30]

Inhabitants of the locality are prone to use private and public road transport in their daily life and only remember railways when closure is threatened. The causes of unprofitability of branch lines lie in history - many were built to keep a rival out of the area or in a burst of enthusiasm engendered by speculators, which took no account of traffic potential. Many were placed badly in relation to villages they were meant to serve. Nobody wants to walk a few hundred yards to a station. [Railway Gazette, 13.4.56, Pages 183/4].

Due to Government's inequitable policies, 1956 was an exceptionally black year for BR. "For nine months, railways will have held their charges constant whilst other industries have been able to increase theirs. Governments have been largely responsible for the accumulated deficits caused by policies of stabilisation and delayed increases in charges. There are two ways forward: Vigorous prosecution of modernisation; Realisation of the greater commercial freedom which still has to be delivered". [Economist 30.6.56, Page 1299].

Improved roads accelerated losses of traffic, not least because roads, unlike railways are justified on the basis of social benefit, calculated on the basis of time which *may* be saved.

## Branch Line Reviews

Under the 1947 Act, executive power was vested solely in the BTC. At their first meeting on 13th August 1947, Chairman Sir Cyril Hurcomb, former civil servant, stated that the "Executives would act as the Commission's agents". [PRO: AN85/1]. Their delegated powers were strictly limited to "operating and maintaining railways" and unifying railways in a real and operative sense. [PRO: AN85/17]. "Much credit is due to the Executive for the smoothness with which the work of unification was effected". This statement in the DoT's Draft of the White Paper for re-organising the BTC, abolishing the Executives and de-nationalising road haulage, was left out of the White Paper. [PRO: MT132/32]. Inclusion would have been an argument for retention of the Executive and abolition of the BTC.

BTC's "Directive N° 1" set out the Railway Executive's "Primary Task": to unify and implement a major organisational change in the control of railways and assume the former role of the General Managers whilst the BTC would carry out the Board's role. This displaced the emergency organisation that had operated successfully from 1939 to 1947. The BTC required the Executive "to obtain prior approval to closing any line to passenger or goods traffic". [PRO: AN85/17]. Consequently the review of unremunerative lines was delayed. The Executive has been criticised for caution in pursuing closures. Critical comparisons of the scale of closures during the brief lifetime of the Executive, ignore the fact that during the first years, they were pre-occupied with the "primary task".

David Blee, a Member of the Executive, set up a Committee in 1949 to expedite consideration of unremunerative lines. Regions were told to appoint officers of standing. The task was not to be approached from a negative view of solely reducing costs. Development of service and light units were to be considered. [PRO: AN4/2, 31.3.49]. Enquiries were to include lightweight diesels, modernised push & pull. [PRO: AN97/21, 3.7.51]. This predates claims that amateurs thought of these first. It undermines a belief that Sir Reginald Wilson, a member of the BTC, initiated the closure programme. BTC minutes prior to Blee's initiative contain no reference to pressure on the Executive to pursue closures. The Executive considered light units, but obviously saw no prospect of viability. The BTC initiated experiments with railbuses, "which were all withdrawn by 1968", [PRO: MT124/150]. As a member of the BTC, Wilson was a party to the experiments. He was lauded in an obituary as the *lone outsider among career railway managers who pressured career managers to effect closures*. He was one of 13 members of the BTC not from a railway background. They out numbered the two career managers on the BTC. Significantly, the unpublished Stedeford Committee report argued that railways should be run by railwaymen, "of whom there were too few on the Commission". [PRO: MT132/85].

Submissions to the BTC had to include all financial data, including long term renewals. Blee pointed out that the case for closure was often clear before all expenditure data had been gathered, and proposed a "shortened procedure". The BTC agreed, but insisted full details be supplied within six months. This directive would do little to accelerate reviews, as no less time would be spent gathering data on each case. [PRO: AN97/20]. The Executive was also told to consult user bodies before submission. [PRO: AN85/4].

In 1954, the MoT wrote to an MP that Wilson had suggested that light railways might be adopted as a solution to closure. In December 1955, the Parliamentary Secretary wrote: "We should investigate every suggestion made if we are to carry public opinion with us". (This meant amateurs' ideas, BR examined all practical options). In 1956, Wilson wrote to the MoT that "whilst there will still be pruning, it will not be fundamental in scale, especially if a smaller unit can be successfully evolved, the further savings to be made by closing may not be sufficiently worthwhile".  He referred to costs his Department had produced on unremunerative services, which were "intended to shock, and should best be forgotten". [PRO: MT113/5].  Critics seized this as proof that BR closure data was inaccurate. However, savings were based on actual costs & planned renewals, less loss of receipts.

If Wilson was convinced of the need for closures, as his obituary states, what prompted his change of view?  Was there pressure from Government? A year later, the BTC wrote to the CTCC of a "reluctance to take the distasteful step of curtailing facilities, which is being effectively demonstrated by planned purchase of railbuses". [PRO: MT113/5]. BTC minutes do not record any dissension. The introduction of railbuses proved ineffective.

The operation by more economic means or elimination of unremunerative passenger services is an essential feature of the Modernisation Plan. The bus, requiring no special track is clearly superior to rail in convenience and cheapness in thinly populated areas. [Cmd 9880: 1956 "Proposals for Railways", Para 50].

Fast and semi fast services can be profitable and suburban services just meet direct costs. Receipts from steam hauled stopping trains do not cover direct costs by tens of millions. Where there is prospect of traffic to be developed, all means of making services earn enough to cover direct costs will be examined before withdrawal proposals are submitted: recasting services to improve rolling stock use, introduction of diesel or electric traction. If diesels doubled receipts and halved costs, a substantial percentage of stopping services would still not cover direct costs.  [BR Memo March 1956, PRO: AN103/3].

## Role of Consultative Committees - CTCC & TUCC's

Local authorities are advised before closures  to take account of any representation they may make before a final decision is made. [BTC 1949 Report, Para. 196].  (The private sector does not do so when closing facilities serving the public). The CTCC "asked the BTC to postpone closure of the East Kent line pending investigation by the CTCC". [CTCC 1950 Report, Para. 25].

The BTC satisfy themselves as to alternatives to closures. With the setting up of the Area Committees (TUCC's), all important proposals are referred to them for their views. [BTC 1951 Report, Para. 11]. TUCC Chairmen will be consulted in certain cases. [BTC Minutes 29.5.51]. They did not foresee public hearings or delays. Soon, all cases were put to them.

The CTCC called for more BR information to *justify* each closure. In 1951, the CTCC had said closures met with their approval so long as satisfactory alternative services were available. [CTCC 1952 Report, Para. 8]. No other business had to justify rationalisation.

In February 1953, the MoT stated: "Since 1948, the BTC have approved closure of 97 branch lines and 216 stations to passenger traffic. Since 1951, there has been a general procedure under which BR advise a TUCC of proposals and no passenger service has been withdrawn without the written approval of a TUCC". [Hansard, vol. 516, col. 103].

"In no cases are withdrawals of unremunerative services recommended unless suitable alternative road facilities are, or will be made available". (At BR's cost). "The provision of diesel units will not necessarily turn an unprofitable line into a profitable one. There is rarely sufficient traffic to provide both road and rail with an economic return where branch traffic is light and stations happen, for historical reasons, to be inconveniently situated". [CTCC 1954 Report, Paras. 12 & 30].

Only limited progress made in freeing the undertaking from the burden of uneconomic services. A survey shows many slow and stopping services fail to cover direct costs by many millions of pounds. There is no remedy except withdrawal. Local opposition is very great. The effect on BTC's competitive position of obsolescent and loss making facilities is serious. The procedure was followed whereby prior approval of a TUCC was sought where a branch service was to be withdrawn. BR have to ensure alternative services are available or can be made available. [BTC 1954 Report, Paras. 7, 18, 181, 182]

The 1954 Report mentioned that since being set up, TUCC's had examined 102 closure schemes with economies of £0.9m. Since then a further 28 schemes secured economies of £0.53m. [BTC 1955 Report, Para 31]. Sixty TUCC meetings dealt with 49 withdrawals or reductions of facilities, and 230 individual station closures saving £0.86m. [BTC 1959 Report, Para. 11].

Consultative Committees are advisory, not judicial, were never intended to usurp management's function, but to consider the effects of BTC proposals on users and whether alternative facilities are reasonably adequate. Too much accountancy detail is irrelevant. The committees are not competent to deal with such detail. It is not their business to do so. If the BTC decided to close against the recommendation of the Committees, the MoT could give Directions under Sec 6 (8) of 1947 Act. [DoT Memo, March 1957 - PRO: MT115/9].

The CTCC told the Stedeford Committee that by June 1960, "Of 919 closure proposals submitted to them by the BTC, 521 were unopposed, 25 were rejected, whilst 55 were 'modified'". The Committee said the closure process was too slow. [PRO: MT132/81, MT132/84]. This was two years after the BTC had reported a speeding-up. Even unopposed closures incurred delay and avoidable losses, as they had to be publicised, and time given for objections. 400 opposed closures represents 40 pa - a big workload for TUCC's.

Sir Leonard Sinclair, member of the BTC, and formerly Chairman of Esso, told the Commission that he opposed outside controls. The BTC ought to be able to say that it had sufficient justification to close. Delays, even of three months were quite wrong. The MoT already exercised control without responsibility. [PRO: AN85/16, 26.1.61]. David Blee had made the same point to the BTC Chairman some years earlier. [AN6/57, 10.2.58].

Alison Munro, of the DoT, in a letter to Mrs. Emmet, MP, wrote that there is a "Tendency of Local Authorities and others to prolong hearings". [PRO: MT115/8]. Despite such objections, 13.5% of route mileage had closed by the time Beeching took over, with more in the pipeline. His plan included closures held up for inclusion in his Report.

There were allegations that the CTCC and TUCC's were not independent, because they were "funded and staffed by BR". They were funded by, but were not *staffed* by BR. The two organisations were "entirely independent and the members are appointed by the Secretary of State from lists of nominees submitted by local authorities, trade unions, agriculture, industry, commerce, tourist boards, women's organisations and organisations for old age pensioners and the disabled". [TUCC for the West Midlands Area]. BR provided a Secretary who had no vote. Having attended TUCC meetings as a non-voting liaison officer representing BR, I can vouch for the integrity of the Members - even if I disagreed with some of their findings. Members received no salary. The membership and funding of the CTCC and TUCC was exactly alike. No body could have opposed BR on closures with more vigour and ingenuity than the CTCC and the TUCC's. Two examples were:-

- The TUCC complained when a line in Yorkshire was severed to avoid heavy engineering costs. BR had to provide a bus link for the severed section and then submit it for closure. [CTCC 1965 Report, Paras. 13-15]. This was in the Mexborough/ Swinton area. BR had diverted trains via a new junction built to connect the former LMS and LNER lines south of those towns. The railways served the same towns on parallel lines. The towns were still served after the diversion. BR had to put on a bus service to/from Swinton Town, to connect with trains at Mexborough, which was less than two miles away. The service carried a total of six passengers a week and ran for three months before the closure was approved.
- The TUCC disputed BR's interpretation of Sec 56 of the 1962 Act regarding those eligible to register objections. BR's Notice stated: "any user of the rail service which it is proposed to discontinue" may lodge an objection. The TUCC said that the Act stated "any user of a service affected" may lodge an objection. BR's view was that to be an objector, a user had to travel over the section of line proposed for closure. BR had to re-issue a Notice in respect of the Goose Hill-Wath Road closure to "broaden the scope for objections". [Yorkshire TUCC 1984 Report, Paras. 8-14]. No retailer would have considered anyone as a customer who did not patronise their premises.

We found it difficult to support recommendations in two or three instances of certain TUCC's who concluded that unremunerative services should continue at a substantial loss. [CTCC 1952 Report, Para. 8]. Evidence to the Stedeford Committee indicated that TUCC's were dealing with an annual average of 40 cases. Hence, two or three did not constitute evidence of persistent over-ruling as one critic said. The CTCC did support uneconomic recommendations in some cases - e.g. re-opening the Wivenhoe-Brightlingsea line that had been severed by sea storms, and in respect of the Westerham branch, told a TUCC to re-hear the case when the TUCC had recommended closure. (See Chapters 6 & 11).

26

"Among suggestions received was one that lines should not be closed until every possible means of making them remunerative at an acceptable level of fares has been tried". [CTCC 1951 Report, Para. 24]. An incredible suggestion which did not specify to whom acceptable, nor for how long trials should continue, nor who would cover losses.

"In many rural areas the traffic needed to make a reasonable service pay is non existent. A line was unremunerative because it was no longer used by those for whom it was provided, and now prefer road transport. Losses on lightly used lines had to be made good by other users of nationalised transport". [CTCC 1951 Report, Paras. 30, 44; 1954 Report, Para. 6].

Some TUCC's initiated 'incredible suggestions'. The West Midlands TUCC suggested "a very light rail coach, with maintenance undertaken by local repair shops which look after railways' road vehicles". [PRO: MT124/65]. Unfortunately, most shops were not rail connected, and none of their staff were trained in maintaining DMU braking and heating systems, driver controls etc., nor would they be qualified in tackling wheel maintenance.

The CTCC went so far as to call for a relaxation of safety regulations on rural branch lines to enable rail buses to run as an alternative to closure. [Times, 15.10.55]. In later years, they were more inclined to call for infinite capital to be spent on new safety measures.

### Ministerial Role

The MoT stated the opening or closing of branch lines was not regarded as affecting national interest. Powers to give direction to the BTC rest on Sec 6 (8), 1947 Act as amended by Sec 29 (2), 1953 Act, whereby when a recommendation of the CTCC or TUCC for Scotland or Wales, was sent to him, he may give a direction. [PRO: MT115/8]. "If the BTC decided to close against the recommendation of the TUCC or CTCC, the MoT could give a Direction under the 1947 Act". [PRO: MT115/9]

In 1956, the MoT stated he had no power to intervene unless the TUCC or CTCC recommended retaining a line which was proposed for closure. If the CTCC supported closure, the Minister could not issue a Direction to the BTC. [Hansard vol. 547, cols. 1575-85].

In June 1962, Parliament was told that no passenger closure would be effected without the Minister's consent. He would have powers to attach conditions to that consent, or to give directions to the Railways Board. These powers would be used to ensure the provision and continuance of alternative bus services, where justified. [Hansard vol. 657, col. 1465].

The TUCC's reported on 18 closure cases to the MoT, who decided that 14 had little or no hardship, but BR must subsidise buses in three cases, four had severe hardship. Since 1954, 44 bus services were subsidised by BR as a condition of closure. Bus services are reviewed annually, eight were discontinued, since it is not justified to support them in perpetuity because the area once had a rail service. Savings on schemes subject to a bus subsidy were £1.5m less subsidies of £86,000. [BTC 1962 Report, Paras. 19, 21]. By the end of August, 20 cases for closure were waiting MoT consideration. [CTCC 1962 Report, Para. 8].

In 1994, on TV, replying to a question about privatisation, a Minister referred to "the one passenger on a line, whom it would have been cheaper to convey by Rolls Royce". Viewers may have gained the impression that BR kept such lines open. Ministers, politicians, objectors and TUCC's played the major part in blocking or delaying closures. The Rolls Royce, like bus subsidies, would have been paid for by BR.

Some authors have compared the rate of closures in the three eras - Railway Executive: 1948-53, BTC: 1953-62 and BRB: post 1962. Comparisons are invalidated by the time required to examine potentially unremunerative lines, and the ensuing delay imparted by the Consultative procedure and by Ministerial involvement, so that many closures effected in the second and third eras had respectively been begun in the earlier era.

## Funding of Branch Line Losses

Losses on lightly used lines had to be made good by the rest of the users of nationalised transport. [CTCC 1954 Report, Para. 6]. Or by wages held below industrial levels.

The BTC was against subsidising railways, but if buses were subsidised, unremunerative rail services should be similarly treated. [BTC Minutes, 11.9.58 - PRO: AN85/12].

Government should decide if unprofitable services are to be provided and bear the cost. [Select Committee Report 1959-60, Para. 16]. The MoT said this affects other Nationalised Industries. [Response to Report, 1960-61, Para. 45]. It didn't. They could avoid uneconomic services by pricing, BR could not. [See *"Blueprints for Bankruptcy"*, Page 43]. He added: "For the time being, such losses will, in practice, be covered by contributions from public funds". This referred to *impending* provision in the 1962 Act for covering the "general railway deficit", (see page 12). It was not intended to subsidise rural services, but to compensate for past interference in pricing. Hitherto, social costs counted as BR "losses", there was no *contribution,* only interest bearing loans. In 1968, Government reluctantly accepted responsibility for funding lines, Ministers had kept open for social reasons. (See page 195).

## Joint Consultation

The BTC set up a Joint Consultative Council. It involved staff representation at local, regional and national levels. [BTC 1948 Report, Para 15]. All proposals, including closures, affecting the number of jobs were *detailed* in writing, showing present & proposed arrangements, including traincrew cover of every train, and revised duty details for staff taking on extra tasks. It was a reasonable development for the 20th century, but not used in industry, where labour walkouts were endemic. It ensured no detail was overlooked.

The time and cost taken to deal with a closure were broadly the same as to consult on a series of piecemeal economies, so often trumpeted by unqualified critics who were obviously totally unaware of this system. Critics lost sight of the fact that figures on closures were put before the staff side at local & regional levels, who readily challenged any weakness in management's case. If management tried to force through an avoidable closure, staff could take appropriate measures, including media publicity and strike action. They knew better than *any* external body or critic whether a line had profitable prospects.

It is claimed that unnamed insiders could cut costs and avoid closures. Managers who could do so "*made a name for themselves*" and benefited therefrom. Ideas put to the Staff Suggestions Scheme were *rewarded* anonymously. Staff could advance alternatives when closures or any operations were discussed under Joint Consultation. Representatives were drawn from those who worked at the depots or stations concerned, and were capable men and women who would advance alternatives aimed at preserving employment if they could. Hence, it is impossible to perceive why they would need to be anonymous.

Sir Frank Ree, General Manager of the L&NWR made the classic observation : "I have never yet met anybody, outside the circle of those who know how it should be done, who has not had a brilliant idea for the managing of railways". [Dow, vol. 3, Page 279].

In 1939, Lord Stamp, President, LMS told the Manchester Chamber of Commerce that they had 'experts' - writing in, telling them how to put railways right - "saying that wagons are loaded to only 20% of capacity. They overlook that a 12 ton wagon was fully loaded with $2^1/_2$ tons of empty beer barrels, 6 cwt of empty pottery crates, 8 tons of loose potatoes or 3 tons of short deals. So all wagons might be fully loaded, and the average load would go down by a reduction in pig iron carryings and an increase in short deals". Lord Stamp said of one 'expert' that "he speaks as a transport man, and apparently had *something* to do with railways at one time - though he must have forgotten a great deal".

Since the war, there has been a proliferation in "expert" advice, especially on branch line economics. Their views are based on a selection of unproven theories. Not one offered to back opinions with their own money, nor promised to travel more often, nor to put a single ton of traffic on rail. Instead, they expected that the cost of retention should be borne by users remote from the line in question, or taxpayer, or by paying low wages. Prominent among critics who had huge volumes of traffic, both passenger and freight but failed to divert it back to rail were local authorities and industrial objectors (See Appendix A).

No activity had more self professed experts than railways. Their ill conceived ideas took up management and staff time which could be used pursuing *real* improvements rather than considering impractical proposals to convince outsiders that BR were not rejecting ideas due to bloody mindedness. No industry, including privatised railways, would spend a fraction of the time on such matters, but they are not likely to be bombarded with allegations that they are 'not prepared to listen to practical suggestions'. These were often presented via the media and almost invariably excluded reference to money. Many must work for employers who fail to give customer satisfaction. They are high on gimmicks and short on expertise. Objectors, who were not using railways, became instant experts offering impractical advice. It is peculiar that the self appointed experts who try to tell railway professionals how to do their job, never seem to do so when other industries are going into receivership, closing loss making factories, closing local shops, or abandoning newspaper production. They muster no experts, retain no QC's to tell *those businesses* that they are wrong - that they are not *really* losing money, or will *not* make savings by closure, and should subsidise customers by profits from some undefined "elsewhere".

In April 1978, I was asked to consider a plan submitted to the BRB by a University lecturer to improve Cambrian line services. It was not costed, had no forecast of revenue, but envisaged "doubling the service", (his train mileage was 50% more, not 100%) and "doubling passenger journeys", (with no market research). I had his 24 page plan costed:-
- Additional signal boxes, locos & new rolling stock to run additional trains, and turntables (for his proposed steam locos) : **£9.2m.**
- New DMU's to replace the existing DMU's to improve reliability : **£4.8m,**

We did not need to go further and estimate the costs of track upgrading for his heavier new locos, coaching stock and higher speeds, nor to estimate additional fuel consumption.

This £14m investment needed revenue to rise by £3.5m - seven times prevailing levels, to pay for it. He did not propose fare increases, but criticised BR policy of "continually increasing fares" (which lagged behind the RPI for the 30th consecutive year).

His plan would increase operating costs by £0.95m pa, requiring revenue to increase by **£4.45 pa** (£3.5m + £0.95m) - *to hold losses at current levels*. He proposed a two year experiment, requiring capital and operating costs - **£15.9m** - to be recovered in *two years*, and that it could be implemented "without much investment" in two months which would "demonstrate or disprove its' viability". Usually, those making suggestions are 100% confident, believing that BR intransigence in refusing to fund brilliant ideas stood in the way of their ultimate glory. The plan required 85 extra staff, whose redeployment would be difficult and costly, if the plan failed - which, in view of the costs, was beyond doubt. He said that better stock and assets would not alone run trains punctually - it required *"benevolent heavenly protection"*, (not least from tidal floods, vehicles smashing into crossing barriers or bridges and other external factors). Unlike most, he sent his plan direct to BR rather than via the media. After quoting the costs to him, we heard no more.

Objectors do not cost 'economies', specify fares, forecast volume, say how to influence it to rail, nor convert all to £. They did not back their views with money. No critic would opt for *losing less*, if his *own money* was involved. BR told the Transport Tribunal in 1966: "We have destructive criticism in fair measure, of constructive suggestions - not a word".

### Pressure Groups

There is an illusion that pressure from external groups kept the railways alive:-
- The Pro Rail movement began to fight back with increasingly sophisticated techniques. [Henshaw, Page 58]. Usually, external groups tended to be *anti-closure* rather than *pro-rail*. The latter demands significantly increased personal user.
- The Railway Development Association (RDA) advocated light railways. [Henshaw, Page 224]. Their ideas were impractical. (See pages 15 & 44). Blee's practical plans and reviews predated the formation of the Association. (See page 23).
- The Serpell Report disappeared because of opposition, including a petition by the Railway Development Society (RDS). [Henshaw, Page 222]. It had 500 members in 1978.

The nature of their "sophisticated techniques" is not clear. They did not seem to include:-
- Raising cash to offset losses - as Associations did to preserve other railways.
- Buying, and donating, leasing or loaning railbuses to BR to use on branch lines.
- Guarantees to make extra journeys themselves *outside the summer peak*.

Some typical ideas and claims are examined. (See pages 219-224 & 228)

Light Railways, (see pages 45 & 159) and petitions (see page 56) are over-rated. BR demolished figures forming the basis of Serpell's Report and discredited it. (See page 227).

The RDA was formed in November 1951. It believed "branch lines could be preserved by applying fresh operating methods". [Railway Magazine, January 1953]. In 1954, a rival group formed - SRUBLUK. (see page 228). Its theories were not dissimilar. It abbreviated its title (see page 222). The two groups merged in 1978 to form the RDS. Their beliefs are akin to production led industry at its worst - to assume that new methods or new products will be profitable, without market research. It was a failing of UK industry. [See "*Blueprints for Bankruptcy*"]. Even worse, in this case, they did not know what the new methods would cost.

"Road transport pressure groups .......... were ranged against a nationalised, yet virtually powerless railway industry. Aided by the MoT, they succeeded by the late 1960's in bringing the railway system to its knees". [Henshaw, Page 10]. In fact, by 1968, prospects began to look brighter. BR's major problems were created by inequitable legislation, the worst features of which were lack of commercial freedom, external interference in closures and fares which trailed the RPI by up to 41 points, and in which objectors: rail pressure groups, industry, professional bodies and councils played a prominent part, thus creating deficits. *They* had far more to do with bringing BR down. Councils objecting to fares increases *and* closures, included Cumberland, Denbighshire, Dorset, Co. Durham, Essex, Kent, Norfolk, Isle of Wight and Somerset - all helped to increase inflation. (See pages 200 & 203). Councils objected to unstaffed halts & modern crossings that would cause job losses.

Denbighshire County Council wrote to BR's manager asking if he would give an undertaking in the next 10-15 years, that the Chester-Mold-Denbigh line would not be closed. "He could not give that undertaking!". [Henshaw, Page 77]. Could they name *one* company that would give such an undertaking? They should first have obtained an assurance that firms and passengers would use the line for 15 years, and promised to do likewise. Would they undertake not to close a school or other facility in the next 10-15 years, without a codicil about Government funding? (See Appendix C for *their* increases).

The National Council for Inland Transport produced a document: "Rail Closure Procedure - Preparing a Case for Objection". It contained not one word urging greater use of railways by objectors - which would have been the most effective method.

## Halts

Unstaffed halts existed long before objectors to closures claimed to make them fashionable. Prior to the development of portable ticket machines, ticket issue was a problem. The essence of halts was the absolute minimum of facilities. When the CTCC had a role for buses, they said: "Provision of bus shelters, at exposed sites, because of cost and usage factors, was primarily one for local authorities to decide". [CTCC 1955 Report, Para 51]. It should have been for BR for the same reasons. Rain falls equally on road and rail.

"The CTCC is more favourably disposed to unstaffed halts than BR. Objectors often suggest reductions to halts. The BTC says that only a limited number of tickets can be issued on trains, children will play on platforms and may fall under trains, and damage windows and lighting, and there may be disturbances by hooligans. The CTCC doubt whether ticket issuing need be complicated and the danger to passengers at unstaffed halts is less than at a bus stop. If trains only use halts in the daytime lighting difficulties can be disregarded.    The CTCC is not opposed to destaffing on grounds of ticket issuing being a bar - there is little for staff to do and vandalism is unlikely in country areas". [CTCC 1962 Report, Paras. 30-32]. Darkness comes early in winter, so services would be very restricted!

"There may be situations in which it would be possible to maintain rail services at little used manned stations by ...... conversion to unstaffed halts rather than closed.  There is no substance in the suggestion that passengers may resent having to re-book at intermediate stations". [CTCC 1963 Report, Paras. 30-33].

"It has been the view of TUCC's for some time that the effect of closures on some communities might be minimised if stations could be retained as unstaffed halts. BR intends to convert to unstaffed halts as many as possible of stations which were to remain open. The CTCC expressed satisfaction with this policy". [CTCC 1964 Report, Paras. 41,46,47]

After some were converted to halts, including some specifically advocated by objectors, there were new objections due to lack of lighting and the absence of staff. (See page 168).

"The CTCC endorsed the TUCC view that destaffing lowers Quality of Service: less assistance to elderly and disabled, no enquiries, no information on punctuality, vandalism, lack of security from attack, and limitations on ticket purchase". [CTCC 1988/89 Report, Page 18]. The CTCC had decried these very problems which BR had warned would occur. The CTCC had advocated unstaffed halts! It is not clear why a single BR employee - male or female - was expected to prevent attacks which are ignored by other members of the public. Loss of facilities is often due to vandalism, which is also a problem at staffed stations.

### Branch lines claimed to be the root of traffic

There was a popular belief that branches fed the main lines. If that were so, they would have been built before the main lines, whereas the first lines to be built were between main towns and cities and in industrial areas. Carried to its logical conclusion, the theory, would mean that main lines and trunk routes had no originating traffic, and hence the towns and cities they joined had none either. A critic advanced the view: "Cut the branches and the tree will die". [Burroughs, Chapter 1]. No gardener would agree with him. Even branch lines with substantial freight traffic in the early days, would become uneconomic when mines and quarries were worked out.

Frequently, local authorities called for BR to do "something" to attract tourists to avoid closures. Hotels, local authorities and others did far too little to encourage tourism, which is why people went abroad. When travelling by car became popular, the blame could not fall on BR, if holiday makers switched to foreign climes. The most compelling reasons were that it was cheaper, service was better and they were not continually being told that food and drink was not available after 2pm, whilst shops, and even Tourist Offices, close at 5.30pm in peak summer months! The practice of boarding house owners requiring tourists to stay out all day, despite the unreliable climate, must have driven many away. Hotels and other businesses stuck their heads in the sand and called for BR to attract tourists to their unattractive facilities. Colleagues told me of coach operators who had complaints when customers found that their mystery tour was to a certain resort famed for its *lack* of attractions and facilities. Why did objectors *always* focus their advice to BR on encouraging more tourism to their desolate areas? Why did they *never* urge local residents to make more use of railways? Perhaps it was because they were too conscious of playing to the gallery. Critics did not address *these* issues.

Public attitudes to the closure of unremunerative lines defied belief. Many owned road vehicles which they naturally used to the maximum, patronising rail rarely. Those who did not possess vehicles, patronised public road transport for most of their journeys and excursions and despatched products by road haulage. Railways were used as an alternative by most people when their own or public road transport was not available, or would be uneconomic. However, when the local line was listed for closure, they expressed surprise and organised petitions which claimed that the line was indispensable.

## Contributory Revenue

The most popular theory advanced by critics is that branch lines contribute revenue to main lines. A branch line whose *movement* costs are as much as five times the revenue is unlikely to make *any* contribution. Critics claimed that fares for journeys from main line stations to a branch would be lost if the branch closed, and hence should be all credited to the branch. They did not dwell on the implications of a journey beginning on one branch, passing over a main line and ending on another branch. Revenue would be counted twice!

The scale of contributory revenue from a main to a branch line, and vice versa, is a matter of subjective judgement. BR's method was approved by an external Accountant. [See Appendix B - Carrington Report]. The fairest allocation as used by BR was pro rata to total journey distance. It was used by the Railway Clearing House to apportion revenue between privately owned railways. Every critic believed it should be more, most did not say how much more, but some claimed it should be 100%. (See page 98). The issue arose most frequently with holiday resorts. If a passenger travelled to an alternative resort paying a similar fare, BR would be no worse off - the lost "contributory revenue" would be zero. If they travelled a longer distance, the "contributory revenue" would be a negative value - i.e., savings from branch line closure would be greater than those quoted by BR, not less. Critics ignored the prospect that passengers may transfer to another rail destination, believing that people are so devoted to resorts on the branch line in question, that, in the event of closure, they will travel by road or not at all. They ignore the fact that main line trains which ran to holiday resorts would be withdrawn if holiday makers did not travel to that resort. Such trains being in the peak season involved higher than average costs.

BR made provision to retain off-line freight revenue by freight spurs, using nearby terminals, or assumed total loss. The effect could be determined because customers were known. The effect on passenger revenue was determined by research or past experience. As excursion passengers were not so devoted to any resort as to decline alternatives, net revenue was retained by running elsewhere. Holidaymakers may also prefer a change. If a branch was losing £10,000 pa, but had off-line traffic earning a *gross* of say, £1,000 pa on the branch line section and a *net* of say, £9,500 on the main line, a gain arises by closing the branch, even if all off-line *net* revenue is lost. A branch not covering its costs cannot have a *net* contribution from off-line traffic *on* the branch. Unless the whole off-line *net* revenue exceeds branch line losses, the branch is unremunerative. Off-line savings arise from reducing costs and assets, thereby cutting the main line loss to a net figure.

Investigation shows that the main centres of production and consumption lie, as one would expect, on main lines. Hence, most traffic remains on such lines. Branch traffic was low: "A third of the system carries 1% of rail traffic". [BRB 1963 Report, Para 4]. Had the Railway Development Association or other critics backed their theories by buying branch lines, they would have been foolish to assume that BR would incur related main line costs, whilst they skimmed the entire throughout revenue, or even a disproportionate share.

Larger companies "snapped up ailing lines and discovered the benefits of contributory revenue". [Henshaw, Page 20]. There was no gain on traffic already passing over their line as they already had a pro rata share in the revenue. If they poached traffic passing over other main lines, there was no national gain. Lines were 'snapped-up' to create a barrier to protect existing profits earned from major industrial centres by blocking encroachment by competitors. What they discovered, but probably already knew, was that they were picking up a railway for less than it cost to build. (See pages 106 & 114). When assets needed replacing, revenue would be insufficient, otherwise they would have not have been ailing in the first place. The consequence was that assets were not replaced, or at best, were replaced by older equipment and rolling stock from main lines, whilst speed restrictions deferred track renewals. The line would then become even more vulnerable to motor vehicles which appeared on the scene within 20-30 years of the absorption of most minor lines by the big league. Pre-war railways did not borrow to modernise branch lines.

There was one way in which the acquisition of an ailing company could contribute to the profits of the predator, and that was by providing a route over which traffic, hitherto routed via a competitor's line, could remain on the parent company's metals for a longer distance, e.g. the S&DR. (See Chapter 13). This retained a greater share of revenue of the parent company's originating traffic. It could be beneficial even where distance travelled was longer or the train loads were lower. Likewise, building an extension was an alternative way to secure a greater share of existing revenue. Thus, an extension may be built which had little to contribute in the way of new profitable traffic, such as the Settle-Carlisle line. Where such lines were built late in the 19th century, no independent company having seized on the idea of building such a line earlier, was clear evidence of a lack of potential traffic. As mergers occurred, some would cease to be of value.

An overlooked cause for "ailing lines" was improvident speculation. (See page 8). Motor transport created other ailing lines. When one company - BR - owned all lines, the scope for closure of lines which had been, or were ailing, would increase. Even without the growth of unregulated road transport, the speed of line closures would have been accelerated in the BR era.

### Loss of main line journeys

Opponents of closures claim that passengers will not travel to the nearest alternative station by bus or car. In some cases, BR pointed out that passengers were already having to use a conveyance to reach the branch line station. (See page 101).

Paradoxically, when it suited their case, objectors would argue that passengers would travel by bus to a branch line station, thence by rail, especially if it was by diesel train, changing again at the end of their rail journey, back to bus, when they could, indeed, in some cases, already were travelling throughout by bus. (See pages 134, 189 & 222).

Objectors, who say passengers would go by road throughout cannot believe that *all* walk, perhaps two miles, to travel by rail on a branch line, to change again at a main line station. It is proved to be absurd by the expansion of carparks at main line stations.

Motorists leave cars at main line stations when they could drive throughout. With the option to drive to a local station, and leave a car there instead of 5-10 miles to a main line station, almost none took the former option. Mr. Steele, MP said that no one will walk to a station if he can get a bus at the door. [Hansard, vol. 547, col. 1602]. "No wants to walk a few hundred yards to a station". [Railway Gazette, 13.4.56, Page 184].

### Never expected to pay

Objectors to the closure of the "Bluebell Line" said that losses were greater than they need have been, and could be reduced (not eliminated) and "it was assumed that a line of this kind was never intended to pay for itself"! [CTCC Inquiry - Cmd 360, Para 11].

Certainly, shareholders expected any line to pay. Users in 1957 expected someone else to subsidise them. This attitude among objectors to closures, that losses could be reduced but not eliminated, was particularly prevalent. In contrast, the private sector does not hesitate to close a *profitable* branch or subsidiary, if by doing so it would increase overall group profit. Some lines that were built were known - by contractors and speculators, but not shareholders - to be unlikely to pay. (See page 8).

If you are not living within your means and tell your bank that you can reduce, but not eliminate, the difference between income and expenditure, so that your overdraft will continue, you will get no sympathy. If you said that to reduce, but not eliminate your overspending, you also needed an interest free loan, to buy an appliance, you would get a very dusty answer. For some illogical and unexplained reason, passengers on lines proposed for closure, expected that these principles should not apply to railways.

### Costs

At every hearing, objectors claimed costs could be reduced. *They* were prudent not to produce audited accounts, which BR was told *it* should have produced, nor to set out *too clearly* how to do so - their self-belief was sufficient proof. In two cases, objectors claimed that by locating men and a steam loco or DMU at the end of a branch, costs would fall. On paper they appeared to do so. Due to lack of expertise, they ignored real issues:-

- Relief cover would be required for holidays, sickness, especially if short notice, and a few other occasions, and hence a depot would need, at least one spare crew to cover those duties. A main line depot typically needed 12.5% cover, a ratio not arithmetically feasible at depots with less than eight men. Sending relief for the first train, from another depot was impractical, as was getting someone home after the arrival of the last train. Larger depots could cover absences more economically.
- Where steam engines were involved, coal stocks would be required, and someone would be needed to unload coal wagons, and reload ashes.
- Someone was needed to raise steam on an engine long before the crew arrived for duty. This specialised task would need relief cover at least for holidays and during sickness. Short notice sickness would present serious problems.
- A spare engine or diesel railcar would be required over and above that required to cover the first train. Inability to open a shop on time, or start a car has limited repercussions, but inability to provide a scheduled train is a different ball game.

- On steam lines, wagons would be tied up with coal, and ashes for disposal.
- To cover a six day service, rest day relief was required. A "rest day" is a weekday off to equate hours to a 40 hour week. Until 1982, eight hour shifts (imposed by Government) usually formed the basic framework. To conform to 40 hours, a day off, not always the Saturday, was a "rest day" to be covered by relief staff. One can see how those living in the sheltered life of industry - which had the five day week long before railways - could fail to comprehend and make allowance for this peculiarity. Covering this element was more costly for a small than a large depot.
- Carriage cleaning & maintenance provision would be required, together with stores.

The obsession that amateurs, including, in one case a road haulier, knew best could be seen in claims that there were "too many staff on a line". Inevitably, they looked at the number of trains to be worked, the number of signal box and station shifts to be covered. Relief costs, for holiday, sickness, vacancies, rest days, etc. can only have been totally disregarded through ignorance of the realities of railway life. Limits on road drivers' hours, imposed by law for safety reasons, are longer than rail drivers' hours and the former are sometimes exceeded. The MoT would not have tolerated comparable standards on rail, so one "opportunity" by the haulier to cut rail costs disappears. (See Appendix A.5).

Only someone who has not been involved in cutting costs could fail to realise that there was a time delay between establishing scope for economy and implementing it. Some economies required capital expenditure or staff training or both. Capital expenditure would only be incurred if there was a perceived return greater than the cost of borrowing *and* the return to be obtained on deploying precious capital on an alternative scheme. If it was unlikely to *eliminate* losses, and almost every critic in the cases reviewed here, admitted that fact, it was a waste of precious time. Staff training and capital costs needed to be brought into the equation. The time involved in preparing an interim scheme would merely prolong the agony. For instance, if £10,000 could be saved by closure, compared to £1,000 by using new equipment or by expenditure on re-training staff, it achieved nothing but delaying the inevitable. No businessman would contemplate it. When Government belatedly accepted it should be responsible for funding transport in rural areas, then it became morally right for any partial economy to be pursued. (See page 195).

In some cases, critics say that staff on a line about to be closed, claim that costs could be cut. Any realistic option would have been raised by their staff representatives at Joint Consultation which preceded every closure, (see page 28). Under the Staff Suggestions Scheme, staff were paid, anonymously, for economy ideas, which were then implemented.

Costs were constantly being cut on main lines where investment in equipment and re-training was justifiable. Each timetable change presented new opportunities to cut costs. It would have worsened BR's position to dissipate these gains to prop up loss making lines. Other "Good-housekeeping" economies were made which did not require investment, but most required staff consultation. These were on-going. When the new boys took over railways, they trumpeted their economies - but former BR managers were not surprised, because they knew that the pursuit of economy is unending, because the "product" - the timetable - and the demand, was constantly under review.

# Fares

The most common fallacy is to believe that cutting rail fares would solve BR's problems. That it may increase travel is possible. However:-

- A 25% fares reduction needs 33% more volume to achieve the same gross revenue, *to hold losses at existing levels*.
- If a train is loaded above 75%, more coaches are required to handle that 33% increase - requiring still more volume to cover these costs, *to hold losses at existing levels*.

In both scenarios, even more volume is needed to cut losses, which theorists claim will follow reductions. Logical minds, seeing that 40-50% volume increases are essential on a 25% fare reduction, must address the down side scenario - who picks up the tab if the experiment fails? Most wish to see reduced prices of every commodity. Some would buy the same quantity, but pay less; some would spend the same, but consume more; few would spend more on any commodity. Savings, especially from low fares, would be used elsewhere. In the goldfish bowl of Courts of Law and Parliament which was BR's environment, prices couldn't be varied quickly up & down as applies in the private sector.

The BTC told the Transport Tribunal in 1951: "Despite extension of cheap tickets in the past year producing 26% more journeys, and 19% more receipts on cheap tickets - total receipts actually fell". Despite this, and evidence that materials prices had increased at a staggering rate, the Tribunal reduced the standard fare in 1951, already below pre-war in real terms from 2.44d per mile (about 1p), by 28% to the 1940 level of 1.75d. Over the next two years, gross passenger revenue rose by £9m *less* than it would have done had it been linked to the RPI. Materials costs were up to 633% above pre-war. [See "*Blueprints for Bankruptcy*", Page 44]. After freight rate increases, there was no change in volume. [BTC 1950 Report, Para 74]. In 1954, the BTC told the Transport Tribunal that cheap evening tickets had produced less rather than more revenue in London. [Manchester Library: PP380.1622.T1]

Rev. T.A. Craggs, Uttoxeter, wrote to the Transport Tribunal in 1957, referring to "a village where people were bus minded - they paid 3/- (15p) for a bus journey of 79 stops taking 72 minutes, rather than 2/- (10p) for a rail journey of 15 stops taking 55 minutes". How could people object to BR fare increases with this comparison - did they want to travel for nothing? Despite this he complained of high fares which "had destroyed a fellowship engendered after the War". [See "*Blueprints for Bankruptcy*", Page 109].

When closure of the Wivenhoe-Brightlingsea line was proposed, objectors said that workers travelling from Brightlingsea would have to pay an extra shilling (5p) per day by bus. (See page 95. So much for high rail fares).

In comparing motoring costs and rail fares, motorists think only of petrol costs, which are but a fraction of the costs. A car left in a garage for 12 months, not having driven a mile, will fall in value. One used for above average mileage, has a lower resale value.

*"BR Season fares per mile were: 1.8p, 1.45p, 1.25p, 1.08p respectively for 10, 20, 30 and 40 miles".*
*"Motoring costs per mile; 'Full Costs': under 1000 cc: 7.47p; 1-1.5 litre: 8.56p; 'Costs excluding depreciation': 3.12p or 3.79p respectively".* [NBPI 1969 Report, Appendix H]

Age and mileage are major factors in value which translate into running costs. A separate figure is irrelevant, but is often used to minimise the disparity, which would be even wider had Government compelled manufacturers to lift cars to BR's safety levels.

"Past experience of resistance to price increases is usually temporary". "Over the past decade, (after the end of the Tribunal's statutory control), fares have been market oriented. BRB estimate that it produces 6-10% more revenue". "It is clear to us from wide ranging studies made by the BR Board and outside bodies that there is no prospect that general reductions in fares as distinct from the Board's practice of making selective reductions might increase revenue". "BR have successfully developed marketing techniques for filling spare off peak seats". [Price Commission, 1978, Paras 15, 16, 18, 19].

In 1982, as Divisional Manager, I varied fares up and down at several locations, to test the market and volume was barely affected. From Crewe, where volume had increased with the introduction of Saver fares, prior to my appointment, but gross revenue fell, I increased fares twice in a year, compared to once on the rest of BR. Volume was unaltered, but revenue increased. In the private sector, this would be applauded.

In September 1982, the Wrexham-Birkenhead Rail Users Association, invited me to address their meeting in a hotel, miles from the nearest station - everyone had to travel by car! The Chairman urged BR to reduce fares. He was told: "In 1946, a return ticket to London from Rotherham (where I worked as a booking clerk) cost £2, a junior booking clerk was paid £2.50 per week. The ticket is now 13 times as much, the salary 25 times as much". Producing a chocolate bar, which had gone up 34 times, and a newspaper 42 times, I said that "Fare increases since the War will stand comparison with anything you can name". They did not name any. (Rail wages were still well below industrial levels)..

"Rail Fan's" letter to the Crewe Chronicle in February 1984, referred to excursions run at fares of £5 to London - 60% below Savers, (half the 1934 average fare per mile). This promotion was aimed at those who had not used rail recently, conducted when spare rolling stock was available. He claimed the solution to BR problems was easy and didn't need a Degree to see that reduced fares would fill trains. Whilst ultra low fares may fill trains, we knew what he didn't - that it would not pay the bills. Whilst he may benefit from such reductions, I called for *equivalent* reductions to benefit everyone else - a new car for £800, petrol at 36p per gallon, and similar price reductions in holidays, food, clothing and newspapers - they were less than 0.5p after the War. All should increase sales *volume*. He was challenged to implement his bankruptcy inducing theories in his own business. There was no response, not even from those business sectors mentioned in my reply to the Chronicle. They kept below the parapet!

BR Chairman Dr. Beeching, from the private sector, stated "During the first 15 years of the inflation which began with the Second World War, fares rose much less than would have been necessary to compensate for the fall in the value of money. Even with the rise in the past ten years the average level of fares on all services remains at or below the pre-war level, though it is widely accepted that prices of services in a modern economy must be expected to rise faster than the prices of manufactured goods". [BRB 1961 Report, Para 260]

A sound way of demonstrating the scale of change in the cost of rail travel is to relate it to average earnings. BR did this in 1957, revealing that the number of minutes work required to pay the fare for a 20 mile journey (then the average journey length), had declined steadily from 51 minutes in 1938 to 29 minutes in 1957. [See BTC 1957 Annual Report, Para 181]. After 40 years of nationalisation, 1988 average industrial earnings were £4.98 per hour (8.3p per minute) and the average BR fare was 8.3p per mile, requiring **20** minutes of work for 20 miles of rail travel. These compare with **29** minutes in 1957, **44** minutes in 1949 and **51** minutes in 1938. [Sources: BTC Accounts and CSO Analysis of Statistics].

BR was criticised for not changing the fixed fare structure, based on mileage, at a time when the all powerful Transport Tribunal still existed. There were six million point to point journey options with several different fare categories for each journey. [BRB 1970 Report, Para 3.13]. If BR had sought to change fixed rate structures by application to the Tribunal, the Hearings would have gone on for ever. Changing the structure was progressed after the overdue demise of the Tribunal in 1969.

Paradoxically, no one argued for the need for a court of law to prevent private sector industry from pushing prices up. It was naively believed that only BR would lose business by raising prices. During those intermittent periods after 1970 when BR enjoyed similar freedom as the private sector to alter its own prices, selective price increases produced over 6% more revenue. [Price Commission Report, Paras 15-18].

When the subject of rail fares is raised, it is not uncommon to hear calls for "reasonable fares". As I wrote in "*Square Deal Denied*" defining "reasonable" must be a lawyer's dream. The definition must depend on the perspective from which the subject is viewed:-

- User - Lower than it is at any given moment; next to nothing; below cost, even free.
- Motorist - less than cost of petrol (also seeks a standard of service far higher than motoring - 100% punctual, 100% reliable).
- Franchisee - above cost, by the highest margin possible.

By the end of the 1980's trains were overpriced and overcrowded. [Henshaw, Page 224]. If trains are overcrowded, they cannot *possibly* be overpriced. If the private sector found demand exceeded supply, it would conclude that it was *underpricing*. When hotel demand increases in the summer, they *increase* prices. Costs do not increase, indeed with light evenings and warm days, costs per head should *fall*. If they adopted the principles urged on BR by critics, hotel prices would be *less* in the summer than the winter.

### Volume

"Turnover is vanity, profit is sanity". It is a moral that BR's critics do not seem to comprehend. A train service carrying a lot of passengers, even if their journeys are converted into cash, cannot be equated with net profit, either now or at some unspecified time in the future. Critics of closure proposals seized on reports that the introduction of diesel multiple unit trains had led to an increase in the number of passengers by 100%. They ignored that when 100% is applied to say six passengers, it produces an underwhelming train load of twelve. Even when they quoted total revenue, they either failed to relate revenue to costs or, argued that covering costs was only a matter of time.

39

A common error was the belief that a line could subsist on high volume on a few summer Saturdays, either from heavily loaded trains run during industrial holidays, or by excursions. Ensuing under utilisation for ten months was ignored by armchair experts.

"Where passenger trains are withdrawn, contact is made with BTC owned or associated buses and where necessary and practicable, additions are made to bus services. Often road transport already conveys the bulk and transfer of a residue creates no problems. BTC are criticised for not closing a large number of branch and secondary lines, yet when after careful study a decision is reached that a line should be closed, opposition is well organised and strong protests are made. Those who protest are never able to offer a solution to securing enough traffic". [BTC 1950 Report, Para 30]

## Subsidise by main line passenger ......

It is ironic that, whilst some were arguing that branch lines were in effect supporting main line services through 'contributory revenue' others could be arguing that uneconomic branch lines should be subsidised by main line passengers. Those passengers who lived near to main line stations were not going to be happy at the prospect of subsidising *anybody*. Moreover, the successful objections to fare increases, which held fares below the rate of inflation and well below the *cost of externally purchased materials for 34 consecutive years* ensured there was no surplus to spare. [See *"Blueprints for Bankruptcy"*].

An MP said that he believed that they (railways) should be sufficiently well run to carry some of the unremunerative branches. [Hansard, vol. 536, col. 1799]. This policy is not pursued in the private sector. Closures are commonplace. When they have hacked off all the dead wood in the UK, it is not uncommon to transfer production to the Far East, leaving derelict factories behind.

## ...... or by Freight traffic

Another popular idea is that freight revenue should subsidise local passenger trains. Due to Government's archaic railway rates policy, profitable freight traffic was being creamed off by road hauliers whilst UK industry exploited the rail freight rates system, and helped to drain away the most profitable flows from rail to road but compelled railways to carry the unprofitable. [See *"Square Deal Denied"*]. Moreover, railway freight rates were decided by a lethal combination of the Minister of Transport and a Court of Law. [See *"Blueprints for Bankruptcy"*]. Users objected to *any* increases, so that the best that could be hoped for was that freight would cover its own costs. Industry and trade demanded that freight should *not* subsidise passengers. [See *"Blueprints for Bankruptcy"*, Page 115].

Freight viability was placed in jeopardy, not only by unwarranted control of railway rates for the first fourteen years of BR's existence, but by being denied a fair share of post-war resources and being encumbered with half a million vintage wagons previously owned by non railway companies - collieries and traders, for which the BTC was told to pay £43m.. These wagons were much older than railway company wagons. To counter creaming-off profitable traffic, BR had to cut rates to curtail losses to a modern road fleet.

"Passenger services were withdrawn from a town in Nottinghamshire where coal traffic paid all track costs". [Henshaw, Page 236]. It should have paid all track costs, but only all *freight* track costs. Having been in management in the BR Divisions which embraced that coalfield, I know the area. Track, signalling and line speeds were adequate for freight services and occasional excursions. Neither the NCB nor their customers would tolerate coal subsidising passengers. The Transport Tribunal could never have been influenced to set coal rates at a level which would provide a surplus for passenger traffic. If passenger traffic shared the line, freight customers would rightly call for passengers to share infrastructure costs and pay all terminal and enhanced signalling costs. They would oppose a new passenger service being given pathing priorities over freight, and causing delay to coal. Without priority, any timetable would be unpredictable. Such priority is costly. Passengers' "share" of track and other joint costs would not be a token amount.

During my spell as a Divisional Manager, a teacher who was a member of a "rail action group", endeavoured to tell me that we should run a frequent freight service on the Cambrian as a means of indirectly subsidising passenger services. I explained:

- Government policy required that BR freight must pay its way independently.
- Our market research of every potential user of freight services, from the corner shop upwards, found no new potentially profitable business. It was hardly surprising that this rural area was lacking the potential to run economic fully loaded freight trains.

He did not identify any traffic which could be influenced to rail. I wondered if he had in mind running wagons up and down to create an *impression* of activity - like model railway trains running in circles with wagons that are never unloaded or reloaded.

### Subsidise from General Railway Deficit

After 1962, some MP's said that losses should be covered from "the General Railway Deficit". They were referring to a provision of the 1962 Act. (See page 12). The Grant was an attempt to allow BR to achieve viability, not to be a licence to keep loss making lines open. Indeed, the Grant was for a limited period, during which they had to take steps, including closures, to live within their means. It was ineffective, because they could not bring themselves to believe that BR needed the *same* freedom as the private sector: total pricing freedom, freedom to close loss making facilities, with no political interference. When an opportunity came for loss making lines to be supported by the taxpayer, some who had objected to closures, and mentioned this clause, voted against the 1968 Act.

### Modernisation

Some critics argued that lightly loaded branch lines were more in need of modernisation than main lines. No business would have considered, for a second, investing scarce capital resources other than where there could be seen, an adequate demand and a good return. Certainly, such resources should not be invested in lines whose historic role had been to poach traffic from lines already handling such traffic, and yet left them unprofitable in the heyday of railways. It is inconceivable that BR should have invested in the Somerset & Dorset line, the M&GN or others, rather than the Euston-Manchester-Liverpool and other main lines for which there was still insufficient capital to replace Victorian signal boxes. Level crossing modernisation was vigorously opposed by local authorities and individual MP's. [PRO: MT114/413]. Belatedly, BR was allowed to adopt principles used safely for decades in mainland Europe. When modernisation was well under way, BR had to modify many newly modernised crossings and install extra phones. Costly changes had to be made after the Hixon accident. Attitudes to traffic lights were lax. Some auto-barriers had to be converted to controlled crossings and CCTV installed in case users, having disregarded lights, became trapped between barriers. I carried out a test over an equivalent distance and found you could crawl and not get trapped, if lights began to flash *after* you began to cross. Government forced BR to make more changes to give more protection to pedestrians. Similar safeguards were not imposed on road crossings. These changes destroyed the economic case for many locations.

"The Eastern Region said: had all services been diesel operated, the *direct* cost of operation would have been covered by revenue, but there would have been no significant contribution to the cost of terminals, track & signalling and general administration. It was a start". [Henshaw, Page 86]. Those four items were 45% of total costs. [BRB 1963 Report, Table 4-A]. That being the average position for all services, means that some were covering even less than 55% of total costs. It was a very discouraging start. Who would cover the balance until traffic could do so, should that ever occur? It could not come from reserves, because BR had never had been given the opportunity to create any. [See "*Blueprints for Bankruptcy*", Page 45].

"The provision of diesel units will not necessarily turn an unprofitable line into a profitable one". [CTCC 1954 Report, Para 30]. "Much of the increase in passengers from dieselisation is in populous areas". "To continue to operate services, the direct costs of which, even using diesels, exceeds their receipts by a large margin, is to waste resources on a scale neither the BTC nor the country can afford. In France and Holland, whose national railways have been revived since the war, passenger services have been withdrawn from a very much larger proportion of their system than in this country". [BTC 1955 Report, Paras 16 & 30]. "In Holland, 691 stations out of 1,000 have been closed". [Hansard vol. 551, col. 1675, 24.5.56].

"There are services which however well modernised, will never pay in any circumstances. There is a tendency to think that all services can and should be dieselised or electrified forthwith, but the magnitude of capital cost is not generally realised". [CTCC 1957 Report, Para 16]. "We are running passenger trains whose costs are more than five times receipts, so that if we halved costs and doubled receipts, they would still lose money". [British Transport Review, April 1956, Page 58]. "The Hooton-West Kirby was a typical rural non-paying line which could not be recovered from losses of £20,000 pa by diesels costing £60,000 pa, so that the 60,000 passenger journeys in 1955 would need to increase by 400,000 to pay for diesels". [CTCC 1956 Report, Para 26].

"The CTCC had visited Ulster and Eire. They noted that the use of diesels had not prevented losses in operation which now threaten the remaining rail services in those places. They appreciate for the sparse traffic of rural areas, railway units are handicapped in comparison with road, by higher capital and running costs and being tied to track, on which stations and halts are often some distance from the places they serve. They state that on railway lines from which services have already been withdrawn, no change in the type of rail unit could have converted loss into profit". [BTC 1956 Report, Para 39].

"Experience has shown that certain services cannot cover their direct costs even when operated by diesels. Gains were achieved on routes where a traffic potential was believed to exist". [BTC 1957 Report, Para 209]. The response of the public to improved DMU services has not been sufficient to turn loss making services into profitable ones. [BTC 1961 Report, Para 302].

This was insufficient proof for objectors who wanted local under-utilised lines to be kept on standby, modernised and under-priced into the bargain. Whereas, other industry would only need to try out a new piece of equipment once, and abandon it immediately it became apparent it was not improving profits, with BR, it had to be seen to be tried out at 50 similar loss making locations, and even then fireside experts would find fault.

### Railbuses

A favourite hobby horse of branch line enthusiasts was that loss making lines could be kept in operation by using lightweight railbuses.

In the Rural Transport Debate (see page 45), an MP took a ten mile branch line as an example for the economic use of railbuses. One railbus would be required to operate an hourly service. On that basis, to operate the 1,535 miles BR had - by then - closed, required 153 plus 27 to cover maintenance, (if all could be based at one depot), based on the 85% availability forecast by manufacturers. A minimum thirty year life is needed to get a return on rolling stock, therefore these would have to be at least that, and probably more because of poorer loadings. Thus the demand would have been for around six units per annum - the number quoted by an MP. (See page 13). There would be no mad rush from manufacturers to fill that demand, especially if demand petered out should experiments prove costly failures. There would be problems arising from movement of vehicles from isolated branch lines over busy main and commuter lines to and from depots, especially as they could not be relied on to actuate track circuits. Contrary to popular opinion, a vehicle could not be located at each branch end without a 100% cover for breakdowns. Any experiment would be costly due to training men for a task that should it prove to be short lived would further increase losses. The self-confident advocates of lightweight railbuses were not, of course, prepared to back their theories by setting up companies to build these vehicles, and sell them on a sale or return basis. (See also page 45).

In September 1959, the BTC told Rural District Councils that a railbus cost £12,000 - three times as much as a road bus. [See "Blueprints for Bankruptcy", Page 75]. The investment required to buy 180 units, and spare parts, would have been over £2m, plus costs for fuelling installations and interest on the loan capital - money that would be at grave risk, as compared with spending it on main line stock. Additional provision would be needed on most routes for mails, parcels, etc., as railbuses had no capacity for such items. Extra units would be required as standby's to cover short notice failure at remote locations.

In the advocated use of lightweight diesels, critics overlooked tail vans containing mails, parcels, luggage in advance for independent schools and holiday resorts, which could be hauled by standard diesel units, but not lightweight buses. If that traffic was sent by road, all infrastructure costs would fall on passengers. They also overlooked the serious problems arising from the unreliability of railbuses to actuate track circuits.

Worse was the belief that they could be mass produced. The car industry tools up to mass produce by the million. Had these vehicles been a practical proposition, BR would have required at the most hundreds, with a life of 30-40 years. I learned from Ford Motors that "mass production" for small diesel engines is a minimum of 300,000 pa. To conceive the prospect of mass production of lightweight diesel railcars was a childish flight of fancy. A private sector company would not have financed such a project, even in the hope of foreign sales. UK industry couldn't produce railcars cheaply enough to make them economic on branch lines. They may have lost an export opportunity by not doing so.

It was astonishing to read that an MP said that "railcars should stop anywhere en route to pick up passengers - not just at stations". [Hansard, vol. 536, col. 1802]. No reliable timetable could be provided. Had he tried to board a train from cess level? Even with steps it is not easy. The repeated emphasis of heavy luggage, prams, cycles etc. was not brought out in *this* aspect of the debate. The concept would have required a special breed of new trains for a handful of lines. It must be obvious that no businessman would contemplate it as a practical solution for a minute. Had the Government been prepared to pick up the tab for this social experiment, it would have been a different matter. Quite clearly they were not, as they did nothing to contribute towards loss making lines until 1968.

One MP "had in mind an eight seater light diesel railcar". [Hansard, vol. 518, col. 1260]. One driver to every eight passengers running on a costly dedicated infrastructure could only be uneconomic. No road operator with such a vehicle could afford to pay for his own road.

An MP, briefed by the Railway Development Association suggested using a railbus, converted from a road bus as used in Ireland. [Hansard, vol. 551, col. 1648]. The CTCC visited Ireland to view railbuses. "Some were ingeniously adapted from obsolescent road buses. In the North of Ireland, they have not succeeded in preventing losses which now threaten the continued operation of many of the remaining rail services". [Times, 4.4.57, Page 7]. Had BR publicised an intention to use vehicles like this converted road bus - of pre-war vintage - when modern vehicles had been appearing on BR for two years, the criticism would have reverberated around the country and in Parliament. The BTC allowed themselves to be pressured into conducting risky experiments. (See page 23).

Great Northern of Ireland Railways can fix flanged wheels on a standard bus, as their gauge is wider than BR's. They have four which have not prevented losses. They can only be driven from one end, requiring a turntable at each end of a branch, (and maintenance depots. UK branch line locos could return without turning). Irish Railways (CIE) are not intending to continue with any experiments and are going back to larger units. It is not clear why those in rural areas would prefer to walk to a station, to use a bus which runs on rails, rather than one which runs on roads. [PRO: MT124/65]. Those on roads would pick up closer to houses. To apply the concept on BR, a narrower bus design was first required !

The Railway Development Association claimed a railbus was cheaper to operate than a road bus, because rail paid no fuel tax or road fund licence. [PRO: MT124/65]. They ignored that these were a contribution towards road costs, whilst railways pay all their costs.

Lightweight units were constrained by safety requirements; many stations are a long way from the nearest community. [BTC 1955 Report, Para 31]. "17 of 22 railbuses ordered have been delivered". "On three branches in 1959, it was found that lightweight units were too small to take care of peak traffic. On another, there was so little traffic, it may have to be closed". [BTC 1958 Report, Para 24; 1959 Report, Para 87].

## Light Railways

As an alternative to modernising branch lines, amateurs advocated conversion to Light Railways, overlooking that conversion needed capital, when there was too little for main lines, and that their low speeds would be no match for road transport competition. The Light Railways Act 1896 allowed lighter construction and simpler signalling and amenities. (See pages 15-16). A maximum speed of 25 mph was commonly imposed to ensure safety was not impaired by any relaxation of safety standards. Preserved railways require a Light Railway Order before passengers are carried.

What the advocates of light railways, especially local authorities overlooked, was that the Act empowered "Any County, Borough or District Council to control and work such a railway". In none of the cases reviewed in this book, did a local authority offer to do so - they were content to stand on the touch lines and urge BR to do so. Why were they so reluctant to prove such lines could make a profit, instead of only criticising? It only needed one local authority with the courage of its convictions.

The concept of Light Railways was developed at a late stage - when the motor vehicle was arriving on the scene. They involved speed restrictions which made them uncompetitive with motor vehicles. The most frequently quoted promoter was Colonel Stephens. His railways do not appear to have been as successful as many latter day admirers seem to believe. Very old rolling stock and other assets, and buildings of low standard, created railways run to standards which were increasingly unacceptable pre-war in competition with road transport. Little wonder they fell into terminal decline.

During a Rural Transport Bill debate, an MP claimed that a railway could be maintained for £60 per mile if operated by light railway methods, a railbus would cost £9,000, £6,000 if mass produced. The MP had been told by an unnamed "*expert*", that running a ten mile line with a railbus costing £9,000, with six journeys each way per weekday covering depreciation, interest, wages and *allowing* £60 per mile for track maintenance would cost 15/- (75p) per journey. [Hansard, vol. 547, cols. 709-710]. Initially, it seemed that the £60 per mile was per *week*, as the Reshaping Report showed the lowest as £2,000 pa for a freight, and £3,500 for a passenger line. I have tracked down the unnamed expert, his paper - and his area of expertise. It was *not* on railways. (See page 221). His "plan" showed that this was the cost per mile per annum! His costs were based on assumptions which were not backed by *any* independent evidence that such costs for construction, maintenance and operation applied *anywhere* in the world. BR's critics who quoted this MP, and these costs, overlook that he also said: "If it is decided branches do not pay, do not tinker, remove them completely". [Hansard, vol. 547, col. 1803].

One critic saw a Light Railway with two obsolete buses welded together as a viable option, with no signalling. This was out of touch with reality. Enthusiasts may flock to travel on it, or more likely just to photograph it, but those who were supposed to benefit - BR passengers - would rightly turn their noses up. Amateurs do not decide what form of basic signalling is acceptable - the MoT's Inspectors will dictate that. In this context, a

Transport Minister said his Officers had told him that "There is no substantial economy from light railways in respect of signalling". [Hansard, vol. 547, col. 769].

An MP stated: "Not a single branch line that has been closed has been converted into a Light Railway". [Hansard, vol. 547, col. 750]. What was holding critics back? Were banks not prepared to entertain their "back of the envelope" plans?.

## Bad Winters

A common objection was that railways were needed in the winter. Spring and bad memories ended support, until closure was threatened. In 1965, a director in the solid fuel business told me that their records showed that bad winters occurred about every seven years. BR were expected to be profit motivated and a Social Service. BR should have been grateful for these rare confirmations that BR kept moving even in blizzards, although the first word from the public was to complain of delays! [See *"Blueprints for Bankruptcy"*, Page 176]. Local authorities and other objectors saw railways as an insurance policy, but didn't want to pay the premium.

In 1956, an MP called for reinstatement of Halifax-Bradford-Keighley services "as moorlands roads are the first to be snowed up, and that in the winter of 1947 (nine years earlier!), one village was cut off for eight weeks". Ministers "had no power to intervene unless the TUCC or CTCC recommended retention of a line. If the CTCC supported closure the Minister could not issue a Direction to the BTC to retain it". [Hansard, vol. 547, col. 1576]. The line was needed on one week in 58!. There was a more logical case for a Ministerial Direction on route retention, with funding, in the national interest - under Sec 4 (1) of the 1947 Act, as amended - than Directions given on selective fare reductions that were not of national interest. [See *"Blueprints for Bankruptcy"*, Page 100].

Praying in aid winters of 7-8 years earlier was not uncommon, as the following chapters show. In one case, they went back 33 years! (See page 150). On some occasions, traffic that never went by rail would miraculously appear. (See pages 107, 167 & 169).

There are areas in the UK that have never had a railway, which suffer worse winters, and are even more isolated than those which are reviewed in this book. Why did objectors to closures expect that main line passengers or taxpayers should single them out for favoured treatment and a subsidised railway? There was an equal case for new railways to be built to serve those more isolated communities - but who would pay?

## "Running down"

Critics referred to "running a line down" or "starving it of traffic" when BR transferred traffic to other routes. These are emotive euphemisms. Translated from amateur to professional and non emotive language, it means transferring traffic to routes, which had the capacity for it. No industry perpetuates loss making, or even marginally profitable, factories if it can divert production to others. No company retains shops if it can divert some sales to another outlet. In any industry but BR, it is seen as good business practice. Some of the case studies in this book make reference to this. Former users are at the root of "starving lines of traffic". Critics who were particularly adept at emotive euphemisms, never applied the same policies towards other industries that were closing down.

What the over enthusiastic amateur and occasional passengers seem incapable of realising was that like any other business activity, railways could only survive if user was profitable. The message to users on all branch lines was "Use it or lose it". Locals preferred not to use it, but didn't want to lose it either - wanting the penny and the bun. When a village shop displays this sign - locals accept the reality of the situation, not that that necessarily makes them use it. What each and every one hopes is that someone else will use it enough to keep it open, so that it is available as a standby on the odd occasion when the car breaks down, or the weather is severe. When it eventually closes there is much shaking of heads, but little else. When the same situation arises with railways, those who make least use, make most noise, and are backed by those who have contributed by a similar lack of patronage to closing UK factories, shops, cinemas, theatres etc. They are supported by those who claim to know everything about running railways, but have not been able to apply their self professed managerial skills to avoid the withdrawal of facilities in other walks of life. With one exception, in every case of closure that I have studied, the common denominator is that *not one* objector undertook to spend more on travelling by rail as a quid pro quo for keeping a line open. The one exception was the Westerham line. They did not go so far as to offer to close the revenue gap, but merely to make a token gesture. (See page 156). Fares throughout BR had been held down, well below the rate of inflation, whilst material costs escalated, and wages rose through necessity to reduce staff turnover or by Government direction. Fares were held down because the self same local authorities and pressure groups who were campaigning to keep lines open, were retaining counsel to object to increases in a Court of Law.

"Even the most determined opponents of closures do not suggest that losses are not made. The issue is whether closure would do more damage to the life and economy of the areas than would be justified to make railways more viable. Some firms make little use of railways. The scale of industry in the area is small. The lines are inadequately used by the present population and industries they serve". [Board of Trade, 10.3.64, PRO: BT213/260].

### Trains re-routed via longer routes

It was rarely so simplistic. Freight traffic over any given route, company trains apart, was not travelling from A to B, but from $A^1$ ...... $A^n$ to $B^1$ ..... $B^n$. Traffic taken from a closed route is spread over different routes, and individual wagons are spread over different trains which cover the range of destinations and origins. Even if the entire wagon flow from a closed route is simply placed on one alternative route, they are often spread onto trains which have spare capacity. Just as not every lorry travels with a 100% load, so the same applies with trains. Moreover, the alternative route may well have better train loads, and, if it is double as opposed to a single line, as was often the case, the length limit imposed by single line loops is overcome by the greater train length permitted on the new route. Spare capacity in loco and crew diagrams (rosters) at depot X can be used up whilst savings are made in those covering the closed route. The percentage "spare cover" element required at smaller depots, tends, for arithmetical reasons to be higher than bigger depots. (See pages 35-36). Bigger locos, which are too heavy for a minor route can operate on the alternative route to create extra capacity. Critics who jump on these diversions as if they have found the holy grail, accept with equanimity that a car may make an overall journey more quickly and at less cost if it travels a longer distance over a motorway instead of a 'B' road. Easier gradients are to be found on trunk routes, because they had the potential flow from the outset to justify greater expenditure on easier gradients, whilst rural routes, for sake of economy, had to accept steeper gradients.

An example of freight traffic re-routed over a longer route at less cost was my plan for Rugby Portland Cement's chalk traffic from Leighton Buzzard to Warwickshire, which by avoiding use of a restrictive single line, increased train size by about 50%, improved wagon and loco utilisation, closed several miles of line, signal boxes and a train crew depot. Having improved our profitability and ensured that the company could send all its traffic in higher capacity wagons, which they had requested, requiring fewer such wagons and releasing 250 standard wagons, it was disappointing to see the traffic diverted to a new pipeline, when they capitalised on cross country trenches being dug by the Gas Board

Another point affecting the obsession of the uninformed on the shorter distance over a branch is that the productivity of train crews was limited by what could be performed in the eight hour day imposed on railways by Government in 1919. [See "*Square Deal Denied*", Page 29]. There could be more waste in a shorter route, crews may get back earlier - but the unused portion of the eight hour day would often be wasted. Those who say you "could find something for them to do", can only have in mind running up and down with the same train, and therefore must have played for too long with model trains.

### Were Managers happy to close lines ?

Some critics alleged that managers were happy to close lines, which, it was claimed, or inferred, could have been made profitable. No hard evidence has been advanced to support such a belief. It is an unlikely scenario which flies in the face of logic. From my personal knowledge, managers made every endeavour to end losses to avoid closures. There is a vast difference between wasting effort on half measures designed only to *reduce* losses, rather than trying to *eliminate* them. If they were not motivated by business, altruistic, personal or operational reasons to keep lines open, they, also, would eventually face redundancy. For some unfathomable reason, critics believed that BR managers, including those recruited from outside the industry, preferred redundancy - even before the introduction of redundancy pay!

Railways were formed into Districts: Operating, Commercial, Motive Power, Civil Engineering, etc. Each was headed by a man, trained and expert in his field, whose salary was related to the size of his responsibility - financially, geographically, distance, manpower, number of depots, assets, etc. A "District" carried a grading, to which his salary was linked. If these criteria are reduced, the District was downgraded or merged with another District. He was then redeployed, into a post with a similar or lower salary structure, which may require him to move home, and be reverted to an Assistant's post. Hence, there were compelling reasons to try to keep lines open.

Some managers opposed closures because an area lacked alternative public transport.

In contrast to those who said that managers didn't try to make branches pay, and hence rushed into premature or avoidable closures, others said managers did not close lines in order to protect their own jobs. There is a more logical prospect that some managers were motivated to keep lines open which should have closed. BR had Luddites, opposed to closure of lines that should never have opened; and were financial disasters in the heyday of railways. Luddite managers were not confined to BR - they could be found in UK manufacturing industry which lost a world lead in so many fields due to its unwillingness to accept the need for change. A BR manager was subject to higher authority, who would monitor his effectiveness in improving standards - *safety, utilisation of assets, manpower and finances.* Hence the scope for Luddite attitudes had its limits.

"No railwayman could contemplate closing down lines unless there was no chance of it ever becoming profitable. For this reason we have experimented with railcars. The track still has to be maintained in safe condition so costs remain high. The railcars have not brought the increase in traffic that was hoped for. It is the only example of modernisation failing to make an impact on the public it serves. Savings on branch line closures come, in fact, to 15% higher than estimates. In earlier times, it was possible to make large profits on some parts and use it to subsidise others. This was at a time of restricted competition". [Evidence to the Select Committee on BR - 1960, PRO: AN116/26].

In 1955, an MP, in a Debate on closures, said: "When a business man finds he is losing business, he does not put up the shutters, he looks around for ways of increasing business". [Hansard, vol. 536 col. 1801]. In fact, the evidence is that they *do* cease to provide a product. One is told: "It is not made any more, no one wants it", when you have just asked for it. Many private sector businesses put up the shutters in 1954 and 1955. The total compulsory and voluntary liquidations in 1954 and 1955 were 3,639 and 3,588 respectively. It is certain that none of them were prevented from increasing prices, nor directed by Government to pay wages they couldn't afford, nor prevented from closing branches to stave off bankruptcy. Companies shut down production here and transfer it to the Far East, then import products under the original well known brand names! A transport example arose at a Transport Tribunal hearing in 1956, when a witness said that his family had operated buses, but gave up because receipts could not be made to match increasing costs. A former Chairman of Esso did not share the MP's views. (See page 25).

"Few were willing to speak out against closures, when they did it was in guarded tones: '*There are those who feel that losses need not have occurred after 1952 at any rate to the extent that they did*', [A.J. Pearson, Assistant General Manager, LMR]. Such criticism hardly amounted to a forthright condemnation of the Beeching regime". [Henshaw, Page 142].

The source was not listed, but this same sentence may be found in Pearson's book. He was not opposed to *closures*, nor saying that *branch line* losses were greater than they should have been. He criticised both the Minister and the BRB in his book. He criticised the BRB for *holding up closures* to embrace them in the Reshaping Plan:-

> "*The Report held up proposals for closures of uneconomic lines and services that would otherwise have gone through their normal processes. They were planned long before 1963 but had to be held up until the first report was issued and approved by Government. Hitherto the practice had been to put forward firm proposals steadily*

*as they were ascertained and patiently plod on with the recommendations. It might have been better if the Board had accelerated the preparation of firm proposals for withdrawing lines and services and pressed them through the machinery instead of dramatising them in a single document".* [Pearson, Page 26].

Losses arose from depressed income and increased expenditure. *"Blueprints for Bankruptcy"* shows that the Government played the major part in both:-

- Fares held down by Government policies and interference, but not materials' prices.
- Wage increases directed by Ministers which the BTC could not afford.
- Delaying all, and preventing some closures of lines that were losing money, many of which should never have opened in the 19th century.

There is further evidence that Pearson did not disapprove of closures, but was critical of continued interference with day to day management: *"After 1954, the financial position deteriorated rapidly, The reason was that receipts failed to keep pace with rising costs, In 1956, the Minister authorised the BTC to increase freight charges by half of the amount proposed, and delayed fare increases".* [Pearson, Page 83]. *"Government instructed the Executive to meet a wage claim declined by the Executive".* [Pearson, Page 49]. *"Marples made silly comments".* [Pearson, Page 103]

Fiennes (General Manager, Eastern Region) developed a scheme for the 'basic railway'. "Similar 'basic railway' proposals had been put forward by the Railway Development Association since the early 1950's". [Henshaw, Page 179]. Despite prolonged research, I have found no reference to a 'basic railway' being advanced externally and the author does not mention a source. It cannot be confused with the Light Railway concept practised by Colonel Stephens, (see page 45). Fiennes envisaged radio signalling - which no one advocated in the 1950's. It is wrong to believe that Fiennes opposed closure of unremunerative lines. Fiennes refers to another expert with a train plan to keep open the Stour Valley line, but Fiennes said this line loses money and cannot be made to pay, and told the 'expert', if you want the line open, what are *you* going to do about it? Fiennes mentions other locations where de-staffing was opposed by local authorities and others. Fiennes was glad to "negotiate with local authorities if they guaranteed extra costs". "I want to run this railway only if it is remunerative - you want it, what are you going to do about it?" [Fiennes Pages 116-120, 102]. You had to be very senior to make comments like this to critics, or you would face threats of questions in the House or a letter to the Minister.

The financial position was set to deteriorate from 1952, when the Transport Tribunal and Government together delayed the first national increase in fares since 1947 for seventeen months, taking some fares back below pre-war levels, and jointly succeeded in holding fares below the RPI for 34 years. No industry, however skilled its managers, could have remained solvent, given the unprecedented interference in prices, whilst suppliers' prices continued their unremitting rise. [See *"Blueprints for Bankruptcy"* for a full account].

In an article entitled "Why BR have to prune dead branches", BR was quoted as saying "We never abandon a service until passengers have abandoned it themselves". The journalist, Brian Hope, wrote: "If people who put their names on petitions had used the stations regularly, they would not be closing". [Manchester Evening News, 12.6.59].

## Losses disputed

To support the claim that managers were happy to close lines which were potentially profitable, critics claimed that BR accounts were inaccurate. By this they didn't mean *the Accounts*, prepared annually in accordance with Directions of the MoT, and audited by independent accountants. That may have brought a legal action by the Auditors. They referred to financial appraisals prepared to assess alternative courses of action. Sir Peter MacDonald, the Isle of Wight MP, told Parliament: "*We hear from commercial industries that if they rendered accounts in the same manner as Nationalised Industries they would find themselves in gaol*". Asked by an MP to substantiate that, he said: "*objectors challenged railways to substantiate accounts* (on closures). *If commercial enterprises were to render accounts without substantiating them, in the same manner they would be up against the Board of Trade and the Companies Act and find themselves in gaol, that is opinion of many people*". [Hansard, vol. 523, cols. 874, 876/7].

No other business in the UK was, is, or ever has been required to prepare "*accounts*" to justify rationalisation. They close branches or cease to provide a service or product to the public, without notice, without Public Inquiries, and without Parliamentary debate. If they did have to perform in a similar circus to BR, they would not, of course, be subject to any accusations as to the accuracy of *their* figures. That *would* lead to legal proceedings. When they see money going down the drain, they, unlike BR, can act unilaterally. Critics who selectively quoted this MP, neglected to mention that, in that debate, he was criticised and told his facts were wrong. An MP said "*In the latter part of his speech, he revealed such ignorance of the Nationalised Industries, that we should set up a Select Committee in order to assist him to learn about them. His facts are wrong*". [Hansard vol. 523, col. 878].

MacDonald was invited to repeat his words outside the House so that he could be sued for slander. He was told that Sir Harold Barton, a public auditor who audits BR accounts, asked if he would supply as much, more or less in the annual reports of a company, said he would not be thanked by shareholders if he burdened them with half the information, the BTC supplies. [Hansard, vol. 547, col. 733]. Objectors who doubted the accuracy of BR figures did not prove the accuracy of *their* figures, indeed, more often than not, they did not produce *any*, opting for vague generalisations and pious hopes, which they expected to be taken on trust. BR was guilty until proved innocent. Councils who were loud in their calls for BR to cut costs, failed to prevent rising costs. (See Appendix C).

Objectors were so obsessed with their own opinions, that they overlooked that BR staff, who, better than any outsider, were well placed to make judgements, were given the same figures, and would have taken action had they been inaccurate. (See page 28).

In 1967, the National Council for Inland Transport wrote: "if £17m has been saved from closure, then more than £17m was lost in other ways". [PRO: EW22/64]. It had! Fares held below the RPI from 1948 to 1967, cost £620m before allowing for inflation and interest imposed by Government on loans which they forced on BR to "compensate" for frozen prices, and more was lost by interference in freight charges. [See *"Blueprints for Bankruptcy"*, Pages 50-52, 63 & 192]. Without interference, there would have been an operating surplus of £132m instead of a loss of £488m. Delays of 2-3 years in closures cost £34-51m, if £17m was an annual gain. Finally, BR was not allowed to modernise for eight years.

It has been claimed that BR's financial plight became worse with each closure. What these armchair critics either did not know or chose to ignore, was that BR's position was becoming worse because, uniquely among all public and private sector industry, they were not allowed to match prices to costs, and were compelled by a dilatory Court of Law to hold prices below the RPI. In its 20 years of power, Transport Tribunal Hearings delayed essential price rises by $12^{3}/_{4}$ years. [See "*Blueprints for Bankruptcy*", Page 91]. Between 1953 and 1955, the rail fares index had fallen from 26 points below the RPI to 34 points below, and by 1957 was 41 points below! [See "*Blueprints for Bankruptcy*", Page 63]. Materials' prices were rocketing up and rail wages being pushed up above affordable levels by Government interference and to cut staff losses to overpaid jobs in industry. Increased industrial wages were passed onto the customer, including BR which was a substantial customer of the private sector. Hence, the margin between income and expenditure would have been even greater without closures and other economies that were being made. As if this inequity was not bad enough, in 1956, the MoT froze rail fares for the sixth year in sixteen consecutive years. Anyone with only primary school arithmetic could predict the outcome. [See "*Blueprints for Bankruptcy*"].

Whilst critics made sweeping unquantified and unproven allegations that savings were over estimated, others stated that BR was not over estimating:-

- BR had been understating potential savings, e.g. on the Carlisle-Edinburgh line. The TUCC were advised of savings of £233,000 pa but potential savings to BR were at least £536,000. [Freeman-Allen, Modern Railways, January 1969, Page 22].
- We are satisfied that the estimated savings were compiled by the BTC on a very conservative basis. [CTCC 1954 Report, Para 10].
- Sixteen lines closed, including two on which savings were confirmed and six had savings greater than forecast: actual £75,606 (+£15,977). [CTCC 1956 Report, Para 6].
- The Stedeford Committee said that "The BTC had cautiously forecast a 5.5% fall in passenger miles - from closures and other factors - between 1957 & 1963, but they had increased by 10%. [See "*Blueprints for Bankruptcy*", Page 79].

Savings always excluded the sale value of land, houses, stations & other property, together with Rates and insurance paid on them, and asset renewal costs due over five years hence.

BR was closing lines before Beeching became Chairman, and continued to do so, following the production of his Reshaping Report. Critics continued to challenge the justification for closure. This flies in the face of logic. Beeching was a director of ICI, one of UK's biggest and most successful companies. Despite BR managers being bitterly criticised for "accounts" which they produced in connection with closures - Beeching reduced the volume of data provided. Logically, anyone from the private sector would have set out to show BR managers how to succeed where they had been said to be failing, especially in the matter of branch lines. If it had been possible for him to show how branch line losses could be eliminated without closures - his logical course would have been to do so. He would have earned huge brownie points by ending the deficit *and* keeping open lines so dear to rural electorates which had a marked Tory affiliation. There was no mileage in pursuing the same policy as BR managers, *unless it was well founded and unavoidable*, since Ministers claimed that BR managers were incompetent, and needed the refreshing air of the private sector. There was every reason for him to find a different way. It is significant that, as a member of the Stedeford Committee, which criticised the BTC organisation created by Government, and whose findings were so embarrassing to Government that they were kept secret for 30 years, Beeching said that the underlying cause of BR problems was fares held below the RPI by the Tribunal. The Committee criticised the delay in effecting closures. Government failure to act on these issues meant that deficits would continue, albeit at a slower rate than would have applied had closures been blocked. It has been suggested that the Minister wanted to see branch line closures expedited because of his road building plans. The road haulage industry would barely notice the traffic diverted to road following rural closures. Their lack of interest in traffic in these areas, by an industry given its highway at sub standard cost, is clear evidence that it was uneconomic. (See page 12). The combined volume of traffic on all closed branch lines would not have justified one mile of motorway.

## Regional Boundaries

Critics claimed that lines were denied investment and only proposed for closure because they crossed a Regional boundary. This belief is undermined by the many cross boundary lines which remained open, e.g.: East and West Coast main lines, Birmingham-Bristol, Birmingham-Oxford, two Manchester-Leeds routes, Sheffield-Manchester, Nottingham-Grantham, Leicester-Peterborough, Derby-Leeds and Newcastle-Carlisle. All are still open and have had some investment. It would have been incredible if a conglomerate in any other field did not eliminate internal competition. It was specifically laid down in the Acts that the BTC was to operate its whole undertaking as one business. A region stood to gain nothing because all costs and all revenue met only at national level. This was implicit in the Transport Acts, and made unavoidable by the inept organisation devised by civil servants in 1948. Instead of keeping the four companies intact, together with a Clearing House structure, under a national Holding Company, which would have maintained individual profitability, they imposed, without consultation an untried organisation, with one set of accounts. Worse they took away from railways, existing control of road transport which would have fostered co-ordination - that phantom policy so often parroted by Government to justify pre-war inaction on legal inequity. [See "*Square Deal Denied*"]

## Our Railways

"People should be allowed to ride in what are supposed to be their *own* trains". [IoW County Press, 5.5.53]. On what is this claim based? The taxpayer had not been called on to pay so much as a penny to buy the railways from the previous owners, despite having benefited both before and especially during the war by the iniquitous Government policies which held charges at levels deliberately designed to subsidise industry and the population. Railways were to be bought out of revenue and donated free of charge and debt to an avaricious Government which had helped itself in wartime, overtly and covertly, to a billion pounds of railway profits, and imposed policies which Ministers admitted would make railways insolvent and incapable of modernising itself, whilst road

53

transport was given a free hand. [See "*Square Deal Denied*"]. Had BR management been allowed the same freedom as every other UK industry to decide its own prices and manage its own affairs, Government would have had no need to impose *repayable interest bearing loans* on BR to "compensate" for frozen fares or fares held below the RPI, and new assets could have been purchased from revenue. [See "*Blueprints for Bankruptcy*"]. Anyone who believes that the below RPI fares which they paid to use railways was, in effect, *buying* BR, must, by analogy, believe they also own every other business in the UK from which they buy goods - often at prices well over the RPI.

"Enthusiasts or local groups would have found it easier to lease operating rights than to purchase a line outright". [Henshaw, Page 229]. The "Big Four" or BR would have found it easier, too! The LNER advanced a similar idea in 1946. If the State had paid for the infrastructure, and taxed BR on the same basis as road transport, BR need not have closed any lines. [See "*Blueprints for Bankruptcy*", Page 90]. There were financial and safety risks for BR, in leasing assets. (See page 217).

In view of the unending claims by critics in general, and self styled pressure groups in particular, of the ease with which a profit could be made on branch lines, it is curious that the Branch Line Re-Invigoration Society and the Railway Development Association did not live up to their names by purchasing 6,940 miles of railway closed by the 1980's.

It was not uncommon for enthusiasts to demand that railway assets be *given* to them, so that they could show how the job should be done. Naturally, they did not expect they would have to face the Transport Tribunal before increasing fares, nor a TUCC Hearing to decide if they should be permitted to reduce services or operate less than 365 days a year or to close should banks cease to honour their cheques. I would have welcomed the opportunity to be given the assets of any unprofitable UK company, with no liabilities or constraints and to have the work performed by unpaid volunteers. It is a "no-lose" situation. In 1955, a Minister, replying to a question about selling BR assets, said: "Provided we have safeguards about the price paid to BR, I see no objection in principle. Rails have been left in the Isle of Wight for two years waiting for some enterprising speculator to start a service - so far no one has come forward". [Hansard, vol. 547, col. 779]. No one could seriously argue that Government was opposed to selling *those* lines at a fair price - there could be no question of running down railways in the isolated Isle of Wight to facilitate the building of motorways. Neither could they argue about the justice of demanding a fair price - critics would soon be on their high horses if BR sold off assets at less than a fair price - unless, to a group of amateurs wanting to play at running railways.

Enthusiasts who were willing to pay, did not expect to pay market value for assets. It was not unusual to read of them suggesting that the price they should pay should be determined by arbitration. Obviously, their enthusiasm for arbitration would stop short of accepting arbitration when *they* sold *their* assets - houses, cars, etc., or re-selling any superfluous railway items that came into their possession - lamps, seats, etc., etc.

Inexplicably, critics believed that the Transport Tribunal, (a Court of Law), should adjudicate on closures. (See page 13). It *precipitated* closures by delaying increases in charges by an aggregate $12^3/_4$ years, and holding fares below the RPI during its 20 year life span. No other industry has, except during wartime, had prices subject to arbitration.

Iniquitously, railways *alone*, were denied that privilege during the war - but had their prices frozen for the duration - whilst the RPI rocketed up 200%. [See *"Square Deal Denied"*].

In July 1958, the MoT said: "Railways are under no obligation to provide all sections of the community with a railway service". [Hansard vol. 592, col. 421].

"Beginning with the Tallyllyn Railway, the principles of running lines through new organisations to provide (free) labour and money has since been applied to the Festiniog, Bluebell, Middleton & Eskdale Railways. It acknowledges that a willingness of members to do a large part of the work can reduce the wages element in its cost so that the whole financial position can be transformed". [Western Mail, 11.6.63].

### Car ownership

Critics claimed that closures precipitated a growth in car ownership. The reverse is the case. A few bought cars due to closures, but far more did so to be "like the Joneses". Many more bought cars for the greater flexibility which follows. Some enjoyed a lift for a share of petrol costs. Councils saw closures as the thin end of a wedge that would drain people away. None foresaw that cars would benefit rural areas. Travelling by car from or to a rural area would always be quicker than by rail. Councils saw only the local issue - "their" branch line - "this one is a special case", fearing that those without a car, may be disadvantaged by closure, if only for an annual journey. Councils wanted to will the end but not the means. Media reports indicate that many buy a car as soon as they can afford it. It is a social symbol. The availability and cost of public transport rarely enters the equation. "Cars were desirable commodities which enhanced the image of their owners". "Every young man should have one". [Transport & Road Research Laboratory Report N° 808].

The following graph shows the rate of growth of car ownership in comparison to the much slower rate of closure of lines and stations.

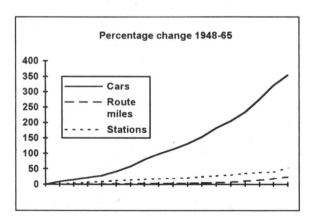

Dreamers would not acknowledge that branch lines, especially with single line sections, with the self imposed limits of end-to-end speed was no match for motor vehicles whose speed had risen dramatically from those of their predecessors, and which could offer door-to-door journeys of higher speed than the branch line could offer. When journeys extend beyond the branch line, the effect of connectional margins, or worse, the connection missed due to the unforeseen, meant there was no contest. The 'commuter' was no longer a slave to the alarm clock. He could arise late and still make it to work - by car. The creation by Ministerial direction of road routes shorter than rail, which had been, so often, made circuitous by the dictates of landowners, tipped the balance further.

Branch line end-to-end speeds could only be increased by massive expenditure, which by definition, had not been justified in their heyday: earthworks, tunnels, curves, gradients, new point & crossing geometry, and doubling of single line sections. To try to keep loss making lines open by singling and replacing gated by open crossings, as some critics advocated, actually made the competitive situation worse by slowing trains further. Clearly the dreamers assumed all users of branch line trains walked to the station, or they would not claim that long distance traffic would be lost if they had to take a bus or car to a main line station. If a passenger walked to a branch station the journey speed was, walk: 4 mph, wait: 0 mph, train: 60 mph, walk: 4 mph, and, if making a connection, wait 0 mph.

## Petitions Against Closures

Petitions are over-rated. Impressive looking petitions were produced objecting to some closures. In no instance, in the cases I have examined, was evidence produced that those asked to sign, were all fare paying passengers, much less regular passengers and that they promised to make more use of the services on a line threatened with closure, nor that they had been fully acquainted with the railways' case, nor that the losses would eventually have to be borne by taxpayers. Whilst those organising petitions state that there were no duplicate signings, it is difficult to see how they can be sure that someone passing on the next day did not sign again, sign his neighbour's name or *sign a different form.*

A man *who wished to be anonymous,* collected 18,625 signatures on an Isle of Wight petition, (see page 72), and avoided argument "as it would waste valuable time". They were warned not to sign twice. In total 81,733 people signed. [Burroughs, Pages 16-17]. Avoiding argument was undemocratic, which since his book mentions a media report that a closure was undemocratic, is ironic. If all had been asked to buy non-refundable season tickets and use a line regularly, it would sort the men from the boys. To coin a term used by the author in another context (see page 68), to claim that it would waste time was a *feeble excuse,* when using more people would have accelerated the task. Warning 18,625 people not to sign twice guaranteed nothing. They were not told not to sign if they were not users

## Future traffic

A common argument put forward by objectors was that railways threatened with closure should be kept open for that "future development" which was always just around the corner. Unfortunately, it was always a long time coming. In many cases, it would be dependent on Government grants to persuade industry to move to a "depressed area".

In few cases was the nature and time scale of this future development spelled out, but in one case, a critic wrote that the Forestry Commission was planting trees which the railway would be able to serve when the trees mature. [Times 23.8.53, 3b]. One thing is certain, no haulier would keep assets lying around waiting for trees to mature!

## The next war

Objectors often said lines should be kept for strategic reasons. Railways entered two world wars blessed with surplus capacity and gained not a penny on either occasion as a result of their investment. Both times, they were screwed by Government, which profited hugely from controlling railways, whilst leaving the companies with their assets in a worse condition. Hanging on to such lines thereafter was not likely to appeal to railway management who were vilified for losses emanating from under used lines. Suggestions by MP's that the Minister of Defence should subsidise rural routes proposed for closure were met by a blank refusal. A Ministerial response that BR was benefiting from the Defence budget served only to emphasise the complete lack of understanding by ministers of the use of this money - which was for journeys made by HM Forces at *sub standard fares*, and for freight at controlled rates. [Hansard, vol. 617, col. 974]. No Government had invested in railway infrastructure, until modest sums were made available just before the 1939-45 war to provide a few facilities and some rolling stock which would be useful in the war. It then seized assets funded by railway shareholders. After the war, Government demanded that nationalised BR should reimburse Government for their modest expenditure. The vital coal industry was not sequestrated in either war, and left free to make handsome profits. [See "*Square Deal Denied*"].

## CTCC alleged to be BR's Agent

"The CTCC ..... hardly an unbiased source". "There was a widespread belief that the CTCC, funded and staffed by the BTC, was not independent". "The TUCC's occasionally opposed closure, but were usually overruled by the CTCC". [Henshaw, Pages 84, 88 & 133].

TUCC opposition to closure can hardly be termed occasional. They opposed or delayed many cases. The CTCC overruled the TUCC's approval of the Westerham line closure and told it to re-convene its hearing. (See also page 26). Other cases prove there was no bias. (See pages 138 & 166). The CTCC was *not* staffed by the BTC. The BTC provided clerical staff, who had no vote, to the CTCC and TUCC's. Members of both bodies were selected by the MoT from lists submitted by various organisations. The BTC funded the CTCC, TUCC's *and* the Transport Tribunal - although the BTC objected to having to do so. No one could claim that the Tribunal was biased in BR's favour - quite the reverse. Records show that from 1948 to 1968, it cut and delayed, for an aggregate of $12^3/_4$ years, virtually every application for increases in charges, despite the fact that fares and charges were trailing well behind inflation rates. [See "*Blueprints for Bankruptcy*"]. Some CTCC and TUCC decisions lacked commercial realism. [See "*Blueprints for Bankruptcy*" and page 137].

There is no reason to question their ability to consider financial data and determine whether it was a fair representation of the situation. No one could conclude that they were biased in BR's favour from an examination of their records and reports. However, as the chairman of the East Anglia TUCC noted, there is a tendency for objectors to believe a conclusion is biased because it did not concur with the views of objectors. (See page 129).

The composition of the CTCC in 1957 was: Agriculture two, Industry and Commerce five, Shipping one, Unions two, Local Authorities four, BTC two. Clearly the BTC members were heavily outnumbered.

# Chapter 5                    Isle of Wight Railways

The history of railways on the Island shows that, even in their heyday, competing with the horse and cart, they were financially unstable. This is hardly surprising, railways were successful when they had a good base load of freight traffic from heavy industry and mining. Some were successful given heavy passenger traffic supplemented by a steady flow of freight traffic. On the Isle of Wight both were conspicuous by their absence. Despite this, pundits in the motor car age were completely blind to the obvious.

The first section opened was Cowes-Newport in 1862, followed 13 years later by the Ryde & Newport. In the same year, a line to Sandown was opened by the Isle of Wight (Newport Junction) Railway. These three lines amalgamated in 1887 as the Isle of Wight Central Railway and it undertook the working of the Freshwater, Yarmouth & Newport Railway from the date of its opening in 1889 until 1913, when they provided their own stock. The Central operated a new branch to Ventnor (from Merstone), in 1900 which it purchased in 1913 to compete with the Isle of Wight Railway, which opened Ryde-Shanklin in 1864, and to Ventnor in 1866. Three railways for only 56 miles. [Sherrington, Pages 44-45]. The cost of the railway to Ventnor was greater than planned. "The tunnel was bored because the Earl of Yarborough resisted the proposal to carry the railway over his land". [Portsmouth Evening News, 12.8.65]. At the opening, Directors stated that, although Ventnor would benefit, "little encouragement had been received from the town itself". [IoW Mercury, 11.3.66].

The Brading-Bembridge line opened in 1882. [Bradshaw's Railway Shareholders Guide].

The Isle of Wight Railway was the only company with a lucrative route, opened Ryde to Shanklin in 1864, and to Ventnor in 1866. It relied on secondhand coaches. [Course, Page 46]

"Once the Isle of Wight Railway was established, it was a financial success. In 1913, a profit of £24,029 was recorded. The Isle of Wight Central paid a dividend for the first time". [Burroughs, Page 11 : IoW County Press, 28.2.14]. The IoW County Press report reveals:

Isle of Wight Central 1st Preference paid 4%. 1st Preference must receive 5% before anything could be paid on 2nd Preference. Nothing was paid on Ordinary shares. They could not reduce costs further. The holiday season should start earlier and finish later.

Isle of Wight Railway paid only 4% on 5% Preference shares, 4% on Preferred Ordinary, 2.75% on Deferred Ordinary and nothing on Ordinary shares.

The Isle of Wight Railway had paid dividends on ordinary shares before. The Isle of Wight Central was struggling to make profits after existing for 26 years, parts of it for 51 years. It had failed to pay on all its Debentures for several years. When it was absorbed by the L&SWR, a £100 share was exchanged for £3 cash. [Bradshaw's Railway Shareholders Guide].

The Freshwater, Yarmouth & Newport Railway took 15 years to complete an eleven mile line. It had an appalling financial record, and by 1896 "could not pay Debenture interest and sought new capital to put the line into a fit state of repair". [PRO: Rail 211/1]. Accrued Debenture interest unpaid amounted to £68,044 by 1914. [Bradshaw's Railway Shareholders Guide]."Judgement was received against the Freshwater, Yarmouth & Newport Railway for arrears of interest on some Debenture stock. The Judgement was not satisfied before Amalgamation into the Southern Railway in 1923". A claim was made against the Southern Railway for the debt. The claim failed. [Law Report Digest, 1921-30, col. 1896].

Overall, the Island's railways' shareholders had an inadequate, many a poor return, on their capital. Even the Ryde-Ventnor section was not well rewarded in the first 20 years. [Bradshaw's Railway Shareholders Guide]. Up to the First War, they were all competing with the horse. Legislation enforced heavy expenditure on all railways to improve signalling and introduce other safety measures. Government imposed the eight hour day in 1919 on all railways, and pressured railway companies to pay better wages. These measures hit rural railways very hard. Yet in the motor car age, and after some "industrial" closures on the Island, locals and their allies were claiming the railways could be made to pay!

"Sir John Blundell Maple had asked Fay to value the railways, none of which paid their way". [Dow, Page 249]. In 1923, under the railway grouping dictated by the 1921 Railways Act, the railways on the Isle of Wight became part of the Southern Railway.

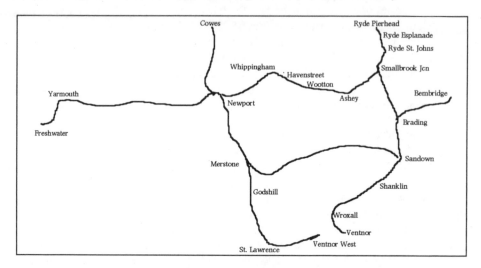

In December 1949, the BTC, in pursuit of its remit to integrate rail and road services asked the Southern Region to set up a working party to look at Isle of Wight services, where the self contained area offered an opportunity for an experiment in integration. They reported in April 1952, after completing their study and liaising with the County Council and other organisations. They concluded that Merstone-Ventnor, Brading-Bembridge, Sandown-Newport and Newport-Freshwater should close immediately, Ryde-Cowes be retained for a few years, and then further reviewed, and Ashey, Wootton and Whippingham stations should close. A census on the Merstone-Ventnor line showed that the maximum number of passengers was five on the worst train and 24 on the best train. The minimum number was zero on the worst. The average was two. They stated that, if all IoW railways, except Ryde-Ventnor and Ryde-Newport-Cowes, were closed, there would be a net revenue increase of £103,000 pa, and there would not be any appreciable extra costs. If Ryde-Newport-Cowes closed, it would save a further £80,500. The Region recommended that the Merstone-Ventnor line should close in September 1952, Brading-Bembridge and Newport-Freshwater in early 1953, Newport-Sandown in September 1953. Ryde-Cowes could be kept on at a reduced loss until 1958.

The BTC approved the proposal to close Merstone-Ventnor in July 1952. In August 1952, the BTC minutes record that the closures should be staged as "It would cause a great deal of ill feeling and raise major issues in Parliament if we were to close down forthwith the whole of the railway services on the Island, however unlikely it may be that they can be made remunerative and however unreasonable it may be that the rest of the country should, in effect, subsidise a well-to-do population". [PRO: AN85/35].

## The First Closure - 1952

The first line to be closed was the Merstone-Ventnor West line. The BTC had sent its proposal to the TUCC. There were eight passenger trains each way on a weekday, some had no passengers at all. It would save £16,000 pa. The TUCC met in July and told the local authority it had no objection, there was no Public Hearing. It closed in September.

"When closure was announced, the hitherto apathetic attitude resolved into one of strong protest". [IoW County Press, 20.9.52]. Not so strong as to use railways - 'protests' always stopped short of opening wallets. Some claimed that closure would adversely effect the island's popularity as a resort. They stood to lose a handful, judging by the loadings.

On the last day, an enthusiast displayed a notice; which read: "If half the people interested in this line today had been as interested in the last two years we should not be closing". [IoW County Press, 20.9.52].

The TUCC invited members of Ventnor UDC to its meeting on 4th December. They said that there were occasions when the line is used to the full. Their spokesman said they had received numerous letters from residents - he would not read them, it would take such a long time, but there was great feeling against closure. (*TUCC files do not include these letters, nor a precis of them*). They were told that there were more villages on the island dependent on buses than trains. The TUCC re-affirmed its earlier closure decision.

The line had opened in 1897, long after the profitable routes were opened, and only a few years before motor road transport came on the scene. Its days were numbered from its inception. The main reason for construction by the Isle of Wight Central Railway, was that it enabled them to avoid transferring passengers to a competitor's route at Sandown to complete their journey to Ventnor. [IoW County Press, 20.9.52]. Obviously, had one company owned both routes, the line would never have opened.

Opposition to subsequent closure proposals by the County Council may have resulted because they were criticised by residents and the Urban District Council for having agreed to the closure of the Merstone-Ventnor line. They put up a very stiff resistance to later closures, even such huge historical loss makers as Newport-Yarmouth-Freshwater.

There were calls to modernise, to electrify the Island's railways. BR were not the only ones to dismiss the proposal as impractical. After all, at this time they were denied materials and finance to make improvements to heavily loaded main lines. "Whether many parts of the Island have any potential traffic in sufficient volume for most of the year is open to doubt". [Railway Magazine, February 1953, Page 73].

## 1953 Closure Proposals

In April 1953, the BTC proposed to close Bembridge-Brading, Freshwater-Newport, Newport-Sandown, and some stations between Newport-Ryde to save £90,500 pa.

The County Council and Chamber of Commerce produced a "*Case for Retention of Island Railways*". "Its proposals should not increase the loss". (*They accepted the loss*).

"Some general economies could be made:-
    (a) Staff could be considerably reduced.
    (b) Push and Pull would reduce costs.
    (c) Signalling could be simplified.
"General considerations - eventually, it will be necessary to consider whether:-
    (a) The loss should be continued indefinitely.
    (b) Losses should be met by a terminal tax.
    (c) Some alternative transport system would be practical".

"A little capital for modernisation will meet Island needs for 20 years and avoid larger expenditure on roads". They advocated "operating the Bembridge branch summer only, with **one new railcar**, capable of carrying 350 on a summer Saturday, which could be used on the Freshwater line in the winter. An extra ferry service should be operated in the summer". *That was a recipe for ruin - IoW railways needed extra passengers in the winter, not the summer*. They advanced no proof that *any* proposal would save more than it cost, nor did they propose to fund assets from the roads budget. 350 passengers required *six* cars (i.e. 3 DMU's) and would need a spare. They did not say where stock from the Freshwater line would be used, when there was a winter surplus already. The source of trained drivers and other staff for the summer was ignored. There was no offer of one extra passenger, ton of traffic, nor parcel by either body. The 52 page Report did not contain *any* financial data to support its claims, but stated that BR's figures were not accepted. Later they issued another report, with a few figures which claimed, without proof, that costs could be cut. There would still be a loss. A QC later said a court would throw out BR's figures - what would they do with a Report with no figures, and one with unvalidated figures? No one criticised *their* extraordinary claims, unlike criticism of the CTCC. (See page 66). No industry would flourish by pursuing such policies - it was the road to bankruptcy.

The TUCC held a meeting on 11-13th May, to which objectors were invited. "It was not their usual practice to meet in public, but having regard to the obvious interest, they had resolved to sit in public". Ironically, the closure was proposed *because of the lack of public interest*! The BTC modified its proposals so as to keep Ashey station as a halt. Mr. Hopkins, the BTC's railway spokesman, said that train loadings varied between one and 105 in the winter on 12 trains; and three and 482 in the summer on 14 trains.

The case cut other new ground. For the first time, objectors were represented by a QC and a junior. Did they consider funding assets as a helpful alternative? BR alone, among all serving the public, had to send executives to justify a management decision. The QC said it was subtle of BR not to send a lawyer. Not really, BR knew it was *not a law court*.

Mr. Bushrod, BTC's bus spokesman stated that 16 extra buses would be required to move passengers displaced by closures. The County Council disputed the figure, and their QC said that such a number was patently absurd. In fact, they acquired 15, and during the next year carried 1.3m more passengers. [Southern Vectis Bulletin]. TUCC files contain no complaints that bus services were inadequate - and there can be no doubt that critics would have missed no opportunity to have a go at the bus company. There would be no difficulty checking the size of the bus fleet. If it had increased by a greater number than forecast, newspapers would, undoubtedly, have been informed of it by gleeful objectors.

The objectors' QC spoke for all parties throughout the hearing:-

- "The justification for placing control of a vast undertaking in the hands of one body was that the public might benefit by unprofitable lines being run at the expense of the more profitable lines". (The undertaking was *transport* not railways, which the BTC was obliged to operate as one unit. No company in an analogous position would keep two subsidiaries, *in the same area,* with one making a loss! The Acts did not specify that unprofitable lines were to be subsidised by profitable lines - *their* users would have objected to paying fares designed to create profits to subsidise others).

- Challenged depreciation costs in relation to the age of rolling stock. (*Historical* depreciation would replace nothing at current prices, unless supported by reserves - of which there were none entirely due to interference by the Transport Tribunal & Government. All prices, except rail fares, had been outstripping the RPI, as if there was no tomorrow).

- "The densest load was on Saturdays in the middle of August and was 80% higher than a July figure quoted by BR". (So what? If even only every *Saturday* throughout the year, had the same load, closure may have been avoided. It is certain no other business nor individual remains viable by having two busy days in 365).

- "Mainland revenue increased because of a desire to get to the extremities. Traffic is likely to increase - unless civilisation on the Island is destroyed by the Railway Executive's proposals". (The destruction of civilisation did not take place).

- "If such inaccurate figures had been presented in a court of law, they would have been thrown out". (In a court, objectors would have had their statements destroyed by BR's QC. Critics did not appreciate that management - in all industries - make decisions from management data, not audited accounts which take too long to prepare when the ship is sinking).

- "The needs of the public demanded continuance of a railway system. BR failed to fulfil its statutory responsibility". (They had *no* statutory responsibility. The BTC was the sole statutory body and their duty was to conduct the undertaking as one business, to integrate road, rail and other transport *which it owned* and pay its way. Avoiding wasteful competition between subsidiaries was mandatory. Even where it had no bus subsidiary, if rail could not be made to pay, it was not obliged to retain services).

- "No one disputed that the Island railways made a loss".

- "A photograph shows 12,000 people waiting to join the ferry at Ryde Pier". (i.e. going away from the island. No evidence was submitted that even one of them actually travelled by rail on the island or on the mainland! BR's spokesman later pointed out that they were waiting because the ferry had been delayed by heavy seas!).

- "A fundamental rule of natural justice was being disregarded". (It was. BR & BTC were guilty until proved innocent - see also page 64).

- "We cannot hope to make any transport system to deal with this peak traffic to pay for itself on present revenue or under the present fare structure".

*Mr. Bright of the Chamber of Commerce appeared as a "witness"* :

- The Island's transport problems could be solved "if the price of rail tickets was reduced to that of buses". (No insolvent business would cut prices in the **unproven hope** that solvency would return. The Receiver would have views on that. By analogy, more visitors could be attracted if hotels reduced prices to match self catering tariffs).
- "The loss could be reduced by taking account of the contributory value of the Island's traffic to the mainland, and traffic from the mainland". They went further by claiming that each of the three lines contributed revenue to the others. Under this principle, the revenue separately attributable to the three lines could aggregate to more than the total revenue of the three lines! (See Contributory Revenue theory on page 33).
- "Savings could be achieved and extra revenue obtained which would cut the loss". (Neither savings nor revenue were quantified. What would have been the reaction to suggestions to members of the Chamber to reducing the cost to their customers?).
- Close Newport-Ryde instead of Newport-Sandown. (The effect would have been to further delay economies, because the alternative would have had to be publicised)
- Did not know how many staff BR had on the lines, but thought it was less than stated!
- Claimed that "the summer peak has always been a profitable source of revenue for BR. BR should run 72 **extra** trains on six Saturdays to relieve pressure on the Pier". (They would stand idle 359 days pa, to deal with existing revenue, thereby increasing losses - it would be economic madness. No other business would have pursued such a policy. Another Chamber of Commerce was trying to run railways - see page 211).

*Other "witnesses" said*:

- County Council proposals would cut costs by £65-70,000 pa with the lines retained against BR's estimate of £90,500 pa gained from total closure. [PRO: MT115/5]. (They did not guarantee to make up the difference if their theories were flawed, much less the residual loss which even their unproven theories would not eliminate).
- The County Council argued that a decision on the Newport-Yarmouth-Freshwater line should not depend on the number of passengers carried. It had a contributory value because it could be used by passengers with runabout tickets. (There was no evidence that even *one person* would not buy a runabout ticket if this line closed).
- More would travel if fares cut but didn't know how many. (A risk no one would take).
- A coal merchant said that the cost of transporting 5,800 tons of coal would increase if it had to be conveyed part by rail and part by British Road Services. (It was 111 tons per week, or a few lorry loads. Why they would not use their own vehicles was not explained. No documentary proof of an increase in cost was tabled).

Critics alleged a court of law would discount BR data. The proceedings were **crammed** with unquantified allegations by objectors, which would not be accepted in a court of law. Had BR retained a QC, he would have made mincemeat of the objectors' "case". Objectors would not have got away with quoting anonymous or absent witnesses or untabled data:-

1. "A statement by a firm (the name of which was withheld) .......".

2.  A company, whose name was not mentioned, lost money on every ton of coal.
3.  A witness's statement being read out, in his absence. (See page 65).
4.  Petitions to retain a facility which they did not guarantee they would begin to use.
5.  The Planning officer claimed people transferred to buses would create more traffic than forecast. He didn't know how many were on a particular train. Asked how he converted them to bus loads: His data was on his desk! (The Chairman did not ask to see it!).

It did not occur to objectors that *they* might do something to attract visitors - off season. As the taxpayer had no obligation to make up losses, nor had done so, the whole circus was unjustified. As potential users were *not* using the lines regularly - even at below RPI fares - they had no moral claim. They wanted to be subsidised by mainland travellers.

BTC managers were interrupted when trying to respond to objectors' comments or to ask questions. BTC managers did not interrupt others.

*   The QC made a caustic remark about BR information, Hopkins tried to reply; "Really, *I must say, Mr. Chairman ...*", but was cut off by the Chairman: "*No, we must get on*".
*   Hopkins (BR) was prevented from responding to a criticism about connections.
*   Bushrod asked the Planning Officer whose **written submission** stated "*this is the equivalent of 80 double deck buses*" to replace closed rail services: "Do you mean 80 journeys?" The QC replied "Oh that is clear!" (The submission had not made it clear).
*   BR's attempts to explain the queue at the pier was caused by heavy seas delaying ferries, was interrupted by the TUCC Chairman who said "It is common knowledge that the peak traffic is something phenomenal".

The QC demanded that he be supplied with details of the financial data which BR had given to the TUCC. They, as the independent adjudicators, had been supplied in accordance with standard practice. Objectors as biased amateurs were not. At the close of the meeting the TUCC decided to call for the details to be supplied at a resumed meeting.

### Resumed TUCC Hearing - 18th June 1953

The QC called witnesses who placed their own interpretation on BR's figures which had been supplied, made their own estimates, and, in some cases related them pro rata to national accounts. One said that BR wages were over stated, but he couldn't say by how much. Hopkins pointed out that single lines required the same amount of labour on banks, fences, drainage etc. (He could have added, that a lengthman walking a single line had to walk back, covering the same distance as a man on a double line). Hopkins also pointed out that some rolling stock or parts were sent to the mainland to main works, and that all materials had to be shipped in, incurring extra handling costs.

BR was criticised for overlooking scholars' seasons on the Newport-Sandown line. It was not mentioned in the Transcript, that they used buses until closure was threatened, [See Newman]. BR's case was prepared much earlier. It does not appear to have been publicised apart from in the Hearing. As a result, it was implied that all BR data was suspect. The sums were quite small and did not approach that required to end losses.

The county council "had engaged an expert witness - Stanley Hill, who arbitrated in the nationalisation of railways". [Henshaw, Page 67]. There was no arbitration. [See "*Square Deal Denied*", Page 180]. In evidence to the Transport Tribunal as a witness for councils objecting to increases in fares which were below the RPI, he did not make this claim. The TUCC's transcript does not say that he arbitrated in nationalisation. (For his background see page 201). He was not present when the hearing began, so the QC read out Hill's nine pages of evidence. Later, Hill stated that, if BTC Accounts had been prepared on the same basis as for the Isle of Wight closures, the profit for 1951 would have been a loss. (See page 203).

"Hill, the expert witness, wisely refused to be drawn on an exact figure as to the financial state of the threatened branch lines". "The QC claimed it was around **£20,000**". "Hopkins (BR) refused to be cross examined". [Henshaw, Page 68]. Why it was wise for *an expert witness* to refuse is unclear. He gave some figures, including "*the contributory value of branch lines to other lines could easily be £10,000 pa*". BR would have been criticised for making such a statement. He said that the lines lost money. By being invited to cross examine, Hopkins was treated as an equal. QC's do not cross examine each other.

As a witness for councils objecting to BR fares increases in 1951, then 30 points behind the RPI, Hill told the Transport Tribunal: "a subsidy was the only answer", he "couldn't devise any other way of making ends meet", the BTC "is not misleading the public".

The transcript states: the QC said that "*if all savings put forward by his clients were achieved*, the loss would be **£20-30,000** pa". Hence, losses were above that level. The practicability of their proposals, which were largely unspecified, was not tested by backing *their* potential savings with *their* money. They did not offer to cover the £20-30,000, despite claiming that greater costs of road improvements would fall on the islanders.

Hopkins (BR) said that "savings did not include items such as loco fuel of £13,500, consumable stores, insurance, municipal rates and publicity, and that diesels would cost £145,000, excluding day to day running and maintenance costs". Who else would risk that sort of money? Neither Cowes Urban District Council nor the County Council offered money. This was in 1953, when BR was being prevented from raising enough capital, whilst charges were held below the rate of inflation, and they had not been allowed to restore track to pre-war standards. Modernisation was two years away, and BR's priority was bound to be main lines. [See "*Blueprints for Bankruptcy*" & "*Square Deal Denied*"].

Hopkins disputed the contributory revenue which Hill and the QC claimed as between the three lines. Because certain trains ran to a certain point, such as Newport, it was more likely to be due to operating convenience, rather than passengers travelling through.

The QC said that "Mr. Bright's figures may be wrong, I do not know, but they are nearer to the loss than BR's figures". (See page 64). He referred to an answer by Hopkins that new sleepers were used on the Island. He had been told that some secondhand sleepers were used on the Bembridge branch. Hopkins made the perfectly rational explanation that costs were rightly based on new sleepers which had always been used. Earlier in the year, a few secondhand sleepers were used on this branch, which BR expected would soon close. BR's costs were not based on the last few months. This admission was seized on as a general measure of the unreliability of statements by the railways. Of one thing, there is *no doubt*, if BR had used brand new materials on a line about to be closed, it would have been front page news - as occurred when stations were repainted in similar circumstances. If UK industry or councils use new materials for a short term purpose, when secondhand ones would suffice, little wonder UK industry folded and Rates always increased! The QC gave a number of complaints to the Chairman, which he had forgotten. No mention was made in the transcript of copies being given to BR.

The chairman asked for a breakdown of an objector's figures, but it was unavailable! The TUCC said that some objections "appeared to be irrelevant". They were unable to agree on closure of the Bembridge branch. They recommended approval of Ashey station as a halt, for Whippingham and Wootton stations and the Newport-Freshwater line to be closed on 21st September, or as soon thereafter as the Executive consider practicable, and that the Cowes-Newport-Sandown line be maintained for a further trial period of not less than two years. (They did not say what they expected to happen in that period - whether residents would start to make use of railways, hoteliers would offer ultra cheap terms for off season visitors, or the Council would divert money needed for road improvements to railways and make the Island *really* attractive to off season visitors).

## CTCC Decision

Island lines were hardly used for nine months each year. The TUCC Hearing was followed by an exhaustive inquiry. They recommended closing Newport-Freshwater, keeping Cowes-Newport-Sandown, closing Whippingham and Wootton stations, but were undecided on the Bembridge branch, which had one sixth of the passengers of competing buses operating a shorter route. The CTCC supported TUCC recommendations and added that the Bembridge branch be closed. They (CTCC) were surprised by the Council's unwillingness to consider improving roads as it seemed that it would be advantageous to have up to date facilities for the increasing number of visitors who provide a principal source of revenue to the Island. Road improvements were overdue and should be undertaken without delay. Fares should be increased to reduce or eliminate the loss, but this required special legislation as present maxima would be inadequate to permit raising fares to an economic level, which would be justified. [CTCC 1953 Report, Paras. 14, 25-39].

BR was not justified in continuing the very unremunerative Bembridge branch as buses were adequate. The railways were operated at a very substantial loss. [CTCC Minute 329].

"The Inquiry was a small victory for free speech. The CTCC made the extraordinary claim that it accepted BR figures and repudiated any claim that the accountancy was questionable. It made a mockery of the consultation procedure and led many to believe the CTCC was an organ of the BTC and not impartial as was claimed". [Henshaw, Page 70]. It would be a mockery, if free speech was denied only to the CTCC. No one criticised the "extraordinary claim" of objectors. (See page 61). If BR figures were wrong, why did objectors not buy lines which were put on sale. It must have been a "no-lose" situation.

In August 1953, a deputation from the Island met the DoT's Permanent Secretary. They were satisfied with the TUCC conduct of the Inquiry, but not that of the CTCC, which, they claimed, "had not examined a transcript of the TUCC Inquiry". Newport Borough Council claimed that BR had "turned down applications for outings". [PRO: MT115/5].

The TUCC's file to the CTCC included transcripts. The Council produced no details, not so much as the name of one organisation refused outings, much less any figures. They may have asked for excursions, on the heaviest Saturday of the year, when all rolling stock would be in use, or at absurd fares which did not approach the cost of provision.

## Closures - 1953

The Bembridge-Brading and Freshwater-Newport lines closed in September 1953. It was forecast that "last trains will be packed with railway fans and islanders making journeys for sentimental reasons". [IoW County Press, 19.9.53]. Had they been using railways regularly, or undertaken to do so in future, closure would have been avoided.

Tourists did not lose, they went elsewhere. [IoW Mercury 29.4.66]. Now we come to it, closure of subsidised lines hit the hotel and tourist trade in the pocket. Some argued that tourists who travelled to the Isle of Wight, with the rail-ship-rail changes, after railway closures, would, *as a consequence* transfer to road throughout, instead of rail-ship-road. If travel throughout by road was feasible, they would already be doing so, direct to their hotel to avoid a double, or even triple, transfer. If passengers transferred to other resorts, BR would retain mainland revenue which may be over longer distances.

On 7th October, the BTC wrote to the MoT that diesels would be too costly, and would stand idle 75% of the year. They had received no proposal for take-over of closed lines. The County Council had been told that unless a firm proposal was made, lines would be lifted. [PRO: MT115/7].

One or two people are interested in forming a company to run trains on closed lines. If nothing comes of that, the County Council will consider operating the branch lines themselves. [Times, 21.10.53]. (One would have expected the County Council, Chamber of Commerce and all others who had claimed that the railways could be made profitable to have fallen over themselves to take the lines over and "show how it could be done". Even if they feared the lines may not make a profit under their management, they had claimed the cost would be less than that required to upgrade roads. They had made it sound like a 'no lose' situation. What caused their disinterest? Unfortunately, I have been unable to access relevant County Council files. Perhaps they realised it was not a 'no lose' situation).

In September 1954, Freshwater Parish Council wrote that "the roads were breaking up under the extra traffic". The DoT replied "There is no such evidence from DoT surveys". There was no further correspondence in the file from the Council. [PRO: MT115/5].

Up to the time of the next stage in the closures - October 1955 - TUCC minutes show that they received no complaints about road transport following the 1953 closures.

## Proposal to Implement Deferred Closure - 1955

BR wrote to the TUCC in September 1955 referring to the recommendation of the TUCC in 1953 that the nine mile Newport-Sandown line should be kept for a trial period of two years. A Joint Consultative Committee, including representatives of rail and road transport, local authorities and other bodies, had been set up on the island in 1953, and had met nine times. Service adjustments had been made, but despite this and other steps to improve traffic, the financial results for the year to 30th September 1954 were no more satisfactory. BR had no option but to close on 6th June 1956. Annual revenue was less than the cost of wages alone.

An internal DoT Memo of the first meeting of the Joint Committee in October 1953, records that "the County Council urged that the BTC should be regarded as a whole. This is a reversal of their own case to the TUCC for a reduction in ferry charges". (See page 79).

"Their case was put in somewhat extravagant terms. The Island representatives asked for the Brading-Bembridge and Newport-Freshwater lines to be left in situ indefinitely - later modified to one year. BR representatives agreed subject to taking out odd rails or crossings if these were required for repairs of lines now open". [PRO: MT115/7]. This forewarning by BR, which was not questioned at the meeting should be seen alongside the criticisms of others - "Staff taking unused crossing to use elsewhere, seemed a feeble excuse". [Burroughs, Page 42]. It is difficult to see how anyone could fail to see the value of using assets standing idle locally, instead of bringing new assets from the mainland.

The TUCC held a meeting to consider the deferred closure on 8th November 1955. BR said that traffic on the Newport-Sandown line was mainly local in nature, only 3% of passengers came from the mainland. Gross costs were £48,300, receipts: £13,900, net loss: £34,400. BR said that traffic would have to treble to make it an economical proposition. No evidence was forthcoming of the prospect of such increases.

Objectors claimed they could save two thirds of the losses. They called for railcars, but BR pointed out some steam would have to remain, which the objectors accepted. BR said facilities to maintain two types of traction would be uneconomic. The scheme would cost £145,000 capital plus operating costs of £78,000 pa.

Which industry would risk that outlay to *reduce* losses? Interest on loans cannot be paid from reduced *losses*. Little wonder that UK industry lost a world lead in every field if they applied these principles. No suggestion was made by objectors as to the source to be tapped to cover the remaining third of the losses, even assuming that their proposals were practical. They made no offer to cover them.

The County Council said they had had 531 objections, 460 from *regular* or frequent users, and a petition of "85 from elsewhere". They suggested that Newport-Ryde be closed instead of Newport-Sandown. BR said that whilst the alternative may work in the winter, it would be impractical on summer Saturdays. The County Council then proposed that trains should be split and run over the two lines instead of one to avoid a closure, claiming that the movement costs would be the same.

The services were losing money over one route, they could not therefore produce a profit over two, with two lots of formation, bridges, track and signalling to maintain. If there were 460 *regular* users it should amount to over 140,000 pa - even the objectors could only claim there were 14-17,000, which equates to about 50 per day! The word "regular" seemed to have taken on a new meaning.

Ventnor Urban District Council urged ratepayers to do something about the proposed closure. They did not advocate the obvious - that they should make more use of, or in most cases, *begin* to use, the railway. Cowes Urban District Council said "modernisation was the answer. Properly handled, holiday traffic alone could no doubt bring in a profit". They did not offer to back their opinions with their own money. One would have thought that they would fall over themselves to invest in this profitable venture!

The Chamber of Commerce criticised BR for not encouraging passengers to travel via a ferry owned by another company, bringing them to an alternative port on the Island. (Their members would not have willingly influenced customers to buy from a competitor).

The TUCC noted that revenue on the Newport-Sandown line was less than the wages. An amendment to defer closure for a year was defeated. The resolution not to object to closure on 6th June 1956 was carried nem con, three members abstained.

The CTCC voted unanimously to support the TUCC decision.

During the Rural Transport Bill debate, Sir Peter MacDonald, the Island's MP stated: "On one day last year, 67,000 people landed and left the Isle of Wight on the ferry. There was a lack of shelter on the pier". It had been under the control of Ryde Corporation for many years, and they had obviously not considered it necessary or economic to provide shelter. (See page 79). An MP pointed out that there are 365 days in a year, 67,000 was irrelevant if there were only 2,000 on the next day. He added, that when the CTCC Report was debated in the House, Sir Peter did not challenge it. [Hansard, vol. 547, col. 739].

## Stage 4

BR's 1963 Reshaping Plan included closure of all lines on the Island. They had been under review before the Plan was initiated. In June 1963, BR told councils and other groups that railways' position was that there was now very little smooth to take with the rough, and it was necessary to equip the island with new rolling stock, but that revenue of the services would not support such investment. It was difficult to get capital for mainland development where the betting was more certain. A councillor said that what they wanted from BR was "every sort of patience". Eleven years after the first closure they were "trying to develop a blueprint for transport on the Island". [IoW County Press, 1.6.63]. BR had exercised extreme patience in waiting for the islanders to start using the railways.

BR formally announced the proposal to withdraw services from the two remaining lines on the Island with effect from 2nd October. The closure of these lines was deferred as a result of objections received by the TUCC.

The number of passengers carried was 2.8m annually, of which 60% is holiday traffic. [Railway Magazine, March 1964, Page 325].

The TUCC sent out an advice in February setting out proposed closures and stated that as objections had already been received, an Inquiry would be held. This was held on 10th-12th June. Objectors included the County Council, Railway Retention Society, Liberal Association, Brading Ratepayers, West Cowes Residents & Ratepayers Association and nine individuals. The Chairman began by saying that "the Committee had read the letters of objection and have concluded there will be hardship, our duty is to quantify that hardship and tell the MoT. We have asked BR to split costs between the two lines. They are Ryde-Ventnor - Earnings: £119,000, Expenses: £142,600; Ryde-Cowes - Earnings: £33,000, Expenses: £121,700. Renewals over the next five years will cost £158,620. The bus company expect a subsidy of £10,000 pa, which they will be asked to split between the two lines. Mr. Baines (County Council) will also represent nearly 50 other organisations and parties, including councils, hotels, women's' institute, caravan owners, Tory Association, traders, ratepayers, NFU and caterers".

Mr. Baines addressed the TUCC Chairman in the formal manner customary in a court of law: "*If you please, Sir*" or "*May it please you, Sir*". It was not a court of law.

- Gave his view on a film of Ryde pier as to what a large number of people were doing there - a worse situation than the Chairman "might have been deluded into thinking".
- It is a betrayal of those for whom the industry exists. These are our railways. (See page 53). The proposals will disrupt the economy for years to come. Over 1m stay each year. 149 objections may look small, but it consists of people. (The Chairman said "we can interpret canvassed objections"). 94,000 Islanders had not objected. BR probably felt betrayed by the inadequate use made of the railways by the Islanders.

Baines praised staff. (BR was criticised for statistics, but statistics generally originated with staff, who collect fares and tickets, pay wages, render accounts and submit returns).

- "We are going to show that the railway can run this system if they modernise, at a loss, no greater than that involved in BR proposals. It will obviate the need for £1m on roads. The line has been run down at the expense - not in the sense of the 'pocket' - but at the expense of the people of the Island". (How one can claim that anything has been done at someone's expense, who has not paid a penny piece to achieve viability, is incomprehensible. They were arguing that new interest bearing loan capital should be invested in a railway, which they admitted would *still* lose money).

He called his witnesses:-

- Councillor Bright had calculated the number of passengers who travelled on the Island as 1.15m. An *approximate* number of journeys had been included for season ticket holders and runabout tickets. Relating this to the total journeys specified by BR, and by using the "Carrington formula", he concluded that BR had understated the number of journeys by over 0.5m. He said that we know the *exact* number of passengers using the ferries.

The TUCC transcript does not expound on the "Carrington formula", nor does it mention that a copy was supplied. There was no copy in the TUCC file. With difficulty I tracked down Sir William Carrington's Report to the MoT in October 1963. He did not advocate his own formula, but endorsed BR's methods. (See page 224).

A few years ago, cross channel ferry companies were criticised on safety because they could not say precisely how many were on each ferry. BR's critics did not establish what percentage of passengers to the Island were on free tickets. Without question, there would have been many. What mattered was the £ sign, not volume.

The Chairman, as if in a courtroom, asked: "Mr. Taylor (BR), Do you wish to cross examine Mr. Bright?". Taylor - *not* prefixing his response with '*If it please you Sir*', replied "These Perry Mason remarks of inviting me to cross examine are likely to cause confusion, as indeed they are intended to do. If he is right in his deductions there may be a boomerang to the question. The film says there are three ferries each hour, but there are not - there are five ferries every two hours, and they are not ferries of maximum capacity. Peak carryings of 2,000 an hour are accepted, all our proposals are based on 2,000 per hour. The real practical issue is the peak carrying, not the annual total. The ferry to train transfer creates problems of large numbers queuing - departures by bus would be more frequent and reduce queues". The Chairman said "I have already reached that conclusion".

Baines resumed his presentation, calling further witnesses :-

- Bus companies were criticised for refusing to issue cheap tickets in the summer. (Hotels, package tours and travel by air and sea *always* cost more in peak periods).
- Southern Vectis bus company had a loss in winter, but a profit in summer. (BR drivers laid off would need to undertake route learning for safety reasons, bus drivers had no such need. Buses laid up paid no road costs, BR 'road' costs continued).
- "His witness" from horticulture & agriculture supplied hotels & caterers and would suffer if tourism fell. Baines asked: "More buses on roads would come as a tremendous impact on farmers?" - "Definitely". (He gave no evidence of using rail).

    Taylor was quick - "*The message is clear, if the holiday trade is affected, it affects farmers' prosperity, but equally, if farmers lower prices, residents will eat more*". The witness replied that is not part of the argument. The Chairman said: "You let Mr. Baines do the arguing!" Baines asked his witness if he wished to answer, and he said: "Not here". (These points do not seem to have been reported).
- The County Surveyor claimed that it would cost £1m for road improvements if the railways closed and the cost would fall on ratepayers. (Most wanted the railway as a standby. They wanted good transport for which others pay - see page 15).
- "You should have the cost of road improvements to compare with rail losses". (He did not say why - the 1962 Act did not require it. It had no bearing on the hardship of *passengers,* there would be no transfer of cash from road to rail budgets if closure did not take place. The Council did not suggest road expenditure be cut to fund railways)
- "The situation was now no different to 1953, when BR said that whilst economics required withdrawal of all services, it was difficult to see how the peak could be overcome in the near future". (Over ten years, whilst tourism to the Island was funded by uneconomic fares, the Council had taken no steps to improve roads. £1m over ten years is £100,000 pa. The MoT would pay 75% of the cost of the roads, Their 25% share would be less than 27p per person pa).

After lunch, the Chairman stated that they had concluded that a case of hardship had been made in respect of the Ryde-Ventnor line. Baines resumed his presentation:-
- Called Professor Hondelink. (*The Chairman said "we are not here to tell railways or Dr. Beeching how to run the railways, but to decide on hardship"*).
- "It will be very brief".

    Q. "*You were Director-General of the Central European Inland Transport Organisation set up to get Europe's transport moving again?*".
    A: Yes. (That was *not* its remit - see Appendix A.2).
- Hondelink said the Island railways could be run without loss:-
    1. *By increasing revenues or reducing costs - costs could be reduced by reducing train length from three coaches to one for nine months of the year, and by signalling and time-tabling, which he did not wish to go into now.* (He had set out his theory in a letter to Mr. Baines - see Appendix A.2)
    2. *By giving a proper service and more advertising. (Both would **increase** costs).*
    3. *The deficit could be wiped out by a 2d tariff on every visitor's fare. It would not cost Islanders a penny.*

The TUCC Chairman blocked an attempt by BR's spokesman to respond immediately to these sweeping generalisations, as it may extend the Hearing!

Unless summer trains were made up by coaches kept in service three times as long as in winter not a penny would be saved in capital. If coaches were rotated, they would be retained until 2044, and incur extra shunting costs. Maintenance based on time rather than mileage would be unaffected - painting, brake tests, etc. They would have to be moved periodically or they would seize up. (See page 204 for his other proposals).

In a Report made in 1965, Hondelink stated that "*railway ..... accounts are recorded to the last detail*"! (See page 209). In the 1964 Transport Tribunal Hearing on London fares, Hill, (the Council's expert in 1953), asked: "Is it any part of your case that BR is mismanaging affairs in *other parts of the country*?", answered: "Oh, no". [Q.2084].

The Chairman *reminded* Baines: "I have a note you were going to refer to 'honouring the pledge' - given by BR not to close any further lines during the next ten years". It was made ten years earlier. [PRO: MT115/7 & Times, 20.10.53] Despite the 1953 statement that all lines should close on economic grounds, the County was unprepared for more closures.

Baines referred to "pledges to keep lines open for 5-7 years". In no political arena do incoming Parties regard themselves as beholden to pledges made by the previous Party, and yet, with policies changed by a new national Government, they expected BR to ignore the requirement to cut losses. The Island was firmly pro-Tory, the Party which passed the 1962 Act, which led to the Reshaping Plan. *They were given 10 years warning in 1953*.

BR could not foresee that Government would freeze *only rail prices* in 1956, ignoring industry which was pushing up the RPI, and cut back Modernisation. Nor would they foresee that the Tribunal would continue to delay fare increases and hold them below the RPI, nor that the Isle of Wight County Council would object to increases in that court of law thereby placing IoW railways at greater risk. BR did not expect it to take two years to implement the Freight Charges Scheme and were surprised when the Tribunal reduced *existing* freight rates on an "appreciable volume of traffic" when BR was supposed to be given the commercial freedom taken for granted by all other businesses.

Baines said that he hoped that BR would not increase fares. Their expert Hondelink had advocated higher fares - for visitors, and the TUCC Chairman suggested it might close the gap - if all fares rose. Baines' part in the proceedings had occupied two of the $2^{1}/_{2}$ days of the Inquiry, and 40 pages of its 74 page Report, the balance included statements and questions by the Chairman, and other objectors. More was to follow.

Mr. Bellamy, Chairman of the Railway Retention Society
- Presented a petition of 81,733 - 58,586 visitors and 23,147 residents. A great proportion would not come again if railways closed.

  *One journey per day would equate to 59m pa - a volume not experienced in its heyday. One per week would have increased it threefold. Without doubt, there were many railway staff and families who travelled to the Island on free passes, who would go elsewhere after closures. It is probable that some had signed the petition. The organisers did not offer assurances that they had cross examined petitioners to exclude non fare paying passengers.*

- "Called *his* witness": Mr Conbeer, a teacher and Secretary of the Society, spoke of many school parties to and from the Island. Asked by the TUCC Deputy Chairman "How many - 2, 20 or 200?", he replied "Only guessing, must be dozens in a year or two".

  *His "statistics" evoked no criticism, in contrast to BR's. His 'evidence' covered five pages, largely on issues which the Chairman said were outside the remit and should have been addressed to the Minister. He then asked for "five more minutes, or ten at the most", was allowed to proceed and went on for another two pages.*

At the end of the second day, the Chairman called three objectors in turn, but they were not present. The fourth Mr. Ross, in the course of his evidence, said that the lines were constructed 100 years ago, and in the process, some went bankrupt.

On the third day, Bellamy interrupted the Chairman, who said "you have been up before us". He said "Yes, as Chairman of the Retention Society, now I appear for myself". He relied on the delivery of goods by rail for his business. The amount or value of the traffic was not mentioned. The Chairman concluded that the objectors had all finished after R.E. Burroughs, who had a one man business - as a photographer and gift shop, strongly objected to closure.

Eventually, the Chairman invited BR to speak. Their involvement covered only nine pages of the 74.

Taylor (British Rail spokesman):-

- The County had a five year plan to spend £100,000 pa on roads.
- BR statistics were based on a total of 2.8m tickets issued, valid for the IoW, including 1.1m for the short journey along Ryde pier, leaving 1.7m. Of these, we estimate 0.88m from the ferry use trains from the pier, the rest are local journeys within the Island. Mr. Bright had expected around 1m boat train passengers of the total 5m carried on ferries. Some 4m ferry passengers do not use rail services. In comparison stage carriages carry 16m, railways do not play a significant part, except at weekends.
- Passengers arriving by ferry would move away more steadily in smaller units - buses - than trains. (In the course of his presentation, there was an *'Uproar'*. No other speaker was interrupted. Only supporters of closures were denied free speech - see page 66).
- "I hope that I am allowed to continue without interruption. Buses at 15 mph, would be $\frac{1}{4}$ mile apart". (Objectors had said they would be head-to-tail) - Taylor said: "*Some head, some tail*".
- Referring to the Council's computer projection of bus journeys, it depends what intelligence is put into the programme, it can produce some surprising results, including empty buses starting in areas of heavy demand.
- If you do not go all the way that railways should be closed, it would be most economical for the remaining line to be Ryde-Sandown or Shanklin. Locos will *have* to be replaced in two years and rolling stock in seven, and there will be heavy capital expenditure. Railways have been chronically short of capital since pre-war days - then and now, the Island has been well down the queue.

- Responding to the Chairman's query about whether an extra 2d (0.8p) on ferry passenger fares would cover the annual loss and 10d (4p), on Island rail fares would take care of £165,000 renewals over the next five years. The short answer is "No". To earn £33,600, every passenger - men, women and children would have to pay it and that is not the full extent of the loss.

The Chairman said: "it was naughty of me to ask". He had told others they should not try to run the railways, and there was absolutely no prospect of public support for such an increase. No objector interrupted to urge such an increase to keep the lines open.

Baines cut in to ask "one or two questions", and posed fifteen over the next two pages. His case had already covered 40 pages. Then later, the Chairman brought him back in again for a summing-up, which covered another four pages.

Baines said we will put evidence before the Minister that you can run the railway without loss and break even. We believe that the whole deficit could be wiped out and it would cost not a penny more. He said that a penny rate would raise £13,000 pa. He had previously said that losses would be no greater if the line was modernised. (See page 70).

This evidence was to be put to the Minister, rather than the TUCC. I have been unable to trace it - it may be held under the 30 year rule. If it involved avoidance of road costs, it was irrelevant as no cash would transfer to BR. It is surprising that the Council did not offer to fund modernisation for a share of the profits, nor buy the lines and reap all profits.

The Inquiry closed at 12.15pm on the third day. BR's allocation of time was less than 20%, and only 12% of the verbatim record covered BR's participation and yet critics claim that the Inquiry was unfair to the objectors!

On 25th August 1964, the TUCC sent a very thick file to the MoT on their findings. It included BR's submission, copies of all written objections and a verbatim record of the Inquiry. **The Report** mentioned, inter alia:-

**BR** stated that receipts totalled £152,000, expenses £264,000 pa, and that renewals over the next five years would be £158,000. They stated that of the 2.8m passengers, 1.1m travelled only from Ryde Pierhead to Ryde Esplanade on the pier tramway.

**Objectors** claimed that the 1.7m journeys should be 2.2m. (The Report contained no independent justification for the higher figure). It was said that visitors spent an average of £15 per head (not, of course, on rail travel). A petition against closure had been signed by 81,733 people - 58,586 visitors and 23,147 residents. (The population was 94,000, so one can only assume that many were unconcerned. Had 23,000 residents made a daily journey, there would have been 8m passenger journeys and viability would have been assured). There were "over 1m visitors each year". The County Council was concerned that increasing road traffic would require an expenditure of £1m, of which 25% would fall on the ratepayers. The Council complained that BR had said in 1956 that they would give five or more years notice of closure, but had not done so. (Doubtless, they were in the same predicament as private sector companies who give no notice of closure). Any serious decline in the number of visitors would reduce property values and cause hardship and loss to hoteliers etc. (One would have thought that this prospect, and the cost of their contribution to road building would have induced them to use railways more, or offer a subsidy. It didn't). Objectors pointed out that rail fares were below bus fares, so closure would increase fares. Most of the travel on the Island was by visitors. The TUCC had received objections from only 24 residents who claimed to be regular users, only *four* travelled daily! 389 scholars could travel by bus without hardship. (If rail fares lower than bus fares couldn't induce people to use rail, what would? - free travel?).

**The TUCC** had considered the option of closing the Cowes line, and retaining Ryde-Ventnor, either throughout or to Shanklin only. They concluded that most of the Ryde-Cowes passengers could travel by bus services, which are more direct than the winding railway route. In respect of the proposed retention which would close the line between Shanklin and Ventnor, objectors pointed out that there are occasional days when frost and ice make it impossible to use the road from Ventnor. (On these *occasional days* BR should be grateful for a few passengers, who normally went by road). The TUCC said that retention from Ryde to Shanklin would alleviate most, but not all hardship.

The MoT issued a press release on 23rd July 1965 that he had decided that the service between Ryde and Shanklin was to be modernised and the rest closed, although he stated even the limited investment would not be justified in normal circumstances. He said that it would be reasonable for BR to increase fares so as to reduce, if not eliminate the loss.

### Stage 4 Closures Implemented
The 14 mile Cowes-Newport-Ryde line closed in February. "Ironically, crowds packed the last trains of a service which failed for lack of support One objector to closure stated: we are sorry to see the Island's railways come to an end and join other extinct landmarks such as destroyers under construction, brick making, disappearance of grain mills, cessation of manufacture of cement". [IoW County Press, 26.2.66]. Islanders were oblivious to the fact that rail closures were a product of industrial decline and road transport growth.

The MoT consented to withdrawal of the Ryde-Cowes and Shanklin-Ventnor lines earlier this year, and directed that the Ryde-Shanklin line must be modernised. The availability of ex London Transport rolling stock was a deciding factor. The cost was estimated at £500,000. Existing signalling was to be simplified. [Railway Magazine, September, 1966, Page 508]. (There was no reference to the source of the finance. Doubtless, it would be represented by an increase in the deficit, as social costs were hidden in railway "losses").

Secondhand London Transport stock was acceptable to the Island's loading gauge with electrical control gear in a suitable position for maintenance. [Course, Page 47]. Tunnel sizes necessitated stock such as used on London Transport. [Portsmouth Evening News, 19.1.66].

The Island's MP said that BR had agreed that modernising Ryde to Shanklin would be profitable and to Ventnor would incur a small loss, but would still leave a net profit. He said that improving Shanklin station approach road would cost £70,000, whereas modernisation to Ventnor would cost £80,000. He said that BR had agreed that the cost of modernisation had been over estimated. The Minister said that it would cost £10,000, not £70,000, to improve Shanklin station approach road. [Hansard, vol. 725, cols. 2347-2352]. A media report states that new figures had been agreed with the County Council. [IoW County Press, 12.3.66]. Unfortunately, papers which would show how and why new figures differed from others, could not be traced by the County Record Office. I suspect that reduced modernisation costs arose because BR had originally costed it on the basis of new stock and equipment, whereas they later proposed to use secondhand LT stock.

BR was criticised because they could make more by terminating trains at Shanklin as keeping the line to Ventnor. (This was standard private sector practice).

The fears of loss of business due to the rail closure do not seem to have materialised. "Most of the people did not know the railway had closed and did not seem to mind". "The seamen's strike had an adverse effect on bookings in the early part of the season". "Southern Vectis had done a marvellous job". "The chairman said the rail closure had not been as bad as they thought it would be". [Hotels Association meeting, IoW County Press, 3.12.66]

### Invalid Criticisms

BR replied to the Railway Retention Association that Government policy had compelled changes to previous forecasts about the life of lines on the Island. [Times, 23.1.64, 3e].

"Hotels on the Island had learned to adopt a flexible approach - why didn't BR?" [Henshaw, Page 230]. Opposition to fares matching the RPI was a very compelling reason, no one held down hotel charges and we all know what *hoteliers* do to prices in the Summer. Any proposal by BR to adopt the flexible policy applied by hoteliers and significantly increase prices in the summer would have been met by vicious criticism. Moreover, it is evident that hoteliers were not as flexible as believed. "One factor in increasing bookings had been the introduction of mid week bookings". "We should do more advertising". "The AA is trying to force hoteliers to provide additional facilities - lifts, more bathrooms, private bathrooms and extra facilities before hotel ratings are increased. It is about time, the AA and RAC did their own job and left hotels to look after their business!". [Hotels Association meeting, IoW County Press, 3.12.66]. (Mid week bookings were common in European small hotels and *Pension* in the early 1950's, and here was the UK's hotel industry following them in 1966. They had not been slow to tell BR how to do their job, but when they were advised to make improvements to benefit the customer, they did not like it!).

Some objectors said that BR had disregarded its paying customers! No business would regard customers who did not cover costs as 'paying customers'. None justified closures or price increases. None faced a public inquiry to close branches making "an inadequate profit", much less a loss nor a court of law to beg permission to increase prices.

A BR warning in 1953 about closure in ten years time, had been read as *sinister* by critics. It was a warning "to use it" - or more precisely pay for it - "or lose it". It is common to see shops warning: use it or lose it. If they didn't respond with ten year's delay, it was clear they did not want a railway system - unless someone else paid for it.

There were criticisms of a lack of point heaters to combat severe weather in November 1967. They are provided to protect heavily used lines in *winter*. It would have been a grievous waste of capital to provide them on lines whose traffic was almost wholly in the *summer*, when thousands of miles used heavily in winter were not equipped due to lack of funds. The line had been kept open as desired at minimum cost, and, as was not uncommon, objectors sought later to impose other costs.

"BR counter proposed that if TUCC was considering retention of the Ryde-Ventnor line, it would be more economic, and losses reduced if the line was terminated at Sandown or Shanklin. The committee were unanimous that closure of Ryde-Ventnor would result in severe hardship, but were not unanimous in their assessment of hardship on the Cowes line. After all this BR put forward a proposal to terminate the Ryde-Ventnor line at Shanklin. No suggestion was made previously". [Burroughs, Page 21]. BR had proposed total closure! When objectors proposed in the middle of an Inquiry, that BR should close Newport-Ryde instead of Newport-Sandown it did not meet with criticism. (See page 68).

It was said that Professor Hondelink, had made a very **close study** of the railway and said it could be made to pay. With regard to the *close study* he would make of the railway, he had written to the County Council, saying that he would spend *one day* on the Island. (See page 204). His proposals for making the line pay were fundamentally flawed. (See pages 71 & 204).

The Regional Labour Party called on the national party to take action in Parliament to preserve, modernise and generally improve railways on the island. [IoW County Press, 27.6.64]. Regrettably, when the Labour Party was previously in power, it passed legislation which ensured BR would become insolvent and worse still, denied to railways the authority and materials to modernise, whilst it turned a blind eye to road transport exceeding Government directives on the number of vehicles to be acquired by the home market. It even directed railways *not* to overtake wartime arrears of maintenance except only in the interests of safety. The effect of this inequitable direction was not overcome until the end of 1954, by which time road transport had eaten heavily into rail freight and passenger business. [See *"Blueprints for Bankruptcy"* & *"Square Deal Denied"*]. The attention of a Labour Minister of Transport was drawn to the fact that post-war rail traffic had been expanding, but rolling stock was less than pre-war, with many vehicles being held abroad by the military, leading to huge numbers of passengers having to stand. [Hansard, vol. 415, col. 1604].

Criticisms were made of a "shutdown of the railway for three months to electrify it". [Burroughs, Page 42]. Closing a section of line for engineering work is, in the long run, usually less expensive than working "between trains" or at weekends. Crewe station, which probably had more passengers than the whole of the Isle of Wight in its heyday, was closed for seven weeks for track alterations. Partial closure coupled with bus links for such a short route would not have been satisfactory. Working between trains carries more safety risks and produces more complaints. He dismissed BR's explanation that the track had to be raised as platforms were too high for London Transport stock. It would have been imprudent to carry out this work "between trains". A 'hump' between lifted and unlifted track, as the work progressed, would have been intolerable and potentially unsafe.

### Amateurs trying to show how to do it

The Isle of Wight Railway Society was formed in 1954 with a capital of *£500* to take over the Freshwater-Newport line, and to take over, when closed, all lines. [PRO: MT115/5].

In 1954, the DoT received a proposal for a narrow gauge railway. "A double track could be laid in the space of the standard gauge, and will lend itself to tremendous improvement in the frequency of passenger traffic to/from Ryde. Each train would carry 350 passengers. Each coach would carry 20 passengers". They would need 17.5 coaches per train, i.e. 18 which would be 540 ft long, compared to 360 ft for a BR train of similar capacity. Trains were to be equipped with the 'Vacuum Air Brake' (sic). [PRO: MT115/7].

The Vectrail Society was formed to acquire and run some closed lines; the primary objective was Ryde-Cowes. It envisaged the council should purchase land and lease it to Vectrail who would buy the track. A frequent passenger service would be provided. It had been given professional advice that it could electrify, overhead, 26.75 miles, with new vehicles for £140,000 more than BR's plan for third rail on an eight mile line. They could reduce the outlay to £250,000 by using ten year old rolling stock. [Burroughs, Pages 45, 28 & 29]. BR's scheme is shown as £680,500. [Burroughs, Page 28]. BR's costs were set out in detail, *including fencing*, in contrast to the complete lack of detail for the overhead schemes.

Another anonymous expert missed an opportunity for free publicity. Both their schemes required huge capital, the interest and forecast return on which is not revealed. The necessity to increase bridge clearances for an overhead system increases costs. It would be interesting to see how much their expert had allowed for these costs. The source of old stock, suitable for the Island's structural gauge, which would save £570,500, was not identified. No reference was made to revenue. Their ambitious plan did not materialise. No one took over their "primary objective". What held them back? The sums involved, lack of detail and disparities make it difficult to take seriously. BR's scheme cost £500,000

BR was criticised for the price asked for selling the railway on the grounds that the net disposable value of land, buildings, permanent way & signalling equipment was £58,200 and BR was asking £85,000. "It was a case for the Prices and Incomes Board". [Burroughs, Page 44]. No other business accepts a third party determining the selling price of assets. The Board did not have a mandate for such matters in either the public or private sector.

In June 1970, the County Council ended negotiations with Vectrail about use of the land when it became apparent that they had not purchased rails for the line, which they had undertaken to do. The Council had bought railway and property comprising the former Ryde to Cowes and Shanklin to Ventnor lines at a cost of £71,610. In 1971, the Council abandoned its 1969 plan for mass transportation. They noted a potential liability of £10,000 pa in interest, fencing and maintenance. In 1973, they agreed to lease the land between Havenstreet and Smallbrook to the Isle of Wight Locomotive Society. Other parcels of the former railway lines were sold to individual householders whose gardens back onto the line, and to Ventnor UDC. [County Record Office: Council minutes]

### Island Ferry Services

Sandown UDC wrote to the TUCC in June 1952 advocating "halving ferry charges in the winter. The Council has every reason to believe that an Island motorist making, say, one journey by car to the mainland would certainly be planning to make two or more if the charge was halved, the experiment might well prove successful". The TUCC minutes noted that it would require twice as many cars to achieve the same revenue.

This proposal was not supported by any market research nor guaranteed against loss. They overlooked that petrol and other motoring costs would not be half price in the winter, so the reduction in ferry charges would be a drop in the bucket. Neither did they realise their faux pas in drawing attention to the fact that Islanders were driving to the mainland instead of using the railways which they claimed were essential!

BR wrote to the TUCC in August 1953 that "car ferry users point out that ferries are more profitable than most BTC activities and claim it is not justified to raise ferry charges in order to subsidise a separate section such as railways". (They had precisely justified cross subsidisation when it came to keeping Island railways operating at a loss).

The BTC wrote to the DoT in June 1954, in response to criticisms made in a recent Debate by the Island's MP regarding charges for cars to/from the Island. They said he is not entitled to describe them as exorbitant, they are 64-111% above pre-war, whereas costs are up 200%. They said that the MP's statement that when the private enterprise Isle of Wight Steam Packet Co. threatened to lower its freight charges, BR threatened to withdraw their ferry service is an objectionable allegation, without the slightest foundation. The truth is that the company would have liked to increase their charges by 10%, and were disappointed to find that we did not consider it justified on our (BTC) route. Responding to criticisms about operations on Ryde Pier, they said it was acquired by the Southern Railway in their 1924 Act and leased to Ryde Corporation, who during the war, took advantage of a "break" clause - in the leasing agreement - and surrendered the lease. The Southern Railway then decided to work the pier. It was the Southern Railway and now the BTC, who have kept the pier going after local authorities were glad enough to surrender all interest when financial prospects appeared to them to be unattractive. The MoT wrote to the MP on these lines. [PRO: MT115/7].

### Postscript

If it was so easy to make a profit on the Island's railways and the MoT had said a private operator could buy them, why did the Railway Development Association or Branch Line Reinvigoration Society or some other group not jump in at once, with Hondelink as chairman, and using some volunteer labour. The County Council may have helped them - all parties would have become household names. It was a golden opportunity to justify claims on the running of a basic, profitable - year round - railway. Were critics uncertain that the lines could be made to pay, or had they endeavoured, unsuccessfully, to raise the capital necessary to buy the formation and track and to run a railway service?

Objectors to closures in 1953 claimed that the loss was £20,000 pa, not the £90,000 pa which BR had announced. The County Council had said that road improvements would cost Islanders £25,000 pa. They would have gained by taking over the lines. Clearly, the objectors did not have the courage of their convictions, or they could not have failed to make a bid, and take them over. Objectors claimed that new trains and lower fares would produce a profit. What held them back from proving it?

Until 1968, branch line losses were carried as a BR deficit. BR was largely subsisting on interest bearing loans. Thereafter, Government made overt Grants to cover losses on socially necessary uneconomic lines and services. (See pages 12 & 197). In 1993, just prior to Privatisation, that was changed by Government to include an "administrative profit". (See page 197).

Under Privatisation, a franchisee on the Isle of Wight receives a subsidy to operate services between Ryde and Shanklin. [OPRAF News Release].

The Isle of Wight Steam Railway's 1999 timetable shows it does not run services on about half of the days in the year. They employ some volunteers.

These two sections of Isle of Wight railways confirm that year round services could not be run at a profit, despite what many critics claimed. No Government subsidy was offered to BR to avoid closures on the Island before 1968.

## New Opportunities for Compensation

Objectors claimed, in this and later cases, that there would be hardship due to property values falling if railways closed. It is an unarguable fact that when railways were built, and again when they were modernised, the value of property and undeveloped land rose dramatically. Not a penny of these profits was offered to railway proprietors to defray constructional costs which had been invariably increased by exorbitant demands for the price of land (developed or undeveloped), by avaricious landowners intent on screwing the railway companies. (See pages 7 & 186).. These were not merely the landed aristocracy, as the long list of those to be compensated in the Loop Line case shows, (see page 184). Now, even objectors who didn't use railways expect to be compensated when a line closed. Needless to say, they would not expect compensation when the last village shop or school closed, despite the effect it must have on property values.

Another objection made under the heading of "hardship", in this and other cases, was that ratepayers would have to fund road improvement costs to take traffic diverted from a closed line. Since councils first became responsible for road maintenance, railways had contributed handsomely to road costs. Indeed for decades, they were, in effect, subsidising road users, especially hauliers who paid little or nothing towards road costs. [See "Square Deal Denied"]. Roads in almost all rural areas in the UK were not improved to the standard warranted by traffic increase. The closure of a railway line seemed to present a second opportunity to exploit railways so as to avoid ratepayers having to pay to improve roads, which had they been adequate 100 years or so earlier, might have avoided local pressure to build railways where there was no real justification. (See pages 184/5). No offer was ever made to transfer to BR, as a subsidy, even part of the amount required to improve roads as a quid pro quo for keeping unremunerative lines open. Objectors sought the improvement of roads at no cost to local Rates.

## Chapter 6                     The Brightlingsea Branch

The branch to Brightlingsea was authorised in 1861 and opened in 1866. It had been planned to extend to St. Oysth, a picturesque village, but was opposed by the GER. Its traffic was mainly seasonal - fish and oysters [C. Langley Aldrich, Railway Magazine, 1947]. The line was worked by the GER. [Bradshaw's Railway Shareholders' Guide, 1880].

There were no intermediate stations, the line existed solely to serve Brightlingsea.

The Chairman of the railway company said : While other railways have lost some of their initial prosperity, the 1880's were good years for us, shares were paying good dividends. Prospects had never been so good or so bright. [Brown, Page 41]. The Chairman's bold words were not borne out by Bradshaw's Railway Shareholders' Guide, which reported on railway results and dividends, and revealed that year after year, there was no record of a dividend on Ordinary shares. They struggled to pay mandatory interest on Debentures and often paid much less than the specified rate on Preference shares.

In 1891, a sale price of £31,000 was agreed and the branch taken over by the GER in 1894 under an 1894 Act. [Bradshaw's Railway Shareholders Guide, 1891 & 1894]. The Guide for 1877 reveals that they had spent £48,942 in capital, including £10,000 on land purchase, so it couldn't have been doing all that well if they let it go for £31,000 sixteen years later.

Costs were increased as Government imposed higher safety standards, shorter hours and standard rates of pay on railways, but not on road transport. Government interfered in the determination of freight rates, and held them down. Railway companies warned the Government that rural branch lines were consequently set to become insolvent. [See "*Square Deal Denied*"]. "Before the coming of the eight hour day, there were arduous examples of 12-14 hours. The normal shift was thirteen hours". [Brown, Page 78].

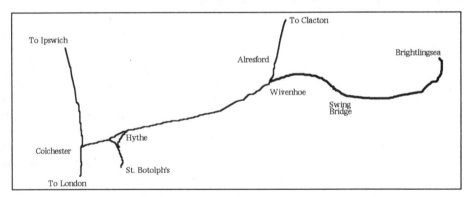

### Closed by Sea Floods

The first serious flooding of the branch occurred in 1897, and continued every few years. 1904 was the seventh in the line's history. Flooding occurred again in 1928, 1949 and 1953 [Brown, Pages 48, 49, 57, 58 & 106].

A substantial section of the branch was destroyed by the sea floods on 31st January and 1st February 1953. This cut the railway line to Brightlingsea. Prior to its destruction, the

BTC had been examining the financial position of the branch with a view to proposing closure as for some time, it had been losing some £8,000 pa. In the circumstances the BTC did not feel justified in repairing the line. On 3rd April, BR informed Brightlingsea Chamber of Commerce that the line would not be re-opened because of losses and that the cost of restoration would not be justified. They set out the alternative arrangements for passenger, parcels and freight traffic. The winter weekday train service consisted of 12 trains each way - 13 on Saturdays. The summer weekday service had two more trains each way on most days. In 1952, an average of 3,000-3,800 tickets were issued monthly, about 100-125 per day. Five trains carried most of the passengers, the rest rarely had more than ten. The trend of traffic was down - 1938 = 100, 1952 = 48. Issues in 1952 had been higher than 1948, due to cheaper tickets, which increased volume, but not receipts.

The matter was brought before the TUCC for consideration. They met on three dates: on 9th June to examine the documents, and on 16th June and 7th July, to hear representations from the Railway Executive and objectors.

These included information on passenger travel, showing that, outside the months of July and August, the daily average was below 130 passengers. (What BR did not want was a further increase in peak month travel. What it needed was a year round increase to bring numbers during ten months up to the peak figure, otherwise assets and trained staff would continue to be provided, for most of the year in excess of needs). In comparison there were about 600 empty seats on BTC buses per day on the parallel route. Gross annual savings were £22,488, net after allowing for traffic which *may* be lost to rail - some of which would transfer to BTC buses - and additional bus and cartage costs of £8,700 pa. They stated "indications of possible increased traffic were without any guarantee and were not sufficiently firm to influence the future of the line". BR's grounds for closure were :- ·

- The operation of the branch before suspension of services due to floods was uneconomic. A net saving can be achieved by closure.
- Prospective revenue obtainable from traffic worked over the branch cannot be expected materially to increase.
- Alternative services proposed are reasonably adequate in relation to volume.
- It is neither reasonable nor in the general public interest to re-open the line and continue an uneconomic service.

*Three* Members of Parliament asked for the hearing to be deferred as they all wished to appear to oppose closure of the line to Brightlingsea, a community of 4,000 people! After they had been heard on 16th June, a deputation of 20 were admitted. Objectors included Essex County Council, Brightlingsea UDC, various traders & businesses and Mr. French of the Union of General & Municipal Workers.

Written objections included :-

*Hotels & Catering Interests* :-

- "*Day trippers* come to Brightlingsea in their thousands, most by train". (Tickets counted by BR staff totalled 1,614 on the busiest Saturday in the year, and included locals, commuters and holidaymakers staying a week or more. If there were *thousands of day trippers*, most must have travelled by road).

- In 1866, one could depart from Brightlingsea at 8.0 am and arrive in London at 10.30. (Railways had no competition in 1866. He neglected to mention how few from this minor resort took advantage of that service in 1866. Nor did he estimate how many would do so, given a similar service in 1953. Any industry providing a service without a reliable indication of take-up would soon be insolvent).
- He was concerned for the effect on smaller boarding houses. (What some boarding houses had to offer in some areas may have lost business. See page 32).

*Regional Board for Industry* :-

- The line should be re-opened for an experimental period of three to five years, during which time it should be the joint responsibility of BR, of industry and of the public generally to place and maintain the service on an economic level. (That objective would have been realised if the losses were jointly shared until the public and industry sufficiently increased user to eliminate losses. Naturally they did not advocate *that*. This was to be a unique partnership, in which only one partner bore any losses).
- BR had failed to provide an adequate and satisfactory service. (Not a word of evidence was advanced. There were 12 trains per day for about 130 people - ten per train. They did not indicate how many more trains were required to cater for the 4,000 population. If they all travelled daily, they would not tax the existing train service).
- "They did not know the financial details". (But it did not prevent them from advancing an opinion. Little wonder we have no manufacturing industry if this is how industry made decisions).
- Brightlingsea was important in two wars, and it was important to preserve the port link in case of a future conflict. (Unfortunately, railways had had their fingers burnt twice for their patriotism and preparedness - see "*Square Deal Denied*").
- The sprat industry was important, and in recent years they have deserted this coast, This has occurred in the past, and it *may well* be that they will return. (How many factories are kept open, in case demand *may* return? The Ministry office at Lowestoft told me that sprats deserted the area due to over-fishing. See also pages 88 & 89).
- The council invested large sums resulting in a large influx of summer visitors. (The problem was that there was too few passengers for ten months of the year!).
- Industry and public should co-operate to ensure that the service is economic or involves a loss sufficiently small to be absorbed in the public interests. (Absorbed by whom is not identified. It was not to be the Board or local authority - Government had no intention of doing so. That left BR who could only do so by cutting wages or increasing losses as fares and charges were held below the RPI by a court of law).
- Should roads be flooded, the town would be isolated if the line closed. (BR was needed as a standby - a variation of the plea that roads may be blocked by snow).
- Congestion would be caused by buses bringing passengers from Colchester. (They may go to a different resort. Locals should have made more use of the line).
- Diesel railcars should operate a fast and economic service on the branch. (One can only wonder if they knew that this was a five mile branch. Assuming that no expenditure was required to make track fit for higher speeds, the odd minute saved on such a short distance would not attract any new custom. The capital cost of the diesels

was ignored - did they know someone who would lease them free of charge? This attitude may explain the demise of UK manufacturing)

- An intensive study is warranted before a decision is taken. (This was not to be funded by the Board, nor the local authority, nor would anyone support losses until the study was complete. If an analogous situation had faced a local employer, and he had been asked to undertake a study - he would have made sure someone else was funding it. It can be little surprise that BR was driven into bankruptcy by external influences).

*Easipower Ltd* :-

- Prepared to switch some traffic to rail if given a preferential rate. This would give a *gross* revenue of £1,500-£2,000 pa. This included "the transfer of £3-400 worth of traffic at present carried on our lorries, and £500 of new production". (So much for the inadequacy of roads and the community's complete dependence on rail. Clearly this could only be a small part of their production. They were not offering to put all their traffic on rail, even if given "undue preference" against the rest of the UK, in direct conflict with the Railway & Canal Traffic Act, 1854, Sec. 2).

*W.J. White & Son* :-

- It is essential for the existence and future development of the fishing industry that a round the clock service be provided. (A standard they had not had in their heyday).
- Fish landings were £42,000 in 1952. (This was a totally valueless & useless statistic. It gave no indication of weight. It didn't even represent *gross* railway receipts).
- Fishing fleets have been encouraged to expand by subsidies and grants. (In addition, they demanded rail transport subsidised by railway staff or other users).
- There are encouraging signs that the once flourishing sprat trade is more hopeful than for several years. (Jam tomorrow. In fact, inquiries of the fishing industry reveal that it never recovered for any appreciable period).
- Our rail carriage has averaged £800 pa over the past three years. (No promise was made of increased carryings. An *existing* £800 **gross** was irrelevant).

*Lyteze Products* :-

- Are forwarding 300 tons by rail pa. It is hoped that output should increase by 50%. (Just over one ton per day, after the **hoped for** increase in business!).

*Shipbuilding* :-

- Approximately 500 tons pa from one yard. (Traffic from the other yard was not mentioned. It is a safe deduction that it was much less, as they were clearly praying in aid every package and parcel sent by rail).

*Other points* :-

- BR *alleges* a loss, but produced no figures to substantiate it. (No other industry had to produce figures to prove it was making a loss, even when sacking thousands).
- The BTC enjoys a monopoly. (It didn't or there would be *no* passenger or freight traffic by road to or from Brightlingsea).
- The BTC has a duty to provide a service adequate to the needs of the local community. (There was no such duty. Under the 1947 Act, the BTC was not required to provide adequate rail *and* road services, only an adequate & economic transport service. Even this obligation ceased with the 1953 Act, except in the London area).

- No opportunity was given to the community to intensify usage of the service. (Not a word of evidence was tabled to guarantee increased usage if given that opportunity).
- If the line was closed some former users would consign by road throughout. (So much for the inadequacy of local roads. The BTC had allowed for traffic loss).
- Restoration of the line should be paid by the Lord Mayor's fund or Government.

Twenty people attended. Colne Fisheries Board and Colchester Corporation, which were represented by Colchester's Town Clerk. A barrister represented all other objectors, including the County Council and the UDC He objected to the lack of figures on which the Executive's *allegations* were based. (This was emotive language. The objectors' case was based on unquantified generalisations, pious hopes, no guarantees and no figures).

He said: If the line is less remunerative than it should be, local interests should be given an opportunity of seeing what could be done to alleviate the position. (Events proved that, this did not mean guaranteeing to make more use if the line, but rather 'playing trains' by trying to show how the service could be improved, in the unproven hope that more investment and more trains would miraculously increase revenue, not merely to overtake existing losses, but to fund additional capital and operating costs).

The QC said that in arriving at the question of net saving, the operating ratio for a branch of this kind should be borne in mind. There was no such thing as a ratio for "a branch of this kind". The ratio - comparing total costs to revenue - was for the system as a whole. There was not one for every branch or main line. It would be wasteful to calculate a ratio for hundreds of lines. Pre-war railways did not do so.

At the hearing on 16th June, further figures were produced by BR. The QC then stated that the convenience of the public should be an over-riding consideration, and that whilst the financial aspect is a major one, it must be subordinated provided that the loss is not so exorbitant as could reasonably be met from the services generally of the Railway Executive. (The Act did not specify that. Defining "exorbitant" and "reasonableness" would have involved protracted and costly legal argument. He was calling for users of this line to be subsidised by others paying higher fares than necessary. As a deficit was being created by the Court of the Transport Tribunal, which was holding fares below the rate of inflation, aided by objections from Essex County Council, the burden would fall on the rail staff whose wages were thereby held down below industrial levels).

He endeavoured to prove that the line was busy by quoting passenger loadings for *one week* in July, when loadings for the whole year showed that 10 months of the year were slack. He claimed that by adjusting train times, 200 workmen could be influenced to travel by rail instead of by bus. (Both were owned by the BTC. Their revenue would not halve the rail loss and would jeopardise bus services).

Mr. French, a union "expert" said that trains departing at 7.22 am and 8.19 am would be more attractive to workers than 7.10 am and 8.15 am buses they were using. As an ex-railwayman (of unspecified expertise), *he* affirmed that the modified service could be operated by one engine and two sets of men from Brightlingsea and one *part-time* crew from Colchester. (He should have known that there was no such thing as a *part time* crew. What he meant was an unproductively employed crew, for whom he *hoped* other work could conveniently be found. Like industry, BR employed part time office cleaners, but not part-time skilled staff). He said workers would be prepared to use the trains which take 23 minutes against 40 minutes by bus at the same price. (Everyone would like something faster for a cheaper price). BR's representative pointed out that "the proposed schedule took no account of connections". As in many other cases, locals expected the main line would be re-scheduled to make good connections for them, but not of course for any other branch, and without regard to the needs of main line passengers. This expert had overlooked the realities of rostering and relief requirements. (See pages 35-36). His service could not have been worked by two crews based at Brightlingsea, because he had overlooked that crews must be given certain periods for safety duties before taking over a steam engine, and do not jump on to engines already conveniently attached to coaches, hence his rosters would be over eight hours, (see Appendix A.3), - the limit forced on railways by Government. [See "Square Deal Denied"]. This means he would have to have his "part-time" crew at Colchester and a crew at Brightlingsea to dispose of, after 22.21, and prepare before 06.40, the steam engine. He could not have had footplate nor rostering experience or he would not have made such a fundamental error. Carriage cleaning and maintenance staff would be required. His sketchy "timetable" (see Appendix A.3), would not have been so described by train planners, as it did not include junction passing times nor other affected trains. Over 50% of existing commuters - about 100 or so - would face a longer day and may be lost to rail. It was a big risk to take to try to attract 200 and at fares which would cut existing revenue. He did not address the effect on the timing of trains on the main line, of extending trains beyond Wivenhoe or by rescheduling the departure of other trains. In typical parochial attitude, he called for one train from Clacton to London to depart three minutes earlier and call additionally at Wivenhoe, to make a connection for Brightlingsea passengers. Leaving aside whether there would be a path without having to re-time other trains and inconvenience thousands of commuters, the idea would go down like a lead balloon in Clacton! Of course, his plan met with acclaim from objectors with equal ignorance of basic railway operating, rostering and allied matters.

The QC enumerated the industrial activity - but the fact is that the traffic was low volume, in total, by *any* standard. If the roads were as bad as they claimed, there couldn't be much to divert to rail anyway. He said that the produce of light industry *might* flow to rail, subject to the offer of rate concessions. These "rate concessions", effectively meant giving Brightlingsea "industry" an undue preference over similar industry elsewhere, in contravention of an Act of 1854. This traffic was another "maybe" not a guarantee.

He drew attention to the number of houses constructed since *1945*. (This was water under the bridge, which had not led to more traffic). He spoke of land being set aside in the Town Development Plan for light industries. (This fell way short of a certainty that they would attract any businesses, much less that it may thereafter lead to more traffic on rail. There cannot be any doubt that no one present would have invested so much as a penny of their own money on such vague prospects). The neglect of the County to improve roads was advanced as a reason for BR to keep an unremunerative service. (The local authority did not offer even 50% of the estimated cost of road improvements to keep the railway. It was noticeable that the TUCC was expected to take on trust that council figures were 100% accurate, and that only BR figures were suspect. The

TUCC never questioned *their figures*. It was sufficient for objectors to claim that BR had taken no steps to improve branch revenue. One would have imagined, from objections based on the inadequacy of roads, that BR was legally responsible for all road construction and maintenance, instead of being merely a heavy contributor to municipal rates).

A representative of the oyster trade spoke of the problems they would face, and quoted the *number* of oysters *sold*, which was not synonymous with despatches by rail. He said that sales had risen to 250,000 oysters in 1952. BR did not charge by number, but by weight. It can be safely assumed that had he quoted by weight, it would have looked less impressive. Inquiries of the Fish Statistics Unit of the Ministry of Agriculture & Fisheries reveal that 15-25 oysters weighed approximately one kilogramme. Hence, 250,000 would weigh 10-16 imperial tons per annum. It would not justify a rail service if it were ten times greater and had all been sent by rail, which the spokesman did not even claim.

The Regional Board for Industry reiterated that the line be kept open for three to five years, as there *might* be prospects of new industry. (Needless to say, they did not offer a subsidy to keep the line open until this Shangri-La situation materialised).

The MP for Colchester said that the closure was not based on economic merits, but on a policy to close all branch lines. (BR policy was to consider all other options before submitting for closure - see page 23). Another MP asked if the public service aspect had been considered, and was reminded that BR introduced alternative services immediately the line was damaged. Referring to another closure, a third MP said that a coal merchant had to collect coal from further afield which cost him 10/- (50p) per ton more. (In contrast to criticisms of BR figures, the merchant's audited accounts were not produced). He argued that diesels on this branch might benefit the export of such vehicles. (He did not identify the source of the capital, nor by how much revenue would have to increase to eliminate existing losses and also cover the cost of borrowing capital).

BR's representative said they did not calculate an operating ratio for a branch in isolation, but credited it with a proportion of off-branch revenue. Costs and savings were checked and verified by accountants. In estimating loss of revenue, BR took a pessimistic view. To have informed local authorities before BR had established the facts would have been counter productive and might have alarmed people unnecessarily had the decision been to retain the line. The economics of the line had been examined in 1948 and 1949, and came under new scrutiny in September 1952. Inquiries had not been completed when the flood occurred. BR decided that spending more to restore a line which was already losing money was not justified. BR was not under a statutory obligation to maintain the sea embankments, although they had done so voluntarily since 1922 and were granted relief from drainage rates in return. He responded to objectors' points as follows:-

• Ministers had indicated that BR would get no sea damage relief from Government or the Lord Mayor's fund.

• The plan of the Union man for a new train service, with a **claimed** saving of **£500** pa, involved re-opening Brightlingsea engine shed - a cost which he had ignored. (The loss was **£10,000** pa. From personal experience of depots with two crews at the end of a branch, the cost of relief cover for holidays and sickness swamped savings which appear to arise from having local men. See pages 35, 36 & 86).

- It is doubtful that there would be 200 passengers, but, if there were, the estimated revenue would be £1,800 pa per 100 passengers. (This would not close the gap).
- The peak day, in the peak week quoted by the QC was Brightlingsea annual regatta day. Objectors had said that the average for that week was 713.
  *BR said that over half of all tickets sold were to workmen at very low fares.*
- Sprats had fallen from 328 tons pa before the war, to 202 tons in 1950, 169 tons in 1951, and nil for 1952 and 1953. All locally generated traffic, and incoming traffic was of low volume. The biggest was agriculture with 53 wagons pa - one per week!
- The number of passengers travelling by rail, after taking account of workmen, did not confirm the development of Brightlingsea had materially affected the amount of railway business over the last five years.
- Additional bus journeys would be small. The BTC were as entitled to use the roads as anybody. (They were more entitled, as they paid annual Rates, far in excess of road transport operators, to contribute to road costs. See "*Square Deal Denied*")
- Diesel railcars needed to be used for high daily mileages, not on isolated short branch lines as one MP suggested. (Standing time would exceed running time on this branch)
- A transfer of revenue from bus to rail was no gain for the BTC which owned the buses. (Objectors had not, of course, urged that buses be withdrawn instead of rail services. The branch line was "essential", but despite "poor" roads, they wanted the buses as well).
- Products from light industry are already conveyed by railhead motors and additional traffic could be conveyed without restoring the line. (Amateurs did not like to hear references to railhead motors. They were unwilling to concede that this system ensured earlier connections from nearby main centres, and reduced handling).
- Regard should be paid to general public interest, whereby economies might be applied for the benefit of users nationally.
- BR should not be called on to incur expenditure and carry the commercial risk on the uncertain prospects dependent on the problematical revival of the sprat industry.

The QC made further comments :-
- "That no special measures had been taken beyond normal contacts to secure additional traffic". (Objectors had admitted that the "potential" they had claimed would not *turn loss into profit*. One may be sure they had listed *every* possibility).
- "No figures had been produced as to the cost of running diesel services over the line". (A detailed costing exercise was not necessary for every line when it was known that the scale of capital cost required intensive user of railcars with good loadings, and that neither was a prospect on this isolated lightly trafficked branch line. It is certain that no industry would repeat trials nor prepare audited accounts in justification)
- "That BR had made no effort to verify or refute the result of the trade union enquiry as to the 200 passengers per day *guaranteed* by the Union expert". (The "expert" had guaranteed *nothing*. Guarantees imply the promise of a refund. If a survey had been conducted and all said they would travel by rail, it would still not close the gap, but would endanger BTC owned bus services, as had already been pointed out).

- "The service could be worked with fewer sets of men". (The passenger service proposed by Mr. French needed *more* men! See pages 35, 86 & 210).
  *BR said the plan ignored freight traffic and time to attach and detach wagons.*

An MP spoke of the prospects of the sprat industry. BR's representative confirmed they had no made no inquiries through the Ministry of Food about the home market or the Board of Trade about foreign markets. He said he would have thought that the merchants should have been the ones to make such inquiries. The TUCC chairman remarked that it was BR which wished to close the line, not the traders. (A more illogical remark is difficult to imagine. Surely the merchants, whose livelihood and future depended on a revival of the industry should have been beating down the doors of the Ministries every week. Their MP's should have been marshalled to badger Ministers in Parliament. But there is no evidence that they did so. One can imagine the outcry about over-staffing if BR increased staff to carry out these inquiries, effectively, on behalf of selected industries).

An examination of Hansard for evidence that the fishing industry had been sufficiently interested in their own welfare to have questions raised about its future prospects, reveals only one entry in the relevant period : 1951-53. "Fishermen were unable to find a market for sprats". A Minister replied "The Herring Board were buying surplus sprats delivered to their factories on the north shore of the Thames". [Hansard, vol. 509, col. 254, 18.12.52]. That presents the sprat industry's prospects in a very different light.

The QC intervened to contend that "BR's spokesman was also the BTC member on the TUCC, and was acting as advocate and judge". The chairman replied that "it was an Act of Parliament which provided for a BTC representative". One voice among 15-20 was not going to make any difference. TUCC's with whom I had contact, did not oppose BR representatives. Why did they think BR representatives were appointed to TUCC's, if not to put the railway view? Perhaps they were expected to be quiet whilst they were criticised, even vilified, by objectors who knew nothing about running a railway. No criticism was levelled at TUCC members from local authorities, who may be objecting to closures. (See page 181). The TUCC recommended that in future, BR should send, in addition to its statutory member on the TUCC, another manager to put the case. Little wonder, costs went up.

Another objector clutched for another straw. He contended that BR was proposing to write off the capital involved in five miles of line. BR replied that capital written off was not material to the issue. If the line was uneconomic, the value of the asset is nil. (Some assets were re-deployed. Some years later, UK industrialists closed down factories and "wrote off capital").

After the deputations withdrew, the TUCC discussed the matter. There was broad agreement on the main issues, BTC dissenting, and the chairman undertook to prepare a draft report for consideration before submission to the CTCC. The TUCC would meet again on 28th July. The TUCC said that this decision presented us with a problem. On the one hand there was the fact that for many years this branch railway had been losing

£8,000 pa, and on the other hand the small coastal town of Brightlingsea, with important **fishing** interests, and certain **industrial** pursuits, situated at the end of this spur line had suddenly lost **valuable** transport facilities. Since January 1953, the railways had had to spend £9,000 to restore the track so as to enable the sea wall to be repaired and for a further expenditure of £4,500 the branch could be completely restored in the course of only a very few weeks. We found that the only road communication was by one indifferent road passing through valuable agricultural country on which there were several villages, and were satisfied that passengers would be better catered for by a bus service which would serve not only Brightlingsea but the villages en route between there and Colchester if this road was suitably improved. We also appreciated that the railways ran through marsh and saltings with no stations en route, that Brightlingsea traffic had to be transhipped at Wivenhoe and very often again at Colchester which was a slow and expensive operation.

Whilst appreciating that for many years, the line had operated at substantial loss, they nevertheless recommended it should be repaired and then kept open for three years, and thereafter the Commission should be free to raise the question of the future of the line.

The chairman said the public should be informed when examination produced a doubtful result neither for nor against. When BR gave early warning of the closure of the M&GN, which inevitably, did not include full financial appraisals - they were roundly criticised for the lack of detail! (See page 123).

The TUCC Draft Report to the CTCC was considered by the TUCC on 28th July and approved. The press were admitted. The TUCC announced it would recommend that the line should re-open as soon as possible for a period of three years from the date of re-opening. On expiry of that period, the Railway Executive would be free to raise the question of the branch's future. Asked by the press if the decision was unanimous - the chairman declined to answer.

The Final Report to the CTCC made the following points :-

*Objectors' case :*

- The convenience of the public should be an over-riding consideration.
- A service adequate to their needs should be retained unless the costs were *exorbitant*. (A word they failed to define).
- The service could be modified to encourage additional user by 200 workers daily and be more economically operated. (They were wrong - see pages 35-36 & 86).
- The council had incurred substantial expenditure to encourage development and improve amenities upon the *expectation* that a rail service would be continued. (As they had not consulted BR to see if there was capacity, it was most unprofessional).
- Railhead services would be less satisfactory. (Experience proved they were faster and due to reduced handling, less damage was caused).
- BR had made no special effort to secure additional traffic. (They produced *no* evidence. One can equally *assume* that *lack of effort* closes shops in town centres).
- The community had no warning to permit an opportunity to intensify user of the service. (By 1963, user had not intensified enough, and losses had increased).

- Arguments on strategic implications were a matter for the Admiralty which was represented at the hearing, but made no comment.
- National interests would be affected if the absence of a railway service resulted in the extinction of the local seafaring population. (It had existed before the railway came).
- Travel arrangements would be less adequately met by the alternative bus service.

*Railway's case* :
- The line was uneconomic before it was closed by sea damage.
- The gain for transferred workers would be only £1,800 for 100 workers, and even if double that figure would only halve the loss, *if* the amended service was not more costly. The BTC would not gain, because any workers would transfer from BTC bus services to BTC rail services.
- BR's road motor services were coping with shellfish and light industry traffic.
- Alternative services proposed are adequate to meet existing and potential demand.
- BR should not be called on to incur further expenditure and continued losses.

The TUCC is firmly convinced that the branch has been unremunerative for a number of years, and is likely to continue to be unremunerative, although possibly to a less extent if it is re-opened with a modified service, and may, indeed, never be self supporting under foreseeable continued competition with modern road transport. It can be argued that the railways have ceased to be a "commercial undertaking", having become a "public service" to which other than commercial criteria can properly apply. By analogy, would there be justification in withdrawing postal services from a village if it was unremunerative. (This was not an analogy. The Post Office had a complete 100% statutory monopoly on mail. The TUCC had acknowledged that BR did not - because it was competing with road transport. Moreover, the Acts quite specifically directed that the BTC must pay its way).

They were "not convinced" of the validity of the BR argument on the relevance of the additional capital expenditure which would be required, "in view of the considerable amount already expended". They referred to the £9,000 spent to put the track in minimum condition to enable BR to repair the sea wall and recover the rolling stock which had become marooned. They noted that a further £4,500 needed to be spent to restore the line to MoT safety requirements appropriate for passenger services.

They were convinced, *beyond doubt*, that the branch was operated at a loss. The shell fishing industry should be sustained. (It was in the doldrums and was to be sustained by BR losses, for which they were later roundly criticised by MP's and others). Brightlingsea has long term plans for development and growth, and wishes to attract holiday visitors. (Unfortunately, ten years later, it hadn't grown. Its population was virtually static, a shipyard had closed and the fishing industry had again declined. Summer holiday traffic could not cross subsidise poor usage during ten months of the year).

They said that there was little likelihood of funds becoming available to improve roads. (The figures quoted by the local authority were not questioned. They may have over estimated the cost). The TUCC have been assured that, if the line is restored, there will be a spirited effort by objectors to popularise the line. Objectors suggested that the modified service put forward by a former railway worker was submitted for consideration by the

TUCC, who are laymen in the technicalities of railway operation. They said that, prima facie, the proposal would reduce costs. The proposal impressed the TUCC. Well, it would since they admitted knowing nothing about railways. "Prima facie" means "at first sight" - i.e. superficially. It was an amazing assumption by "laymen" that someone who used to work in an unspecified capacity on railways was automatically accepted to be the fountain of all railway knowledge, surpassing that of those employed on train planning. They did not dwell on there being "little likelihood of funds becoming available to BR".

The TUCC noted the explanation of fishing industry spokesmen that the sprat industry had declined in recent years because shoals had moved elsewhere which was a recognised phenomena and to foreign currency problems. (In fact, my inquiries of the Ministry has established that it was due to over fishing, and it did not recover for many years). BR told the TUCC they had been awaiting a revival of that industry and it had not done so. The TUCC criticised BR for not making inquiries of the Ministry as to the objector's assertion that the shoals would return in abundance. BR was also criticised for not making inquiries as to the possibility of foreign exchange controls being relaxed to facilitate export of sprats should they become available! (This is truly incredible. The fishing industry itself had clearly not been sufficiently confident or they would never have been off the phone with Government on these two issues. One can well imagine the reaction if BR told the MoT that they were planning to employ extra staff throughout the country to constantly monitor these complex trends. There can be no doubt that no one, but no one, would be given advance notice by Government of plans to alter currency regulations - for reasons which ought to be perfectly obvious to anyone. They should have realised that relaxing currency regulations would give a boost to holidays abroad at the expense of resorts such as Brightlingsea).

The TUCC said that BR normally gave twelve months notice of intention to close. (BTC Annual Reports show that it then took 2-3 years to effect closure. Little wonder, BR was losing money). The TUCC said that "prophesies" in relation to the sprat trade could be expected to justify themselves. They, therefore, recommended :-

> *The Brightlingsea-Wivenhoe branch line should be re-opened as soon as possible for a period of at least three years from the date of such re-opening. On the expiry of that period the Railway Executive will, of course, be free to raise the question of the branch's future, de novo.*

BR pointed out that the small amount of increased road user would not tax local roads, which had been coping with the traffic by road, since the line had been cut by the sea several months earlier.

The TUCC Report recommending re-instatement was considered by the CTCC on 13th October and supported, with the proviso that roads should be improved as a matter of urgency to enable this unremunerative branch line to be closed before the termination of the three year period. The BTC had to accept the CTCC finding and the branch was restored from 7th December 1953

The question as we saw it was - should the town of Brightlingsea, which had suddenly lost its railway communications through no fault of its own, be required to continue to rely on indifferent road communications for an indefinite period or should we recommend the additional expenditure of £4,500 for repairing the line which we were satisfied *could only be operated at a substantial loss*. We felt that logically, taking the long view, there was no justification for additional expenditure on the railway, but that in all the circumstances, and not least the time factor, it would be reasonable for rail facilities to be restored as soon as possible and kept open for a period of three years, and that in the meantime the road between Brightlingsea and the trunk road system should be brought up to date so that efficient passenger and freight road services could be established as these would serve Brightlingsea far better than the railway. We therefore supported the recommendation of the East Anglia Committee. [CTCC 1953 Report, Paras. 32-35].

They said it was not the fault of the locals, but had they used the branch as much as they had pre-war, BR would have restored the line in days. It was certainly not BR's fault - the sea had breached sea walls all the way down the east coast. No one suggested that the damage caused by the exceptionally high tides was the fault of the many local authorities responsible for other sea walls. If J. Bloggs & Co., employing hundreds of people had been washed out by the flood, and decided it was not economic to re-open, it would have been tough luck. It is amazing that the local authority had not improved roads to serve isolated villages in the area, which had never had a rail service.

"A reprieve was granted for three years. In that time, with no marked success, efforts were made to encourage more passenger and freight traffic on the line. The reprieve was expected to terminate next month and prospects have not been considered favourable for retention of the line, as residents understood the situation". [Essex County Standard, 2.11.56].

A final attempt to make the Brightlingsea branch a paying proposition is to be made by introducing diesel trains in the near future. Traffic has not developed on the line as hoped. The service will have to be justified economically and traffic on the line must be increased. [Essex County Standard, 11.1.57].

On 4th March 1957, the branch line services were dieselised. [TUCC min 236]. It would have been madness to provide DMU's earlier, when busier lines still lacked them.

### 1963 Hearing
In 1963, the Brightlingsea -Wivenhoe line was again being considered for closure

The TUCC considered a proposal to withdraw passenger services from the branch from 4th November 1963. 27 objections were received by 22nd July, and a public hearing was convened on 17th September. The Brightlingsea Rail Closure Appeal Committee sponsored by the UDC was formed and represented by counsel. The hearing was attended by 35 persons. The chairman explained they would report to the MoT on hardship, and suggestions for alleviation. Sixteen people spoke in support of written representations. BR and bus company representatives replied.

BR stated that the line was earning £8,000 pa, had expenses of £18,000 pa, and faced renewals over the next five years of £10,000. Total BR savings from closure were therefore £12,000 pa, of which a maximum of £5,000 pa would be paid to the nationalised bus company for additional services. At the 1953 hearing, the objectors' QC had said that local interests should have an opportunity to see what could be done. A ten year reprieve - six with diesels, and a service of 30.6% more train miles, proved "*what had been done by local interests*": losses ***increased***, whilst precious capital was wasted on providing diesels.

37 workmen* travelled to Wivenhoe, an unquantified number of children to school, four season holders to Chelmsford, 23 to London and there were some visitors in the summer. Fifteen trains carried 3-400 passengers. The bus service was 20 journeys in each direction, passing close to Alresford station which had 36 trains each day. The oyster and sprat traffic, such as it now was, was carried by road. No volume was mentioned.

*\* In 1953, objectors claimed that 200 workmen would use the line if services were improved and fares were no higher than by bus. It was now dieselised - and bus fares were higher.*

*Objections*
- £18,000 would be spent on extending the Town Hall. (Did they envisage this being a tourist attraction? If not, what relevance did it have to closure?)
- "A development scheme has been prepared for the construction of a yacht centre in a disused shipyard". Aside from the improbability of the wealthy yachting fraternity making any noticeable use of rail instead of their cars, the plan went on to make it more improbable by adding that the plan included "petrol filling stations and a motel, carparks and a caravan site". "It would include 30,000 square feet of industrial buildings". There was no assertion that these would be taken up, much less that they would produce so much as a single ton of traffic, nor one passenger.
- Closure of the line would mean less visitors. (There was not a word about market research. The uneconomic line had been given an unwarranted new lease of life ten years earlier, and here they were still talking about jam tomorrow, and they had not even commissioned market research to back up their claims).
- Population would increase from 4,200 to 6,000 by 1981, which would be debatable if the line closed. If this increase did not take place, existing ratepayers would have to meet the cost of improvements in the town. (As they were the beneficiaries, they, not BR, ought to fund these costs. How much of the council budget for Essex or the town went on rail travel? As they tabled no evidence of having done anything to transfer any traffic at all to the line since 1953, it can only be concluded to be zero).
- Ratepayers would have to pay more to save the taxpayer a small sum. (The taxpayer was not covering losses. They were increasing BR's debt to the Treasury, which they wanted repaying. With hundreds of similar pleas, the small amount becomes large).
- Children on trains are not at risk from accidents which may occur on roads. (That can only be apply if they alight directly into school grounds, without passing along a road. As no such locations were mentioned, it can be safely assumed that there were none).
- The roads have not been improved since 1953. (BR could not be held responsible for that. How were they hoping to attract car owning yachting fraternity? They could not ***seriously*** expect that they would carry all their clothing and other gear on a train, and then hump it down to the marina? It was out of touch with reality).
- They feared the loss of day trippers. (This was seasonal traffic, which if they were happy with rail travel, would go to another resort by rail. The line's problem was that

it was too seasonal - all year traffic was needed, and 37 workers who could not get a lift in a friend's car were not going to tip the balance).

- Some 14 acres of land are *scheduled* for industrial development. (More jam tomorrow - which other towns did they hope to denude of their industry, and what would tempt them to move to the end of a branch line?).
- If the road is blocked, the railway line is the only link. (No statistics were provided to indicate the frequency of road blockages. The line was seen as a standby).
- The line should be kept in case there is another war. (36 years on, it would still be losing money waiting for the next invasion).
- The council has co-operated with BR in suggesting alterations to services and fares. (But not a mention of one parcel, nor one passenger at council expense. How many attending meetings in Colchester or elsewhere travelled by train? The absence of data suggests there were none. The requirement to co-operate was not limited to trying to show how to run the line, for whose ensuing increased costs or decreased revenue, they excluded themselves. No other industry would have accepted such an attitude).
- Other suggestions were in hand to develop local activities. (Why had these rail travel generating ideas not come to fruition before now, after a ten year reprieve?).
- 37 workmen in Wivenhoe shipyard would pay 66% more to travel by bus. (If more could not be attracted to diesels - so often claimed to be the solution - at fares at this level, what would? It is the proof positive of the fallacy of unqualified claims that new trains and lower fares were the solution. Had fares been allowed to keep pace with inflation, many lines could have been kept open. Local authorities, including Essex County Council had opposed that. Users wanted to "have their cake and eat it").
- Porters at Alresford would be unable to handle the extra passengers. (This council had called ten years earlier for a reduction in costs and an increase in passengers).

"An observer reported poor loadings on five trains - in October 1963, varying between four and 30. So it can be seen that the appeal for people to use the line was just not working. The case for the closure was a good one". [Brown, Page 120].

The TUCC sent a Report to the MoT on 8th November, summarising BR's case and the basis of objections. It mentioned that the line was reprieved in 1953 for a period of three years, with a stipulation that improvements should be carried out to the road leading out of the town. It stated that it is alleged that little improvement had been effected. The line closed in 1964.

"It is still said locally that the line should have been kept, I would like to agree, but can't". [Brown, Page 123].

# Chapter 7                    The "Bluebell line"

The line was promoted by local residents, led by the Earl of Sheffield, who became the first Chairman. They examined proposals for a ruling gradient of 1 in 100 and 1 in 70 and opted for the latter. (A company with good prospects would have opted for less demanding gradients). They approached the LB&SCR in 1876, who said that it would not oppose a line from Lewes to East Grinstead, but would oppose extension beyond East Grinstead. The minutes of the company reveal "If the line when constructed did not earn enough to pay the income on the capital, the LB&SCR would make up the deficiency". The company was incorporated in 1877, and empowered to raise £533,000. These powers were abrogated by the 1878 Act whereby the LB&SCR found the money necessary to build the line. The minutes contain details of land compensation costs, including one from the Earl for £5,662. Under the LB&SCR Act 1878, the undertaking was amalgamated with that company which agreed to provide the requisite capital and operate the line. The minutes record that the LB&SCR was asked for £50,000 in July 1878. A short extension from Horsted Keynes to Haywards Heath was authorised by another LB&SCR Act of 1880. The line opened in 1882. [PRO : Rail 364/2]. The stations were built on a lavish scale, costing an average of £17,000. Gradients ranged from 1 in 50 to 1 in 75. Most of the route was single track. Formerly, there was substantial milk traffic from a private siding and stations, but it has been transported by road for many years. [R.C.Riley, Railway Magazine, October 1954].

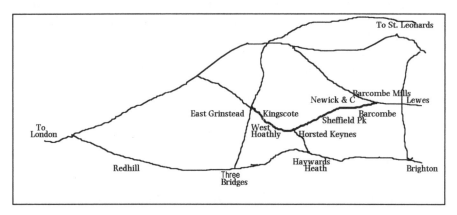

## The First Closure

BR concluded in 1953 that the line was uneconomic, and informed the TUCC, which sent details of the closure proposal to 22 councils and individuals. Six stations would close: Kingscote, West Hoathly, Horsted Keynes, Sheffield Park, Newick & Chailey and Barcombe. There were seven passenger trains each way, with an extra one on Wednesdays and Saturdays. Freight consisted of one trip daily. Minimum gross savings were put at £68,000. Loss of receipts at £8,000 and extra cartage costs of £1,000, would leave a net saving of £59,000. Total wagons dealt with on the line were: forwarded 148 pa, received 1,754 pa. The main traffic was timber, coal, sugar beet, and ashes for a tennis court.

A public meeting of objectors on 16th June 1954 appointed Mr. Peck as spokesman. Eighteen objectors attended a meeting of the TUCC on 30th November, representing six local authorities, a chamber of commerce, a ratepayers association, two coal merchants, a coal merchants federation and eight individuals. Objectors doubted the level of economy could be achieved and claimed that greater efficiency would increase revenue. (They offered no proof, nor did they back their claim with money). They prayed in aid, that horny old favourite, its value in time of war. The TUCC had received a petition of 1,400 names from Barcombe (which had about 100 daily passengers). They were told by BR that the line used to pay until buses came and passengers transferred to them. BR's representative said that diesels were only justified with volume which did not exist on this line, and he "had seen two trains on that day each with one passenger. If people want the line they must be prepared to support it". (No one guaranteed to do so. They could have signed up for non-refundable annual season tickets). He said that BR ran an excursion to Brighton, it took £20 in receipts, having been advertised in the media and on Notices.

*Objectors' views:-*

- "It was needed in the event of war. It was used by a hospital train in 1940 from Newhaven". (Activity was so light, a siding was unused in the war - see below).
- A timber merchant said he was not allowed to use a private siding *alongside* his premises, as it had been allowed to fall into disrepair during the war. He said "it should be brought up to standard by the various parties". (The need for the line in war was emphasised, and this siding was not used during the war. Clearly it was not *his* private siding as it was alongside - not into his premises. He hadn't grasped that, like a private road, maintenance of a private siding was funded by the industry or trader which owned it). His *inward* traffic amounted to 1950/1: £320, 1951/2: £550, 1952/3: £750. "There had been outward traffic from time to time, but this is not sufficiently impressive to be worth quoting. Outward traffic goes by road". He made the excuse that there were problems if sent by rail to London Docks for export, but did not mention problems with inland traffic. He had a 65 year old employee who came by rail to work and that a lack of rail service would hamper recruitment prospects.
  **BR stated that he took all outward traffic on his own vehicles.**
  (It would be astounding if his entire inward traffic was represented by £750 pa of rail carriage. My dealings with timber merchants revealed a lack of foresight and a failure to modernise - see "*Blueprints for Bankruptcy*", Page 167. Was there no local labour to replace his employee? He should have sent more by rail if he wanted to keep the service. Others sent huge volumes by rail to London Docks).
- When people move to the area, they ask about train services. (Doubtless, to see if there is a standby when it snows, or the car breaks down).
- The Ratepayers Association said that if a line closes, BR ceases to be a ratepayer (a saving never mentioned by BR, who were usually accused of over estimating savings).
- A former Land Agent had sent sugar beet by rail, having now returned *may* wish to do the same again. (His comment emphasised that agricultural traffic had ceased, and he likewise missed a golden opportunity to *guarantee* traffic by rail).

- BR's proposal would increase road traffic. (It was the local residents who had done that on the grand scale, and destroyed railway viability).
- The line should be electrified and a frequent service operated. (There was no offer to share the costs and profits - or losses, nor even to guarantee additional user).
- BR was asked how savings could arise if men were moved elsewhere. BR's representative explained that they would fill vacancies elsewhere (which would be costing 50% above base rate due to rest day and overtime working).
- The line was important to agriculture. (Traffic figures disprove that, and they had been among the first to desert railways).
- Criticised having a Station Master for a group of stations as a survival of a bygone age. (Clearly he had *no* idea of the need for a trained man to deal with emergencies).
- The Civil Defence for the area saw problems in securing volunteers if the line closed.
- BR hadn't tried to make it pay, they could run more trains. (As usual, not a *scrap* of evidence was advanced and there was no offer to back these claims with money).
- There were many allegations that the proposed alternative bus services would be inadequate.

*By 18th October 1955, no complaints had been made to the TUCC - see page 99.*

*Miss Bessemer* :-

"Viewed with concern BR's refusal to provide more *information*". (The private sector provide *no* information when closing factories and shops which deprive communities of facilities and jobs, leading to eyesores, and they do not justify any managerial decision).

*Colonel D.H. Bessemer* :-

Quoted sections of the 1947 Act which required the BTC to provide services, (but .did not quote sections which required it to pay its way, and empowered it to dispose of any part not required - see page 11) He claimed that all revenue for a throughout journey should be credited to the line. He said that locos were too powerful for the line. (*The uneconomic alternative was for BR to build a couple of small locos, plus a spare loco to keep on this line, instead of drawing from a fleet covering a wider area*). He quoted 1953 profits, but ignored the accumulated deficit of £27.3m, "because it was irrelevant, partly illusory and may even be non existent". (BR's external auditors clearly did not agree. Neither did the Treasury, which wanted its £27m loan refunding, and interest paid on it).

*BR replied to Colonel Bessemer that if the trains could be operated without cost, the revenue would still not cover other costs.*

The transcript makes no reference to the Bessemers being users of the line. (See page 99).


After the objectors withdrew from the meeting, a vote was put to the meeting to approve the proposed closure and carried by a majority of 8-5.

The CTCC had received the Area (TUCC) Report submitted to them in February 1955. [PRO: MT115/9]. The TUCC's recommendation to close the Lewes-East Grinstead was supported by the CTCC. [CTCC Minute 113, 8.2.55].

Closure would save £59,000 at 1953 prices. The CTCC conclude it is unreasonable to place on other users of Nationalised Transport, the burden of subsidising this line. The present light use of this line is due to more suitable road facilities. [MoT Memo, 22.6.56, PRO: MT115/9]

The line closed on 13th June 1955. "No complaints had been received as to the inadequacy of the alternative (bus) services". [TUCC meeting 18.10.55, minute 116g].

## The Line Reopens

Miss Bessemer pointed out that the LB&SCR Act 1878, Sec. 35, effectively stipulated that four trains per day must run each way, stopping at four named stations. "The BTC's Chief Solicitor has taken counsel's opinion. He advised that to avoid a possible infringement of old enactments, a minimum service ·of four trains per day should be restored. This will be done from 7th August". [PRO: AN103/3]. To end the obligation, required that part of that Act be repealed. This was sought through the next British Transport Commission Bill, sponsored by the MoT, and debated in Parliament in 1957.

A DoT Memo - Munro to Willis - of 21st June 1956 stated: The BTC have undertaken, on legal advice, to reopen the line. The decision is lamentable. That they should use scarce staff and coal - no matter how few or how little - to provide a service that has been proved redundant, indicates the attitude of mind to the whole question of redundant facilities which we are trying to combat. However, the BTC must decide. [PRO: MT115/9]

The line re-opened 7th August 1956. The re-introduced service of four trains cost £18,000 pa plus civil engineering & signalling costs of £14,000. Receipts were £1,000 pa. Only one person petitioned against closure - local authorities didn't do so. [PRO: MT115/9]

In a four page Petition to Parliament for the Session 1956-7 seeking to prevent repeal of the LB&SCR Act 1878 Sec. 35 until a Public Inquiry was held, Miss Bessemer said she was injuriously affected. She criticised BR for having fulfilled its obligation to the letter, instead of re-instating the former service. She did not say that she was a user, much less a regular user, nor guarantee to be a user in future. (Shakespeare's female attorney had called for the *precise* execution of a contract, neither more nor less). She "normally travelled by private car". [R. Jones, *"Heritage Railway"*, January 2000, CMS Publishing].

Due to Tory backbench opposition, the BTC had to make a costly and wasteful concession, agreeing not to close the line if their Bill was passed until the case had been resubmitted to the TUCC. The MoT announced that he had requested the TUCC to hold an Inquiry locally, and to admit the public, so that they can be convinced of the BTC's case. It seems unfortunate that the BTC should be put to the trouble and expense of re-submitting its case and the time of members of the TUCC so unnecessarily occupied when they are unpaid and acting from a sense of duty. In presenting its Modernisation Plan, the BTC made it clear that it assumed it would be free to eliminate services for which there was no longer public need. [Railway Gazette 22.3.57, Page 327]. Representatives of the public *had been admitted* to the 1954 Hearing. Did he envisage admitting several thousands?

On 25th April 1957, the MoT wrote to the TUCC suggesting that they convene a meeting to consider closure, adding that the local MP had suggested it should be held in Lewes not East Grinstead. The MoT said that the requirement to give three months notice of an Inquiry could be shortened to two months. The TUCC Chairman replied that he agreed to do so, adding that members are "very resentful of the allegations". The TUCC went ahead and arranged a suitable venue. However, within a week, the MoT wrote again that a Committee of the House had urged an independent Public Inquiry. He had decided to ask the CTCC to conduct a local Public Inquiry, adding that he entertained no doubts about the competence of your Committee or its ability to reconsider the case thoroughly or fairly. There is no need for you to proceed with your arrangements for the Inquiry.

On the same day, the MoT wrote to the CTCC Chairman, noting that the Chairman had serious misgivings on hearing the case. The MoT had been advised by Treasury Solicitors that he has no powers to hold a public ministerial inquiry under Sec.122 of the 1947 Act and suggested that a sub committee of four or five people drawn from the CTCC would be adequate. The Chairman replied on 16th May : If the CTCC do hold another inquiry it is tantamount to endorsing Parliament's censure vote. [PRO: MT115/9]

On 9th May 1957, Alison Munro of the Department of Transport, wrote: "On the Isle of Wight 'Precedent', the Minister, Lennox Boyd, did convene a meeting, but flatly refused to reopen any question considered by the TUCC. The CTCC examined the TUCC recommendations and refused a further public inquiry, and went further by deciding to approve the Brading-Bembridge closure. The MoT was involved only on the issue of roads expenditure. The Parliamentary Committee on the BTC Bill 9th May 1957 admitted that they had no power to lay down procedures to the MoT". [PRO: MT115/9].

TUCC minutes of 20th May 1957 refer to Hansard on 13th March when Sir Charles Taylor stated : "Some Hon Members feel that local people, local authorities and users were not given a fair hearing when the case was submitted to the TUCC". The Chairman referred to the criticism in Parliament that it had not given a fair hearing and asked "can we with any self respect continue to function?" He then went on to recap the history:

> "A memo of 59 pages had been circulated setting out in full BTC's proposals and objections thereto. The TUCC made an inspection of the line before the Inquiry. 22 invitations to the Inquiry were sent out, but only 18 attended including Mr. D. Peck QC who represented the deputation appointed at a public meeting on 16th June 1954. Two petitions - of 77 and 67 were considered. During the meeting a further petition of 1,400 from Barcombe was handed over. We had a long Inquiry, hearing from the QC and eleven others, and when no one else desired to address us, the Inquiry closed. During the Inquiry, the QC passed several complimentary remarks concerning our handling of the case. We discussed the matter at great length and as a result approved the closure. We wrote to the QC, who replied : 'The deputation and other objectors to whom I have spoken, have all said how impressed they were by the friendliness of our reception by the Committee, and the courtesy with which we were heard'" . The Chairman noted that "the MoT had repudiated the suggestion that the BTC case was phoney, but no defence was put up on behalf of the TUCC. He moved to suspend activities of this Committee until they have considered the findings of the new Inquiry".

The TUCC, having been congratulated by the objectors' QC on their conduct of the Inquiry, voted to suspend activities, because of the unjust vote of censure. The TUCC regarded the MoT decision on a public inquiry as a reprimand. They had considered the matter on 30th November 1954 and travelled over the line. They had circulated with the agenda, 59 typed foolscap sheets setting out the BTC proposals and the written objections thereto. [PRO: MT115/9].

A Memo from Munro to the Parliamentary Secretary stated: Lord Coleraine, CTCC Chairman, has asked the MoT not to let the procedure for another public inquiry become a precedent. This request is reasonable. Consultative Committees are not in a position to undertake Public Inquiries - such a practice would change the entire character of Consultative Machinery which has - hitherto - worked well. [PRO: MT115/9]

Munro wrote on 21st May 1957: The TUCC are angry at what they regard as a vote of censure. They have resolved not to sit again until something is done to vindicate them. On 25th May, Stedman (DoT) wrote : The Select Committee and Parliament would not be satisfied with an inquiry by the Area TUCC. An Inquiry by the CTCC is the only course. Memo from Munro to Goodison 27th May: This Committee has taken umbrage at the way they have been treated by the House of Commons. At their meeting on 20th May, they unanimously resolved that their activities would be suspended. [PRO: MT115/9]

In discussing the 1957 Bill, Mr. W. Vane Tory MP, Westmoreland: "It is greatly to the credit of the Railways that they had operated as well as they did". [Hansard vol. 566 col. 1216]. In the debate on the 1957 BTC Bill, "The Minister surrendered to pressure from a few backbenchers, rather than stand by the decision of TUCC's he appoints and the BTC for which he is responsible. If such opposition is allowed, the chances of the BTC paying its way was made that much more difficult, if not impossible". [Railway Gazette, 22.3.57. Page 326]. The Government's majority was nearly 60.

The British Transport Commission Act 1957, Sec. 73, passed 31st July, repealed Sec. 35 of the 1878 Act. Closure was deferred pending the outcome of a further inquiry.

### Formal Public Inquiry : 9-11 October 1957
The MoT asked the CTCC to hold a Public Inquiry on 13th May. On 2nd July, he told Parliament: "I have asked the CTCC to take the exceptional course of conducting a Public Inquiry into this proposal when it is submitted again", adding, (to placate the TUCC): "but have the fullest confidence in the ability and integrity of Area TUCC's who normally review proposals for closures and in particular the South East Committee which has already been concerned with this scheme". [Hansard, vol. 572, col. 133].

*BR's case, was presented by a QC, as this was a formal Public Inquiry:*
- The service from 1948 to 1955 had been at the same level as pre-war.
- There were staff shortages in the South East. (Closure would facilitate re-deployment and reduce the number of vacancies. Inflationary industrial wages in the south had precipitated the shortages on BR, where wages were constrained by below RPI fares).
- Closure would relieve fare paying passengers and freight customers on the railway generally.
- With one exception, the stations are some distance from the villages whose names they bear. Consequently, passengers have to use a conveyance to get to the stations.
- The BTC was a shareholder in Southdown Motor Services, and hence, any transfer of passengers to buses would not be a total revenue loss to the BTC.

- Costs have gone up more than fares in the period since 1953, so the loss is greater.
- Regardless of the closure, freight - except bulk traffic - would be transferred to the Zonal system. (Collection and delivery over a wide area by railhead motor transport).
- All local passenger traffic would be lost, but BR expected to retain 75% of non-local traffic. (Even if all revenue was lost, there would still be a substantial economy).
- One could not, as suggested, take as the number of locos required, those required to run the trains - additional provision had to be made to cover down-time in main works and on depots. (This should not surprise anyone with industrial experience).
- Before the closure announcement, there were no complaints about the adequacy of the service and "no amateurs had come forward to say that they could do a better job".
- Despite the accumulated deficit, BR had not had a penny from the taxpayer to date. Government advanced interest bearing loans to cover the deficit. (The deficit was caused by Government's inequitable policies - see "*Blueprints for Bankruptcy*").
- No credit was taken for consequential economy in coaches, nor for any sale of land.
- If every individual loco, coach or other asset was assessed for its actual life, instead of taking the average for a particular type of asset, BR would have to incur extra costs to record them.
- It is impractical to cost each branch line in detail. Some averages have to be used.
- BR explained that one had to take average coal consumption per mile for a class of locos, because it was impractical to weigh and record every pound of coal used by each loco. (It is incredible that even the uninformed argued otherwise).
- BR's witness told the objectors' counsel that a track maintenance cost which was in the submission did not include renewals.

*Mr S.W. Hill appeared as a witness for the objectors* (see also Appendix A.1) :-
- He took average figures from BR Annual Accounts to try to prove the line was not as costly to operate as BR stated. (However, this was undermined when it was revealed later in the Inquiry that average Southern Region costs were higher than average BR costs - which is not surprising, because severe staff shortages in the south east had to be covered by overtime which increased average earnings in that Region).
- He stated that the number of track staff employed per mile was above the national average, given that some of the line was single track. (Later evidence pointed out that the work on fencing, drainage and many other tasks does not vary between double and single track - there being fences on both sides, and the same amount of drainage etc. Variation in the stability of the sub structure affected costs).
- He questioned why trains ran beyond the end of the branch.
    *BR explained that this facilitated maintenance of locos and coaches.*
- He said that it would be "probably be cheaper to provide somewhere" to keep them. (It was a common theory - that there was a cheaper alternative by having a local depot. It overlooks the cost of localised maintenance and staff costs. See pages 35-36).
- Asked by a CTCC member if he was going to quantify the savings which would be achieved by applying his methods, he admitted he could not do so. (In effect, BR was guilty until it proved itself innocent).

- He said that the fares and freight rates which the BTC charged were geared to its outgoings. (BTC submissions to the Transport Tribunal, before which he appeared as an objector's witness on several occasions, were geared to outgoings, but the Tribunal reduced them on virtually every occasion and delayed increases by an aggregate $12^3/_4$ years. The end product was that charges were inadequate to cover outgoings. See Appendix A.1 & "*Blueprints for Bankruptcy*")
- Asked about maintenance of fencing - he assumed it was properly maintained. (It would cost labour time, materials and money).
- He said that if a person starts his journey on a bus, he will finish it on a bus.
  *BR had pointed out - and it was not refuted that the villages were so far away from the stations that almost all passengers had to use a 'conveyance' to get to the station, hence, the local practice proved him wrong.*
- Asked by the BTC's counsel if he had ever managed a railway - he said No, he did not have time to run things as well ! He admitted that he had not been responsible for railway engineering policy.
- He did not dispute that BR had brought in the contributory value of off-line traffic.
- He said that when he worked on Railway Rating (Municipal Rates), they used to bring in much smaller figures on assets - by extending their lives.
  That may have been what led to the Railways paying higher Rates than they should have - until they were reduced by about 50% by the Appeal Court. (See pages 201-2).
- Asked whether the line is likely to be profitable - he said "No, there is bound to be a loss on this line, as there is on half of the lines on BR".

The BTC's counsel said at the end : "Can we believe that the opposition you have had to listen to will ever be satisfied by the figures?" He pointed out that the objectors had made statements without any cross-examination by him. He said that it was unthinkable that a line of this length should have to keep invoices or receipts for every item of expenditure. He stated that you can afford a big experiment if you can expect big savings, but you cannot afford even a modest experiment on a line which has a traffic potential of £5,000 pa. (Who but a spendthrift would do so. Managers would be criticised if they went around getting experimental stock on lines, only to find they were ineffectual).

Nine members of the CTCC took part in the Inquiry. Ten members of the public appeared and eleven had written. (Little wonder the line lost money). The record of evidence ran to 83 pages. They agreed on 10th December, a 36 page Report [Cmd 360], including 28 pages of financial data from BR :-

Para. 7: Exonerated the TUCC from allegations of unfairness to objectors.
Para. 9: BR put savings in 1953 at £67,936 gross, net £59,736 plus avoidance of renewals. BR said losses had increased "no estimates were submitted". (Wages had risen faster than fares).
Para. 11: Objectors said that losses were greater than they need be and could be reduced (not eliminated) and "it was assumed that a line of this kind was never intended to pay for itself"! (No shareholder would have funded a line given that assumption).

Para. 16: BR estimated a DMU service would cost £45,000 capital plus £40,000 pa; with no diesels in the area, maintenance would be costly. The CTCC said that a diesel service could not have shown a return adequate to justify the service.

Para. 20: BR said the line could not be electrified except at very heavy expense, and there was no traffic potential. The CTCC accepted BR's view that it was better to improve the main line.

Para. 26: Dismisses the need for renewal costs, as 75 year old buildings were in good condition, and as there was no depreciation fund, it was unreasonable to allow for renewals. (Accounts provided for depreciation. Government policy prevented creation of reserves. Renewals cost money whatever paper transactions show. Perhaps objectors hoped infrastructure & trains would give timely warning of their final demise giving time to make a third closure proposal).

Para. 31: "The inconvenience and expense to individuals caused by closing the line is not in itself an overriding consideration, unless of exceptional proportions. We must recommend that in the public interest the service between East Grinstead and Lewes be withdrawn".

The MoT received the Report on 10th January 1958. The line closed for the second time in March 1958, after avoidable losses.


## Subsequent Debate

Major Tufton Beamish, MP, wrote to the MoT on 20th January 1957 about the "typically unanswered question as to savings which would be achieved by a frequent service of diesels". [PRO: MT115/9]. He failed to define "frequent". He did not say that he would accept the answer, if it demonstrated that it would not turn loss into profit, nor suggest who would make up the residual loss, if diesels would not eliminate losses. He could have asked Government to do so. Alternatively, losses could have been paid by councils or objectors who believed their local lines should keep open, despite the losses.

In June 1957, Major Beamish demanded a copy of the TUCC minutes, which he had "supposed would record detailed reasons why the BTC case was accepted and the objectors' case not accepted". The TUCC replied that the minutes did not record the reasons, merely the decision. This followed reading submissions, a visit to the area and a public inquiry. (He may have been confusing the TUCC's with a court of law). They also bluntly told him that they "resented the statement that you and other local people, local authorities and users were not given a fair hearing". "The system is one for which Parliament are responsible, and it was for this reason that my Committee resented the statement attributed to Sir Charles Taylor - in Hansard - that you and others thought that the local people had not been given a fair hearing". The correspondence ended.

TUCC minutes for 18th March noted the CTCC Report and, in particular, Para. 7: "The TUCC acted throughout with absolute fairness. The charges of unfairness bandied about would never have been made, if those making them had taken the trouble to inform themselves of the facts".


## The Preservation Society

A Preservation Society was formed to re-open the line. Miss Bessemer told the inaugural meeting that 500 people per day used the line, and more in summer. (*In fact, the daily average, for the whole line, throughout the year was 300*). It was hoped that BR would lease the line to them. They would purchase a GWR diesel railcar to run Horsted Keynes-Sheffield Park, 4.5 miles during summer as a beginning. Appeals were made for public donations from local councils and public bodies. [Times 16.3.59, 14e].

The Lewes-East Grinstead Railway Preservation Society said that £30,000 was required to buy the portion of line from Horsted Keynes to Sheffield Park. The cost of the whole line would be prohibitive. The Society had £89. They proposed to sell sleepers at £1 each, gradient posts at £5, chairs at 10/-, (50p). [Times, 15.6.59, 6g].

The Preservation Society have been offered the line for £34,000. BR are being very co-operative. [Newspaper clipping, 16.2.60 - PRO : Rail 1005/352].

Members of the Bluebell Railway were told they will have to pay £2,250 pa to keep the line open, the Horsted Keynes fare from Sheffield Park will be 2/6d, (12.5p). 10,000 members will be needed to keep it open. [Times, 20.2.60]. (With that number of passengers, the line would have been kept open by BR).

The Society secured for £11,250 a five year lease on a five mile length of line, with the option to buy for £34,000. It is better patronised than under BR (probably by enthusiasts, rather than commuters). The line pays its way on almost entirely voluntary labour. [Economist, 1.9.62, Page 755].

The BTC went to considerable trouble to facilitate the transfer of the line to the Preservation Group. The BTC proposed to the MoT that a Light Railway Order and Amending Order be applied for simultaneously as part of the transfer with a lease, but the MoT said "there were legal obstacles. The first must be published and approved - there may be objections. If amended, it would affect the second Order. The BTC would have to apply for the Order under Sec.18 of the 1896 Act, and then an Amending Order would be required to authorise the lease". At BTC's suggestion, the MoT agreed to reduce the period for objections to the application from three months to thirty days. On 20th June 1960, the MoT wrote that it had not yet received a formal application from the Bluebell Company, which will authorise lease or transfer of the railway from the BTC to the Company. The Company put the required notice in the London Gazette, but gave an incorrect date and had to re-advertise. They did so on 17th June. [PRO: MT124/83].

The line made a profit of £2,844 profit in its first year, from 1st April to 29th October : 91,000 journeys Sheffield Park to Horsted Keynes. [Times, 4.12.65, 6c]. Their fare at 30d (12.5p) for 4.5 miles return = 3.3d per mile. BR's average in 1965 was 2.2d per mile. They charged 50% more for a similar distance, and had free labour *and* membership fees.

## Postscript

"As a result of simplification at East Grinstead - facilitated by the closure - and utilising rolling stock and crews released by closing the line, improved regular interval services will be introduced on the remaining lines in the East Grinstead area, viz. regular hourly interval services outside the business period between Victoria and Tunbridge Wells West via East Grinstead with connecting services from Oxted to Tunbridge Wells West and from East Grinstead to Three Bridges". [BR. Officers Conference March 1955, PRO : AN103/1].

BR received a £35,943 credit for assets recovered from the East Grinstead-Horsted Keynes line. [PRO: AN103/28 - Southern Region Board Minutes, May 1964]. No complaint was received by the TUCC on the adequacy of bus services up to 1962.

# Chapter 8                    The Princetown Branch

The branch opened in 1883, and the station at Yelverton in 1885. The line begins with a mile long gradient of 1 in 40. Except for a short piece, the entire branch was steeper than 1 in 75, with stretches of 1 in 41/47. [J.B. Baron Collins, Railway Magazine, vol. 23].

The branch was worked by the GWR from its opening but did not become part of the GWR until 1922. The increasing cost of operation, isolation and road motor competition spelled out redundancy long before the Beeching axe. The GWR was clearly dissatisfied with the finances of the company. 1931 saw the peak of passenger traffic, but the following year, buses to Dousland were introduced and rail traffic suffered as a result. An increase of traffic came in 1939. [Kingdom, Pages 6, 75 & 88].

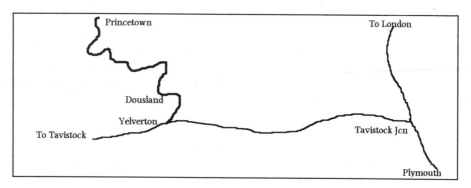

From 1903 to 1920 inclusive, the Railway did not pay a dividend, and frequently failed to pay interest on bank loans. It managed only to cover the 4.5% due on Debentures. Its General Reserve was "Nil". By 1920, unpaid interest due on Lloyds Bonds was £20,186, other debts totalled £8,250. Annual gross receipts were around £3,200, net £900. Annual interest on £19,900 Debentures took £895. To pay interest and general charges, the Company required £1,562 net pa, before sums could be set aside to pay dividends. From 1898 to 1920 it was incurring annual debts of around £600. In 1914, the GWR, which had been operating the line on behalf of the Company, offered to take them over. They would pay £7 cash for each £100 of Princetown stock. Princetown £100 4.5% Debentures would be exchanged for 4% GWR Debentures. The Princetown Company wrote to its shareholders: "Owing to the unsatisfactory state and financial position of this company, and no prospect of improvement, it is desirable to arrange absorption by the GWR". This was approved by a General Meeting of the Company in April 1914, most shareholders accepted. In 1921, the GWR had second thoughts. "Although it might be questioned whether the terms offered in 1914 would now be justified, having regard to the provisions in the 1921 Act, it would be difficult to depart from those terms inasmuch as the majority have settled on that basis. The total outstanding cost is £500". The final purchase of Princetown shares was approved by the GWR Board in March 1922. [PRO: Rail 253/758].

The Princetown Company reported a deficiency of £20,435 on the half year to June 1913. After deducting the GWR proportion of 70% of receipts for working the line, the balance fell short of the amount required to pay interest on loans and other outgoings. A year later, their revenue debt had risen to £21,032. [PRO: Rail 1110/386]

The writing was on the wall as early as 1954. Staff were informed of impending closure in 1955. All through 1955 and the early part of 1956 traffic was augmented by people making the journey as an act of sentimentality. [Kingdom, Page 91].

## TUCC Hearing

In 1955, BR proposed closure as it was costing £7 to earn £1. Savings were established at £11,000. If the line is not closed, £6,500 would have to be spent over and above the savings mentioned. BR said bus services would be over a shorter distance than rail. BR records passed to the South Western TUCC set out the losses and showed that:-

• The 7.35 am Princetown-Yelverton carried an average of 32 passengers in May 1954, 21 in June 1955, 19 in July 1955 and 15 in August 1955. These included 4-6 BTC staff.

• Traffic conveyed from Yelverton in severe weather on five days in early 1955 included bread, milk, meat, vegetables and bales of hay - traffic which did not pass by rail before the onset of severe weather and ceased immediately roads were clear. The bad weather was on 4-5th January and 23-25th February.

• The branch was a circuitous route rising to 1,300 ft above sea level to Princetown.

Bus records supplied to the TUCC were as follows:-
The Tavistock-Princetown-Yelverton service did not run due to ice and snow:-

    1952/3 : Saturday 14th February : two journeys out of six;

    1953/4 : Saturday 9th January : two journeys out of six;

    1954/5 : Service withdrawn - Tuesday 4th January, Friday 18th February, Tuesday 22nd February, Friday 25th February, Saturday 26th February.

The average loading of the last Yelverton-Princetown-Tavistock bus (10.40 pm) up to Saturday 11th June over 12 months was ten, with no appreciable seasonal variation. The average load of the 9.17pm Yelverton-Princetown-Tavistock bus service which began on 18th June was fourteen. Other bus services had average loads between eight and thirteen.

*Services were withdrawn on five days, to cover which, BR was expected to maintain loss making services for 365 days pa, and had been bitterly criticised for those same losses. No other industry would have put up with it for a second.*

A hearing was arranged for 8th July 1955, when an opportunity was given to objectors to present information. From facts supplied and current data, the number of passengers are tending to decrease, freight traffic is negligible. [TUCC Annual Report, Para. 10].

## The Objectors' case

*Modernise the line*

The local MP, Henry Studholme had written, that he "had been in touch with an independent expert on traffic problems who knows the Princetown line and has convinced me that it would probably be possible to use a small diesel or electric train which could negotiate the gradients and curves of the line. The effect would be to considerably reduce the running costs and the staff required".

He did not name the expert nor send a copy of his document, so that his sums - if any - and qualifications were there for all to see. No expert worthy of the name could have seriously proposed, that, here in the middle of nowhere, with the nearest electric traction depots and sub stations 120 miles away as the crow flies, it would be economic to have an island of electric traction, with its own power supply sub station, maintenance facilities and specialised maintenance staff. Did no one, outside BR, understand that new capital equipment - diesel or electric - required funding, and that the interest and depreciation costs alone would not be covered by any potential savings, and would actually increase losses? No suggestion was proffered as to who would fund the new trains, including one spare unit to cover down time. Government's interest bearing loans were BR's only source of funds. The MP did not undertake to call on Government to fund uneconomic services.

A suggestion had been received by the TUCC that 6-7,000 miles pa were being covered unnecessarily and asked if it was not possible to cut expenses by reducing the distance - i.e. by creating a new shorter rail route between Yelverton and Princetown.

*Reduce costs*

A Prison Officers Association spokesman said that the line was over staffed. (What would he have said, had a railway union representative told him that the prison was over staffed?). He aired his views on the benefits of using diesels - a knowledge which would hardly come from prison work. He said there was no reason to suppose that any attempt had been made to reduce the loss, that there was no equal to the railways, and it wouldn't have happened in GWR days. (His presumption that no effort had been made to cut costs was arrogant. One could say the same about prison costs. He didn't explain why people weren't using the branch, nor how to get them to walk past a bus stop to a station for a train which took longer than the bus. The line was in financial trouble when it was privately owned, and motor transport was beginning to abstract traffic in GWR days).

*Inconvenience*

The MP said the saving by BR of £11,000 from closure, could not be compared with the inconvenience to residents. There is an onus on the BTC to provide Princetown and the prison with adequate transport facilities. (There was no such obligation after 1953).

The prison Governor said that closure would be detrimental to officers and families. A prison officer said that they had been offered a bus to Plymouth in 1935 but had rejected it because they knew it would close the line. (This probably made them unique in the whole of the UK. In no other case studied, did anyone else claim to have done likewise. It made no difference in this case, because the prison took its coal off rail, and buses brought trippers into the moors who had previously travelled by rail).

*Increase traffic*

BR was asked what had been done to promote the service. (It was idle to pretend that in a small place such as Princetown, there was anyone who didn't know there was a train service, so why didn't they use it? The line was insolvent when competing against the horse in this exceptionally difficult terrain).

*Winter problems*

Snow closed local roads for "weeks at a time". A spokesman for Tavistock RDC said that roads were icebound in the early morning about twenty times pa. (If any occasions were at weekends, schoolchildren and most workers would suffer no inconvenience).

Devon County Council had written to the TUCC that "The Yelverton-Princetown road was completely closed for 18 days in 1947". (*Eight years earlier*. They overlooked that the line was also blocked by snow during the same winter).

## BR's Responses to Objectors

*Modernise the line*

Dieselisation had been considered. Unless there was a substantial traffic potential a diesel service will not pay and this was proven when the BR ran an experimental service for six months between Usk and Monmouth which resulted in few additional passengers, but the loss was doubled. Diesels were not the answer for all poorly patronised lines. The proposal presupposed that BR would dispense with goods, but retain passenger services. Light weight diesels could not handle goods traffic nor negotiate the acute curves. Two forms of locomotion would be necessary, thereby worsening the finances. It was also suggested that crossings would be operated by the driver, and signalmen be dispensed with, but they have other duties so no economy would ensue.

To create a new shorter route - contours must be taken into account when building railways and if the route suggested was used, a gradient of 1 in 10 would be encountered.

*Increase traffic*

To promote the service, there had been press advertisements, posters on stations and a fare of 3/- (15p), which was one third cheaper than by road and had still been unable to attract more passengers. On the last bank holiday, only 300 used the line in perfect weather, whereas in the distant past 20-25,000 were conveyed on a bank holiday. During very severe weather, the number of passengers was very small and the amount of merchandise carried to Princetown was such that it would appear the population was on hunger strike. If prison authorities wanted to keep the line, why did they, several years ago, divert coal from rail to road?

Half day fares are cheaper than road, but the public do not use the railway. Comment was made about a late service being needed. It is not borne out by experience. A written request was received for a late service when Plymouth Argyle played at home - it carried *four* passengers. Western National Omnibus Company used to run a service at 10.0 pm up to 11th June - it was not supported. Passengers had fallen off in 1954. Recently, a coach excursion was arranged to Looe - railways had not been approached.

*Winter problems*

Weather difficulties were no worse than in Scotland where 30 branch lines had closed, but life went on. Many places exist where railways have never been available but life goes on. The BTC was being asked to subsidise this line in order that road users would have an alternative means of transport on those odd occasions when the road is impassable. BR pointed out that coal and newspapers all went by road, without difficulty. In the recent railway strike, no complaints were received and Princetown managed to live.

*Alternative services*

The TUCC was being unreasonable in expecting a replacement bus service to be 100% reliable. No transport undertaking in the world would give a 100% guarantee of reliability. (No business would. A guarantee to replace a defective product should not be confused with a 100% guarantee not to provide an unreliable product in the first place)

## The Evidence Reviewed

After objectors, BR and bus spokesmen withdrew, TUCC members commented:-

- The morning bus could depart later as the route was shorter and quicker.
- One member thought that no attempt had been made to make it pay. He was told that the line had the minimum number of staff, and there was no real traffic potential.
- A councillor among the members said that the BTC must pay its way.
- Prison authorities could use the line more than they do, and if they were prepared to give a guarantee of extra traffic over three years, the case would on an entirely different basis. A guarantee could be given in respect of goods and/or passenger.
- The Chairman doubted that even that would make the line profitable, but it would show that they were willing to help. Coal goes by road because it comes by sea to Plymouth where it is put into lorries. If it came by rail, it would have to be put into lorries at Princetown to take to the prison, lorries run direct from Plymouth. (*It could have been sent direct from colliery to Princetown, as it originally was, saving transhipment at two ports*)
- Closure proposals had been published for a long while and despite strong opposition, rail revenue had not increased. One would have anticipated that objectors would have put their business on rail to show they were willing to help as much as they could.
- During the last few weeks, with exceptionally fine weather, a few more passengers have been carried - some said they were taking an opportunity to travel on the line before it closed. (Obviously, the line did not lack publicity).
- Is it not possible to supply a light weight diesel and review it in 12 months time? (BR had explained to the TUCC that light weight diesels could not haul freight. Moreover, he did not address the question as to which manufacturer would loan a diesel for 12 months. BR would not transfer units from where they were presently in use, leaving them short - that would bring reaction from other users).
- Objectors to the closure should use the railway. The remedy is in their own hands.
- On road alternatives, reference was made to the winter of 1947 and this last winter, one member pointed out, there were only two bad winters over a long period.
- The variation in the passengers during bad and normal weather was practically nil.
- Whilst appreciating the concern about prison officers, they do not travel by rail very often.
- Railway staff get to work in the morning to run trains despite adverse weather
- The Chief Constable had supplied a report from a police sergeant stationed at Princetown from 1950 until Spring 1955: "There were very few occasions when the road was completely blocked by snow. The last occasion was during last winter when the Princetown-Tavistock road was blocked for 36 hours and the Princetown-

Yelverton road for a slightly longer period. In early 1951 the latter was blocked for a night by a heavy snowfall. Almost every year, during the months of January and February, there were falls of snow that made the roads dangerous, but usually passable with care. There have been occasions when ice formed on the roads during early mornings, but these occasions have not been numerous. Fog should present no real obstacle to road transport, it is never of the London 'pea soup' type. It will never bring traffic to a complete standstill as it does in London. The number of occasions when the route is impassable can be counted on the fingers of one hand".

Finally, one member said that, although the railways had made a good case, the motion be put that:-

*"While the Committee recognise that it is unlikely the Princetown branch can be run on an economic basis, they feel there are certain particular circumstances which justify special consideration. Owing to the geographical location of Princetown, the Committee are not satisfied that alternative bus services can be entirely satisfactory. Furthermore, the fact that HM Prison is located in Princetown, introduces an exceptional set of circumstances which cannot be ignored. Therefore, the Committee recommends the line remain in operation".*

Five voted in favour, five against, the Chairman gave the deciding vote for retention. Had such a narrow vote been for closure, and become known, there would have been a public outcry. Needless to say, they did not say who was to pick up the tab. The Home Office should have covered losses if they required a service for the prison.

After making their decision, the Press and some objectors were re-admitted. Sir Henry Slessor, spokesman for Devon County Council said that there were 300 staff at the prison, with families - about 1,000 - most of whom depend on public transport to Plymouth. Closing would make it difficult to recruit officers. He said the alternative bus service was entirely unsuitable, and there was no way anybody in Plymouth or west of Princetown would be able to get to the moor. It is our duty to provide people with facilities for using the park and to close the line would deprive them of that opportunity. He went on to say that the money which the local community would lose was greater than BR's loss of £9,000 on the line. (In that case, the Council should have offered a subsidy and urged more use by prison staff and locals. There is no mention of either in the TUCC transcript. BR had said that rail travel to the moor was down from 25,000 to a few hundreds).

A TUCC meeting on 9th September 1955 dealt with the proposed closure of Princetown branch. "Ample opportunity had been given to any interested council or organisation to express their views on the proposed closure and for BR to state their case. Tavistock RDC had phoned on 1st September seeking a later hearing as additional information was now available and was told this was not possible, but if it was submitted in writing every consideration would be given. This was accepted and an assurance given that the details would be submitted before the meeting. Nothing further had been heard from the RDC".
[TUCC min. 215]

111

## CTCC Decision

On 31st December, the CTCC overturned the TUCC's recommendation, subject to reasonable alternative arrangements being arrived at between the prison authorities and the BTC. It was considered that the augmented bus service proposed would reasonably meet existing needs. [CTCC minute 516, 11.10.55].

"At both Princetown and Yelverton stations, many tickets, some dating back to GWR days were sold as souvenirs". [Times, 5.3.56, 3e].

## Postscript

The line closed on 3rd March 1956.

Hundreds took a last trip. Instead of the normal one coach, three were required. Driver Bill Gough said: "You can't run lines at a loss". His view was shared by Fireman Cyril Stephens. Watching the crowds of people milling about the station platform, after the arrival of one of the trains, one of the railway staff observed: "If only they had always used it so frequently we should never have been closed down". [Western Evening Herald, 3.3.56].

It is a great pity that the line could not have been kept open by some private company, but the upkeep no doubt would have proved too expensive. Many people gathered together to ride on this train before the line closed and we all bemoaned its passing, but we had done very little to justify its retention. [Kingdom, Foreword].

The line was difficult and expensive to operate with little indigenous traffic and seemed ideal for closure, but there were special circumstances. Traffic to and from the prison, the atrocious Dartmoor weather and the spectre of tourism. The Dartmoor weather was to wreak wicked revenge on the authorities. In the winter of 1963, Princetown was cut off for three days. [Henshaw, Pages 80 & 82]. Henshaw quotes a 1971 estimate of possible tourist levels in 1981 - *25 years after the line closed.*

Prison traffic was negligible. If the atrocious weather wreaked revenge on anyone, it must surely have been on those who failed to make regular use of the line, and only turned to it when a severe winter came. It is unreasonable to argue that the line should have been kept open for a bad winter eight years later, to carry supplies normally conveyed by road, to the ungrateful villagers and to the prison, which didn't make full use of the railway throughout the year. Critics seem to believe that the line should have remained open in perpetuity to be used every 7-8 years for three days and subsidised by passengers elsewhere or by BR staff. *Estimated* tourist levels, hopefully producing a return to solvency in 25 years time, would have cut no ice with any private sector company. It is doubtful, any would have even been influenced by a *guarantee* so far into the future.

The effect of the line closure on the prison was stupendously less than critics claimed. "A contract to be provided for 200 (passenger) journeys pa. Arrangements to be made for the conveyance of prisoners on release, to Yelverton, when the branch closes in March 1956. The additional cost will be £70 pa". [PRO: PCOM9/1884].

The route began as the Norwich & Spalding Railway - the first section opened in 1858, but never reached Norwich. The Lynn & Sutton Bridge Railway opened in 1861. The Spalding & Bourne Railway opened in 1862 and took over the lease of the Norwich & Spalding in 1877 under the name of the Midland & Eastern. In 1883, they amalgamated with Lynn & Fakenham, Peterborough, Wisbech & Sutton Bridge, Yarmouth Union, Yarmouth & North Norfolk to form the Eastern & Midland Railway. The Eastern & Midlands Railway was taken over jointly by the Midland & Great Northern in 1893. [Sherrington, Page 130].

The M&GN was formed by the amalgamation of a number of small independent companies. The oldest was from Spalding to Holbeach, built by the Norwich & Spalding Railway in 1858, extended to Sutton Bridge in 1862. The Lynn & Sutton Bridge and Spalding & Bourne sections followed. The Midland & Eastern Railway was formed to take over the Bourne to Kings Lynn line. Various lines from Norwich and Yarmouth were built in sections. In 1882, the Eastern & Midlands was formed to amalgamate these minor companies. They were finally taken over by the M&GN in 1893. It was an alternative to the GER. [BTC Closure Booklet September 1958].

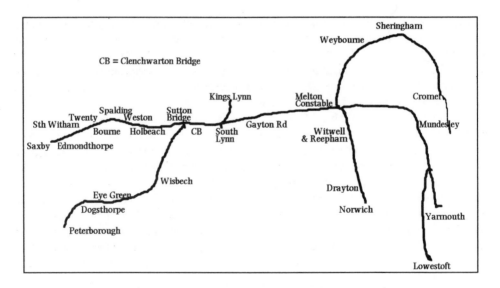

In 1884, the Eastern & Midlands Railway complained to the Railway Commissioners about the small amount of traffic received from the Midland over the Peterborough-Lynn route. Their Inquiry revealed that most of Midland Railway's East Anglian traffic was going via the GER from Peterborough as that route was quicker. Goods sent in the morning via the GER would be at Norwich by midday, but via Sutton and Melton would not arrive until evening. [Rhodes, Page 13]. That the Midland, which had a working relationship with the Eastern & Midlands Railway, should find it advantageous to route some traffic via the GER is a strong indication of the shortcomings of the M&GN route.

Due to financial burdens, the Eastern & Midlands had to be content with what rolling stock it could get, giving a miscellaneous collection. [H.L. Hopwood, Railway Magazine, vol. 23].

Year after year, during the ten years it controlled lines from Peterborough/Saxby to the coast, the company failed to pay dividends and often had insufficient to meet all mandatory interest payments on Debentures. In 1891, a Receiver & Manager was appointed to run the company. He continued until the company was taken over. The total capital raised by the company was £1.93m in stock and £1.1m in loans. To take over this £3m railway, the Midland & GNR companies issued a total of only £1.2m, a clear demonstration of its poor prospects. New M&GN shares & debentures were, in many cases, exchanged for old stock at less than par. [Bradshaw's Shareholders Guide, 1883 to 1893].

Before the Great War (1914-18), the company had an annual gross profit of £80,000. [Railway Year Book, 1914]. The finances of the line were in deficit between the wars. A net loss of £1,302 for 1928 had risen to £10,603 pa for 1938. [PRO: Rail 1110/323].

The M&GN, although not a branch line in terms of length, had all the attributes of a rural branch line with little originating traffic, and little inward traffic and was very dependent on the Midland and GNR. It was a collection of branch lines merged to form one system to compete with the GER. Had the GNR and GER been merged into one company, as they attempted to do early in the century, it cannot be doubted that the M&GN could not have been sustained by Midland traffic alone. It suffered from the high proportion of single line sections which made it very vulnerable to cumulative delay.

### The Cause of Decline

It was never prosperous, even before the advent of road competition. That must be ascribed largely to the fact that Wisbech, Spalding, Lynn, Norwich, Cromer and Yarmouth are the only towns over 10,000 inhabitants in an area which is otherwise sparsely populated. Many of the M&GN stations served only small villages. Three *weekends* before and after August Bank Holiday, it is very busy. [BTC Closure Booklet].

Traffic loss to road between the wars would have led to closure, but for war in 1939. The LNER, which ran the line from 1936, suffered more than the other railways from trade depression in the 1930's. and could not have continued indefinitely to subsidise it from profits elsewhere. I worked on the line in 1953 and recall that traffic was light.

For years the line had operated at a considerable loss and closure of Melton Constable to Yarmouth was being considered as early as 1954. Other closures led management to believe it would lead to a public outcry. Proposals were delayed when it was thought that the new charges scheme might check the swing of mainly agricultural traffic to road. Relaying and other maintenance was delayed as long as prudent. The condition of Clenchwarton Bridge brought matters to a head. [NRM: BTC Internal Relations Paper]

The M&GN was "a product of the over extravagant and over optimistic period of railway development in the 19th century". "The M&GN was a less efficient route. It suffered by comparison with the GER. It was restricted over two-thirds of its route to engines of route availability '4' whereas to all principal competitive towns, the GER could work the most powerful freight and any passenger engine except Pacifics. The competitive distances from London were heavily on the side of the GER, and with the Midlands only slightly on the side of the M&GN". "Road competition began to take its toll between the wars". "The M&GN depended more on the LMS after the Grouping". [M.J. Clark, Railway World Special, Pages 3, 6 & 14]

Under the 1923 Grouping, the GNR and GER became part of the LNER - hence M&GN traffic would be reduced by diversion of GNR traffic to GER routes.

Since lines in the Western section ran on the level, and roads did the same there were many level crossings. The M&GN had 140, of which 74 were on the Western Section - an average of one per mile, each requiring a keeper's cottage. M&GN stations were often uncomfortably distant from the communities they served. Weston, Weybourne and Reepham were all about $1^1/_2$ miles distant. North Drove was isolated, with hardly a house in sight. [Rhodes, Pages 17 & 24].

"An observer at Melton Constable yesterday said in $1^1/_2$ hours on the platform, he saw no passengers at all". [Times, 13.6.58]. It was said to be one of the busiest stations.

"Tickets printed with the original name of M&GN were being sold at booking offices on the line". [Times, 16.8.58]. This tells the story of insufficient demand to have failed to clear ticket stock of such vintage.

### BR's Proposal

The Eastern Area Board stated: "No effort has been spared during the last few years to maintain the widest practicable network of services in the Region. Experiments have been made with cheaper methods of operation. Losses on non-paying sectors have been reduced. On certain sections there are still big losses, and the extent to which these can be financed out of proceeds of profitable services has been limited by recent trends. No place served by the M&GN is more than a few miles from the GER line and there are bus services throughout the area. This duplication and a sparse traffic has been responsible for poor loading on the line. Traffic can be transferred elsewhere. Reduced costs and improved receipts from diesels have not been sufficient to bring the services into financial equilibrium, and the M&GN offers a less favourable ground for experiment. There is sufficient experience of diesel operation to establish that to make this type of stopping passenger service profitable, there must be a very substantial increase in the carryings. Such increases in the area served by the M&GN are not available. *In many cases, stations are a long way from the villages they serve.* Freight traffic is insufficient to justify the line as a separate through route". *Area Boards included outside businessmen.*

The plan to close the line was initially advised to TUCC's and press on 12th June and local authorities on 19th August. The BTC circulated a Booklet, to press and local authorities, containing full details of the plan, on 16th September 1958, stating inter alia:-

- There is insufficient traffic for two railways - rationalisation is overdue and there is no statutory obligation to keep it open or run any trains. There are certain covenants for stopping trains on request or for the provision of sidings. Steps are being taken to secure release from these.

- Ironstone workings at Edmondthorpe and South Witham will still be served, also brick-fields at Eye Green and Dogsthorpe, sand at Gayton Road, South Lynn sugar beet factory and Wisbech quayside.
- At retained freight stations, 100% of traffic is expected to remain. At those to be closed, 70% is forecast to be retained at other stations nearby. The cost of additional cartage and additional rail services over the GER have been calculated.
- During week ending 21st June, no station except Bourne on the Saxby-Spalding route had more than four passengers per day. 40% of stations between Spalding and Yarmouth had fewer than 20 per day Monday-Friday, although weekends were better. The only route which could claim viability was Melton Constable-Norwich where weekday averages were 33 at Drayton, 188 at Melton and 324 at Norwich.
- Local passenger receipts will be lost and those to some other destinations. Where an alternative station is available, an allowance of 12% has been taken as traffic likely to be retained and 88% lost.
- Through traffic - all principal towns on the M&GN, are also on the GER. For the most part, all services to the rest of the country are adequate. The principal loss on through services via the M&GN will be between Yarmouth and the industrial Midlands. Alternative services are expected to retain 73% of the traffic.
- A special problem exists with seasonal peak holiday traffic. This traffic is not merely of a peak character, but contains a "peak within a peak". Superimposed on the normal summer weekend peak, is a special peak on the three weekends immediately preceding and following the August Bank Holiday. It will be carried over the Great Eastern route. Yarmouth Vauxhall will be improved to cope with diverted holiday traffic and carriage sidings enlarged.
- Dieselisation has been considered, but would cost £125,000 pa. Based on experience on the Melton Constable-Norwich service since September 1957, it is unlikely that it would produce enough revenue to justify the investment.
- 174 miles of passenger and 116 miles of freight route are proposed for closure. The estimated net benefit is £640,000. Immediate and short term savings were £826,000, with renewals of £913,000 over the next five years equating to £183,000 pa, totalling £1,009,000. It is estimated that £265,000 in receipts would be lost, and £104,000 incurred for additional services : road £1,400; rail £94,000. The net saving was £640,000. No savings have been taken into account for direct costs of train movement off the M&GN in respect of traffic which will be lost. Therefore £640,000 is a conservative estimate.

**Public Reaction**

Councils and organisations set up a body to co-ordinate objections to closure. [Times, 26.8.58]. They did not co-ordinate traffic back to the *essential*, seriously under used line.

Despite much traditional rail traffic having been transferred to road transport over the years, there was still some limited reaction to closure from the remaining clientele.

Not everyone was against closure, a spokesman for the Sugar Beet industry said that only 5% of beet was brought in by rail at Spalding in 1957. Wisbech & District Fruit

Growers Association said 80% of their produce was carried by road. The closure attracted a lot of publicity and the impression was gained that the whole area was up in arms, but in reality, most people were unaffected. A public gathering in Melton, badly affected by the proposal, attracted only 70, which even the convenors of the meeting found "disappointing". [Rhodes, Page 30].

Heacham Parish Council feared holidaymakers would be diverted to the Lincolnshire coast (a loss to Norfolk, not railways). They said "In any large undertaking, it is necessary that those services which are unremunerative should be subsidised by remunerative ones". [Rhodes, Page 35]. This does not apply to retail chains or banks. The council expected that tourists to that area should be subsidised by those travelling elsewhere.

Media reports and correspondence with the TUCC's make no reference to the need for railways to convey highly perishable traffic such as fruit, flowers and allied produce, which used to be conveyed by overnight express freight.

An NFU spokesman said the main asset of the M&GN to agriculture was through Lynn to the Midlands. [Times, 21.8.58]. Agriculture was among the first to desert the railways.

### Consideration by TUCC's
Preliminary notification was received from BR of a proposal to close the M&GN. A large number of objections are expected. A tour of the line was made by TUCC's on 26th September. A joint meeting was arranged with the TUCC for East Anglia at Peterborough on 30th September. [TUCC-East Midlands 15.7.58, min 461].

### Peterborough meeting
Present at the meeting were the General Manager and six others from BR-Eastern Region, and 33 people from the two TUCC's. BR said that public bodies throughout the area had been told of the proposals. BR would retain certain sections of line for freight.
*BR comments*:-

- The MoT had stated in Parliament on 23rd July that Government intend to support plans for eliminating hopelessly uneconomic services. Railways are no longer a monopoly with an obligation to provide all sections of the community with a railway service. On 1st August a Minister said that the BTC has a duty as a commercial organisation, it is not a social service.
- The bus, car and lorry had largely destroyed any local or contributory revenue which may have existed. Paragraph 124 of the Modernisation Plan mentioned a reduction in stopping services and branch line services which are little used by the public. This was part and parcel of modernisation.
- The statement stressed cash savings and left out items of a purely accountancy nature which may be debatable. Where cash - wages and payments for materials are concerned - there can be little room for argument. There is a clear gap of £640,000 pa. which is very much a minimum figure. Savings from renewal of rolling stock are worth £35,000 pa. and there are additional savings at motive power depots away from the M&GN which now provide loco power for trains to the M&GN. BR would not be surprised if the net final saving is £1m rather than £640,000.

- Many coaches are used only for Saturdays in Summer. The holiday peak needed to be spread. Diesels were not a universal panacea for loss making lines. They had their uses and the BTC was very pleased with results in certain areas. They cost so much, that a potential must exist to pick up far more traffic. Diesels between Norwich and Melton increased passengers by only 10%. Elsewhere on the M&GN it is doubted that there would be even this. An improvement of £125,000 pa could be made by dieselising the whole of the M&GN - far short of estimated savings from closure.
- There are alternative routes for holiday trains with running times which compare favourably with M&GN lines.
- Regarding freight, BR consider that spurs : Saxby-Edmondthorpe, South Witham-Spalding-Sutton Bridge, Peterborough-Wisbech and South Lynn-Gayton Rd would cater for most worthwhile freight on the line. The cost of routing coal to Norwich via Cromer and Melton Constable was not a problem, it would be in train loads, with small costs in relation to savings. (The latter route was shortened - see page 130).
- Clenchwarton Bridge was nearly life expired, and due to its condition, has a 5mph speed limit. Rebuilding would cost £270,000. To invest this in a line which loses money does not make sense. Every week that closure is deferred, costs BR £10,000.

## TUCC-East Anglia Public Hearing

The TUCC had received 64 written objections by 14th October. Some objectors attended the Hearing to make verbal protests. (Some reports said there were 55 written objections, but TUCC papers include a total of 64).

The Hearing took place at Norwich on 14th/15th October. Oral objections were heard on the first day, whilst on the second, written objections were considered. The full list of objectors - oral & written totalled 84, including forty-one local authorities, two local authority organisations, two Chambers of Commerce, (one later withdrew), four Holiday camps, two NFU groups, four trade organisations, ten other organisations, eleven local firms, (one later withdrew), and eight individuals. The Chairman of the TUCC said in all cases checked so far, savings had been equal to or in excess of estimated amounts and no errors had been found over a long period. He explained the functions of the Committee, reminding objectors that they were there to help the Committee to arrive at a recommendation which will best serve the general public interest, including that of the taxpayer. It was not a legal tribunal, and there would be no cross-examination. Questions could be put through him and he would decide if they were admissible.

BR's spokesman was asked to present their case. He said that BR had given the earliest intimation possible on 12th June, quoted the financial implications of the 1947 and 1953 Acts, and referred to statements by Ministers that railways must shed non-paying services. Obligations borne in days of near monopoly could no longer be maintained. They re-iterated points made at Peterborough, including potential savings, the Clenchwarton bridge, the retention of freight spurs and that dieselisation was not a better option. and added :-

- The estimate of likely traffic loss was on the pessimistic side. Other savings could have been included, but the case was amply proved on the figures quoted.

- BR has been maintaining a very large stock of coaches which are only used on a few Saturdays in each Summer. This is unduly expensive and is being tackled - the Yarmouth traffic is typical. The holiday trains would be diverted into Yarmouth Vauxhall, but some measure of spreading arrivals and departures would be necessary. Whilst the longer route for some trains would tend to increase fares, BR planned only to increase by 50% of the difference.
- Local traffic can be well provided for by buses.
- Most of the economic freight traffic can be retained by the proposed spurs. The BTC is prepared to assist traders with the expense of transferring to other locations.

The Counsel for Norfolk County Council, also represented five UDC's, eight RDC's, 21 Parish Councils, three County Boroughs and the Norfolk Farmers Union. The County Council had decided not to oppose the closure, but to oppose the time scale for it to be carried out. "The opposition did not seriously contest BR's estimate that they had been losing £640,000 a year by keeping the line open nor that they might save nearly a million by closing it. Instead the local authorities took the more practical step of pleading for delay". [Eastern Daily Press 15.10.58].

*The Counsel stated* :-

- The County Council did not object to the closure itself, but at the speed, and urged it be deferred for a couple of years so that adequate alternatives could be worked out. The County Council realised that closure was inevitable, it would be idle to argue against the proposal.
- The additional 500,000 bus miles pa on the roads would not present any real difficulty, but redundant railway staff would add to rural unemployment.
- Cromer, Sheringham and Mundesley had suffered over the past five years due to a fall in the number of visitors, which would be aggravated by a reduction of travel facilities. (The drop in holiday travel would have had an impact on rail revenue. It was a plea for BR to lose even more money to keep these resorts in business. No mention was made of any action *they* had taken to build business back up. BR couldn't force holiday makers to go to a particular resort).
- Yarmouth had 80-100,000 visitors per week in the peak months. The capacity and facilities at Vauxhall would need improvement. (BR had already said that this was in hand. There was no reference as to how many of these visitors arrived by road).
- Crab traffic from North Norfolk amounted to 4,000 cwt's pa from Cromer, Sheringham & Mundesley. "Because of irregular forwardings it would be difficult to contract with road hauliers". (200 tons pa from three places! Yet again, leaving BR with the uneconomic 'tiddlers' whilst hauliers got the highly profitable full loads).
- Diesel trains should be run at routine hours: morning, lunch-hour and evening between Melton Constable and Norwich City. "If a substantial loss continues, the BTC could *renew* the application to withdraw passenger services". (i.e. start all over again. Any other company would have closed without warning in May when the facts were clear. It would have been uneconomic to run railcars three times a day - a total daily distance of 150 miles, especially as BR maintained its own "highway").

119

- It would be better in everyone's interests to run for a year or two, even at a loss, with reduced services. (It was only the interests of those locally, who were not making full use of the line. There wasn't another company in the UK which would do so).

He said "No one can say logically and sensibly that the line should not be closed eventually, but the time was not yet ripe". [Lynn News & Advertiser 17.10.58]. "If the line still made a loss, the BTC would have a better case for closure". [East Anglian Daily Times 15.10.58].

*Objectors' comments* :-

- The spokesman for holiday camps said that "in the peak 2,250 stayed, 80% from London, the rest from the Midlands. Quite a number travelled by rail". In answer to a question, he said it was about 25%. (One wonders why the camps did not offer a discount to those who arrived by rail if they wanted to keep the line). He said that the committee should satisfy themselves about the accuracy of BR figures. (In contrast, his statement that 25% travelled by rail was expected to be taken on trust).
- East Anglian Grain Co. sent 2,614 tons by rail last year, all to Burton, because consignees required it by rail. It was less than one third of forwardings. They bought land in 1947, but did not commence building until 1949, and completed it in 1954. They paid £1,500 for a private siding at East Rudham, which would be lost. - *BR said it was £1,057, which was not disputed.* (The criticism which would have been hurled at BR for such a faux-pas was conspicuous by its absence. The inference was, that but for requirements at Burton, there would be none by rail).
- Yarmouth Chamber of Commerce criticised Vauxhall station, but were satisfied with arrangements for freight traffic. They made a plea for BR to protect Yarmouth from worsening unemployment. (Tackling unemployment was the Government's job).
- Two coal merchants received 1,500 tons pa by rail and would have to take coal an extra eight miles by road. (Thirty tons - two wagons - per week).
- Another coal merchant would have to transport 3,940 tons of coal by road for seven to eight miles. A fourth would transport an undisclosed tonnage eight miles by road. (The merchants made no mention of tonnage received by road. Rail tonnages could not have kept them fully occupied six days a week).
- Broadlands Mushroom Farms grew 20 tons pa. During part of the year they are disposed of locally. (They did not disclose what percentage went by road).
- Suppliers of agricultural products expressed concern about the loss of rail services.
- A turkey breeder said that they send traffic by rail *almost daily*. (He gave no details of volume, nor of the percentage sent by road).
- A Wisbech fruit & potato merchant received at least a truck of bananas per week by rail. (No reference was made to the rest of his business which obviously was by road).
- Stalham Parish Council feared that in the next war, they would be "in the front line" with an invasion. (It was nearly twice as far, across the sea, as the distance travelled in the 1944 landings in Normandy - a more unlikely prospect is difficult to imagine, and irrelevant, since Governments had never paid railways for such contingencies).
- Briston Parish Council thought that the coast near them was more likely to be the invasion beach. (It was much further from the continent than Stalham).

- The same council referred to roads being very bad, but went on to admit that 75% of people visiting the boatyards came by road!
- Weston Longville Parish Council were concerned about a company making materials for road construction, which were carried by rail. (Only until the road was made!)
- Felmingham Parish council saw the solution as single car diesels. (Others who sent parcels and fish by train did not. The council was advocating spending scarce interest bearing capital on new specialised diesels *in the hope of* reducing the loss!)
- Sea Fisheries Joint Committee, sending 20 tons pa from four towns, said temperatures in diesels were much higher and detrimental to fish. Diesels had limited capacity for parcels, and cannot be sufficient at times. (These were two car units. The widely advocated single cars would have had no space at all).
- Other councils thought that freight spurs could be used by railbuses. (They were obviously unaware of the lower standards and, hence costs, of freight lines).
- The Norfolk Federation of Women's Institutes called on the BTC to ensure that alternative transport was adequate and permanent. ("The resolution was sent before the Federation discussed it, in order to get it to the TUCC Inquiry at Norwich. It was necessary to anticipate the delegates' decision!") [Lynn News & Advertiser 17.10.58]. They said that railways were subsidised by taxpayers, and as they were taxpayers, the line should remain. This was a popular illusion. Government made interest bearing loans to cover losses created by Government policy. [See "*Blueprints for Bankruptcy*"].

King's Lynn Chamber of Commerce withdrew its objection and stated: "Having ascertained the facts, this Chamber considers that the economic benefits of closing the line are overwhelming and therefore wishes to withdraw its previous objection".

*BR responses and comments* :-
- The private car had taken much of the coastal traffic and there could be no justification for both train and bus services for so limited a business.
- Melton Constable-Norwich DMU earnings were £17,000; direct movement costs were £21,000, producing a loss of £4,000, to which must be added terminal costs of £11,000. To run trains only at times needed for workers would give a less satisfactory result. (This was acknowledged by objectors to be one of the busiest sections)
- All trawlers using Lowestoft are now oil fired, no coal is used, reducing freight traffic
- On deferment of closure 'because there had been little notice' : "Proposals were made known in June, and it is a very long time when you are losing £640,000 pa"
- BR had already stated that Vauxhall facilities would be improved by next summer. The most essential change (unperceived by objectors) was increased carriage sidings.
- The present rate for coal to Norwich City would remain unaltered.
- The submission by the holiday camp proprietors was in respect of one train per week which does not regularly convey 4-500 people. Many people for the camps do not use this service, but travel to Yarmouth and go forward by buses provided by the camps.
- The only crab traffic affected was from Cromer and Sheringham via Melton Constable. It could be dealt with via Norwich and would get a better service.

- With one exception, the journey time of Saturday holiday trains would be improved. The GER route was faster. There would be two additional through trains from Derby and Leicester to Cromer.
- It was usual for road hauliers to take agricultural products to main markets on alternate days and for traffic to be forwarded by rail on Fridays at the commencement and end of the season when there was insufficient traffic to attract hauliers.

The East Anglian TUCC stated that it would not announce its decision until the East Midlands Inquiry had been held. After withdrawal of BR representatives and objectors, they reached the following conclusions :-
- The financial details submitted by BR were accepted. It was agreed that savings would be in the region of £640,000, and probably more.
- They could not recommend deferment of closure for two years as suggested. It would cost BR about £2m. Nor could they recommend a continuance of the present or a modified diesel service from Melton Constable to Norwich.
- Alternative services are fair and reasonable. Some may be worse off, but others would be better off. They noted that the bus mileage would not be a problem on the roads
- They were unconvinced by objectors' arguments relating to holiday traffic. Proposed services are adequate, but Yarmouth Vauxhall needs improvement.
- They could not accept at face value all the claims of extra costs put forward by coal merchants. There was a case for some assistance by BR.
- Bus services from Murrow required to be improved.

### TUCC - East Midlands Inquiry
The East Midlands TUCC arranged to hold an Inquiry at Bourne on 27th October and invited written objections.

A conference of local authorities and other organisations had been convened by Holland County Council on 25th August. It resolved that the interests of users of the line can only be effectively safeguarded by continuance of full operation as a whole. (Nothing was said to pressure users to put more traffic onto the line and non users to begin to use the line).
*East Elloe submission* :-
- Diesel experiments should have been given a fair trial before a decision was taken to obtain evidence as to savings before closure. (See page 43)
- The line could be more economically run and, therefore, losses are greater than they need have been. Automatic devices could have reduced the high cost of manning level crossings on little used roads. (They tacitly accepted that there were losses. Many level crossings had resident keepers, whose wages were never sufficient to fund any form of modernisation. When BR sought to replace men with automation, the principal objectors were councils who alleged they were unsafe, but were trying to protect rural employment and Rates income. - See pages 41/42, 200 & 226)
- Increases in road congestion should be offset against savings. Cost of traffic delays is increasing at 14% pa. (There would be, of course, no transfer of cash to railways from the Government or local authorities).

- The savings are vague. More details are called for. (They were jumping the gun, they had been promised details would follow the preliminary notification).
- Alternative bus services are inadequate and no assurance was given on long term reduction of buses.
- The alternative rail route to the coast was not adequate, and no assurance was given on long term reduction of rail freight.
- Closure would be detrimental to life, amenities and travel, would cause disturbance, inconvenience, hardship and would jeopardise employment. (Usually, councils were thinking of the loss of employment prospects for railway staff, not commuters).

*Spalding RDC submission* :-
- Referred to new housing at Tongue End.
- The BTC had allocated £104,000 for alternative bus services.
    *BR said it was £1,400, which was set out in the circulated booklet.*

*Bourne UDC submission* :-
- Claimed that the BTC had failed to carry out the statutory duty imposed on them. (It quoted provisions in the 1947 Act, overlooking that it was modified by the 1953 Act).
- Appreciated that the number of passengers using the line was small.
- Referred to a large monopolistic undertaking charging what the traffic will bear and as a consequence remunerative routes should subsidise uneconomic routes. (How could they talk of monopoly and also admit few people used trains, and be aware of amount of freight going from the area by road? Local Authorities have awesome monopoly powers. They made no offer to put any Council traffic on rail).
- Criticised railways for seeking to change established habits  (The established habit of travel by rail had been changed by *users* transferring to other modes, and it was likely that they would continue to do so, despite fares then trailing the RPI by 41 points).
- Pressed for diesels to see if it would improve finances. (If it was a policy of councils to repeatedly invest in non redeemable assets to see *if* they would reduce costs, little wonder Rates never went down. See page 43 & Appendix C).
- It serves to connect to the main line and withdrawal of freight facilities would be detrimental to the economy of the district. Approximately 25,000 tons of freight pa was conveyed in or out of Bourne or from sidings within the Urban District. Agriculture was important, not only are raw materials necessary, but for distribution of the product. (They were *first* to desert railways. 25,000 tons equated to 80 tons per day - 40 in 40 out and would hardly keep two or three lorries occupied, much less one train. No mention was made of how much freight for the Council came in by road. Rail freight rates were also controlled with the NFU prominent among objectors to increases.  Councils objected to fares being increased when they trailed the RPI).
- They claimed, without advancing any evidence, that BR had not tried to attract traffic to the line and referred to traffic diverted off the line. (They were, perhaps, looking for traffic on *other* lines to be diverted to the M&GN, rather than attracting *new* local traffic, of which neither they, nor anyone, offered to contribute any).

*South Kesteven submission* :-

- Set out statistics of potato production and then admitted that virtually all went by road. Argued that BR should be able to get it back. Assumed if BR cut rates they will get all the traffic back. (They did not postulate a level of rates which would secure the traffic. Significantly, there was no offer to divert to rail at a reduced rate. There was no evidence that lorries would be scrapped, and quite obviously, if the traffic was attracted to rail, lorries would become unproductive)
- Sack hire influenced traffic to rail. (Much traffic in sacks went by road, making them difficult to trace. Independent consultants had recommended dropping sack hire).
- Rail transport was vital for sugar beet. (Only a small part went by rail, much at night, weekends and holiday periods - to give factories a reserve pool to draw on when the lorry flow dried up. Wagon detention was excessive).
- Railways are well equipped to handle cattle. It is an advantage to have them brought by rail to the local station. (Instead of lorries taking them direct, it would involve double transhipment. See below for their contradictory objection in the same written submission. They didn't explain why cattle had all transferred to road).
- If lorries are used to take freight a little further to a station because the local station is closed, traffic will go direct. The greatest single factor in the past has been the inability of railways to quote competitive rates. (Local Authority objections had held down fares so that freight traffic had to bear a bigger share of joint costs).

*Other submissions* :-

- East Elloe coal merchants association members had 40,000 tons pa, and claimed that "charges for solid fuel are 100% higher than other freight". (No evidence was tabled. Receipts per ton mile for coal was 11% *less* than for all other freight traffic in 1957 and 5% less in 1958). [BTC Accounts, Tables IX-8 & X-6]. A possible explanation for their belief was that coal factors - the middlemen between the NCB and merchants had inflated the price of coal and blamed BR for it.
- One coal merchant had a coal business with 700 tons pa by rail. (He didn't reveal how much was brought in by road. He was unlikely to survive on 700 tons pa).
- Another coal merchant had 3,126 tons pa at five depots. (one train load per depot pa).
- A timber merchant received hundreds of tons pa from Kings Lynn Docks to sidings at Sutton Bridge. (It was 5,000 tons pa. They were satisfied with an alternative route)
  *No mention was made of how much was by road.* (See reference to timber trade - page 97).
- A Bourne resident said: "many cross country lines serve sparse areas and this is one and cannot really be expected *ever* to pay its way. Each evening, I have got on the train a small number of people - three or four - have got on the 6.35 pm from Twenty to Bourne to spend the evening and return on the 9.5 pm".
- A corn merchant "had placed traffic on rail where it was a condition of delivery".

The TUCC meeting at Bourne on 27th October was attended by BR and the objectors - ten local authorities, four trade organisations, thirteen merchants, two individuals and the NUR. The objectors supplemented their written objections with oral presentations.

*BR responses and comments* :-

They repeated the principal points made at Peterborough and Norwich and added :-

- Responding to complaints about "vague figures", BR had given early notice but had no obligation to do so. When formal notice was given, it contained all the facts.
- Referring to a petition signed by 535 people, BR asked how many of them used the railway, particularly how many used it regularly? There was no answer. (There was probably an embarrassing shuffling of feet, and a sudden interest in the ceiling).
- Compared the small potato figures from a small number of farmers, and asked what of the others - a quarter of a million tons was available.
- Only 6% of sugar beet was sent to the Spalding factory last year by rail.
- The Clerk to Bourne RDC had said railways was a big factor in the economic life of the town, but on the figures, BR questioned that.
- Referring to criticism on the timing of the singling of Little Bytham - Bourne line, it was done in the light of what was known then. No apology was appropriate. All businesses made investments which at some later time did not pay off.
- Responding to references to a loss of service for passengers regularly travelling from Spalding to London, BR said it amounted to one or two passengers each year.

*Holland County Council* :-
- Did not propose to raise any very strong objections.

*Bourne UDC* :
- Agriculture and horticulture need speedy transport. They will lose some of their best markets. Wherry's have their own large road haulage fleet but dispatch approximately 800 tons pa by rail from Bourne and receive 60 tons pa. (Doesn't mention their road tonnage, which must have eclipsed this many times over. They were a big company which had once depended on rail. Even then, the line had financial problems).
- Mays send 350 tons pa and receive 50 tons. Moody nurseries despatch 40,000 chips watercress. It is true to say large consignments are sent by road, it is neither economical nor possible to convey small consignments to the smaller towns. Howard watercress send 12-15 tons pa. (No reference was made to the amount sent by road. It must have been very embarrassing to admit that large consignments went by road, having said that rail was essential. 40,000 chips was only 50 tons pa).
- Banks received 100 tons of seed potatoes in 1957, despatched 1,000 tons wheat in 1956*, despatched 250 tons wheat and 1,000 tons sugar beet in 1958. Stafford's sent ten tons pa. These tonnages are small but small firms are as much entitled to a service as large users. (Large firms weren't using the M&GN, except for inconvenient oddments. Companies with mega customers do not give Joe Bloggs the same service)

   .* *1956 was the year of the oil shortage due to the Suez invasion.*
- BR should use "one engine in steam" - it would save four or five signal boxes and three or four crossings on the Bourne-Billingborough line. (Why did he assume that railway managers had not thought of that, when they employed it at hundreds of locations throughout BR, not least in East Anglia. It smacked of grandmothers and

eggs. The same train had to return before another could use the route and involved stopping to open and close crossing gates. If it reduced, but did not *eliminate* loss, it was not an acceptable alternative).

- Rail traffic had increased recently and within the next 2-3 years additional tonnage would justify retention. (Or 20-30 years? They did not underwrite their prophecy).

- "£826,000 is a once and for all saving". (It included £0.5m wages plus other costs which would be incurred every single year in future, if the line remained open. Little wonder council costs always go up if they see wages economies as "once and for all").

- No alternative for reducing costs such as single line working has been considered. (How did they know what had been considered? They wanted speedy transits!)

- In any large undertaking it is necessary that services which are unremunerative should be subsidised by more remunerative services especially when the unremunerative services are essential to feed the main remunerative services. (I know no company which accepts losses on one product should be covered by profits from another. Unremunerative services couldn't support their own costs - how could they contribute to main lines? They lost the thread of the argument they were trying to make, for on the one hand they speak of unremunerative lines being subsidised by main lines and then try to claim the former feeds the latter!).

*South Kesteven RDC* :
- Severe winter conditions interfered with road traffic.
- Traffic received and forwarded to Billingborough in 1957 was 8,200 tons goods, 5,900 tons minerals and 5,300 tons coal, totalling 19,400 tons. (373 tons, or 25 wagons, per week - half a train load).
- *If* the export of machinery and motor cars continue at the same high rate, ironstone will be needed in large quantities for many years. *If* mining commenced south of Bourne the Bourne-Saxby line would be invaluable. *If* mining takes place in the Ashlocky area, the nearest railhead would be Billingborough. (Too many "if"s).
- Part of the Cohen committee's 2nd report dealt with BR: "There has been a tendency in recent discussions to lump together economies obtained by producing services more efficiently and economies obtained by abolishing services as though they were the same thing ... but from the point of view of the public, they are opposite things. Abolishing a service has the same effect as raising its price to a prohibitive level, with the convenient difference that no index number of the cost of living is affected". (The sentence was quoted out of context, and did not refer to BR - see page 225).

*Others* :-
- Various objectors raised the old standby used when all other objections are shown to be of little significance - "Defence considerations". (This had arisen twice in railway's 100 year history, and the Government did not feel obliged to pay anything approaching a fair price for the conveyance of its billions of tons of war traffic. Forty years after this closure, railways would still be carrying surplus under-used assets waiting for Government to sequestrate them for a third time for next to nothing).

- Sutton Bridge parish council claimed that all operating costs were wholly M&GN which was responsible for all working costs. (That was not the case. Train working costs incurred by Midlands depots were not debited to the M&GN. The principle of such transfer debits was not practical in pre-computer days. The M&GN had been credited with off line revenue which might be lost, but not debited with off line costs).

A Chamber of Commerce spokesman said : "As regards freight, he was satisfied with the efforts the BTC were making which were as satisfactory as could be under the circumstances. He had no complaints to make".

The Lincolnshire Road Car Co. had no hesitation in saying that the company had sufficient buses for diverted traffic and excursions.

It was noticeable that no offer was made by *any* business to revert their traffic to rail, nor by *any* local authority to insist on suppliers sending by rail to M&GN destinations. Nor did local authorities offer a penny towards the costs of services, although they would later happily subsidise buses, and *their* owners would not take kindly to allegations that such services were not unprofitable and didn't need a subsidy.

The TUCC Chairman said he was "impressed by the extent to which traffic had left the railways, rather than by the extent to which railways were proposing to leave the traffic. It was difficult to say how this trend was likely to stop or be reduced".

At a resumed meeting on 11th November, the Committee gave full consideration to the proposal as submitted by the BTC, to objections and to BTC responses thereto. BTC representatives said "The game was given away when someone talked about small consignments not being economical by road. That implied that the railway could have the small lots but the big lots would go by road. On possible ironstone deposits, the Iron & Steel Federation with whom BR had close contact did not object to the closure". After BTC representatives had withdrawn, the Committee agreed to approve the proposal as it affected the East Midlands area, subject to qualifications and agreed the following statement being given jointly with the East Anglia TUCC:-

> "The East Anglian TUCC and TUCC for East Midlands jointly agree to the proposal of the BTC to close the former M&GN line subject to certain provisions indicated in the two separate Reports of the two Committees"

The Reports of the two TUCC's embraced the following additional points:-
1. We approve the proposal to close the former M&GN line as submitted by the BTC on 16th September, subject to certain proposals.
2. We welcome the BTC decision to retain certain freight spurs.
3. Although withdrawal will cause inconvenience to certain individuals and places, alternative road transport provides reasonable alternatives and in some cases will be an improved service.
4. The last bus from Bourne to Spalding at 6.32pm would not be satisfactory, as the last train leaves at 9.15pm. The first bus from Spalding to Bourne at 9.32am deprives

early passengers. There should be fresh consultation between the local authorities, individuals and bus companies

5. Alternatives for passengers from the Midlands to the coast are reasonably adequate. The proposal to improve accommodation at Yarmouth Vauxhall is welcomed.

6. Regarding freight - we are satisfied that BR has made serious efforts to meet most of the problems likely to arise.

7. There is no evidence to support the contention that alleged new ironstone deposits in South Kesteven area are likely to lead to a considerable increase in demand for freight in the foreseeable future.

8. We welcome the BTC statement that there was no doubt about the statutory responsibility for the bridge at Sutton Bridge. It may be possible to double the road over the bridge. (It had a single railway line and a single road carriageway on it).

9. We are concerned about Bourne - population 5,000 - its prestige and importance will be affected by withdrawal.

10. We are impressed by freight traffic at Bourne and believe it might be considerably increased having regard to the closure of collection and delivery points in the area.

11. We believe Bourne should be retained as a freight railhead and that lines from Billingborough to Bourne and Bourne to Spalding should be retained as spurs. This is the only major proviso the Committee wish to make as affecting the East Midlands Committee. They feel it should be a condition of their approval of the proposal.

12. Retention of these spurs will be a challenge to users and BR to ensure an increase in rail freight. Further retention will, of course, depend on users. (*Use it or lose it*).

13. Some farmers and coal merchants were concerned about loading docks constructed at their expense being rendered useless by closure. Problems can be avoided by retention of the freight spurs, If there are others the BTC should negotiate compensation.

14. Thanks are expressed to the BTC, Lincolnshire Road Car Co. and Eastern Counties Omnibus Co. for efforts to ease the task by offering alternative facilities, which are generally satisfactory.

TUCC-East Midlands minutes for 1st December record that South Kesteven Council had expressed appreciation of the TUCC's consideration of the question.

## CTCC Recommendation

By mid November, the TUCC's had approved closure. On 25th November the CTCC confirmed closure, all in ten weeks. [BTC 1958 Report, Para. 9]. (Ten weeks losses = £0.12m).

Objectors presented cases sensibly and moderately in welcome contrast to some exaggerated attacks in the past on the capacity and honesty of the BTC. [CTCC 1958 Report, Para. 35]

## Post Inquiry Comment

The secretary of North Walsham Chamber of Trade & Commerce said : "As a body of businessmen we cannot object to any organisation closing down any unprofitable section of its business, we would ourselves adopt the same course". [Eastern Daily News 13.11.58].

In contrast, the secretary of Aylsham Chamber of Trade & Commerce spoke of the difficulties which would be faced should a stoppage or reduction of oil supplies upset road transport. [Eastern Daily News 13.11.58]. This is the attitude which left railways without traffic - to regard them as a standby. Since the 1939-45 war, there had been no interruption to oil supplies except that precipitated by the 1956 invasion of Suez by Anglo-French armies. The next such occurrence might be 100 years coming.

The chairman of Stalham Parish council referred to hitting agriculture and many who have relied on rail transport. He said that any body should lay the facts before an independent committee or tribunal composed of people affected by the decision! If you can't carry on a business successfully, you should get out and let someone who can, do the job. [Eastern Daily News 13.11.58]. BR had just laid the facts before an independent body and were now getting out, but there were no offers to buy up the line. This was a new definition of "independent" - usually it is taken to mean having no pecuniary or beneficial interest. Agriculture had been among the first to desert railways for the motor vehicle.

Erpingham RDC referred to the "widely held view that the line could be operated at a profit", and claimed that figures were not produced by BR. [North Norfolk News 2.1.59]. It was not a view shared by Norfolk County Council and others represented by a QC at the Inquiry. Figures were, of course, produced by BR - and scores of copies of the comprehensive booklet were sent out to local authorities and other organisations. The figures were referred to several times by the TUCC, BR and objectors at the Inquiries. RDC's and other councils faced no public inquiry to judge their performance, and certainly no objectors led by a QC. The RDC produced no figures for its claim.

At the East Anglian TUCC meeting on 13th January, reference was made to a request by Walsingham RDC for an inquiry into the running of the line. Mr. Easton said that an inquiry would ensure that confidence in the TUCC and the unbiased way in which it operated would be restored. The chairman said : "if confidence was lost if it did not agree with everyone an intolerable state of affairs would be reached. We are independent. All interests are represented. If they want a committee appointed which will only agree with their point of view, then that is not an unbiased committee. People are assuming that our job is to get the maximum facilities for one section of the community without reference to its effects on other sections or the BTC. That is wrong". [Eastern Daily Press 14.1.59].

### Postscript

The line closed on 28th February 1959.

At Peterborough 200 people packed the platform on the last day. [Rhodes, Page 40]. (Nearly half of the normal level for the whole line!). As a postscript to the promise of improved bus services, and underlining that perhaps the railway was not as vital in the late 1950's as some suggested, a substitute bus service from Melton Mowbray to Spalding, following very closely the route of the M&GN, had from the start run into difficulties because of poor patronage. On the first day the 7.50 am bus left Spalding with only five people on board and these got off before Bourne was reached. The return trip later in the morning arrived at Spalding with only one passenger. After warnings in the press that this could not continue the service eventually ceased in the early 1960's. [Rhodes, Page 46]

The Tongue End-Spalding bus service introduced when M&GN closed, was poorly used. The Eastern Counties Omnibus Co. had met local authorities and agreed a journey on market day in Spalding. The local authority was not pursuing an objection to withdrawal of Monday-Friday bus services. The Saturday service was unaltered. [TUCC - East Midlands 15.7.59]. Aside from this item, the minutes of both TUCC's contained no reference to correspondence from users regarding the operation of alternative services, suggesting that fears that they would be inadequate were not substantiated.

If bus companies operate loss making services as a result of a council objection, local authorities know that they will have to pick up the tab, unlike losses on railways, where BR had to fund the loss. Hence councils objected more vociferously to BR closures, because it was a "no-lose" situation. The cessation of a bus service was equally inconvenient to users - if not more so.

"We must agree that we have insufficiently patronised our 'Joint'". We have largely forsaken it, so economies decree that it now forsakes us. [Lynn News & Advertiser 27.2.59].

In 1959, BR secured planning approval to connect the former Central Norfolk section of the GER, west of Wroxham, with the former M&GN line from Melton Constable to Norwich City in the vicinity of a village called Temelthorpe. This cut the distance for coal traffic from 64 miles to 40 miles to give access to the extensive coal yards at Norwich City station. It saved 100,000 miles pa. According to the Eastern Daily News, there had been a proposal almost 60 years earlier to connect Thorpe and City stations via Cathedral Close, but it was defeated by the Dean and Chapter. The new link became operational in September 1960. [M.J. Clark, Railway World Special]

The line originated as the South Durham & Lancashire Union Railway, and was completed in 1861, from two junctions with the NER at Darlington and West Auckland and crossed the Pennines at Stainmore Pass, joining the L&NWR at Tebay. At the same time, the Eden Valley line was constructed from Kirkby Stephen to Eden Valley Junction, four miles south of Penrith. The lines comprised 28 miles of double and 27 miles of single line. [BR Memo, York TUCC T/203].

Teesside ironworks were obliged to obtain ore from Ulverston in Cumberland via Leeds & Normanton. Completion of the Darlington & Barnard Castle Railway opened up the prospect of a direct link with Ulverston, launching the South Durham & Lancashire Union Railway in 1856 to link the Stockton & Darlington with the Lancaster & Carlisle Railway at Tebay in Westmoreland. The railway encountered little opposition. The line needed new locos to cope with the severe gradients. It opened for mineral traffic on 4th July, 1861. The Eden Valley Railway provided a line from Clifton to the south of Penrith to Kirkby Stephen. It opened on 8th April 1862 when it began to feed ore from Whitehaven through to Teesside via the South Durham & Lancashire Union Railway. [Kirby, Pages 160-162 & 171]. The lack of opposition probably indicated little prospect of profit.

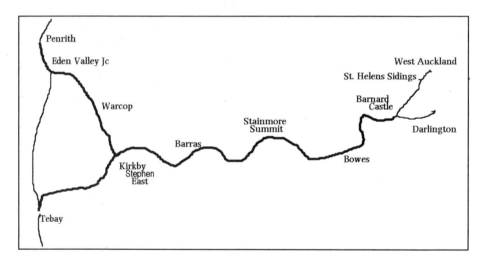

### Closure Proposals

The proposed withdrawal of passenger and re-routing of freight trains on the Barnard Castle - Penrith route was considered by two TUCC's on twelve occasions, and the CTCC on four occasions, over two years. Objectors said re-routing freight was not in customers' best interests, but the customers said they were satisfied!

"The line was built in the 1860's to carry freight. Passenger services served the sparse population, but never at any time were these run at a profit, and by 1960 were losing £25,000 pa". [CTCC 1961 Report, Para. 28].

The London Midland and North Eastern Regions made a joint submission to the BTC on 30th June 1959 to close the line. On 2nd October, the BTC approved the proposal to withdraw services and recover track and redundant assets. [PRO: AN116/5].

"When the BTC submitted its proposal, it did not say if the line was running at a loss or a profit. It came out that it was probably profitable, but that more profit could be made and substantial economies achieved by diverting freight traffic". [North East TUCC meeting 9.12.60]. *(That was standard private sector practice).*

On 3rd December, BR sent out 123 copies of a 28 page Memo setting out details of its proposed closure of the line between Barnard Castle and Penrith/Tebay. It stated that DMU's had been introduced on the route in January 1958 to improve the finances of a passenger service which was known to be unremunerative. This had reduced costs and there had been an increase in receipts of £1,400, but this had not been maintained in 1959. There were three passenger trains each way. The average number of passengers joining and alighting daily at stations varied between one and 56. The heavier totals were at stations at either end of the line, those en route were largely in single figures.

Freight traffic can use alternative routes. Through traffic would be routed via Newcastle and Carlisle or Northallerton and Skipton. Due to a ruling gradient of 1 in 57, double heading of, and assistance to freight trains was necessary, making loco working expensive and difficult, especially in the winter. Apart from through summer passenger traffic, the principal reason for the continued existence of the line was the movement of coke from Co. Durham to Barrow in Furness and Millom steelworks. Volume had declined in the past year, coke being obtained from alternative sources in Yorkshire, and due to a fall off in the demand by steelworks. Eastbound freight was mainly limestone. The through freight would pass via Newcastle and Carlisle. The ruling gradient via the alternative route was 1 in 96. Little of the Stainmore route was better than 1 in 98, whilst the alternative was mainly of 1 in 240 or better. Track would be recovered.

*Forecast Savings* :-

After allowing for the loss of passenger and freight traffic of £19,000, savings would be £103,000. No credit was taken for repairs due on the permanent way and signalling west of Kirkby Stephen as data was not readily available nor for removal of bridges although this is likely to be substantial. Apart from annual savings, recovery of redundant assets will realise a credit of £257,000. In addition, closure of the motive power depot at Kirkby Stephen will avoid capital expenditure of £45,000 on the provision of a new roof and staff amenities, Capital of £9,000 is required at Millom to cater for traffic arriving via Carlisle.

## Objections to Closure

Objections were sent to the TUCC for Yorkshire and the TUCC for the North West from individuals, companies, trade associations, 55 local authorities and several others.

*The MP for Bishop Auckland*

- "There is a greater number of fatalities on road than rail". (The MoT Directive on the preparation of BR Accounts made no provision for BR to take credit for fewer deaths)
- "Closure should be deferred and reviewed in three years time". (No suggestion was made as to who would cover the losses over the next three years. The method of

accounting meant that these social costs would simply inflate BR losses, for which, needless to say, BR, not Parliament, was criticised).

- "One million tons of coal was not moved in the last quarter of 1959 due to wagon shortage". (The imbalance between summer and winter meant that BR had to store tens of thousands of coal wagons for months at enormous cost. In the Sheffield Division, we had to store around 7,000 each summer, as did other Divisions. We knew that tonnage was grounded at collieries because of altered orders, poor quality coal, insufficient wagons being ordered or congestion at consignee's sidings. I blew apart NCB claims on coal not moved, when I pointed out, in 1980, that weekly totals of coal not moved should not be aggregated over a year, because it was being counted again and again. When coal was not moved this week, wagon orders were adjusted to reflect current production plus arrears. The tonnage not moved in a year, was that which was not moved in the final week of the year. Wagon turnround by industry was a disgrace. It was common to give priority to unloading lorries before rail wagons. Ministers could have directed the NCB and industry to modernise facilities to handle larger wagons but that would have reduced jobs in those industries).

*Kirkby Stephen Chamber of Trade* :-

- There would be a loss of employment of 100 railway staff. (Chambers of trade or commerce do not call on unprofitable private sector companies to remain open to maintain employment).
- Passenger services might have paid their way if properly timed. Not satisfied railways had tried to attract business and alleged an early morning train from Kirkby Stephen and a late train from Darlington had not been tried out.

    *BR told the TUCC that such trains had been experimented with and withdrawn due to poor use.*

*Lake District Hotels & Catering Association* :-

- "If private industry displayed the same lack of energy or initiative, the nation as a whole would be in the same state as BR". (UK hoteliers had no room to criticise *anyone* given the drift of holidaymakers to Europe and elsewhere - clear evidence of a lack of initiative. Why had hoteliers not halved rates to attract tourists and created or sponsored entertainment? This may have increased rail travel).

*Westmoreland County Council* :-

- "The future of railways is about to receive the highest Government consideration". (They had been saying this since 1928, and had done nothing, enabling hauliers to cream-off rail traffic. Legislation requiring BR to plead in a Law Court for permission to increase prices to match inflation fuelled by suppliers was the last straw).

*Appleby and Penrith councils*:-

- "Three trains per day with an average of not less than 30 wagons, *assuming* an average of 13 tons per wagon = 365,040 tons pa. *Assuming* an average of 25 shillings (£1.25) per ton, the *through* freight traffic would earn £456,000 pa". (They confused this with profit, because they did not quote costs which would be heavy due to the steep gradients. They did not identify the source of their *assumed* charge. Coal, coke and mineral traffic - the traffic on this line - was conveyed at rates well below average. Average receipts per ton for all freight was below £1, the average for coal & coke was £0.73, and minerals £0.81. [BTC 1960 Accounts Table IX-8]. Their annual tonnage equates to three trains per day, 312 days pa. BR did not work freight on bank holidays or a full freight service on Saturdays. The service was based on spreading tonnage over 5-5$\frac{1}{2}$ days. Collieries and much of industry worked only a five day week).

*Ramblers Association* :-

- Losses could be ***avoided*** by using bigger locos or diesels. (They didn't guarantee to use the line en masse out of season, nor make one extra annual journey. They wrongly assumed that freight customers should subsidise passengers. A diesel would still haul more via Carlisle. There were too few diesels to haul expresses - See page 218. West Coast expresses got them in 1961 - See Cumberland & Westmoreland Herald, 11.2.61)

*Other objections* :-

- "It was BR's fault for putting fares up". (As if other UK prices were in a 1940's time warp. In 1958, the average fare was **6%** over 1948. The RPI had risen **47%**. BR fares were **41** points behind! Every increase sought was delayed and reduced by the Transport Tribunal, so that the change was minuscule, and the delay catastrophic - a fact pointed out and criticised in 1960 by the MoT's Advisory Group, - the "Stedeford Committee" - composed of top private sector people. Rail fares were 14% below bus fares for a journey which was 29% faster! [Cumberland & Westmoreland Herald, 21.1.61]).

    For Stedeford views & fares/RPI data see "*Blueprints for Bankruptcy*", Pages 42 & 63.

- "Diversion of freight over a longer route would cost more".

    *BR explained that the alternative route had easier gradients, hence payloads were higher.*
    (Motorways are used rather than the shortest route because gradients are easier and journeys quicker).

- "There was a strong case for a subsidy, and the line should be kept open until Parliament decided to pay subsidies". (It came seven years later. Users and objectors - who are not necessarily the same - held back from underwriting losses until then).

- "Connections were poor at both ends of the line". (Clearly they thought that this line should be the start point for timing all main line trains throughout the UK, because that is the only way in which good connections could have been made at both ends).

Perhaps the most ingenuous objector was the one who, by claiming that people could travel by bus over a wide area, and then by train managed to extrapolate the potential population in the area around the line, from the actual few thousand to two million. He had not realised that the main thrust of objections was that people would not do that.


## Other Views

One member of the TUCC set out to "gain knowledge of the line by using it extensively week by week". He found that between Barnard Castle and Penrith on each occasion the train was empty but for himself and sometimes one other.

Another member pointed out that freight going via Carlisle was, in some cases, arriving 2-3 hours earlier than it did on the Tebay branch. He did not think firms would lose by diversion, but would find it an advantage.

## TUCC Initial Inquiry

A joint meeting of the TUCC's for the North West and North East Areas took place at Carlisle on 24th February 1960. Among the objectors present were seven local authorities, two hotel associations and two trade associations. Three of the councils were represented by a barrister. TUCC papers reveal that one objector was "verbose and always asking for five minutes more".

A solicitor for the Hotels & Caterers Association said that no steps had been taken to encourage the use of the line. (That was it! The TUCC's files show that they advanced no evidence to substantiate this claim. BR was guilty until proved innocent. This reversal of basic principles did not even apply at Nuremberg. The Association did not offer discounts to customers travelling by rail - to demonstrate real support for rail services). The TUCC's were told, "that last year, 186 of the visitors to one of the smaller hotels came from the east coast area, but it was not possible to identify the means of travel". (A more useless piece of 'evidence' would be difficult to conceive. They did not even reveal which *part* of the east coast they came from and whether around Newcastle or south of York. It is unclear why they could produce figures for only one hotel. All must have registers showing car registrations. By deduction, they would have known how many came by public transport. Little wonder, UK hotels lost business if they did not keep records of the source of their clientele. How else could they determine which areas to target with publicity?). They mentioned that "there were 56 passengers to Keswick over the Eden Valley line on 1st August". The TUCC Chairman pointed out that this was one bus load and suggested that the hotel industry might provide one. Their solicitor replied that "if they started running buses they would be up against certain difficulties, and it was outside the terms of reference of the Inquiry". (Supermarkets provide buses for customers. It is noticeable that, in reports and criticisms of BR closures, remarks such as this which infer that critics had no room to talk were rarely published. When BR was criticised, nothing was deemed outside the terms of reference, but when the criticism was turned back on objectors, it was a different matter - see reference to farmers on page 71).

A chamber of trade spokesman said the loss was not large when it came to keeping the line open. (In that case, why did councils not make up the loss? With a catchment area of two million population claimed, it would be a few pence per head. Chambers of trade are not noted for keeping loss making businesses afloat, when "the loss was not large")

An objector speaking on behalf of a trades council, said that he felt the railway did pay. The line did pay - with freight traffic on it, subsidising sparse passenger traffic, but freight operating costs could be reduced by re-routing the through freight traffic. The passsenger service could not then support the infrastructure costs. (*Such action was precisely analogous to the private sector practice of factory rationalisation*).

Yet another amateur pitched in an idea to reduce the cost of freight train working. "Two locos are required to haul 24 wagons over Stainmore, whilst BR said one would haul 34 via Carlisle. By replacing one of the two locos by a class 9, 50 wagons could be taken forward from the top of Stainmore". (Assuming that his facts were right, to get 50 wagons, would require two trains of 24 to be combined, plus two off a third train. As there were three trains per day, 22 wagons of the third train would have to stand overnight, to be made up to 50, by 24 off one train and four off the next. Delaying wagons in this way would not be welcomed by the industries concerned. The theorist presupposes that a similar technique at the summit on the alternative route would not produce even bigger loads. He overlooked that the Kirkby Stephen turntable was too small for a class 9).

The two TUCC's decided that :-
- Complete closure of the line be postponed and reconsidered in eighteen months.
- The DMU service to continue.
- Practicability of freight diversion should be proved for 12 months.
- BR to increase efforts to attract tourists.

Their reasons for the Decision:-
1. Whilst accepting that there was a financial case for closure, they noted the strength and volume of the opposition.
2. The existence of Iron & Steel company traffic.
3. Probable industrial developments.
4. The potential for travellers from the rapidly expanding Teesside to the Lakes.
5. The wind of change which is becoming apparent in Government policy, both in regard to railways and the provision of transport in rural areas could not be ignored.
   *"The BTC believe that they misinterpreted the Government's attitude on this question as represented by the Prime Minister's recent speech"*. [PRO: AN155/208].

It is amazing that they could see increased *summer* loadings as the solution to round the year losses, when the problem was the poor loadings outside the summer peak - tourists were conspicuous by their absence in the winter. Local authorities and hoteliers should have been pressured to attract off-season tourists. Regrettably, a "rapidly expanding Teesside" was more likely to produce travellers to "the Lakes" in Europe or the USA. "Probable industrial developments" were always seen as something which should influence BR to hang on in there - it never influenced any private sector company which was feeling the pinch. This decision was out of touch with commercial reality. No calculation was made as to how many passengers would be required, and at what fares, in order to break even. It was an ill founded judgement.

## CTCC Review

The CTCC considered the case on 10th May, [CTCC min. 990], both TUCC chairmen were present. It concluded that the freight should be diverted and passenger traffic retained until the two Area Committees were satisfied that a satisfactory service could be maintained via Carlisle. If, and when, a satisfactory service could be demonstrated to the satisfaction of the Committee, the passenger service from Barnard Castle to Penrith should be withdrawn and the line closed. The TUCC's informed the objectors of this decision in June 1960.

Barnard Castle UDC wrote to the CTCC on 5th July : "We object to the closure - residents are to be denied the train service to which they feel they are entitled". They meant, of course, at subsidised fares, as they made no offer to pay more or travel more. As we all know to our cost, Councils will quickly tell residents that if they want a service to which they feel entitled, the rates - or taxes - will go up. (See Appendix C)

## Media Reports

A local MP said that the line was of great economic and military significance. [Yorkshire Post, 25.2.60]. (In that case, the Minister of Defence should have contributed to the cost of retaining the route. There was no prospect of that. Cabinet Minutes in March 1951 show that, after the war, when rail fares were held down well below the rate of inflation for electoral reasons, the Chancellor advocated that the BR should be relieved of the £3m pa cost of subsidising fares of HM Forces. The Minister of Defence objected and no action was taken). The MP asked the Minister of Defence "if he will reassess the military importance of BR to the Service Departments, with a view to estimating what capital and current costs they should contribute to the BTC in respect of services needs". The Minister replied "No, BR will recover £13m from the Ministry for the Defence role". [Hansard, vol. 617, col. 430]. BR did not recover money for the "*defence role*", but for conveying men and materials at the sub standard charges imposed on them by law and Government policy.

W.E. Sayer, a haulier, offered to lease the line, confident that it could make a profit He proposed to rent it for a year, using BR rolling stock with BR paying for traffic delivered between Penrith and Darlington. He did not believe that the diverted freight can be carried at the same rate. He could run the line with less staff and use two or three powerful diesel locos to replace steam locos. He offered to manage the line without pay to prove it could make a profit. [Cumberland & Westmoreland Herald, 13.8.60]. He ignored the cost of diesels and costs of fitting automatic brakes to wagons. His theory was flawed. (See Appendix A.5).

BR wrote to the TUCC that "diesel locos had problems controlling loads on falling gradients". Consequently, it was necessary to fit large numbers of wagons with automatic brakes.

Moreover, we, on BR, were aware that the economies forecast from diesel locos would not be realised if we used them on lines which did not operate around the clock. If locos worked on other lines, they could not all be used at other times on three shift lines. Diesels were more expensive, and a major factor in their adoption was that they did not have to spend as much time out of service as steam, leading to fewer locos being required. If they weren't used to maximum availability, they would be uneconomic. Diesel locos for freight working were only just coming into operation on main routes. Even some main line passenger services were still steam hauled. This line was years down the list, without doubt, after the three shifted Newcastle-Carlisle line. (See page 218 for size of diesel fleet).

## Freight Diversion

On 17th March 1960, the CTCC wrote to the TUCC's: "Losses after freight diversion will still be £36,000, which is not a frightening figure". (Not if someone else funds it. This attitude undermines allegations that the CTCC was in BR's pocket. See page 57).

In May 1960, the Chairman of the North East TUCC told the CTCC that a £36,000 loss to the BTC was not an excessive insurance to ensure blast furnaces are not closed. He did not think that the working of traffic via Carlisle had been sufficiently studied by BR. A member of the CTCC said that they should let BR try and if the customer was satisfied, then that would be OK. The CTCC Chairman said it was the TUCC who had to be satisfied! The CTCC agreed to recommend that if BR could maintain a satisfactory freight service, the passenger service could be withdrawn. [CTCC Minutes, 10th May 1960]. (If £36,000 was not excessive to protect the steel industry, then it was for them, not BR, to fund, otherwise they would receive a hidden subsidy).

BR wrote to the TUCC's on 30th May that freight diversions would begin on 4th July. They pointed out that the effects of snow are felt much more on the Penrith than the Carlisle route. 75% of freight traffic was in train loads. [BR memo to TUCC's 25.2.61, & min 742].

In due course, BR wrote "The transit times of diverted freight are mainly much better than before. Every person engaged in transport knows that the shortest distance between two places is not necessarily the quickest nor the most economic".

A report said that "a meeting was taking place between BR and the haulier today". [Cumberland & Westmoreland Herald 27.8.60]. The TUCC papers included a letter from BR which explained that the greater load via the alternative route had resulted in fewer engine miles than was necessary over the much steeper Stainmore route.

Sir Hedworth Williamson Limeworks wrote: "On the whole, we feel that the new system is workable". A note from the North East TUCC chairman to the secretary stated that he had expected them to say the diversion was a failure, but this was not the case.

W.E. Sayer wrote to the TUCC that diverting freight traffic would incur all traffic in an additional 100 miles. He went on to relate what he *claimed* the total traffic was, and then applied to it 2d per ton, not merely on the traffic, but also on the tare weight of empties. Customers did not pay for empty mileage, charges were only for loaded miles. He wrote that his traffic over the line totalled 3,000 tons per week. [See also Appendix A.5]

In response to a request from the TUCC, BR replied: The claim about increased mileage is wrong - *none* is subject to 100 miles, the highest is 90 miles and the lowest is 30 miles. His calculations are therefore invalidated. BR has never made a secret of the fact that train and wagon miles will be greater, but engine miles will fall. Trials have proved that transits are no worse, and often better. There is no additional cost, but there is a saving arising from reduced engine miles. In a later letter to the TUCC, Sayer replaced his reference to 100 miles, by 90 miles. (That was the maximum, not the average).

On 18th October, the County Borough of Darlington wrote to the North East TUCC expressing fears of increased freight rates due to the diversion of traffic. BR's reply to the TUCC's request for an answer was: "The BTC has explained that the unit of cost in train working is the engine miles, and loads which can be hauled via Newcastle & Carlisle by one loco are about double those via Kirkby Stephen. Fewer engine miles would be required to work traffic via the alternative route, despite the increased mileage. Rates are based on competitive commercial considerations and closing of this line would not alter the competitive position with regard to road transport".

Durham Steel & Iron Co. wrote to the TUCC on 20th October 1960 that railways have agreed not to increase rates due to the increased mileage.

The County Borough of Darlington wrote to the North East TUCC on 25th October: "I assure you that I appreciate your position and I should be happy for you to ignore the flatulent objections that we have made on the subject of freight traffic. There really is no substance in them. I am obliged to put them forward because a particular member of my Council keeps hammering the question. He has no evidence that would stand up for half a minute and I have the greatest difficulty in persuading him to that effect. There may be some substance in our observation about passenger traffic, but, of course, I cannot prove that, it is purely a subjective impression".

Kirkby Stephen Chamber of Trade claimed that BR had said two locos were required to pull 22 trucks via Stainmore as against 34 via Carlisle. According to BR's Instruction Book the load of two class 4 locos over Stainmore is 27 not 22. BR told the TUCC that the chamber's memo was headed "Loading of limestone", but BR comments on loads referred to east-west coke. For this traffic the two engine load stated on 9th December to be 22 via Stainmore and 34 via Carlisle is correct. They refer to 27 standard wagons, but a calculation had to be made to convert this to coke traffic, which reduced it to 22. The two engine load from Kirkby Stephen to St. Helens was 18 wagons limestone, while with the assistance of a banker for 13 miles, from Carlisle the single engine load via Carlisle-Newcastle is 32. There is no need for additional wagons, because the transit time is no greater. No excessive payments are made to crews compared to the previous route.

"BR began freight diversions on 4th July. They are now operating satisfactorily and we consider the passenger services should be withdrawn. Savings are estimated at £36,000 after allowing £19,000 loss of receipts". [North West TUCC letter to North East TUCC 6.11.60]

On 21st November, the North West TUCC replied to a letter from W.M.F. Vane, MP, "The statement that the diversion of freight traffic is now satisfactory is not based solely on the view expressed by BR. I already hold a letter from Sir Hedworth Williamson's Limeworks to that effect, and both I and the North East TUCC have other letters from freight users on both sides of the Pennines expressing similar views".

On 22nd December, a memo noted: The TUCC's have carefully considered the evidence offered by the BTC and are satisfied that the diversion of freight traffic has proved satisfactory to the industries concerned with the bulk of the traffic. All major firms are satisfied with services. The Stainmore route at 1,480 ft above sea level is the highest in England. Not only had transits in general shown an improvement, but some 100,000 engine hours pa had been saved.

On 22nd March, the TUCC asked Sayer for details of delayed consignments. They repeated their letter on 10th April. Three days later, they received a reply giving details in the form of advice notes from Consett Iron Works. BR investigated and found that they were not complaints, but notifications that certain wagons had, notwithstanding arrival, not so far been drawn from the Standage Pool* and in accordance with standard practice, not paid for by consignees. Both Consett Iron Co. and Dorman Long have written to the BTC saying they have no complaints on delay. The service is as good as, if not better, than before. The TUCC wrote to Sayer on 22nd April asking, if in view of above, he still maintains allegations of delay. A reply is still awaited. It was never received.

*The basis of Standage schemes was that customers did not pay detention on individual wagons, but on the total number in the pool. Hence, wagons could be called forward, out of sequence, by them without paying detention charges, provided that the clearance rate was adequate.

The records of Dorman Long - a major freight customer - show that there has been no deterioration and in many cases a very substantial improvement. Delays which have occurred were local to the Teesside area. Consett Iron Co. had reported that transits are about the same, and that they do not object to diversion. [CTCC letter 27.4.61].

Consett Iron Co. wrote to BR on 29th May, with a copy to the TUCC, : "As I have said previously, the transits you are giving us are satisfactory by the new route. On occasions, we are not able to pay sender's accounts because owing to necessary accumulation of stock at Consett, it sometimes happens that wagons that have arrived here in reasonable time, have not taken their proper turn in tipping. Until a wagon is tipped and tared it is not our practice to pay accounts. Mr Sayer is not correct in assuming that non arrival of wagons from Warcop can always be considered as complaints of delay to traffic".

Kirkby Stephen & District Chamber of Trade wrote on 29th September 1961 to the MoT that they knew that Sir Hedworth Williamson's Limeworks had not made any strong objection to the closure, but would be far happier if the proposal was not implemented. (The Company had not told the TUCC Inquiry this, indeed they had said that they were satisfied with the new arrangements. Hitherto, they had spoken for themselves).

Dr Ashby of the Ramblers Association, wrote to the MoT that he "had checked freight train loads with railway staff concerned and claimed the load was 27 heavy wagons not 22 eastbound". [PRO: MT115/255]. (One can understand him not quoting names, but he could *without risk* have given their grades. Most staff did not understand the load book because they did not need to. There was no copy of the relevant pages of the book. As each member of the staff who had to apply the provisions of the book had a personal copy, there would have been no problem. Anyone who 'lost' his book would have been given a replacement). BR explained the 27>22 conversion to the MoT. (See page 139).

In September 1961, Dr Ashby wrote to the TUCC that a railway official had told him that the whole basis of train loads had been destroyed because in August 1960, regulations were changed to allow heavier locos via Stainmore. The letter was passed to BR, who replied that he had "once again based extended arguments on a misunderstanding of the facts. The instructions were amended in July 1958, and the calculations on diversion were related to that, although the heaviest locos were not actually used because of the limitations of turntable size. Whilst diesels would increase the load via Stainmore, they would do so likewise via Carlisle, which route being three shifted gives better utilisation. There were difficulties in braking loose coupled trains on severe gradients which would further widen the margin between train loads on the two routes. The details were set out in a comprehensive memo which was presented to the TUCC's at the Leeds meeting".

None of the critics had the grace to admit that freight diversion did work.

### More Objections

Penrith UDC wrote to the TUCC that they intend to support Appleby Borough in any action they may take to keep the line open. They said that a rail excursion last Sunday from Darlington to Penrith had only twelve passengers, and there were no advertisements except handbills on stations. [North East TUCC 3.8.60, min 765]. Neither council mentioned *increased user* of the line among "any action they may take".

In response to a request from the TUCC, BR replied: The train was not an excursion, but a normal Sunday service on 19th June. Excursion bookings were available on the train. Publicity was given in the Northern Echo, Northern Dispatch, Northern Daily Mail, and Middlesbrough Evening Gazette; on posters on stations in Darlington, Marske, Middlesbrough, Stockton, West Hartlepool; handbills were distributed to clubs, hotels and factories and placed on stations in the area. They were also placed at Kirkby Stephen and Appleby, and distributed to clubs, institutes and put on station blackboards. The TUCC informed Penrith Council, no apology was received in reply.

Boyden wrote that the TUCC "should not recommend closure until Government plans for subsidies had been worked out. *If* only part of the proffered advice proved effective, the loss would be considerably less. Development of alternative industries was essential". Hitherto, Government had opposed subsidies for loss making branch lines which they had required BR to keep open. Against opposition, the Labour Government introduced subsidies eight years later. Boyden was admitting that the line would still lose money *if* the unqualified advice was implemented and *if* it proved to be effective.

Boyden asked the MoT if he would consult industrial and other organisations to plan greater co-ordination of rail & road transport so that traffic can be diverted from the most dangerous roads. He replied: Transport by road is a more convenient way of taking traffic door to door, which is the attraction rather than the cost. [Hansard vol. 616, col. 974 3.2.60].

In 1956, the MoT, to justify freezing only rail prices which were already trailing the inflation rate, in a feeble 'explanation' of the meaning of *enlightened private enterprise*, said price was important. He never mentioned "door to door". Road transport was more attractive because UK industry is formed in such small units that bulk conveyance was irrelevant. Had industry merged into the groups which international experts advocated, rail transit would have been imperative to avoid nose to tail lorry convoys. UK industry did not do so, and industry became uneconomic and vanished. Indeed Government worsened the problem by subsidising industry to fragment production and locate in areas of high unemployment.

Boyden asked: "Will the Minister give a direction to the BTC to consult with the Board of Trade and Minister of Defence as to the economic and strategic importance of lines being considered for closure and to obtain from them estimates of the economic value of such lines to their respective Departments". The MoT was brief: "No, Sir". Boyden persisted: "Does the BTC inform the Minister of Defence of proposed closures". MoT: "All Ministries are informed and can object if they so wish". [Hansard vol. 616, col. 990, 3.2.60]

Boyden asked the Minister of Defence if he would re-assess the military importance of BR to the Service Departments with a view to estimating, in conjunction with the BTC, what capital and current costs the Service Departments should contribute to the BTC in respect of service needs. The Minister replied: "No, Sir". [Hansard vol. 617, col. 430, 10.2.60]

Boyden presented petitions signed by 2,000 members of six organisations to the MoT. As representatives of 1m people they fear closure will cause damage, hardship and deprivation. [Hansard vol. 645, col. 1115]. No reference was made of guarantees to make increased use of the line. Given a million people, the cost of keeping the line would have been a few pence per head, but the local authorities did not propose to provide that sum.

Boyden also wrote to the MoT that a number of objectors "who know the working of the line intimately have made many suggestions to cut costs. *If* only part of the advice proved effective, the loss would be considerably less". [PRO: MT115/255]. No details of the cost cutting measures were enclosed with the letter. The loss would not be eliminated, but reduced *if* the advice proved effective. Needless to say, there was no offer to back this unsolicited advice with a wager equal to the continuing losses whilst their experiment was tried out. Nor did he say who was to carry the burden of the residual loss.

Boyden tried again to get Government to keep the line open, asking: "Will Government offer a subsidy. Before diversion of freight, revenue was £378,000 and costs £418,000. Given economy, enterprise and *a better steel and coal trade*, the £40,000 deficit could be considerably reduced. Government is spending millions on a subsidy on a Cunard liner, surely, they can invest a few thousands on maintaining and improving this line". [Hansard, vol. 643, cols. 1202-08, 3.7.61]. The Minister did not agree. The MP was now saying that retention needed heavy industry to pick up. A year earlier, the huge Consett Iron & Steel company said that it was working at full capacity! [Northern Echo, 10.8.60].

### TUCC Public Meeting at Newcastle

In consequence of freight diversion which had produced economies, BR tabled a Memo at the meeting on 9th December, setting out the revised situation. It stated that £36,000 could be saved by withdrawing the passenger service and closing the line. In addition £70,000 renewals expenditure would be avoided in the next five years, and £257,000 realised from recovery of track etc. If the line had been singled, closure would produce £30,000 pa savings, £50,000 renewals savings and £159,000 recoveries. Figures had not been adjusted to reflect a recent wage increase and a fares increase. (They would show the gap had widened because wages rose by a greater percentage than fares. Government had set up a wages inquiry which recommended that wages go up by 8-10%. Their Court of Law had limited the average fare rise to 7%. when it was trailing the RPI by 30 points).

A TUCC memo dated 22nd December 1960 stated that the TUCC's are satisfied that the diversion of freight traffic has proved satisfactory to the industries concerned. All major firms are satisfied with the service. Not only had transits in general shown an improvement, but some 100,000 engine hours pa had been saved. They concluded that BR have proved the case that there is insufficient potential to justify retention of the passenger services on financial grounds. They recommended that the passenger service be withdrawn at an early date to coincide with improved bus services. They realised that user on a few summer weekends is not nearly sufficient to cover the costs for the year. (This should have been obvious from the beginning). The North West TUCC considered this memo and voted 7-1 (BTC members abstaining) to recommend passenger services be withdrawn at an early date. [North West TUCC 16.1.61, min 801].

WE Sayer, a haulier, quarry owner etc., said that he had written to BR who declined to accept his proposal (see Appendix A.5), to take over the line, or rent it and run it for a year. Sayer also said that he feared competition from opening of new quarries on the Carlisle-

Newcastle line and undercutting him. He claimed that 15 wagons between 17th October and 8th June were delayed. BR replied that they were held up by consignees restriction on acceptance. The "delays" related to the Consett Iron Co., who had made no complaints, and neither had Dorman Long.

An objector claimed a Dartington Hall survey said: *"running expenses of rural lines were unnecessarily high and maintenance expenditure could be reduced. Automatic barriers would reduce costs. Signalling costs could be reduced by centralised signalling"*. He said: "Twenty miles of double line could be singled. The Cockermouth, Keswick & Penrith line was reprieved* by being singled. *If* the service is still not economic, it could be operated *summer only* for passenger, and freight diverted throughout the year".

*It later closed, exposing the folly of staged economies, and incurring investment to get them*

The TUCC had no copy of the survey. I tracked it down. It did not refer to this route. Its views did not accord with my experience which included major and minor modernisation of signalling, crossings and traction. It said rural subsidies were inevitable. (See page 226)

Capital costs for centralised signalling, auto barriers and singling had to produce a return which exceeded the cost of borrowing, and would also eliminate losses, otherwise it was ineffective. Singling of lines on these gradients would produce extra signalling costs as *worked* catch points at fourteen locations would be mandatory and expensive. (See page 16). As BR's investment expenditure was limited by Government in every year, it would have to exceed the rate of return obtainable from main line schemes. For objectors to advocate running the line for a *summer only* passenger service, when infrastructure maintenance costs carry on throughout the year, was out of touch with reality.

BR said the line could be singled, (see page 142), but it would still lose money. The costs of opening on Sundays exceeded gross receipts and could not possibly pay. Critics said that there may have been an increase in revenue since the closure was first raised. BR said there was no increase in traffic, but wages had been increased 8-10% by the Guillebaud award. (It was appointed by Government who accepted the award with undue alacrity).

Objectors referred to cattle sent by rail. They didn't say how much was going by road and why it had been taken off rail, where it had been for decades before the advent of the motor vehicle. They said that trees were sent by rail three nights each week earning £45 per night - gross! They didn't say how much went by road and why so little by rail. It is inconceivable that this amount was the Forestry Commission's entire output.

Some local authorities called for more trains and cheaper fares. Needless to say, they did not offer to underwrite their ambitious plans. There are no prizes for guessing what response there would have been from making analogous suggestions to local authorities.

The subject of holiday traffic was raised. The North West TUCC chairman said that well under 1% of visitors to Keswick arrived by train.

An objector said that a sleeping car train should be run from Middlesbrough to Heysham every night in the summer - it would be packed with Irish workers. BR's spokesman said it would be unlikely to carry more than six, and most of the Irish workers in the area were from Eire and would find that route inconvenient. The objector said he didn't believe it, BR should try and see. He didn't produce any figures, offer to fund the experiment, nor agree to pick up the losses if he was proved to be wrong.

One objector said that one loco could pull a train of 16 wagons over Stainmore. One loco hauled 34 wagons via Newcastle-Carlisle. He was trying to keep the route, but was making a case for diversion. Another had "seen diesels running practically empty on the Durham-Bishop Auckland line". He was arguing they could be deployed on the Stainmore route. (He did not concede that trains and buses were poorly loaded on this rural outpost)

The owner of GNE buses said he could cope, and would see what the demand was, but did not expect to make a fortune. He was asked what would happen if Darlington Rambling Club turned up on a Sunday morning to go to the Lake District, and he said that they carried them regularly and they usually gave warning that they were coming! (His comments were not reported by critics. The objector had been trying to prove that the bus company could not cope, but was hoist with his own petard. What this showed was that all those ramblers, to whom the existence of the railway was vital, were in fact using road, when they could have gone by rail, and even worse, they expected rail to have resources to carry them without warning, whilst bus companies were given advance warning).

Another objector said that the Low Committee had said that the BTC had inadequate statistics to evaluate the financial standing of parts of the railway. It found a strong case for subsidy to branch lines. The Report presents a different picture. (See page 227).

Boyden said that a White Paper on the Stedeford Inquiry was awaited. It was not issued. They criticised Government policy in a report closed for 30 years. They said the closure process was slow. They did not advocate subsidy, but called for an end to statutory control of fares. Government ignored most recommendations. (See "*Blueprints for Bankruptcy*").

After a break for lunch, the TUCC's concluded they could not make a decision that day, and after hearing further objections, would defer for another month to sift evidence. After hearing further submissions, the meeting was adjourned and a private meeting re-convened at Leeds on 16th January 1961 - it involved 30 people being accommodated overnight at the Queens hotel. BR would be asked to demonstrate the diverted freight service was satisfactory and BR would seek a final decision on the passenger service.

### TUCC Meeting at Leeds

On freight diversion, BR said that, in addition to saving 105,000 loco miles pa, they had saved nine drivers, nine firemen, three carriage & wagon staff, with no additions on the Carlisle route. Although some transits were worse, it is known that the delays caused were due to Newport Yard being under reconstruction, and that affected all routes. Even so, average transits were improved by 4.6%. There was no truth in the rumour that Toledo Springs traffic had been diverted to road. The company owns "C" Licence vehicles which they use to the maximum. Responding to suggestions about using modern traction, BR said the cost of a 3-car DMU was £48,600, a 2-car was £35,000 and a light weight diesel car was £12,745. The idea of replacing station masters by lower graded staff had been considered, but the economy is outweighed by the advantage of having people who can deal with emergencies. The potential loss of revenue was now less because travel by servicemen from Barnard Castle to Lancashire had ceased, reducing BR revenue by £6,000 pa on this route alone. (Conscription had just ended. They had been the biggest groups travelling at weekends throughout the year)

The TUCC chairman said that savings would therefore be nearer £50,000 than £30,000. He said that objectors had not grasped the nettle of off-season travel. The line is busy on summer Saturdays and fairly busy on summer weekdays, but for eight months it was not busy at all. The average number of passengers on a winter weekday is about 20 and as 40-50 people were on duty for that, they would be better dealt with by bus. The taxpayer paid £2 for every £1 spent on fares. (The taxpayer was only *loaning* BR that £2).

BR representatives pointed out that no economy could be made at stations where signalmen issued tickets. If people were desirous of keeping the line, they could have proved it by using it more. (The two year media publicity about closure was ample to acquaint people with the existence of the line, if they were *really* interested in using it).

The BR representatives then left the meeting. The TUCC then convened in private. The chairman thought that by economies, higher fares and more traffic the loss might be cut by £5,000, but could not see there was sufficient revenue to keep the line open, and the loss was not justified, but on the other hand, none of the local authorities and big users were happy about the line being closed and might consider subsidies. He thought it unlikely that they would. Opinions recorded by members of the TUCC comprised:-

- During the rail strike limestone moved by road satisfactorily.
- People should have shown more interest by using the line - traffic had not increased.
- Not convinced that a longer route was cheaper. (Only where a rail route is involved. Longer motorway routes were justified by the savings they would generate).
- With the suggestions, the line could be made to pay. (They were not even evaluated).
- A White Paper suggests that "borrowing from public funds for certain services which did not pay" might be a solution. (They weren't a solution, they had to be repaid. The interest payments on the loan would cause the annual loss to increase!).
- Had long experience of working the line, would be sorry to see it close, but there must be savings on the Carlisle route. (He was a councillor who had been a BR employee).
- Satisfied that GNE buses could cope winter and summer.
- Having agricultural interests, hated the word 'subsidy' - agriculture had got a bad name through it. How many members used this line regularly? He had. The only section made use of was Barnard Castle to Darlington. There would be no hardship and the TUCC's were wasting public money in having these meetings.

Meanwhile, the Chairman of the BTC wrote to the MoT on 27th January 1961. drawing attention to the delay. The proposal was first put to the TUCC's in December 1959. He pointed out that the track and equipment will deteriorate quickly on an exposed line such as this. The MoT replied that he had to consider all the issues.

The North West TUCC said the line should be closed, the North East TUCC said keep it, and the Government to subsidise it. The BTC deplored the further delay and frustration in this case. [BTC Minutes, February 1961].

### The Debate Continues
The North West TUCC wrote to the North East TUCC on 29th March that the case had been referred back by the CTCC, [CTCC min 1070] for further consideration as our

recommendations were contradictory and having heard a deputation of users from both areas, are now in doubt as to whether full information of the freight services via Carlisle & Newcastle had been made available to them. They queried the comment about Kirkby Stephen motive power depot and drew attention to Boyden's criticism of the hearing.

A North East TUCC meeting took place on 4th May "To finalise and agree to the closure". A member who was a councillor proposed that they defer a decision. It was agreed to defer a decision until June. (Needless to say, deferment wouldn't have been proposed and approved if the members of the TUCC and the organisations they represented had been picking up the tab. As always, the delay increased BR losses, for which everyone blamed BR management, rather than those making the crucial decisions).

The North West TUCC re-affirmed their previous decision, and decided, on reflection, to delete their previous criticism that BR could have closed Kirkby Stephen motive power depot earlier. The chairman referred to a remark by the MP that "objectors had not had a proper hearing; it had been hasty and confused". He said it was neither hasty nor confused ample opportunity was given for everybody who had a point to bring it up. [11.5.61, min 848].

The North East TUCC wrote on 9th June to the CTCC: At the meeting in Darlington, my Committee reversed their decision and agreed to the BTC proposal that the line should be closed. The outstanding questions on freight delays, BR figures and rates, addressed by the CTCC to the two TUCC's on 21st March 1961 were :-

1. Diversion of mineral traffic via Carlisle and Penrith. It is working satisfactorily. When Mr. Sayer was given another opportunity at yesterday's meeting to provide evidence of complaint from the area with which we are concerned, he could produce nothing to support his case.

2. (a) We have no evidence of delayed transit of mineral traffic in either direction. .

(b) We are satisfied that the BTC revenue figures have not misled us.

3. Mr. Sayer asked for assurances on rates and that if traffic was moving satisfactorily, it would be allowed to continue to do so. BR gave assurances on both points. (There was no further mention of his offer to run the line).

## CTCC Decision

The North West TUCC noted that the North East TUCC had now agreed the passenger service be withdrawn and the line closed which accorded with our recommendation. The CTCC had written to the TUCC's: They had considered most carefully the analysis supplied by the BTC dealing with Mr. Sayer's traffic. It appeared that the root of his previous statements in regard to the reduction and late delivery of his traffic since diversion via Carlisle were without substance. The alleged "complaint forms" which he had produced regarding delays of traffic to Teesside were not, in fact, complaints at all. The North East TUCC had decided to investigate the matter again with Mr. Sayer who had been invited to attend their next meeting. The TUCC Secretary reported that notwithstanding repeated requests, Mr Sayer had so far produced no new evidence of delays to either of the TUCC's. [North West TUCC min. 852, June 1961].

The CTCC agreed to recommend to the MoT that all train services between Barnard Castle and Penrith be withdrawn and the line closed. [North West TUCC, 11.7.61 min. 877].

# The Proof

In the beginning there were doubts about the prosperity of this line. Now we can look back, it seems clear misfortunes which attended it in the early days may be at the root of its troubles. The demise of Cumberland mineral trains over 30 years ago left the line almost entirely dependent on scanty local traffic, which even before road competition, would scarcely have justified its existence. [Cumberland & Westmoreland Herald, 5.8.61].

If a bus is full, it leaves passengers behind to wait for the next service. [Kirkby Stephen Chamber of Trade letter]. (BR were vilified unless they increase the capacity which is adequate for 364 days to that which will ensure no one is left behind on the 365th). Buses to Kirkby Stephen are running at a loss - and we can only run more services if given a subsidy. [GNE bus company letter to the TUCC 19.2.62]. (Everyone had been saying BR could provide a service at a profit - and BR was paying for its own infrastructure, whilst road operators paid next to nothing for theirs. At that time bus licences cost little more than that for a car).

A local bus operator threatened to abandon operations unless Government steps in to share the load. [Penrith Observer, 1.3.60]. (By 'load', he meant the cost. No one told *him* that his business *was* profitable, he *lacked* initiative, or wasn't *trying* to attract business).

A Ramblers' special bus extended to make up for the railway closure is now in danger of suffering the same fate and for the same reason. The GNE company is not being supported. They added that BR said the railway was only paying for two months in the year, and it is the same for us. [Middlesbrough Evening News 7.8.62].

Ramblers could have guaranteed to travel ten or twenty times as often as a constructive way of keeping the line, instead of tendering advice on a subject of which they had no knowledge or experience. Objecting councils did not promise to place so much as a ton of freight on the line nor buy one extra ticket. Neither did Mr. Sayer.

The Lake District Planning Board minutes record: "It is difficult to believe that railways carried any appreciable traffic to the Lakes. Figures produced by our clerk in one week in July last year show only 27 passengers left Barnard Castle in one day on *three trains*. The Board did not dispute BR's figures and said that BR had a good case. The Board intend to take no action". [PRO: MT115/254 - closed to 1992].

The MoT's Chief Inspector of Railways told the MP for Westmoreland "there are many factors in assessing manpower required for track maintenance. Barnard Castle-Penrith is class 4, and Kirkby Stephen-Tebay class 5. This is reasonable and cannot be reduced if the line was kept in use for traffic. If it is kept open with no trains, ten men would be required for statutory obligations - maintenance, undergrowth clearance and fences. The most serious problem was the two very high viaducts with cast iron pieces that were getting into bad condition and would require extensive strengthening in the next ten years if kept open, at a cost of £1m". The MP said it was the first he had heard of it, and "agreed such expenditure could not be justified". The £1m was not disclosed as the BTC are directed to quote expenditure only over the next five years for TUCC hearings. [PRO: MT115/255].

Revenue had shown an increase of £1,400 pa following the introduction of DMU's in February 1958. [Walton, Page 189]. It did not scratch the surface of the loss, nor cover interest on the cost of two units required for the service. BR said the increase was not maintained in the following year. (See page 132). A bank looking at losses of £36,000 would be unexcited about £1,400 pa when two diesels cost £70,000. Savings from single manning etc. would not pay the interest, nor redeem the loan nor fund maintenance & fuelling facilities. If off-line facilities were used, costs would be incurred in movements to such depots. No self respecting businessman would delay more than a few minutes before deciding to stop throwing good money after bad and re-deploy assets to a location offering a better return. When British Midland re-deployed aircraft away from Liverpool due to substantial losses on the route, wisely, no one accused them of not trying.

The Commission is concerned by the delay on this closure. The MoT had asked the BTC to give adequate notice of closure, should the CTCC endorse the TUCC view to close. No irrevocable action was to be taken before he had an opportunity to consider the matter further. It is already over 12 months since submission. [BTC Minutes, January 1961].

The final proof of the unprofitability of the line is that Sayer, who had said he was *"confident the line could make a substantial profit"*, did not make an offer to **buy** the line. He could have kept his traffic on the line and canvassed other traffic with low rates.

### Postscript

The line closed January 1962. In 1969, the London Midland Region obtained £69,975 for sale of assets on the Eden Valley line for an outlay of £4,650. [PRO: AN155/208]. This was for assets *sold*. It excluded assets re-deployed. North Eastern Region papers on asset recovery are not yet available in the Public Record Office.

"£257,000 was disclosed by the BTC as the amount to be realised by recovery of redundant assets. This should have had no bearing as this credit was a capital asset already paid for". [Walton, Page 194]. It had a major bearing. One assumes that the private sector recovers or sells assets from closed factories. Track, points & crossings, bridges, signals, plant, cranes etc. from closed lines were transferred to other locations to avoid expenditure on new materials. Such was the scale of recovery that concrete beams from dismantled bridges were used as sea defences avoiding purchase of quarried block stone.

Boyden asked why the MoT had refused to meet a deputation from the Stainmore Line Protest Committee. He replied that he received the letter more than a month after closure was announced and ten days before closure day, and that the TUCC's and the CTCC had held six meetings. Boyden said the original case was based on a 25% error as to the freight which could be hauled over Stainmore. [Hansard, vol. 653, cols. 1296-91]. A comparison of gradients was enough to prove a better load could be hauled via Carlisle. There was no error, except in the minds of those who did not understand freight train loads. (See page 139).

Sayer was "one of chief users of the line and has transferred the whole of his output from Brough to Teesside from rail to road. *2,000* tons per week at current freight rates - a loss to BR of £104,000". [Guardian 26.4.63]. His traffic was on rail because it benefited him, not for altruistic reasons. Rates in BR Accounts show this was *gross* income. BR would *not* lose that sum, as costs involved in conveying his traffic would cease. The traffic was among the lowest rated and the profit margin would be tight. He gave no reason for a change, 15 months after closure, having been given assurances on rates and with transits as good or better. When he first objected to closure, his said his tonnage was *3,000* tons per week. A drop to *2,000* tons would have boded ill for the line had it remained open.

**Chapter 11**                    **Westerham Valley Branch**

The Westerham Valley Railway was incorporated in 1876. An extension to Oxted to join the LB&SCR was envisaged, but the SER objected. After that idea was abandoned, the SER agreed to work the line, provide equipment and operate the line at 50% of gross receipts. They guaranteed that the Westerham Company's share of net profits would be at least £2,750 pa, with the excess, if any, divided equally. It was agreed that the SER would have a right to purchase at a reasonable figure. The line was brought into use in July 1881, by which time it had been absorbed by the SER. It was constructed as a single line, but sufficient land was obtained to enable it to be doubled, and bridges were built to allow for a double line. When it opened there were stations at Brasted and Westerham. In 1907, Chevening Halt was opened. Brasted was later reduced to the status of a halt. In 1955, the line was reduced to one engine in steam, involving a two coach push & pull train. [PRO: Rail 1057/3166]. Clearly, SER interest in the line was a blocking tactic. (See page 7).

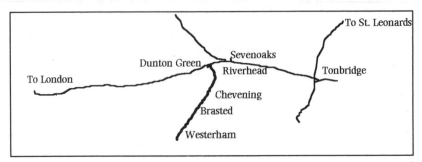

**The TUCC's First Hearings - 1960**

BR submitted a proposal to close the 4.75 mile branch on 30th March. The TUCC for London appointed a working party which made a visit to view the line on 20th June. There were 60 written objections to the TUCC. Local Authorities asked for more time, so the TUCC deferred consideration until the 21st July, when the TUCC met to discuss the proposal and received deputations of the Sevenoaks UDC, Sevenoaks RDC, Kent County Council, Westerham Railway Passengers Association, Ramblers Association and others. There were 42 people at the meeting in addition to the TUCC. The deputations had submitted letters and a petition of 617 names.

They were told that train loadings vary between four and 84. The typical train load was 20 passengers. Seven trains were being run for 167 passengers. BR said there were immediate and short term savings of £9,915, plus renewals of £22,655 over five years. With a loss of receipts of £3,500 and bus subventions of £6,500 and cartage, it produced a net of £11,600. BR said there would be colour light signals inside Sevenoaks tunnel which steam and smoke would obscure. To keep and maintain the loco at Dunton Green, would be costly and impractical. Replacement by diesels would be costly. Existing maintenance and spares provision is based on a fleet of three car trains. If a two car, or single car train was provided, it would need a full time spare because there were no others available.

*Written Objections* :-

- In *1927*, the roads in and out of Westerham were snowed up and impassable. Even the railway was closed for five days. Such a thing could happen again!

Kent County Council:

- Journeys by bus and rail to London would be 55 minutes longer.
- Savings achievable from diesels had not been explored - they might well reduce loss to an insignificant figure. (*Only a loss borne by someone else is insignificant*).

Sevenoaks RDC :

- Losses are greater than they need be. Savings of £11,600 are an over estimate compared with the number of regular passengers. (The thinking behind this comparison is unclear).
- Under County plans there appears to be no substantial potential increase on the branch but the number of commuters justifies a rail service. (It didn't justify *one* train)
- The number of passengers is less than those of an ***independent*** census taken by the Westerham Railway Passengers Association. (In no other walk of life would it be regarded as independent, as they stood to gain. They did not specify the difference - it may have been one or two, which would have no impact on the case).
- The line is an essential business line, unlike the "Bluebell line" which was a relatively unessential or pleasure line. (It was later claimed the branch had tourist potential).
- The main line is heavily trafficked, closure would increase passengers on certain peak trains. (***Every*** train on which the commuters travelled from Dunton Green, called at or started from Sevenoaks. The same capacity would still be available).

Westerham Railway Passengers Association - 152 members :

- Alternative services are inadequate, slower and would cost £16-18 pa more.
- Believe savings could be made by using diesels and other economies. (They ignored capital cost and interest on the borrowings).
- The branch has a considerable future traffic potential given a good diesel service. (There was no offer to underwrite the capital costs, or losses if they were wrong).
- It is clear that diesels would effect considerable economies. Do not accept the maintenance problem, there are diesels on Tonbridge-Brighton services. Alternatively, they could use battery trains. They could abolish all signals and the signalmen at Westerham, convert Westerham to an unstaffed halt and dispense with all staff. (This would result in no station lighting, unless they envisaged borrowing more interest bearing capital to install time controlled lighting. There would be no station cleaning. Issuing season tickets on the train would have presented problems).
- The cost of £19,915 could be reduced to £14,914. In this they reduced permanent way, bridge, building and signalling maintenance from £2,192 to £1,500, but it may be less - in the absence of details, they "didn't know". (They did not explain how it could be done. A figure was pulled from the air, and BR left to disprove it).
- Interest figures on the diesels would decrease progressively owing to depreciation on capital. (They hadn't grasped that the interest was on the initial loan to buy the diesels. If you take out a loan to buy a car, the interest on the initial loan does not decrease as the car becomes older).

- The loss remaining would be small and could be covered by increased profits from main line electric train services. (Neither the TUCC nor Supporters reported any support from main line passengers to pay fares sufficient to subsidise this branch).
- They called for a practical test, with every effort made to reduce cost over a reasonable period of time. (There was no offer to repay all losses over a reasonable period, if it failed, nor to take, what would then be, a superfluous diesel unit, with no other use, off BR's hands at initial cost).

*BR Response* :-
- Brasted and Chevening halts are well away from the main centres of population.
- The total population near to the branch was 9,330 in 1951 and 9,530 in 1958.
- Daily average loadings are 1953: 139, 1955: 143, 1958: 147, 1960: 155. There are 140 season ticket holders and 14 scholars.
- The Passengers Association has confused costs with short term savings. Relative annual costs are steam: £29,652, diesel loco train: £29,040, electric units: £23,764, diesel units: £24,070. Additional off peak trains would increase costs for the three modern alternatives by £2,130, £1,724 and £2,670 pa respectively. All would be based on "one engine in steam regulations". Losses will increase.
- Despite regular Sunday services, there is no evidence of tourists increasing, Sunday traffic is not heavy.

During the meeting the following points were raised :-
- Kent County Council said that planning permission had been given for 84 additional houses near to stations, which may produce 80 additional commuters. (How they could assume that these houses would all produce one commuter, when a population of 9,530 produces 147 was not explained. On that basis, assuming an average of four people per house, there ought to have been 2,250 daily commuters already).
- The Council also said that the track had recently been relaid. At the meeting, BR said most had not, but later stated that only 55 chains was still to be done and that is what the £7,300 over the next five years relates to.
- The Passengers Association said there were two car units elsewhere on BR. There was scope to increase tourism. (*They had said it was a business, not a pleasure line*. A two car unit would need a spare. Knowing the area, its tourist potential by rail was low).
- The Ramblers Association criticised BR for not running special trains. They wanted special trains "to form friendships". (Wisely, they did not claim it would reduce net losses, much less turn loss into profit).

BR said the service could not remain steam operated as an isolated pocket, it must be diesel or electric and these involved heavy capital costs. A railbus would require a spare. A loss would remain. It was not justified. They pointed out that there were 617 signatures on a petition, but only 167 of them used the train. BR explained that running special trains did not produce additional revenue when the scheduled service was underused. The Ramblers were free to charter an excursion, fix their own fares and pocket the profit.

151

There was no response. If Westerham was destaffed, an additional parcels van would be needed at Sevenoaks. BR had advertised the line but there was little tourism.

A decision on the closure was deferred pending provision of further BR data on costs of operating the branch with diesels, and operating records by London Transport. The objectors thanked the Chairman of the TUCC at the end of the meeting.

A TUCC meeting was held on 4th October when it again considered the proposed closure of the Westerham branch. The BTC forecast a saving of £8,860 pa. The Deputy Chairman (a councillor) "was not satisfied that losses could not be further reduced. He would like to see the money saved, but some people would be inconvenienced. He was especially concerned for families who had bought houses in the area in the expectation that branch line services would continue". [TUCC min 757]. The poor user suggests that most wanted the line to provide a standby for the next period of bad weather.

The TUCC Chairman said "some people felt that BR should be prepared to support a loss on feeder services". He said that the cheapest railbus would cost £20,900 pa, branch earnings did not exceed £3,500 pa, and would need a capital outlay of £32,822 including £4,690 for signals. If the line closed London Transport would provide two additional buses and BR would require a van for conveying parcels requiring a capital outlay £1,006.

Other members views comprised :-
- This feeder service was much more expensive, pro rata. than others. To maintain it, considerable expenditure would have to be incurred and he failed to see how the committee could possibly recommend that it be kept open if they were satisfied a reasonably adequate bus service would be available. The concept of using a railbus is completely outweighed by the capital cost and the loss involved in continued operation. Alternative facilities were reasonable and the cost must be less. He moved that the committee recommend closure. (He was a representative of UK industry).
- BR could use diesel shunt engines for passenger trains. (He was in shipping. Finding paths for a 25 mph shunt loco would be very difficult on a heavily occupied main line. These locos could not heat trains, so there would be no heat in winter).
- Opposed to closure. (He was with LEP transport. No one compelled private sector industry to provide uneconomic services).
- It was "grievous to ask the BTC to bear the burden of this line - it should be closed, despite inconvenience to passengers". She, an LCC Alderman, seconded the motion.
- An Inquiry had been held, and objectors given ample time to submit evidence.

The chairman called for deferment and to invite leaders of the deputation of objectors to attend a further meeting. This was opposed by others who said the TUCC had had an all day meeting at which objectors were present on 21st July, after they had been given ample time to submit evidence. They had had a very good hearing. A decision should be taken now. A clear majority favoured closure, one disagreed but would go with the majority decision. The vote was nine in favour, one against, the BTC representatives abstained.

The TUCC agreed to inform principal objectors of the decision to recommend closure:-
1. The BTC have shown withdrawal will save £8,860 pa.
2. There will be savings during the next five years of £7,300 on renewals of track and £6,000 for sheet steel earmarked for remedial measures against earth slips in the Brasted area.
3. Modernisation provided for the elimination of steam in BR's South East Division within two years. To maintain a steam pocket would be costly even if practicable. The loco would be based at Tonbridge, requiring two journeys per day. By 1962, with the improved signalling for the more intensive service, steam would not be desirable for safety reasons in Sevenoaks tunnel.
4. Diesel railbuses would reduce the cost of working by £8,752. Objectors had argued that the difference between saving from diesels and the projected saving of £8,860 should be related to inconvenience and hardship which will be caused. The argument is unacceptable because conversion to diesel is a separate and difficult proposition which can only be judged on the basis of a full account of revenue and expenses. Costs for five alternative forms of traction are :-
    - Diesel mechanical railbus - £20,900 pa; Capital outlay £32,822
    - Battery powered unit - £26,296 pa; Capital outlay £84,222
    - 1550 hp loco & a two car set - £29,040 pa; Capital outlay £51,300
    - Two car electric multiple unit - £23,764 pa; Capital outlay £72,000
    - Three car diesel electric multiple unit - £24.070 pa; Capital outlay £61,000
    - These compare with steam at £29,652 pa
The first two forms would require a spare unit. The present total revenue is £3,500. Assuming no increase in revenue and a tolerance of 10% in costs, the minimum loss would be £15,310.
5. In view of the alternative bus services, it is unreasonable to ask the BTC to invest capital required under any of these schemes in order to maintain a service which would be certain to involve them with further heavy deficits next year.
6. Sevenoaks RDC foresee "no substantial regular potential increase in passenger traffic on the branch". Kent County Council point out that the line is in the Green Belt, and do not anticipate expansion. The most optimistic estimate of additional traffic likely to be produced could not have any significant effect on finances of the branch.
7. London Transport have undertaken to supplement route 403 by four additional trips per day from Westerham to Sevenoaks in the morning and six returning in the evening. Total capacity exceeds the maximum recorded capacity of traffic on the branch.
8. London Transport foresee no staffing difficulties. On two occasions only in the past year has part of the weekday 403 service been cancelled, one for staff shortage, one due to congestion.
9. Objectors' concern at longer journeys to London is due to incomplete knowledge of bus timings and the faster trains from Sevenoaks. The maximum increase in journey time is 19/20 minutes. They will benefit by bus stops being closer to homes, affecting door to door journey times.
10 The additional cost of £16-18 pa season cost is not unreasonable when one considers the loss BTC would incur in keeping the line open. The Committee hope that the BTC will ease the impact by issuing joint road/rail seasons to present branch line users for a year.
11. The MoT does not believe the additional road traffic will overload the A21 and A25.
12. It may aggravate the car park shortage at Sevenoaks, but space is available at Dunton Green.
The capital cost for diesels would produce a negative return on investment - no industry would consider it for more than a second.

## The TUCC's Second Hearing - 1961

Objectors petitioned the CTCC, who referred it back to us on the grounds that the objectors should have been given an opportunity to comment on additional information. [TUCC 1961 Report]. The branch was just over 4 miles long, carrying only 167 passengers. The TUCC had considered it "at great length in 1960" and recommended closure, but the CTCC put it back to TUCC to reconsider. [CTCC 1961 Report, Para 33].

On 14th November, BR wrote to the TUCC asking for an early decision because steam could not continue indefinitely - it must cease. The CTCC wrote to the TUCC on 2nd December that objectors should have been given an opportunity of commenting on the additional evidence* submitted on 21st July before the TUCC reached their decision.

     *The word is significant, it smacked of trying to act like a court of law.*

Arising from the CTCC remit, on 8th December 1960, the TUCC again discussed the branch closure and set up a working party to review the evidence, consider BTC observations and prepare views on further objections.

The **Working Party** met on 5th January. They could find no fault with BTC figures.
- We do not think there remain any reasonable grounds to doubt that annual savings of the order of £8,860 pa would be achieved by the closure and that the expenditure on capital renewals amounting to £13,000 during the next five years would be avoided.
- We are pleased that the BTC agreed to permit season ticket passengers to travel by bus to Sevenoaks and thence by train for one year at the same fare.
- There were 167 passengers per day - Westerham: 113, Brasted: 20, Chevening: 34.
- The saving from destaffing Westerham was not worth pursuing.
- There is nothing to be achieved by restoring an off-peak service.
- Passengers would spread departures by bus to take advantage of more trains from Sevenoaks. Risks of inadequacy of any bus journey are safeguarded by assurances.
- We dismiss the view that the original submission should stand, and accept BR's view that the case must rest on the cheapest alternative to steam - viz. diesel railbus.
- County Council estimates of road congestion were based on applying the increase noted elsewhere to the 1954 census on the A25. It is evident that road congestion is largely a weekend problem. (Hence it would not affect commuters).
- County Council representatives agree that the claim about extended journeys of 55 minutes was calculated without knowledge of the timing of additional bus journeys. The BTC show that additional times would be reduced by additional bus journeys and faster trains from Sevenoaks. A table attached to the Report shows the difference from using bus/rail services in the morning varied from -1 to +29 minutes, with an overall average of +10. On the return, they vary from -17 to + 20 minutes, an average of +4. (The average was much less than the Council's times. Some would be quicker as there were more and faster trains from Sevenoaks, as compared to Dunton Green, at which station Westerham passengers changed to all-stations trains to London).
- It is difficult to tell what petitioners have in mind when referring to a great deal of financial and other relevant evidence being heard after objectors have presented their case. The only material evidence given verbally at the hearings - additional to that circulated before the hearing - was the statement of the capital cost of introducing any of the alternative forms of traction. In the main, the BTC confined themselves to rebutting the objections put forward by the deputations.

- The County Council complain that they were not afforded an opportunity to test and answer the additional evidence submitted after the meeting in July. At the end of that meeting, the chairman asked objectors to state whether they considered they had had a fair, reasonable and proper hearing. He intimated that the TUCC would receive further evidence from the BTC and consider it when making their recommendation. No request was made by any objectors - or on their behalf - for copies of such additional evidence to be made available to them. The chairman and the committee were thanked for their patient hearing of the case.
- On 25th July, objectors were informed that the TUCC had deferred consideration of the proposal pending submission of an analysis of the cost of operating services with a diesel railbus, alternative bus services and traffic conditions on roads; adding that objectors would be advised of the TUCC recommendations. Between 25th July and the announcement of TUCC recommendations on 5th October, no request was received from any objector for an opportunity to comment on additional evidence.
- Sevenoaks RDC claimed that the MoT speech on 26th October [Times, 27.10.60] meant that a decision to close the line would be contrary to advice given to the Government by the MoT. We have studied the speech and failed to detect any evidence that the MoT stated what advice he was going to give. He did say "The railways must be viable. They must meet operating costs and interest on capital".
- We dismiss the Passengers Association view that this is the first closure of a line used by commuters and would create a precedent. Crystal Palace High Level and Alexandra Palace lines have been closed with TUCC approval. In any case, TUCC's are not influenced by previous decisions, each is judged on its own merits.
- The Passengers Association advanced inaccurate figures for the full cost of railbus services which would be £32,000 not £29,000 and would result in a loss of £15-17,000. Our enquiries have not suggested that BR's estimate of minimum annual loss can be materially reduced. They complain that the BTC has included interest charges on capital investment in estimates of operating a diesel railbus service. We find no fault with the BTC in respect of those figures. (One wonders in what line of business these London commuters were engaged if they found it strange that interest on loan capital was included as a cost against providing a service or product).
- The Passengers Association is confident that traffic would increase given diesels. The County Council criticise the BTC for not admitting the possibility of an increase. Their optimistic views are discounted by Sevenoaks RDC : "There appears to be no substantial regular potential increase in traffic on the branch line". We are not convinced that a short ride in a railbus is likely to induce large numbers of residents to increase to any significant extent the number of journeys they make to London for shopping, amusement or visiting. The branch has no value for journeys to Sevenoaks.
- The Passengers Association expressed doubts about London Transport's ability to staff additional buses. The TUCC accept London Transport evidence that in the previous year only on one occasion had part of a bus journey been lost between Sevenoaks and Westerham on Mondays to Fridays due to staff shortage. (It is almost inconceivable that in 12 months, not one train had been cancelled, but this was not mentioned).

155

- BR had calculated that each commuter would have to pay an extra £104 pa to cover the losses of the cheapest alternative. BR said the offer made by the Association is no offer at all. (They had offered to pay an extra £22 pa per head to keep the branch).
- Taking out all staff would save £1,484 but additional cartage costs would be £1,036, leaving a net of £450. An unstaffed station $4^1/_2$ miles from base is unsatisfactory.
- The Select Committee on Nationalised Industries said BR had not asked branch line users to pay higher fares to end losses. We consider it impractical to ask users to pay an additional £104 pa per head to meet the cost of the branch using a railbus.
- Diesel railbuses accommodate 46-56 passengers and would be inadequate for the limited peak. There is no scope elsewhere for such a vehicle to be used - it would be a limited pocket. A spare vehicle would be required for backup for this branch alone. It would need to run to St. Leonards for maintenance and Tonbridge for fuelling. As these vehicles are too light to be relied on to work track circuits, special arrangements would be necessary. It would produce an annual loss of £17,000.

BR had written that the electrification advocated in a newspaper, had no chance of paying. The shortest train - two cars - would cost £23,000 pa for the existing service, and £25,500 if an off-peak service was re-introduced. The suggested half-hourly off-peak service cost would greatly exceed £25,500. Extensive track and signalling alterations would be required at Dunton Green to permit direct access to the branch in the Down direction. The signal box only opened for the freight train. It would be an extra expense. The suggestion says it would cost £100,000 - even half that could not be justified. There is no comparison between the potential of the Westerham branch and the well populated lines of Chelmsford and Margate which the reader had attempted to portray.

Kent County Council wrote to the TUCC that steam cost £29,652 pa, a railbus £20,900 pa, so it would be £8,752 pa cheaper, and that BR's estimated saving of £11,600 less £8,752 leaves £2,845 loss. (They made no provision for the cost of borrowing, nor depreciation. They did not offer to buy one and lease it on a short term to BR at 0%. The Council was confusing short term savings on the existing, with full costs for new stock).

A special TUCC meeting took place on 8th February 1961 to which objectors, including Sevenoaks RDC, Westerham Railway Passengers Association, Kent County Council, Sevenoaks UDC, the MP and Orpington UDC were invited. The latter wrote that it had had ample opportunity to comment at the earlier stage. The Report of the Working Party was accepted. [TUCC min. 785]. The secretary gave additional information about bus times.
The Passengers' Association made the following points :-
- The diesel could go off the branch for maintenance and fuelling when the freight train went off. (They did not identify an opportunity for it to return!).
- Guards were not needed because "On a single line trains did not need protection in the rear". (BR replied "On single lines both ends are the rear and have to be protected in the event of a breakdown").
- As most season ticket holders worked in London, the branch should be considered an integral part of the Greater London network.

- If it was necessary, railbuses could transfer *elsewhere*. (This emphasises the unreality which underlies objections - that the cost ceases because the asset is hidden from view, by moving it *elsewhere*. If "*elsewhere*" justified one, they would have one).
- Had never denied it ran at a loss, but it could be reduced to £2,845. BR boggle at capital costs of £32,000 which will still make a loss, but they deprive a town of 4,000. (Capital incurs interest. To boggle at improvidence was an unintended compliment).
- Referred to the money required for bank stabilisation, and asked if "earth slips" had occurred? (They seemed to believe the time for action was after a bank had collapsed and commuters began to complain that they couldn't get to work. See BR reply).

Kent County Council :-
- Criticised BR for the reluctance to admit the possibility of increased traffic. (It was discounted by Sevenoaks RDC at the earlier meeting)
- It did not wish to criticise the TUCC - it had been a fair hearing.

Sevenoaks RDC :-
- 388 houses had been occupied in three years. (The past had no bearing. Only a huge inflow could increase user, and that was ruled out by councils - see BR reply).
- Passengers had been told that the increase would be £1.10.4d (£1.51) per month from Westerham to London, it would now be £2.4.0d (£2.20), an increase of 50%.

Further BR comments :-
- BR said that the objective of providing metal sheeting was to *prevent* slips!.
- BR said that of 388 houses, 106 at Riverhead had no access to the branch.
- All fares were rising. Seasons would rise from £6.2.1d (£6.14) to £8.3.7d (£8.18) per month: a 33% increase. (The original figure was quoted a year earlier. It represented the cost of travelling by bus to Sevenoaks, and by rail from there. The greater distance increased the cost. In the past year, all fares - and other prices - had increased. Fares were still trailing the 1948 RPI by 27 points).
- It would need a massive increase in housing to produce a worthwhile increase in revenue. If the line was kept open, BR would have to spend £32,000 on railbuses and £13,000 on other renewals in two years. BR had to borrow from the Government at 6% and they expect 10% return.
- In closure cases, only Heads of Information data was required to be supplied. But if the BTC was asked to consider alternatives, they were obliged to use full costing, including interest, and the 4% postulated by objectors was unrealistic.
- Only if no one used the buses was it right to count £3,500 as a loss. BR had assumed some commuters would not use buses, but if BR had underestimated bus usage, the subsidy to London Transport would be less, because they would be taking extra fares.
- The present cost was £29,625 pa and gross receipts £3,500. BR could save £20,000 pa immediately. Bus and cartage costs would still leave a short term saving of £9,000 pa. No Highway Authority would provide a road for 170 passengers per day in 5-6 buses.

TUCC members' views :-
- A member with shipping experience asked if BR could not transfer two diesels in temporarily and transfer them *elsewhere* when the South Orbital Road is open. (Where did he expect them to come from, and what would happen to traffic in the

157

area temporarily without them? Does the shipping industry act like this, transferring assets from full time use *elsewhere* to cater for loss making business? If so, it may explain the decline in UK owned shipping).

- Calls were made to re-instate off-peak services. (BR said that they had withdrawn the off-peak service because people ceased to use it. A projected income of £1,800-£2,000 pa would not even cover the extra costs incurred and, hence, would not cut the loss).
- A member with industrial experience said that Westerham was not a commuter area - only 150 were regular travellers out of a population numbered in thousands.
- There would be hardship from using buses which were less dependable. Regard should be paid to future housing development and station parking.

The member who worked for LEP Transport suddenly moved that the line should remain open, and it was seconded by a member who was a Croydon Alderman. It was abruptly carried six to one, with two abstentions.
Those in favour gave their reasons as:-
1. Social need.
2. Passengers had bought houses, with the railway near. *
3. Buses are less dependable.
4. Journey length increased by 19 minutes  (The Working Party Report contradicted that).
5. Higher season fares.
6. Some 84 new houses had been approved. (They wouldn't scratch the surface).
7. Transfer from rail to road is undesirable. (Councils had taken no action to curtail road traffic).
8. Diesels should be provided, the off peak service should be resumed, it might make a contribution. (If it didn't, the TUCC would not reimburse the loss).
9. Passengers would pay £3,800 more to keep the line, the amount they would pay to use buses via Sevenoaks. (Not enough to cover current losses much less the cost of replacing steam)
    * *Apart from the 167 using the line, the remainder who lived in the area were obviously only interested in a rail service as a standby.*

The TUCC accepted the view that the location of the line and the railway commuter use constituted a social need. Using buses would cause hardship. They had regard to subsidiary factors such as potential housing, congested roads and influenced by additional information and arguments put forward after the original inquiry in 1960. In the committee's view diesels held reasonable prospect of increased revenue. The BTC would have to make a capital investment of £19,571 for an *additional* loss of £5,123 pa, which in their view was justified. [TUCC Annual Report 1961].

One would have thought it would be the rational view of any businessman that it was *totally unjustified*. The reasons which the TUCC and its Working Party tabulated (see pages 153-156), for recommending closure were unchanged. It was a totally irrational reversal. They didn't underwrite their revenue forecasts with their own money.

The CTCC wrote to the MoT that the line should remain open on social grounds - it is doubtful that it could ever be made profitable. [Times, 10.5.61, 17b]. The CTCC were criticised for not supporting a TUCC recommendation to oppose closure, [see Henshaw, Page 81], but in this case, they told them to re-hear the case when the TUCC had recommended closure.

The TUCC noted the CTCC minute 1083 of 8th May 1961 recommending to the MoT that the Westerham line should be retained on the grounds that to close it would cause undue hardship. They also noted the reply given in Parliament by the MoT on 2nd August that he was unable to agree with the CTCC conclusion and had informed the BTC that it was free to proceed with the closure as soon as arrangements had been made for the necessary augmentation of the bus service. [TUCC minute 343, 16.8.61]

The Westerham branch was $4^{1}/_{2}$ miles long, with only 167 passengers. The TUCC considered it "at great length in 1960" and recommended closure, but the CTCC put it back to them to reconsider and they changed their minds. The CTCC supported them, but the MoT decided to close. It was the first time that the MoT had ignored a CTCC recommendation. [CTCC 1961 Report, Para 33].

The branch closed on 30th October 1961. BR offered to sell the line to the Passengers Association on condition that they operated a daily service, which would avoid BR having to subsidise replacement buses. It was a reasonable condition - the Association had argued that the line could be made to pay, and given free labour, it ought to have been child's play

## Postscript
Lord Stanhope and others deplored that the MoT had ignored the recommendations of its advisors - a body "appointed to advise him and the Commission". [Times, 8.8.61, 9f].

Acts did not name the CTCC as advisors to the BTC unless the BTC asked for their views. They were not asking for advice on closures, but were informing of an intention to close. The MoT failed to accept CTCC advice that proposed fare increases in 1952 were fair. No complaint was registered by anyone that the MoT was not listening to *that* advice, and the increases were the first for four years for 80% of passengers, despite a 20% rise in inflation. The MoT appointed the Special Advisory Group in 1960 and ignored all recommendations which favoured the BTC. There were no protests. It is a curious that no external voice protested against Government decisions which would increase deficits, whilst the noise to oppose actions which would reduce deficits was deafening.

## Cost free labour
Closures created groups seeking to show professionals how to make "profits", using *unpaid* labour.

One author stated that BR had not investigated whether the line could be run more cheaply. He mentioned a suggestion which had been made, that an old bus, with flanged wheels could be used on the branch. The suggestion envisaged that the driver - perhaps an old retired BR driver - would sell tickets on the train.

No evidence was advanced that BR had not investigated if it could be run *more cheaply*, which was irrelevant if it still lost money, unless someone was going to cover the residual loss. To eliminate losses, required the average train load to increase fourfold to the national average, or costs to be cut by 75%. A local group could not keep it in service even with cost free labour! It was not stated why "an old retired driver" would be sought instead of a redundant or active driver attracted by good pay and a 'Golden Hello'. The likeliest reason was a hope that he would work for little or nothing applying training and expertise funded by BR. Collecting fares would extend journey times longer than decried alternatives. The prospect of an old bus converted to a railcar equipped with a deadman's control defies belief, and there was little prospect that the MoT would permit a single manned *rail* vehicle conveying fare paying passengers without a safety aid - and rightly so. It would have to be an *old* motor coach, because new buses fitted with flanged wheels would not fit BR's gauge. (See page 44). It would need a turntable at each end of the branch.

The chairman of the Westerham Railway Passengers Association claimed the branch could run at a profit. Estimates showed that a service for commuters, tourists and enthusiasts would make an *estimated* profit of **£1,977** during the first four years. [Times, 18.5.62, 9a]. There was no indication of the envisaged costs of drivers, maintenance, materials and interest on loans for the purchase of the line and a railcar. They did not venture what they would do, if the railcar broke down at 06.00. There were no plans for clearing the line of snow on weekday mornings in those winters which they feared, nor any mention of a schedule, although there were hints elsewhere that it would be similar to BR - which would rule out one man driving *and* taking fares. No indication was given of research data which enabled them to forecast traffic levels. That no bank loan was obtained is proof positive of the unviability of the scheme, even with some free labour.

"Negotiations are to begin between BR and a passenger association for sale of a branch line at Westerham which closed last October. BR told the Westerham Branch Railway Passenger Association that they were prepared to sell the branch line for £30,000, which the Association has offered, subject to a condition that they would run a service which would make the extra buses provided - as a condition of closure - unnecessary. The £30,000 was for track, buildings, some land and part of the main platform at Dunton Green. A 500 strong Association had been formed". [Times 7.9.62, 6c].

The Association wrote : "Our solution would be to back up, by practical advice, finance and other assistance, societies seeking to run lines under private auspices". They "were hoping to run Mondays to Fridays, perhaps Saturdays, a diesel service catering for 200 or so commuters - operated by *retired* railwaymen, and 400 enthusiasts. With careful management, it could pay its way or make a small profit. If it ran at a profit, publicity would be given that one more 'hopelessly uneconomic line' is paying its way". [Railway Gazette, June 1962, Page 733]. They spoke of 200 or so commuters, when the current level was 167. No proof was given that the number would increase. BR had a handful of staff, not 400 unpaid. Running "profitably" under such conditions would be child's play. It exposes the fallacy of many closure objections. UK would have no export problems if industry operated with unpaid labour.

Another author, claimed that BR were obstructive, and thereby frustrated plans for the Association to run the line. He did not spell out what actions were taken by BR which could be deemed obstructive. Clearly, they - like he and I - would have to obey the law, and if the Council obtained approval by the MoT for a new road - which they did - and threatened compulsory purchase which they were empowered to do, whether to demolish privately owned houses or buy up a closed railway - BR would have had to acquiesce. In one case, BR was required to divert a main line at Colwyn Bay to build a new road. It is also pertinent to note that in a similar case - the Bluebell line - BR bent over backwards to help them to take over the line, and they found the money. (See page 105). The Association's own minutes indicate that BR was prepared to sell the line for *less than its value*.

The MoT published a draft Order for the South Orbital Road - objections to be reported to him by 27th December 1963. [Kent County Council Planning Committee 10.10.63]. Clearly supporters of the railway could not muster enough support to block the development and its effect on their plans. Had the idea been practical, and beneficial, it should not have failed to secure support. They had had *over two years*, since closure, to organise themselves and raise the money for this line which, given cost free labour should have been "profitable" to them. Blame rests with themselves not the County Council, nor BR.

A favourable picture is painted of BR's role by the Westerham Valley Railway Association itself. At its 1962 AGM, it was reported that the value of the land has been estimated at well over the price accepted by BR, and so the capital outlay will be fully covered. BR had valued the property at £80,000, and had reduced the price asked, first to £53,000, then to £30,000. A member asked what would happen if the venture were to fail, and was told by the chairman that the company would have to bear the loss. (*Hitherto, the impression had been created that the venture could not fail*). Others asked why they were 'giving away too much' in allowing an independent investor to provide much of the capital, and would he accept a 50% holding. They were told that the Association had tried for six months, without success to raise the money, and had never been in a position to take a 50% holding. At their 1963 AGM, members were told:-

- All efforts to raise the £40,000 needed to purchase land and equipment had failed. Only £2,000 had been promised. (*Over 2,000 people had petitioned their MP. They ought to have been able to raise far more than that*).
- The Association had tried to raise the money as Debentures, but had failed.
- Kent County Council, which had shelved its original plans of using the land for road development to enable us to acquire the line, had now decided to re-open negotiations with BR. The BRB was seeking assurances that we had the money to purchase. If the money could be raised, they could stop the Council getting the line.
- To proceed with purchase, there were two options - to sell the Westerham station site, and open a new station outside the existing station area, but this would be unacceptable to commuters; or to obtain a loan of £35,000.
- The prospective investor withdrew support when planning permission for development of land at Westerham and Brasted was rejected. Other backers were approached, but their interest was dependent on relocating Westerham station some way down the line, and obtaining planning permission.
- Many members were not pulling their weight. (*Snow clearance would be a problem*!).
- A member understood that if they were willing to run a commuter service, the County Council would have no option but to stand aside. It was accepted that the commuter service would not pay, but we should be prepared to subsidise it if the line was obtained. (*If they couldn't make it pay with voluntary labour, how could BR?*).

# Chapter 12                     Haltwhistle - Alston Branch

In 1841, directories show that Alston parish had a population of over 6,000, the town itself about 1,650, with an extensive and productive lead mining industry. Other minerals including iron ore, coal and copper were mined. The line opened in 1852 to handle this traffic.

Before the end of the century, the population of the parish was down to 3,384. The lead industry and coal mining had virtually disappeared. This left agriculture, and that industry was among the first to desert railways for road motor transport.

There were only 2,678 people in the parish in 1931. By 1938, the remaining mineral trade was effectively uneconomic. The branch was a typically unprofitable rural line.

The nature of the line, with its severe gradients - the 13 mile branch line had a ruling gradient of 1 in 56 - its many bridges and Lambley viaduct would make it more costly to operate than lines of comparable length, whilst its pastoral nature would produce little revenue. It must have been accelerating towards closure, even before the War.

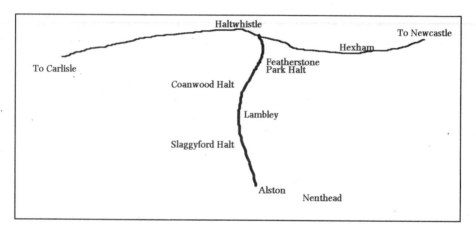

In 1959, the TUCC was advised that passenger services were running at a loss and in an attempt to avoid closure, steam would be replaced by DMU's from November. It was known that the savings from using diesels would not be sufficient to balance receipts and expenditure, and cheap fares were suspended. Costs were reduced and there was a small increase in receipts. As there was little scope for economies which would eliminate the loss, complete closure was recommended by the North Eastern Region to the Rail Board.

BR was criticised because cheap tickets were abolished. BR said that revenue from them was insufficient to fund the new DMU's. One would expect to pay more for a better product, especially as fares were trailing the RPI by 39 points. [See "Blueprints for Bankruptcy", Page 63]

The Anglo/Austral Mill, (which objectors said had sent traffic by rail), closed in 1961. Its weekly output was 160 tons. [Cumberland & Westmoreland Herald, 28.1.61]. That did not justify a *weekly* train. Little wonder the line was unremunerative.

## The First Closure Proposal - 1962

BR submitted a twelve page proposal on 26th January 1962, to close the line with a saving of £5,865 and to avoid £10,992 being spent on renewals in the next five years. Five stations and unstaffed halts would close. Redundant assets worth £60,559 would be recovered. BR sent copies of the papers on the proposed closure to 41 bodies and organisations. Alston was the only place within the jurisdiction of the North West TUCC, so they left the North East TUCC to pursue the matter. [North East TUCC 17.4.62, min 941]. The TUCC's received 21 written objections.

The TUCC set up a sub committee to consider objections. The sub committee invited objectors and BR to meetings at Alston on 11th April and Haltwhistle on 11th May.

**Objections** :-

*Haltwhistle RDC*

- Revenue could be increased by restoring cheap tickets; costs reduced by cutting out less well patronised midday trains, introducing railbuses & halts. (Not a single statistic was advanced to prove how many extra passengers, much less, how much more revenue could be expected in order to pay for building halts, never mind reducing losses. Is this how councils make investment decisions? It may stimulate volume, but that is not the same as net receipts. Noticeably they were insufficiently sure of their ground to guarantee the experiment with hard cash. Nor did they suggest who should cover the loss. Neither did they offer to take it over - at valuation, and obtain a Light Railway Order to run it themselves).
- A saving of £850 pa could be made if traincrew lived at Haltwhistle and the DMU stabled there, reducing the £5,865 saving to £5,015 or even to £1,605. (They did not explain how the further reduction would be achieved).

    *At a Sub committee meeting of the RDC, Mr. Wright of Hexham said that the reason for the DMU being located at Hexham is that some use is made of it on the main line, and also for maintenance reasons. BR said that the RDC's proposal did not allow for relief for covering rest days, sickness, etc., and highlighted the problem of short notice absence, maintenance, fuelling costs, and the implications of replacing the one and only unit at 6.00 am in the event of a breakdown.* (See also pages 35-36).

- Criticised BR because Rampgill Mills at Nenthead *has* to take traffic by road to Haydon Bridge for onward rail transit deliberately diverting traffic from the line.

    *BR explained that the company had **requested** that this be arranged!.*

    Nenthead was not connected to the branch. Had it been taken by road to Alston, the train load would have been less. Taking it to Haydon Bridge would benefit the customer and BR, because train loads were greater, and the customer paid less. By inference, they were erroneously assuming that freight traffic should be priced high enough to subsidise passenger services. Bus services were not subsidised by freight, they were subsidised by councils.

- Produced a list of passengers - it was so small that they could list everyone by name and journey on two pages. They claimed 113 would suffer hardship using buses.

*Alston Parish Council*
- Had passed a unanimous motion to protest against the closure. The Board of Trade had given financial assistance to *two* companies in the area! They were confident that with fewer trains, increased traffic from Precision Products, and cheap fares, the loss could be halved at least. It could be that whatever economies are made the line will not be self supporting, but over **90** depend on the line to get to work. (They were not so confident as to back their claims with money, nor with themselves making increased use of the line. They produced no figures. They expected freight to subsidise passengers. That would be unacceptable to freight customers, who wanted to pay the absolute minimum rate. Precision Products' traffic was very small - see page 165).

*Cumberland County Council*
- Their Surveyor's Report stated that the railway is the only means of ensuring communication with Alston. (Even the railway was blocked by snow at times).

*Northumberland Association of Parish Councils*
- Revenue would increase if a lightweight railbus was based at Alston with a one man crew. Lambley should be an unstaffed halt. Signalling on a 13 mile branch need not be elaborate. (Were *they* qualified in signalling? They had overlooked capital and working costs for fuelling & maintenance, which would easily exceed the "savings" - See pages 35-36).

  A BTC Report stated: "*Cannot dispense with the guard, as a railbus will sometimes run onto a line where protection, in the event of failure, must be carried out on an adjoining line. Railbus design does not lend itself to the driver issuing tickets. There would be delays. The range of ticket issues on rail is far wider than on road transport*". [PRO: AN85/47, 20.3.58].

*All Local authorities*
- Disagreed with BR that each halt would cost £3,000 - a set of steps would suffice. (The MoT would have to approve that. A one man crew would have to attend gates, collect fares, put steps up, assist passengers with those inevitable prams, heavy luggage and babies in arms, which arise on every line proposed for closure, remove steps and clear snow. The schedule would be unpredictable).
- The cost of alternative road improvements was greater than BR savings. The railway should continue to operate as a social service whether some losses are incurred or not. (They didn't offer a penny towards BR losses to avoid road costs and avoided suggesting who would pay the subsidy - passengers on other lines or staff).

*Northumberland Education Committee*
- Would cost an extra £370 pa for school transport. (Rail fares were said to be too high)

*MP's*
- Mr. Whitelaw referred to 70 passengers from Alston and said the loss should be met by taxpayers as part of the *general railway deficit*. (See page 12. That was not to subsidise branches. Losses were to be eliminated in five years. BR still had to pay its way, albeit Government policy ensured that could not be achieved. BR had been advanced interest bearing *loans* to compensate for losses on such lines. He voted against the 1968 Act which introduced funding of socially necessary lines).

- Mr. Spiers drew attention to the winter problems and made the same point about the deficit being met by the taxpayer.

*Industry*
- **Alston Foundry** criticised the lack of an early train to bring labour in.
    (In this area of high unemployment and light industry, the prospective volume of labour by train was not going to be of levels which would pay for extra trains).
- **Cascelloid Ltd** said "it could well be that as we extend, facilities for workers to travel from further afield may be essential".
    (*If* and *Maybe*. No other industry would be expected to maintain production because someone *may* want to buy their products on an unspecified date)
- **Precision Products of Alston** found it difficult to reconcile two facets of Government policy. The *Board of Trade gave them financial assistance*, but it is now proposed to withdraw this vital transport facility. BR should reduce fares!
    (In contrast, BR got no Government finance. BR had been subsisting since 1948 on interest bearing loans from Government to keep open loss making lines, hold fares well below the RPI, and compelled to freeze prices when industry didn't).
    *BR said that their rail traffic amounted to **two tons per month** and was irregular.*

*Other objectors*
- J.M. Clark, Chartered Land Agents: costs could be reduced by cutting out staff at Featherstone, Coanwood and Slaggyford level crossings as they were at stations, and traincrews could open gates. It should be retained at a loss as a public service. (No other company offers loss making services as a public service. Perhaps they were unaware of the effect on schedules of such methods, especially if snow had to be cleared to enable gates to be opened. Coanwood *was an unstaffed* farmer's crossing!).
- Major Joicey - doesn't think that because the number of days lost due to people being unable to get to work due to snow is small, it is an argument for not keeping the line.
- J.S. Joicey of Blenkinsopp Hall, argued that the BTC should tell the NUR branch that wages on the line would be cut. (The days when employees in any industry were brusquely told their wages would be cut had long gone. No industry in the UK had been brave enough to tell its workers to take a cut in wages to keep their jobs. That came 30 years later, when Directors increased their own pay at the same time).
- The line is the only means of travel when roads are blocked by snow and ice.
- A return fare of 2/6d (12.5p) on Saturdays instead of 6/6d (32.5p) would attract additional traffic to travel to the cinema in Alston. (It required 160% more passengers to preserve existing revenue. They did not guarantee that increase with cash).
    *BR said they have tried cheap Saturday fares - it was not beneficial to revenue. Numbers were down, but revenue was up since cheap fares were withdrawn.*
- Mr. Hedley said fares should be reduced for a six month trial down to 4/- (20p) from Alston to Haltwhistle. (He did not propose who would cover increased losses if his theory reduced revenue. See his complaint on destaffing - page 168)
- Oakwood - population 90 and 30 in outlying areas sent a petition with 123 signatures, and Lambley, population 64, one of 56. (Clearly, they were not all regular travellers).
- Wives need trains for shopping. Others advocated cutting out off-peak trains.

The closure proposal had some support:-

- The community can hardly expect BR to operate this service when it is only supported during wintry conditions. If Alston RDC have ratepayers' interests at heart, why do they not offer a payment to BR to operate this service. [Reader's letter "*The Journal*" 9.1.63].
- "The line does not pay. The social service plea, community interest, rural area, no alternative transport are irrelevant from the Minister's and BR's viewpoint. Will the farmers, Post Office, councils, schools services offer more support for rail transport, or in the absence of a subsidy, the branch line will die". [Mr. W. Owen, MP 13.1.62].
- Regional Board for Industry wrote to the TUCC on similar lines to Mr. Owen.

## TUCC and CTCC Decisions

The Sub Committee's Report stated that "It is thinly populated. Apart from Alston with 1,400, eleven other communities had populations between 30 and 500 with an average of 212. Savings were originally £5,865 are now £4,955. Renewals of £10,992 would be avoided by closure, and credits of £60,559 gained from recovery of redundant assets". (Alston's population had declined dramatically since the line was built to compete with the horse). "We are satisfied that without a subsidy the service cannot continue, but we don't want the service to stop in the interests of people here. There was no direct evidence that costs could be reduced and receipts increased sufficiently to make the service pay its way. On purely economic grounds, BR had a case for closure. They doubted the adequacy of proposed alternative services. Withdrawal would produce undue hardship".

A private bus operator said that buses would need to be subsidised.

The motion was put, and carried that: "This Sub Committee, having examined the proposal to withdraw rail facilities recommends the service be maintained and the Minister asked to make a Grant. Failing this, the road to be made safe for a bus service, no alteration to be made until satisfactory alternative transport arrangements are made, on account of hardship which users would suffer".

The full TUCC accepted the Sub Committee's Report and agreed to recommend that the MoT makes a grant to the BTC in respect of losses. Failing this, roads to be made safe for a bus service before closure. "The economic case for closure is accepted". "Withdrawal would result in hardship". [North East TUCC, 19.6.62, min 372].

The MoT was asked to make a grant. Failing this roads to be made safe for a bus service, no alteration to be made until the TUCC are satisfied alternative transport arrangements have been made, on account of the hardship users would suffer. Members said, after travelling over the proposed bus route, that £1,000 for road improvements was inadequate, it would be nearer to £20,000, a new bridge was needed. [TUCC min 972].

The CTCC endorses the TUCC recommendation that the service be maintained or roads made safe for a bus service. The CTCC did not endorse the suggestion that a grant be made to the BTC in respect of losses. [North East TUCC 17.12.62, min 988].

## Railways Needed in Bad Weather

A recent snowfall proves there is a need for a train service. Alston station reported an increase in passengers carried. [Haltwhistle Echo, March 1962]. *Until roads were clear*!.

Haltwhistle RDC wrote to the TUCC expressing appreciation for keeping the line open. All food and necessities were handled on the line, and earned warm praise They didn't say it would earn more use by the grateful population *and* the council. The praise should have been directed to BR - the TUCC did not supply any staff to clear snow.

Roads were blocked for five days by snow. Milk was being put (back) on trains, bread was brought in by train. [Newcastle Journal 4.1.63]. This was a common basis for objections. Spring and bad memories ended support for such lines, until closure was threatened. ["*Blueprints for Bankruptcy*", Page 80].

BR wrote to the TUCC: "BR staff worked continuously under arduous conditions and at great expense to keep the line open". Needless to say, BR was not overwhelmed with offers of financial help. As soon as the crisis was over, passengers, bread and milk reverted without delay to normal methods.

Those who called for staff cuts, took no account of the need for increased staff in winter nor did they consider, in the midst of proffering their unsolicited and inexpert advice, whence staff were to be drawn to tackle such problems. Neither did they acknowledge that these extra staff had to be paid. Doubtless, they would challenge every penny debited to the branch for such activity. The effect of traincrew getting down to open gates, move forward, stop and close gates could not have crossed many minds. If there was snow, they would first have to shovel the snow sufficiently to enable the gates to be opened.

The MoT, responding to information on the effect and use of the railway in winter, stated: "As a general rule, we could hardly expect that railways should provide services throughout the year with all the heavy capital cost involved just as an insurance against exceptional weather conditions. The case for retention of service would normally have to be decided in the light of use made of the line throughout the year". [Hexham Courant 1.2.63].

### Reprieved

On 22nd July 1963, the MoT wrote to the CTCC: "The Minister has considered the recommendation and the alternative facilities for passengers if closure takes place. He has decided to accept the Committee's recommendation that the passenger service should be continued".

The first decision made by the MoT on a proposed line closure since the Beeching Report was published, was to accept the recommendation of the North East TUCC, endorsed by the CTCC that the Haltwhistle-Alston line, some thirteen miles long, should remain open. [Times 25.7.63, 10a]. There was to be no Government subsidy for the users of this line - BR losses would continue to be inflated by this social need.

Tyne Valley Coaches Ltd wrote to the TUCC in January 1969: "In 1964, BR was quoted for a bus to be provided when Lambley viaduct was being repaired. A bus would still be a practicable prospect. However, a large subsidy would be required".

Clearly had the line closed in 1962, the viaduct expense would have been avoided. These are the renewal costs which objectors and TUCC's had tended to dismiss as something too far in the future and remote to take into account.

## Interim Economies

In March 1966, Mr. Hedley objected to destaffing Lambley station as an economy - consequent on the MoT's refusal to authorise closure - for the following reasons :-

1. It would cause great inconvenience to the travelling public.

2. If trains are cancelled, staff can inform passengers of alternative arrangements.

3. The station is half a mile from the village.

4. There are several season ticket holders.

5. BR may say problems don't happen often, but the public is entitled to expect, no matter when they travel, they should be able to do so without inconvenience.

He was at the meeting of Haltwhistle RDC which proposed halts. There was no opposition. Having got the Minister to decree that the line should stay open, the very economies which objectors said should be made, when made, were subject to objections! Partial economies made earlier would still leave losses to be carried by BR. (See page 36).

Haltwhistle RDC wrote on 7th March 1966 to the TUCC that they "had asked BR, without success, to introduce workmen's concessionary fares in the *hope* that it would increase revenue and be an added attraction for workmen to travel by rail, *if* either Alston or Haltwhistle be successful in attracting industry to the area upon closure of Bordon Mill colliery. They said that cheaper fares would *tend* to increase the number of passengers". No one would argue with that, but there was clear evidence that it caused revenue to *fall*, whilst costs continued to rise - see "*Blueprints for Bankruptcy*". There was no codicil that if reduced fares led to reduced revenue, the RDC would make up the difference.

BR proposed to convert Featherstone and Slaggyford manned crossings into Open Crossings. Trains would stop at a distance from them, "Halt" signs would be placed on roads. There would be no lighting, they would be like cross-roads. Councillors said that there should be some indication to show that a person was going to cross, because drivers may not stop. It is the same on roads. One said he was not worried about expenditure when it comes to human life. [Hexham Courant, 16.10.64]. There are millions of locations where pedestrians cross and walk on roads which have neither pavements nor lighting nor any "indication" because most councils have *not* put human life before expenditure limits. When BR was criticised for modernising a crossing near a playground, I replied that if children were too young to cross the line safely, they were too young to walk along the road which had no footpath on the playground side, to get to a playground beyond the crossing. The frequency of motor vehicles, which leave one just as dead, is many times greater than the frequency of trains on branch lines. [See "*Blueprints for Bankruptcy*", Page 145].

In 1969, councils informed the TUCC that, "justifiably all stations had been converted to unstaffed halts, but buildings had not been replaced by bus shelters nor electric lighting provided". The objective was to make modest savings, not dissipate them by re-deploying them on extra capital projects and running costs. When the same people advocated these measures, they did not mention this additional investment would be needed. (See page 31).

## Grant Aid

The 1968 Transport Act introduced Government subsidies for the first time, to compensate BR for being compelled by successive Governments to keep open lines for social reasons. Under the Act, the line was grant aided for a period of one year and there-after was subject to annual review.  In 1969 it was £40,000, in 1970: £41,000, in 1971: £54,000, rising to £61,000 in 1973. After 1973, grants were not separately identified. [BRB Accounts]. Costs had been driven up by inflation, fired by local authorities' wage policies.

The MoT told Parliament on 18th December 1969 : On the information available it would not be justified in continuing the grant paid for services between Haltwhistle and Alston without some evidence of social and economic need. [Hansard, vol. 793, col. 397].

"Last December, the MoT, Fred Mulley allocated a £43,000 grant, but said the line would close at the end of 1971, because he believed a grant for more than two years was not justified. A Hexham RDC councillor said 'lives had been saved by this line'". [The Journal 21.8.70].    Not a penny was credited to BR for "saving lives". Criticism of BR for Government initiated losses was undiminished. [See "Blueprints for Bankruptcy"].

### The second closure proposal - 1970
The MoT advised BRB it is unlikely there will be a renewal of grant unless consent to closure of this service is refused. Accordingly BR gave notice in September 1970 of a new proposal to withdraw the passenger train service between Haltwhistle and Alston, and said that Ribble will provide alternative bus services.  [Cumberland & Westmoreland Herald, 26.9.70]

When BR gave notice to close, there was an immediate outcry of objections:-
- When the roads are blocked, the school bus is unable to run, and the train is their only means of transport! (Their gall was only eclipsed by the farmers - see below).
- Alston Foundry said it operated an efficient mini bus service to convey employees to work, but "it cannot operate in winter when roads are blocked by snow"! (This smacks of treating the railway as an insurance - but only paying the "premium" when there is a need to make a claim on the "policy").
- North Pennines Rural Development Board: When roads out of Alston are blocked with snow, 23 farms depend on rail services to bring bread, meat, fuel and fodder. Under such conditions nine farms rely on the railways to take milk to Stocksfield Dairy. The alternative is a helicopter which would cost farmers several hundred pounds. (One has to marvel at their cheek, but *they* were accustomed to subsidies).
- Cumberland County Council: Since the last decision to spare the line, there has been no very severe winter.  For an average of 5-6 days pa, roads in the area are closed.
- Northumberland County Council: 35 people use the line daily or several times per week. Non regular use is 153.  21 use it in bad weather! (This presumably meant the last bad winter in 1963. Why did they not use this 'essential' line all the time?)

Local Authorities in rural Northumberland have been told to subsidise country buses by 31st December or lose the bus services. A subsidy of more than £9,000 would be needed from Hexham RDC to maintain a bus service.[The Journal 20.10.70 & 22.10.70].

The TUCC held a public inquiry into the proposed closure of the line on 17th February 1971.  BR's spokesman said that the line earned only £3,000 pa and survived on a £50,000

Grant from the MoT. Each user is subsidised at the rate of 50p per mile. Since closure was last considered in 1962, there had been a fall in passengers from 180 to 111 on weekdays and 209 to 124 on Saturdays. Economies had been made in signalling, fuel and staff costs and the number of trains had been reduced. A reduced weekday fare system designed to attract passengers had lost money. The Grant will be discontinued at the end of the year. There were over 40 objections, 13 from local authorities. Haltwhistle RDC said the line had proved its worth time and time again to the elderly and sick of the area. Northumberland County Council said that proposed road improvements had never been discussed between BR and the Council. [Cumberland News, 19.2.71]. If only the elderly and sick were using rail, little wonder it was losing money. BR had no remit for roads.

Cumberland County Council said that to withdraw the rail link before a new road was built would be a betrayal. [Cumberland News, 19.2.71]. The betrayal had been by those who called for reduced costs, reduced fares, retention of the line - got them, and then used the line *less* than before, thus not making the line viable as they had claimed it would be.

Alston RDC accused BR of doing nothing to keep the line. [The Journal, 18.2.71]. They tabled no evidence to demonstrate that they, or most of the local populace, had done, or would do, *anything* to keep the line, other than to use it in extreme weather conditions.

The English Lakes Counties Travel Association said that the population of Alston doubled between May and September, because of holidaymakers, **many** came by train. [Cumberland News, 19.2.71]. That was it - not a single statistic to back up this claim. The population was over 2,000. With even 51% (i.e. "many"), of the *extra* 2,000 people using trains, the line would have been carrying eight times as many as recorded on Saturdays.

Ribble Bus Company's spokesman said that a bus service would run at an even bigger loss than other rural services and would need local authority subsidies and fares would be higher than current rail fares. [Evening News 18.2.71].

The Inquiry on 17th February 1971 was told that the service was operated by one diesel multiple unit as a pay-train; there was no signalling on the line. The TUCC chairman said that BR had experimented with cheap fares, but they had cost money. Passengers had dropped, since 1962, from 180 to 111 on weekdays and 209 to 124 on Saturdays. BR said the bus services would provide alternatives for nearly all regular users of railways, but recognised that there would be time difficulties. Seven people in Coanwood would not be served by bus and a similar number from Alston who use the 08.50 train to Haltwhistle. There would be £3,000 in short term savings. Northumberland County Council said that road improvements would cost £290,000. Thirty people per day use the line to get to work and another 20-30 for shopping. Of 152 users, one third were pensioners. Schoolchildren from Slaggyford to Alston travelled by train *when the weather was bad*. [Hexham Courant 19.2.71]. The Government would save £61,000 pa.

A report issued by the TUCC this week says: "The TUCC has examined the proposed withdrawal of the passenger train service and are of the opinion that should the service be withdrawn, without extensive road improvements being carried out to allow a suitably timed bus service to be introduced, the hardship which would be caused to the whole of the area served by this line would be severe. The TUCC have not been able to suggest any way of alleviating the hardship". [Cumberland & Westmoreland Herald, 16.4.71].

On 22nd January, 1973, the Minister notified County Councils that he had agreed to BR's proposal to close the line, but to facilitate the introduction of a bus service, the closure would not take place until 1st May 1975. The Government would meet the cost of roadworks up to a maximum of £300,000 at current prices. This was later raised to £400,000. [Northumberland County Council Memo, 4.4.74].

The MoT told MP's the line will not close until adequate provision for alternative transport including road improvements has been made. [Hansard vol. 866, col. 41].

A deputation from the area was seen by the MoT in March 1975. They pointed out that Alston depended on the railway line *in winter*. Under blizzard conditions, the railway had been the only way to transport people to hospital and bring in supplies. It was hoped that local people would support the Preservation Society in its attempt to save the railway. [Cumberland & Westmoreland Herald, 22.3.75]. Local people had given inadequate support to the line or it would not have closed. Usage in bad winters was not enough.

The line eventually closed on 3rd May 1976. On the last day, a five coach train, organised by *Carlisle* Round Table, carried passengers at £2.75 each. BR had been offering journeys from *London* for 5-6 weeks at £5 each, 100 had made the journey each weekend! Line closure has meant something of a tourist boom. The line closed after the last train on 1st May 1976. It was hoped that the South Tynedale Company in conjunction with the County Council will run a service. BR had offered the land and line for £150,000, but failing an immediate offer, the line would be removed. The County Council's request for a deferment was rejected by BR, as the council had known, since 1973, that the line would close. BR pointed out that the assets were worth more than £150,000, but they would deteriorate if not removed. The South Tynedale Company announced the public would have an opportunity to buy shares, and expected a widespread and international response. [Cumberland & Westmoreland Herald, 1.5.76]. These "tourists" were using the line because it was about to close. Such people were not otherwise to be seen on the line in meaningful numbers.

## Postscript

Two local rail enthusiasts - Councillor Bill Weeks and John Arnott Brown - would like to take over the line and run it as a tourist attraction. Northumberland County Council said: If private enterprise are prepared to take over the line and provide a service which BR cannot, then it might be possible to subsidise them! [The Journal 18.3.71]. They could not have recognised the irony of this remark. Private enterprise needed a subsidy and would get it. The branch could only operate with a subsidy, but under BR, would not get one.

A Preservation Society was later formed to buy a section of the route and operate a service. "A diesel made its first trip of $1^1/_2$ miles on what was the Haltwhistle-Alston line, With the help of the Manpower Services Commission, they have constructed a narrow gauge railway. They have two wooden bodied coaches and an industrial diesel loco". [Hexham Courant, 5.8.83].

The Society opened a short section of narrow gauge railway in 1983. North Pennine Heritage Trust gave them a Grant of £9,000. [Cumberland News, 4.8.95, Page 7].

# Chapter 13        Somerset & Dorset Joint Line

It was originally the Somerset Central and the Dorset Central. The former received the Royal Assent in July 1852 for a line from Highbridge to Glastonbury. Extensions to Cole, Wells and Burnham followed. Connection was made at Cole with the Dorset Central. The S&DR (Somerset & Dorset Railway) formed in 1862, experienced financial difficulties in the late 1860's. In 1874, it opened lines to join the Midland at Bath. Further financial difficulties were experienced in 1875. The Midland and the L&SWR leased the line for 999 years. They formed the Somerset & Dorset Joint Railway - from Bath to Broadstone Junction near Poole - 100 miles. Less than 50% was double track. A branch to Bridgwater opened in 1890. The most important development was an increase in coal traffic handled in the Radstock area of the Somerset coalfield. [Sherrington, Pages 46/47].

The company lacked the essential features which made other railways viable. It had steep gradients, was largely single line and ran through a sparsely populated region, with little industry. Hence, despite its length, it had more affinity with branch than trunk lines.

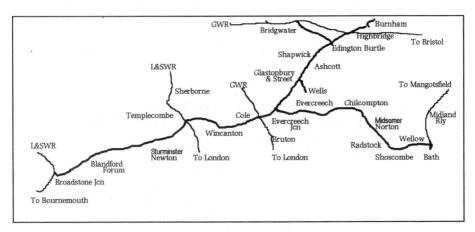

## Financial Record

The Salisbury & Yeovil directors were not disposed to throw out branches, which have proved to be a source of embarrassment - including - that most unfortunate of railways - the Somerset & Dorset. At Templecombe, the best paying line in the Kingdom is brought into connection with the worst. A direct line of 40 miles, unencumbered with branches pays 14% : Salisbury & Yeovil. A pretentious undertaking which sought to exchange the mineral wealth of South Wales for the products of France - Somerset & Dorset, has found many additions to its originally modest aim to be so many clogs to success. [Ruegg, Page 56].

The company was in such a bad state in 1875 they asked the Bristol & Exeter Railway Company to lease it, but they seemed not inclined to do so. [The Railway Year Book, 1913].

The line was not a financial success from its earliest days. Its rolling stock and assets were inferior or inadequate. One of its tunnels was badly constructed. It had insufficient capacity, limited by single lines and severe gradients - 1 in 46 and 1 in 50 - which required banking engines. Its financial structure was unsound - nearly 50% of capital was in Debentures and Loans on which it often failed to meet interest. Arrears accumulated forcing it into Receiver's hands. It was struggling to compete with the horse.

The company struggled to attract investors, who clearly saw its poor prospects. Of £645,000 of Ordinary Stock, £300,000 was issued at 50% discount. Some Preference and Bath Extension shares were also issued at a discount. The latter included some accepted by the contractor who built the Extension in part payment, because the company was short of cash. [Bradshaw's Shareholders Guide 1876 & Herapath's Railway Journal, 1874, Page 1101]. A company which had to sell shares at a discount was in deep trouble. Its ambitious project to extend to Bath was a financial disaster. They were rescued from Receivership by the Lease. Despite the lease terms, of fifteen classes of Stock, in 1883, seven had no dividend paid on them. The remaining Stock, Debentures and Preference shares were largely covered. 1884 presented a similar depressing picture. [Bradshaw's Shareholders Guide, 1883-4]

The effect of leasing the line can be gleaned from the operating ratios, (the percentage of gross receipts taken up by expenditure), before and after the lease :-

|  | 1865 | 1900 | 1922 |
|---|---|---|---|
| Midland | 44% | 62% | 79% |
| L&SWR | 52% | 62% | 78% |
| Source : Sherrington, Pages 49 & 117 | | | |

The finances of the S&DR Joint line became progressively worse, between the Wars. A deficiency of £20-23,000 pa was recorded each year 1924-28 inclusive. Directors Reports show the net loss had worsened to £36,196 by 1934. [PRO: Rail 1110/419].

### Traffic Decline

Early hopes of hordes of people crossing by steamer from South Wales to continue their journey via Burnham and the S&DR to the South Coast did not materialise. Mechanical transport was cheaper and more convenient, and as the years passed, passengers and freight grew less. Buses took most of the passengers, but they in turn have lost to private transport. [Poole & Dorset Herald, 1.1.64].

In 1951, passenger trains were withdrawn from the Highbridge to Burnham line and the Wells branch closed. In 1952 the Bridgwater branch also closed for passenger traffic

Somerset coalfields suffered from the availability of cheaper alternatives such as oil, and were failing to attract sufficient labour to work the pits thus reducing potential output. [Hawkins, Page 9]. (*Potential output* does not equate to *sales* of a more expensive product).

New Rock colliery ceased operation before the end of 1965. At that time Norton Hill colliery was working and was the most modern in North Somerset, but during 1965 it began to lose money at such a rate that the NCB had to close it in February 1966. This was convenient for BR. [Deacon, Page 25]. No criticism was made about closing a colliery nor was the accuracy of NCB figures questioned - they did not face a public inquisition.

The line was doomed from the start. All through history, one source of traffic after another dried up. They decided to try the Mendip coalfields but that soon ceased. They had to rely on milk traffic, but that now moves by lorry. It is useless to keep a line open for brief hours of glory each summer. Rural buses do not pay, there is no point in allowing two forms of public transport to compete for a limited traffic. Bus is the most effective form in a sparsely populated rural area. [Poole & Dorset Herald, 10.4.63 & 1.1.64].

## Traffic Diversion

That a line such as the S&DR Joint Railway should have been *believed* to prosper as part of the Midland and L&SWR, and later under the LMS and Southern Railway, does not mean that it was essential in a national undertaking. If the traffic reverted to original routes, following nationalisation, then the S&DR was rightly and sensibly shown to be superfluous. When BR owned all railways, they were bound to look at concentrating traffic on fewer routes. Critics saw this logical policy - pursued without criticism by industry - to concentrate activity on fewer locations - when practised by BR - as an action to make a line avoidably unprofitable. This is all the more incredible since critics acknowledged that traffic had been lost to road, or due to cessation of production.

BR was criticised for re-routing beer traffic to the West of England via Taunton, which critics claimed had gone via the S&DR since 1874. (It had almost certainly been on the Taunton route before that. Re-routing after the Midland secured joint control would have increased Midland's net profit, but not that of railways as a whole).

One by one through freight trains ceased to run : fertilisers from Avonmouth to Blandford were re-routed via Bath Spa, Westbury, Southampton, and Bournemouth - 135 miles from Bristol against 65 over the "Dorset". [Deacon, Page 16].

Mileage was not the most significant factor. (See page 138). The line's severe gradients made operations more costly than a longer less steep route :-

- Double headed operation on heavy trains on the ruling 1 in 50 gradient played an important part in diverting traffic from this line particularly because of the extra manpower needed. Enthusiasts would not see the sight of five pilot locos waiting in the central siding at Evercreech Junction to assist trains over the Mendips. [Hawkins, Page 10].
- One wonders how much a busy summer Saturday must have cost to operate with every through working having a pilot as well as a train loco; a large number of pilot locos awaiting their next turn of duty; light engine running; extra train crews and locos. The time taken for an express from Bath (Green Park) to Bournemouth West was poor. They had to reverse at Bath and at Templecombe Junction. With severe gradients and tight curves, overall speed was low and the time taken to travel the line was greater than lines of similar length elsewhere. [Deacon, Page 17].

The advent of the motor age, with the undeniable advantage of door step departure inevitably poached a crucial proportion of local traffic. Only its use for through traffic from its two owning companies kept it alive, otherwise, it must have died in the thirties. When all became one corporation, the justification for routing trunk traffic disappeared.

In 1962, BR re-routed the "Pines Express" via Basingstoke and Oxford. The TUCC criticised BR for doing so without informing them. (The 1962 Act did not require such action). BR explained that it had been done due to the heavy programme of engineering work involving electrification and rebuilding of Birmingham New Street. The service pattern after electrification would make it difficult to restore to its present route. The principal traffic was between Bournemouth, Birmingham and the North. The routing was a relic from pre-war days, because the line was a direct link between the LMS and the Southern, without passing over the GWR, which would have had to have a share of the receipts. Although stops were made on the S&DR, user was slight and the train is in no sense a stopping train. The economics of the line were being investigated, and if this leads to a proposal for closure, a submission may be made to the TUCC at the end of September. (Those involved in electrification knew diversion during construction was unavoidable).

### Non Closure "Solutions"

Critics said that signalman Ernie Cross produced a plan to save the line and gave it to the media. It is not clear why this came three years *after* closure was proposed. The Joint Consultation Agreement (see page 28), required staff to co-operate in improving efficiency. It could have been tabled years earlier by his elected representatives under that procedure or at the meeting held to discuss closure. Management would have had to consider it. He could have used the Suggestion Scheme and been paid anonymously. Details of his plan were not set out by those who praised him, neither was there an indication of a newspaper which published it. It required prolonged research of many newspapers for the area before finding a report of his *five page* "plan", for which I am grateful to Somerset Library Service. Not all staff blamed management. (See page 183).

It envisaged a two hourly DMU Bournemouth-Bristol service plus two semi-fast trains each way, one steam hauled to Birmingham to cater for enthusiasts. (*It was unwelcome 'under the wires', as staff had been electrocuted*). 40 men could operate the line instead of 100. It would save £50,000 pa. Another £50,000 would be saved by closing the Evercreech Jcn to Burnham line. (*It was to be closed under BR's proposal*). The line would be capable of handling its rightful share of local and through freight traffic. Four depots would be provided for coal, goods, parcels and livestock. A three year experiment would be necessary to prove that it can serve traders and public. He called on rail unions to support him. [Shepton Mallet Journal, 21.1.66]. No letters of support were published. His service required more trains than that proposed by the Branch Line Society. (See page 222).

He did not claim that the line would be profitable, "more efficient" means losing less. It was losing £290,000 pa, and he wanted diesels costing over £122,000 (see page 223), plus costs for maintenance, fuelling facilities and re-training of staff to undertake diesel driving and maintenance. Under his plan, losses would fall to £190,000 pa, to which must be added interest on capital of £6,000 pa. Through traffic was not its, as of *right*. If it could be moved via other routes and the line closed, it was morally right to do so and avoid losses. There was no guarantee that new depots would receive so much as one parcel between them. It did not involve staff, traders or public backing the plan with money. Who was to finance it? The public could have bought non-refundable annual season tickets. Without forecasting revenue, it was valueless. A three year experiment may fail. Who would refund the ensuing £588,000 losses plus the cost of diesels and new depots?

Managers and staff, who considered any economy plan, required details of present & proposed rosters and traction & rolling stock "diagrams" to prove it. (See page 28). I handled many proposals for economy - none was containable within five pages. Financial justification for capital, including savings and revenue forecasts, would fill several pages.

If proper marketing techniques had been applied from the early 1960's the line might have been able to survive. It would have been important to introduce large scale modernisation of the line. Not just diesel, but signalling, unmanned stations and possibly singling. [Deacon, Page 20]. A line which struggled in competition with the horse, would not be made viable by infinite capital and imagination not shown in private enterprise days.

"Cross-border lines fell into the hands of the *enemy* and were largely ignored for investment", e.g. S&D Joint Railway. [Henshaw, Page 43]. (This theory is dealt with on page 53).

As early as 1962, the Branch Line Re-Invigoration Society put forward proposals aimed at restoring it to health, convinced that it could become viable and profitable. It was an imaginative plan, and with a few signalling and operating economies, might have saved the line. Inevitably, the report was ignored and the line wasted away. [Henshaw, Page 183].

***Their 1962 plan was not even costed.*** They produced a "costed" report in 1963, but it was completely unsound. (See Appendix B). They were not so convinced as to set out to raise capital and take over the line, nor even to offer any contribution towards the costs.

## TUCC Hearings

BR told the TUCC's that revenue attributable to the line amounted to £108,600 pa, with direct costs of £398,000 pa. On 26th June 1963, the South East TUCC noted that they had been advised of BR's proposal to withdraw passenger trains from the S&DR: Bristol-Bath-Bournemouth and Evercreech Junction-Highbridge. An official announcement was placed in the media on 15th and 22nd June. [South East TUCC min 427].

The Branch Line Re-invigoration Society objected to closure on behalf of members - but neglected to say how many were regular users. Letters in the media told people how to object to closure, but none called on them to use the line more to secure its future. [Poole & Dorset Herald, 10.7.63, 17.7.63, 24.7.63 & 31.7.63]. One group said that regular excursions from the Midlands had been withdrawn. They did not consider the prospect that Midlands people had no overwhelming desire to spend their every free day travelling via the S&D, and had rejected the south coast by electing to go on excursions to other destinations.

South West TUCC received 114 objections, many in general terms, 48 of them appeared at Hearings on 25th September and 18th October. They included Somerset County Council, thirteen councils, a chamber of commerce, women's institute, a trades council, an MP, and some individuals. South East TUCC received 94 objections and held a Hearing at Blandford on 8th October. Objectors included Dorset County Council, several councils - RDC, UDC, Borough & Parish - a chamber of trade, a trades council - 120 persons attended. Similar objections were advanced at all hearings:-
*County Councils*
- An attempt should be made to make the line profitable, by putting on diesels to test the argument that the line can be made economic. (They appear not to have realised that you do not need to bang yourself twice on the head to learn that it hurts. It is

unnecessary to repeat the same experiment time after time after time in every rural area to gather data on the prospect of making a return on precious capital).

- Extra buses were called for, above those proposed, if the closure was implemented.
- One person in five had a car. (In broad terms that is one per household). It left 16,000 dependent on public transport or "cadging a lift". (The latter must be a substantial number, or travel by train would have been much higher, since objectors were saying how much more convenient trains were than buses).
- Wanted to attract new industry, and would be held back with no railway. (It is curious that in all closures, local authorities only ventilated the idea of attracting *new* industry *after* a line was proposed for closure. The same people were criticising BR for not attracting new business!).
- Rural areas were entitled to a modern railway as much as an urban area. (This did not mean that the Councils were willing to see urban railway modernisation delayed *in their area*, for a year or two whilst BR experimented with modernising rural lines).
- Difficulties would arise with boarding school pupils and their luggage six times pa, losses to small hotels, traders dependent on railways (they did not identify one), surgery visits etc. (If rural areas were "entitled to a modern railway as much as an urban area", rural patients were entitled to the same service as urban patients - with surgeries located in villages. TUCC reports do not indicate that councils had unsuccessfully pursued that more vital angle).

*Poole Borough Council*
- Called for additional buses as set out in a document, not circulated in advance of the meeting. (BR was criticised for making new proposals during a meeting. See page 77)

*Other objections*
- Called for a full Public Inquiry under Sec. 90 of the 1962 Act. (That did not give the MoT powers to compel railways to keep open a loss making line. The MoT could recover the costs of such an inquiry from those calling for it - See page 10).
- A company "forwarded 127,000 small and 69,000 large baskets of watercress by rail, 60% on the S&D line". (Converted to weight, which was the basis of charging - the volume looked much less impressive. A small basket, including the weight of the basket was about 2.5 kilos, and a large 3.5 kilos. The total conveyed on this line would equal about 335 tonnes pa, or about one tonne per day. No reference was made to the amount forwarded by road).
- One objector "travelled on the line twelve times every year".
- No reason given, but just registering an objection.
- It has been starved into submission. (Given such bad roads, it must be by lack of use).
- Should be dieselised. (If steam was faster than road, why would there be more user?)
- Bus routes are longer.
- Should be more excursions. (Does not say who would use nor back them with finance)
- Would use it if given the incentive to do so. (No indication was given of the desired incentives. One would have thought that the *greater convenience of rail*, which was frequently emphasised by objectors, was incentive enough).
- No account taken of freight revenue. (Every closure with traffic at risk always did so)

- Every winter, road transport is useless. Last winter all supplies for the village shop came by rail. (An offer to use the service when it snows? - see page 46).
- Prams can't be taken on buses. (Generally, pram ticket issues were the lowest of all)
- Needs a fast through service several times per day. (He didn't specify at which stations trains should not call. A more useless piece of advice is difficult to conceive).
- One trader received 422 parcels - in one year !
- Trains are moderately well patronised, except in a few notoriously bad cases. Improved services should be run for a specified period to ascertain the real usage the railway would receive. (Whence these new passengers would come given the bad roads which were a deterrent to road travel was not made clear. Nor was any suggestion made as to who would pick up the tab during the *unspecified* period).

## Bus Company responses

Services proposed by the County were completely unworkable with vehicles springing up out of the ground which never go anywhere else. These proposals had only been placed in the hands of the bus company and the TUCC at the very last moment - during the meeting. (In another case, an author criticised BR for suggesting a variation of a plan during a Hearing - see page 77).

The South East TUCC concluded that there would be some hardship, notably with longer journeys, but that hardship could be alleviated by:-
    1. Bus services proposed by BR.
    2. Additional buses proposed by the County Council should be further considered.
    3. Provision of bus shelters suggested by the County are desirable.
    4. BR to give special attention to alternative services for watercress.
Referring to the call for a Public Inquiry, the TUCC stated that it gave a full and patient hearing to every objection, any further evidence of hardship is unlikely to be tendered at a Public Inquiry.

Blandford Council later criticised the handling of the meeting on 8th October, on the grounds that objections could only be made on hardship grounds and they were not allowed to cross examine BR on finances. They called for a Government Inquiry under the 1962 Act, Sec.90. The TUCC dissented - they had heard all the relevant representations on hardship. The chairman only closed the meeting when objectors tried to raise issues outside the terms of reference. Dorset County Council had written that their Clerk who was present at the meeting said it had been quite properly conducted, and every opportunity given to every possible objection, and in his opinion the complaint was quite unjustified. The County has decided to take no further action. [South East TUCC min 449]. Objectors quickly rejected criticism which was outside the terms. (See pages 71 & 135).

A summary prepared by the South West TUCC shows that bus proposals, with amendments made after suggestions or objections, were accepted by the objectors. After hearing objections, the South West TUCC set out its conclusions separately for the following five sections of line. They sent a Report, to the MoT on 31st December 1963.

1. **Bristol-Bath** : An adequate bus service exists and the TUCC is satisfied that closure would cause no hardship to local travellers including workers at Mangotsfield.
2. **Bath-Radstock** : Is mostly in a valley, with steep hills on both sides. Closure would cause severe hardship to 30-40 people living in or near the villages of Shoscombe and Wellow who with present bus services would have no public transport to or from Bath for school or work. The Bristol Omnibus Company is willing, if authorised and *subsidised*, to run four buses daily in each direction between these villages and Bath. A dozen people would have a steep climb of $\frac{1}{4}$ mile to the nearest point a bus could reach. Some say bus services could not operate throughout the year due to steep roads. A majority of the TUCC concluded that the hardship of those at Shoscombe could not be substantially removed by providing buses.
3. **Radstock-Cole** : The problem is mainly one of 50 children attending schools in Cole and Bruton. For those travelling from Midsomer Norton, Chilcompton and other places, the present rail services are the most convenient and safe and although alternative bus services could be provided and were suggested by bus company representatives, they would have to leave before 6.30 am. TUCC members consider this would impose hardship to the children and parents concerned. Withdrawal of train services would tend to make parents hesitate to enrol children at Cole and Bruton, which will tend to run down with consequential loss to many people in those places who rely for their livelihoods on these schools. (The TUCC did not establish how many had cars which they used for work, and whether they would change to rail to cut rail losses, or whether they would take children to school by car).
4. **Cole-Templecombe** : With present bus services, there would be severe hardship in two main ways. Seventy children in and near Templecombe and Wincanton would lose their most convenient rail service to schools in Cole and Bruton. People in Bruton and Wincanton would be denied a convenient rail service via Templecombe to and from Sherborne, Yeovil and other places for work, shopping, hospital visiting and other purposes. The TUCC considers that in the event of closure, arrangements should be made with the Western National Omnibus Company and an independent operator which would substantially remove hardship under both headings.
5. **Evercreech Junction-Highbridge** : People in Street, Glastonbury and a few in Highbridge would lose a convenient rail service to Bristol, Bath, Bournemouth and other places including London, but the TUCC thinks a reasonable alternative bus service could be made available. The TUCC cannot see how hardship or serious inconvenience could be avoided for a few - up to six or twelve - who use Edington Burtle, Shapwick and Ashcott stations who would have to walk a mile or two to a bus. (*Shapwick and Ashcott stations were two miles from their respective villages!*).

The South East TUCC Report to the MoT on 24th December made the following points:-

- For many years, a daily fast service in each direction over the S&DR was provided by the "Pines Express": Bournemouth-Liverpool/Manchester via Birmingham, From September 1962 it was re-routed via Basingstoke & Oxford. Journey times from

Bournemouth to Birmingham and beyond are now shorter and so there is no hardship in this respect. Journey times from Poole are a little longer, but not seriously so.

- Local passengers in Dorset are well served by bus. Blandford has a direct bus service to Salisbury with connection to London and many other destinations. It is more direct than the all rail route via Templecombe or Bath. There is a through Bristol-Bath-Bournemouth bus service.
- Additional bus services are proposed, including one along the S&DR route to Bristol Temple Meads station which is quicker than most trains.
- On the line as a whole, direct costs are in excess of revenue by £290,000 pa.
- Objectors say that there has been a lack of apparent effort to attract traffic. Freight diversions were cited as evidence of a run down.
- Objectors contended that faster modern services would increase traffic and substantially reduce if not eliminate the loss.

There were no promises to make increased use of the line: not a single passenger, a ton of traffic or even a parcel. It was to be attracted to the line from *elsewhere*, by robbing another line. It flies in the face of reality to believe that motorists would be attracted to a train service with a two hourly frequency, which is the most ambitious even the Branch Line Society could envisage. If a train was just missed because of a late running meeting, a wait of two hours would go down like a lead balloon. Objectors advanced no evidence, no business forecast, no assessment of costs or capital and interest payments thereon.

The TUCC's issued a Press release on 9th January: Existing and proposed bus services would provide reasonably adequate alternatives for some passengers, but there may be cases of hardship through longer journeys, extra cost, heavy luggage and prams.

The MoT asked the South East TUCC to meet the County Council, Poole Borough Council, BR and the bus companies and make a further Report. [South East TUCC min. 469].

On 18th March 1964, Dorset County Council submitted further proposals "calling for toilets on long distance buses, more buses, and shelters equipped with toilets to be provided of adequate capacity for the number of potential users. When these proposals are gone into, it will be seen that it will be cheaper to keep the railway open. Difficulties would arise with the Blandford-Poole bus service, but we could not say how many would be affected". They called for a railbus to be provided from Blandford to the south, or if possible from Sturminster Newton.

Responding to the County's 18 proposals, which envisaged extra services, extensions of services and services "starting back from .............", the bus company answers included:-

- No need is known to exist from a study of rail carryings.
- No train exists at this time.
- No requirement is known.
- Purpose not apparent.
- No comparable train.
- There is an adequate connection.

County proposals were well in excess of needs arising from the closure. Shelters, with toilets capable of holding large numbers were not provided in the past, nor were they conspicuous over the next thirty years. Bus shelters were funded by councils, but rail facilities were not. They were looking for BR to fund these. Councils usually demanded better facilities for rail - and, in this case, ex-rail passengers - than bus passengers

Five months later, Templecombe Parish Council informed the TUCC that they had spotted *one* wagon incorrectly routed via Bristol which ought to have passed over the S&DR. They referred to the "greater mileage and thus greater expense". BR replied that a member of the staff had made a mistake. The TUCC said that neither the consignee nor the consignor had complained.

Rail staff probably made no more mistakes than those who worked for the council. Unless the wagon was conveyed on its own special one wagon train, the extra cost, for all practical purposes, was almost certainly zero.

On 17th September, Dorset County Council again called for a railbus to be provided, "which would reduce the costs". (There was no financially evaluated plan attached to their letter to validate this assumption. Do councils usually invest on this basis?).

On 30th October, the County submitted a formal looking document headed "Proof of Evidence of A.J. Wallis". He agreed that local journeys would be best by bus as stops were nearer to houses and shops etc., journeys over 20 miles would take longer. He also criticised the "impossibility of buses coping with unexpected crowds". ("Unexpected crowds" could stand on trains - but, of course, they, and their councillors, complained).

On 3rd November 1964, a sub committee of the South East TUCC met Dorset County Council, BR and the Southern National bus company for further discussions on the revised alternative bus services which had been circulated by the bus companies in advance of the meeting. The Council rejected the revised schedules, and without prior warning, tabled proposals prepared by their Senior Engineer. The bus company spokesman criticised the Engineer - "an amateur without any experience of operating buses or preparing timetables". Bus company proposals were based on known facts about existing rail travel. Lord Basing, representing the County Council on the TUCC suggested that as the line from Blandford was being retained for freight, that a diesel railcar could be operated on it. BR replied that it would not be economic to operate such a service. (There was no forecast of usage. Track costs would be greater if used by a passenger train).

After all others had withdrawn, the sub committee unanimously agreed that the County proposals, which sought connection with every main line train, could not be justified. They recommended that, if the MoT decides to close the line, the BR/Bus company proposals be accepted. The Report of the sub committee was unanimously adopted for transmission to the MoT. [South East TUCC min. 524].

Among the members of the South East TUCC, there were at least two Councillors, who were from local authorities objecting to the BR proposal. Clearly, there should be one rule for the "plaintiffs" and another for the "defendant". In the Brightlingsea case, a bitter complaint was made when the BTC member on the TUCC also spoke in support of BR's proposals. He was accused of being advocate and judge. His one voice would have been easily outvoted by representatives of local authorities, and others. BR did not criticise councillors being in a potentially analogous position. (See page 89).

Replying to a question about the delay in making a decision on the closure, the MoT said : "My predecessor asked the South East TUCC for a further Report in January 1964, it was not received until December 1964. I have now given the Economic Planning Committee an opportunity to comment before deciding". [Hansard vol. 711, col. 424, 28.4.65].

The delay had not been caused by the TUCC. Being a voluntary committee, with outside interests, they met about six times each year. TUCC papers show that some delay had been caused by the Dorset County Council, which pleaded "other commitments".

BR sent to the TUCC's, a survey for five days to 30th April 1965 - during which all day schools in the area were open - with long distance traffic slightly inflated by students returning to boarding schools after the vacation. From conversations with considerable numbers of staff of all grades and members of the public during the investigation, it is apparent that the pattern of carrying which emerges is fully representative of the position at present obtaining insofar as the general traffic trends on the section of line are concerned. BR responded to suggestions to alter proposed bus services and to identify the cost thereof at just over £9,100 pa. Wakes Bus Company could provide services, it has six each way between Wincanton and Templecombe. Average carryings per working day in January and April of local rail passengers from Wincanton to and via Templecombe :-

Wincanton-Gillingham : less than one per day
Wincanton-Sherborne : less than one per day
Wincanton-Yeovil : six per day - mostly pupils for whom a bus is proposed.
Wincanton-Templecombe : six per day
Templecombe-Wincanton : 21 per day - spread over ten trains.

The MoT wrote to the TUCC's on 6th September 1965 : I have considered the Reports of the South West and South East TUCC's and all the relevant factors including the advice of the Economic Planning Council for the South West Region on the proposal to withdraw rail services, and have given consent to closure - but not until additional bus services are provided as proposed. The TUCC's were reminded that the additional bus services are dependent on licences being granted by Traffic Commissioners.

"The Wakes Bus Company withdrew its application to run buses on the approximate route of the S&DR", due, among other reasons "to a justifiable fear that it would prove unprofitable"! [Henshaw, Page 181].

If there was a "*justifiable fear*" for the road operator, using publicly funded infrastructure, including bus shelters and layby's, but making an insufficient financial contribution thereto, and picking up near to houses and shops, there was absolutely *no* chance that a railway could have been made profitable by BR investing in DMU's which cost several times as much as a bus, and paying for its own infrastructure. It is difficult to comprehend why the available traffic should be unprofitable for a bus company, but ought to be profitable for BR catering for the same clientele.

The main reasons given for withdrawal by the Wakes Bus Company was that it was due "to shortage of staff and shortage of time". [Bath & Wilts Evening Chronicle 14.12.65].

BR was criticised for reducing services from 3rd January - when the line was due to close. It was alleged to be due to a fear that closure would not be permitted. There was no reason for such fear. It was due to "staff leaving in anticipation of closure", and to "transfer of staff to other vacancies, which it was impossible to reverse completely". [Shepton Mallet Journal, 21.1.66]. Recruitment would have been suspended some time earlier when closure seemed likely. Had it continued up to the last minute, BR would have been subject to the same criticism as if they continued to maintain assets up to the last minute - "*the station had just been painted*!" Paradoxically, there was criticism when assets were not maintained in anticipation of closure. [Branch Line Society 1962 Report - see also page 222].

On 11th October, Sturminster RDC wrote to the MoT asking for "the line to remain in situ, and for railway land and buildings to be transferred to them at nominal cost to enable them to provide an adequate bus depot". This would deny BR the opportunity to secure rents or sell at full market value. Why they should expect to acquire assets below cost was not explained. The MoT replied that he "cannot intervene in day to day management".

On 29th December, Sturminster RDC complained to the MoT of "BR's precipitate action in announcing closure from 3rd January 1966, and called for another Inquiry". How it could be *precipitate* when BR had wanted to close it *three years earlier* is incomprehensible. The RDC informed the TUCC on 14th January 1966 of a case of hardship: *A passenger* travels from Stalbridge by train in bad weather ........!"

A few days later, a TUCC member wrote to the Chairman: "However sympathetic we are, we cannot ask for trains to run to take three girls five miles, and two for two miles. It would be cheaper to give them cycles". Hopefully, not at BR's cost, as applies with buses.

South West TUCC Chairman referred to the consent of the MoT regarding cessation of passenger services as from 3rd January 1966 and to the withdrawal by Wakes Services Ltd from undertaking to provide buses in the Templecombe and Wincanton areas. The operator's decision was passed to the Traffic Commissioners only two days before the Public Inquiry into granting licences was due to convene, and this was only two weeks before implementation. Time did not permit for another operator to obtain the necessary authority from the Traffic Commissioner. BR was obliged to introduce emergency services. These were limited owing to shortage of staff, etc. and a number of protests were received from Wellow and Shoscombe and a few from Templecombe and Wincanton. Additional facilities were implemented by BR on 17th January. [TUCC minute 864].

The TUCC noted on 28th January, that BR had found an operator to replace Wakes. His licence application will be heard on 14th February. "Councils objected to the application, regarding it as a means of blocking the closure". [Dorset Evening Echo, 15.2.66].


When the line closed, one railwayman said the crowds who turned up were like a family who had not seen their parents for 20 years and turned up when the old man was on his last breath. Afterwards, the crowd moved off in their cars which had gone a long way towards putting paid to lines like the S&DR. [Shepton Mallet Journal 11.3.66].

The value of the line was put into clear perspective by the local media : "It will be a loss to the railway enthusiast if no one else". [Poole & Dorset Herald, 26.6.63].

# Chapter 14            North Staffordshire Loop Line

In 1861, the North Staffordshire Railway opened a short branch to Hanley from Etruria on its main line. The Loop was to be created by extending from Hanley to Kidsgrove, through towns built on hills, so that Etruria-Hanley-Kidsgrove would form a "Loop" alongside, and not very distant from the main line between Stoke and Kidsgrove.

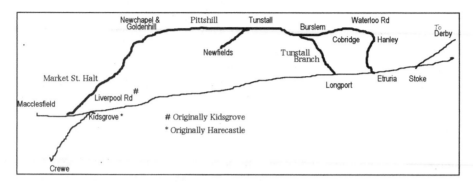

At a Special Shareholders Meeting on 30th May 1865, the Directors tabled a Bill for building the Loop at a cost of £150,000. Despite opposition, it was passed. [PRO: Rail532/1]. .

The estimate of expenses including purchase of the land for the Loop Line was £150,000. The company's application listed 245 owners, of whom only 87 assented to the proposal. 483 occupiers were involved in 1,014 properties held by the owners. Incredibly, the Burslem Board of Health which was leading the campaign for the Loop to be built, had not assented to the proposal. [House of Lords Record Office, DP 1865 N17]. They could only be holding back agreement to secure the highest price and terms possible for their land. The North Staffordshire Railways (Potteries Loop Line) Act was passed in 1865.

On 13th February 1868, a Shareholders Meeting was called to consider abandonment of this line, which received shareholders' support. On 24th June, shareholders were told that the Board of Trade had declined the application to abandon. The Tunstall branch and Loop line were not yet contracted for. The Directors obtained overwhelming support to an application to the Board of Trade for extension of time to build under the "Railway Extension of Time" Act, 1868, which they are authorised to grant. This application was made and favourably received. The Directors did not intend to enter into any contract for building these lines without again consulting the shareholders. [PRO: Rail532/1].

In September, 1869, Directors were sent a Report on the probable prospects of traffic on the Loop. The next Board meeting decided that it was expedient to apply to abandon the Loop. [PRO: Rail532/6]. On 10th November, the Directors told a Special Meeting that they intended to make another application to abandon the Loop and other lines. The motion was carried. [PRO: Rail532/1]. The Burslem Board of Health regretted the attempt to abandon. Manufacturers, ironmasters, *landowners* are ready to combine and spare no funds to oppose the application. Repairing the road from Tunstall to Longport station would cost ratepayers £5-600. [Staffordshire Sentinel, 13.11.1869]. Building the Loop would avoid that cost and produce profits from land sold to the railway company. There was no local desire to invest in the line. Traffic would be loaded at Tunstall at Longport rates.

Directors were probably influenced by losses on an existing branch (see page 186), and because shares for building two branch lines had to be offered at a discount, [Staffordshire Advertiser, 15.8.1868]. The prospects were not good for raising capital nor making profits.

The company's Chairman told a Commons Committee on 23rd March 1870 that he and some directors never had confidence in the Loop, which was promoted after local pressure from manufacturers who promised support, but it had not materialised. None offered to find funds. In his opinion, it would never pay. Most available mineral deposits were near to existing lines. Trade has fallen off. The Loop would, in effect, compete with their own lines. Ordinary share dividends had already fallen from 4-4$\frac{1}{2}$% to 2$\frac{1}{2}$-3% and would fall further as 5% would have to be paid on Preference shares. They wished to abandon the project. Only a small proportion of shares were held in the Potteries, and land would be very expensive and the rate for traffic would be the same whether it came from the Loop or the existing line. [House of Lords Record Office, HC, 1870, vol. 23].

Tunstall Board of Health said abandonment could only have been advanced by those having no connection with or interest in the advancement of the Potteries. [Staffordshire Sentinel, 13.11.1869]. Local interests could have built the Loop, or bought shares and benefited from the profits which they forecast. They could have secured a majority of votes. Failure to do either is proof of the riskiness of the project. The Directors' duty was to shareholders not the Potteries. Their dividends were the "smallest in England, having regard to the size of the railway". [Staffordshire Sentinel, 15.8.1868].

At the Directors' meeting on 30th March 1870, reference was made to an Abandonment Bill brought before the House of Commons. By a unanimous decision, the case was not proved and therefore, it was necessary to make the Potteries Loop, Tunstall line and the Burslem branch. The Authorised capital was £366,000, to be raised by 5% Preference Stock to rank with Preference shares already created. [PRO: Rail532/6].

On 4th May 1870, a Special Meeting of shareholders was told that the House of Commons had rejected the application to abandon. It was now necessary to proceed and raise the capital authorised. It was passed that £300,000 be raised for the Loop line and £66,000 for the Tunstall branch. New Preference stock would be issued. [PRO: Rail532/1]. On 30th July 1870, they approved £144,468 for works for the Loop line. By July, of the £366,000 5% Preference shares, only £155,000 had been taken up. In 1871, Debenture Stock at 4.25% was being issued. In 1872, due to a deficiency of assets to cover liabilities, the Board of Trade was asked to approve powers to raise £200,000. [PRO: Rail532/6].

On 15th February 1872, the Directors were authorised to borrow £122,000 for work on the Loop and Tunstall branch. On 17th February 1877, Directors reported that £400,000 had already been spent on the Loop, a further £25,000 was required. On 7th August 1878, they reported that nine miles of Loop and branches had cost £493,976 The rate fixed by Parliament of 1.75d per ton per mile did not take account of stopping at everybody's siding. On 13th February 1880, shareholders were told that the Loop had cost £60,000 per mile. [PRO: Rail532/1]. This compares to a UK average of £34,000. (See page 7).

Clearly, it was not a good investment. It cost three times the estimate, and freight rates did not recompense them for the work. The Directors had forebodings. At a shareholders' meeting in February 1878, the Chairman said the company does "a great deal of work for little return". [PRO: Rail532/1]. Some said that the Loop was a financial success: "*In time it proved a veritable gold mine, and before trams and buses followed by lorry and car robbed it of its business, it earned good profits for owners*". [Baker, Page 5].

Profitability was not ascertainable from traffic volume nor even gross revenue. Revenue must be compared with costs. There was no such data for the Loop. The Company Secretary told a Commons Committee in March 1870 that they "did not know if branch lines paid, because railway accounts are drawn up en bloc. We would have to employ extra staff to draw up accounts". [House of Lords Record Office, HC 1870, vol. 23]. In 1882, shareholders were told: "Only one branch had separate accounts and that was the Macclesfield, Bollington & Marple line due to the joint interest with the MS&LR, and it was losing £33 per mile". [PRO: Rail532/1]. In 1869, it had been forecast that the Macclesfield, Bollington & Marple line would become profitable. [Staffordshire Sentinel, 14.8.1869].

The effect of opening the Loop line can be judged by the worsenment in the Operating ratio. In the five years before it opened, the ratio averaged 49.9%, worsening to 54.1% over the next five years. [NRM: Directors Reports]. The higher the ratio, the lower the profit. The company's financial position was significantly worse.

Some railway promoters tended to overestimate, rather than underestimate, the rate of return and many collapsed. Hence, I am inclined to believe that the Directors had good reason to have second thoughts about the potential profitability of the projected Loop line. I searched in vain through the Directors Reports to find evidence that the Loop was ever regarded as a financial success. The 1875 Directors Report referred to a constant increase in assessments for local rates and taxes. Clearly, pressure was not merely aimed at improving transport in the area at no cost to the community, but as a means to levy taxes on the company. There was a Gold mine - for the Councils and landowners. Locals saw it as *their* gold mine - an opportunity to milk the railway. This was not unusual. "Landowners regarded railways as a ***golden mine*** to them". (See pages 6-7). "Some demands from landowners had been astounding and exorbitant". [Herapath's Railway Journal, 1873]

It was a sign of poor prospects that they were in talks with other companies. The L&NWR offered amalgamation with a guarantee of half the L&NWR dividend - 4%. Shareholders agreed in 1871, that a committee be set up to explore the possibility of being leased by, or amalgamated with, "one of the Great Companies adjoining it". The year after completion of the Loop, Directors reported on a proposal to amalgamate with the MS&LR. A majority of shareholders were in favour.    [PRO: Rail532/1]. The North Staffordshire operating ratio was six points worse than the MS&LR ratio of 49%. "Directors recognised the advantage that would result from amalgamation. Sooner or later amalgamation was inevitable". [Staffordshire Sentinel, 24.12.1875]. These are not the words of a prosperous company. The chairman favoured amalgamation with the MS&LR. [PRO: Rail532/6]. In the 1923 amalgamation, a £100 share became £74 of LMS stock. [NRM].

The chairman said that mismanagement in the past was in the making of new lines and that receipts are less from an increased mileage. [Staffordshire Sentinel, 20.2.1875].

On 7th November 1876, the Traffic & Finance Committee minute reads (and I quote verbatim): "*Submitted, Statement of the Gross Receipts of the Loop line, Etruria to Kidsgrove, including the Tunstall & Newfields branches, for the half year ending June last, amounting to £13,573.13.11*". [PRO: Rail532/19, Committee Minute Nº 9379]. No costs were quoted to determine profitability. There were no separate costs for branches, (see page 186). Nearly £500,000 was spent to build the line. Directors Reports note the company's Operating Ratio was 55%. At 55%, costs incurred to earn £13,573 would be £7,465, leaving £6,108 net. A return of £12,216 per full year (based on £6,108 per half year), on £500,000 would be 2.4%, much less than 4.25% which *had to be paid* on Debentures and 5% on Preference shares. Ordinary share dividend - already the lowest for such a company - with which shareholders were dissatisfied - was bound to fall. Directors would be aware of the significance of a rise in the Operating Ratio - a commonly used yardstick. Given the Loop's severe gradients, it was likely to be more costly to operate than the system as a whole. The results are worse, when one realises that £13,573 included receipts for traffic previously put on rail at Longport and elsewhere. Over the next five years, dividends fell by an average 25%. The company had no grounds for rejoicing. The Loop was a financial disaster and should not have been built. I could find no favourable comment in Committee or Board minutes on the adequacy of receipts. Any public statements on the prospects of the Loop could only be aimed at pacifying shareholders and bolstering share prices.

The shareholders were told in February 1876, that mileage had increased by one quarter since 1870-1, but costs had risen by 50%. [Staffordshire Advertiser, 19.2.76].

Director's Reports show that net railway receipts, for 1876, after expenditure were £800 down on 1875, net company receipts - including canals - were £6,000 down. [NRM].

On 19th December, 1876 - it was recorded that all the Capital authorised for the Loop had all been spent, £20,000 in land compensation had not yet been paid. [PRO: Rail532/6].

The half yearly meeting of shareholders was told in February 1878, that surrounding companies made profits from good mileage, but the North Staffordshire had to do a great deal of work for comparatively little return. It was a collecting line for the big companies, Shareholders expressed dissatisfaction at the poor dividend. [PRO: Rail532/1].

### Road competition

Trams required no fences, gates or crossing keepers, picked up passengers close to homes and workplaces, enabling them to capture passengers. In 1869, the horse drawn Potteries Street Railway paid 5%, compared to the North Staffordshire $2^3/_4$%. [Staffordshire Sentinel, 6.2.1869]. In 1880 trams were steam powered and by 1899 were electric.

In February 1882, shareholders were told that the company had had to "increase train frequency and reduce fares to compete with trams to maintain our position". [PRO: Rail532/1]. Increasing costs and cutting fares to retain existing traffic could only be a recipe for ruin, unless they thought to drive trams quickly out of business and then increase fares.

Competition from electric trams serving the same towns as the Loop, caused railway passenger traffic to fall. Although reductions were made in passenger train mileage, it would not necessarily reduce Loop costs to a comparable or better degree, as some have assumed. Net total railway receipts for 1901 were down by £6,000. [NRM]. The railway's

General Manager told a Public Inquiry in 1901 that "last year passenger traffic fell by 400,000 entirely due to tram competition". A breakdown by section of route, indicated that some losses were for the half year following introduction of new tram services. [Staffordshire Advertiser, 23.2.01]. Equated to a full year, losses would thus come to 673,800.

The Deputy Chairman told Shareholders on 7th August 1901 that it was almost impossible to compete with the electric tramway. Their lines were laid on public roads - they did not have to buy land like railways. They crossed all roads on the level without the same requirement which applied to trains. [Staffordshire Sentinel, 8.8.01].

The Chairman told Shareholders that in his 27 years as a Director, no company had opened its mouth to eat them up. [Staffordshire Sentinel, 1.3.19]. Had they possessed a "Gold Mine", it would have been inundated by offers from major companies. The Staffordshire company was interested in being leased by or merged with others. (See page 186). However, one by one, the bigger companies withdrew their expressions of interest.

### Traffic Decline

The Chairman told shareholders in 1869 that the Tunstall and Burslem branches would be purely mineral lines, and the Loop for minerals and passengers. When opened, the Loop served small potteries and a number of mines and carried local workers. The area's minerals were mostly very short distance traffic, producing poor wagon utilisation - not traffic best suited to rail. Traffic fell as mines became worked out or closed. When the area began to face cheap imports, potteries tried to cut costs by introducing the new tunnel oven concept, many were unable to do so because of lack of finance or lack of space.

The loss of these industries also led to a fall in passengers. In June 1956, a check on passenger train loads revealed they were low - one train carried a maximum of four passengers including three railwaymen travelling free of charge. [Evening Sentinel, 28.6.56].

A major factor in traffic decline, was the replacement of old housing, which was near the line, by new estates constructed well away from the railway. Tram and bus services ran much nearer to these new homes and direct to towns not served directly by the Loop.

### Initial economies

In view of the overall deficit and to effect immediate savings, the BTC announced its intention to withdraw certain local services in the Stoke on Trent District from the 1956/7 winter timetable, including trains on the Loop line with peak loads of 15-28 passengers.

On 2nd July, Stoke on Trent Council wrote to the TUCC: "Local traffic formerly carried by the Loop line is now largely carried by bus. The Council feel the time has arrived when an effort should be made to transfer some back to rail. It is felt that diesel units have great advantage over steam - giving quick service station to station, and if a more frequent service was given, passengers would use trains. The idea is to have services of such frequency that timetables would be unnecessary. BR has said diesel would not be justified on the Loop and could not be supplied for at least two years. The Corporation do not accept the views of BR". *BR did not accept the Corporation's views.* (See page 189).

They did not offer to back their opinions with money, neither did they tell BR which manufacturers could supply in less than two years without diverting units already promised to lines which had greater prospects. They did not say if they had ever objected to bus companies being granted licences on the grounds that there was adequate capacity on the railway - an objection they were legally empowered to make. BR objected, usually without effect. The local authority did not advance this view of reversing trends until BR proposed to cut services on this lightly used line. They did not spell out the frequency necessary to dispense with public timetables - although BR would have to time the trains, and ensure there were main line paths for them to Stoke on Trent. To match bus frequencies of six minutes, the service would have to be increased from 12 trains per day to 20 per hour! The two mile section of single line would have to be doubled and modern signalling provided throughout. Main line occupation, especially at Etruria Junction would be excessive. Additional tracks to Stoke would be needed. A round trip of, say, an hour, would require ten units, plus one to cover downtime for maintenance and servicing. The capital cost of units was then around £35,000 each, giving a total of £385,000. The interest on the loan for purchasing eleven units would have been a minimum of £19,250 pa, which exceeded gross earnings by over 50% before allowing for signalling, fuel, maintenance, wages and materials. At least 24 extra crews would be required.

Most potential passengers would have had to take a bus to the nearest station or halt. They had referred to diesels being faster, but the gain on journeys would be a minute or so at most. What would induce passengers to take a bus to a station or walk considerable distances, past several bus stops, to reach a station, and walk at the other end to their place of work or to shops? One can only imagine it would need a savage reduction in fares. If fares were halved, passengers would have to increase by *over 300%* merely to cover interest charges on the new diesel units. To eliminate losses (see page 191), as well, they would need to increase by *over 4,000%*, even before allowance for other costs besides the diesel units. In all other closures, objectors told BR that people would not travel by bus to a station, if a branch line was closed, but, by inference, this local authority was claiming that passengers *would* travel by bus to a branch line station, to travel on a diesel service with, at best, no greater frequency than the throughout bus. It was inconceivable. There wasn't an industry in the country which would have made such an investment without having someone underwrite the risk. The local authority made no such offer.

The TUCC asked BR for comments on the council's proposal, and were told: "The fortunes of the Loop have declined since pre-war through rapid co-ordination of local buses. Potteries Motor Traction is the principal, almost exclusive carrier in North Staffordshire. Rapid post-war housing development mainly on higher ground at a sufficient distance from railway stations has encouraged transport users to travel throughout by bus rather than railway for short distances. Agitation for diesels comes from a group led by an Alderman who is a railway employee. The views he expounds are not accepted by management as economic".

A TUCC member who was in industrial transport, wrote to the TUCC secretary on 17th August: I am sure that BR would not miss an opportunity to increase profitable traffic, and cannot help feeling that if BR do not consider an augmented service justified, it is naive of Stoke on Trent City Council to say they do not accept those views.

"Stoke Corporation called for diesels on the Loop. They were not convinced of their own case for a diesel service Kidsgrove-Hanley-Longton. The use of the railway had progressively declined with competition from buses. The TUCC Sub Committee had seen ribbon development with four to five bus stops to the mile. Hillside estates put railways at a disadvantage. The Chief Constable would like to see road traffic halved, but there was little doubt that people would continue to patronise buses. There was no case for diesels, the rail position was hopeless. People would not use them, they were too far from their homes. It was agreed that it was delicate, but the proposed expenditure would be completely unjustified. The only convincing way was to expend money on a pilot scheme to prove once and for all that it could not be made a paying proposition. BR's representative told the TUCC that railways could not match the three minute frequency of buses. The Sub Committee had recommended to tell Stoke Council that the TUCC could not support the application. The full TUCC approved the recommendation". [TUCC 22.10.56 min 245]. What they meant by a pilot scheme is not clear. One unit would have proved nothing. Without a six minute frequency throughout the day, it stood no chance of competing with buses. A "pilot scheme" would require eleven units. (See page 189).

The TUCC wrote to the Corporation and told them that there was ample evidence of decline in the use of rail, as road services are much more popular and convenient and could meet all the requirements of the area. There is no evidence that diesel services would be supported to the extent required to make them a paying proposition. The TUCC could not support the application for dieselisation.

In 1957, TUCC minutes [min 308, 16.10.57] show that Stoke City Council had again raised the matter of providing diesels on the Loop, giving as their reasons:-
- "BTC had said the problem was delivery, there now seems to be no problem".
- "The Crewe-Derby service has been dieselised. The Council suggest that some could be diverted via the Loop". (*Trains would reverse twice, causing delay to other services and requiring signalling changes at two locations to provide for regular passenger train movements - see map on page 184. The longer Crewe-Derby journey would be likely to jeopardise viability*).
- "A recent bus strike showed there was potential". (*Bus strikes were an infrequent occurrence and at the end of the strike, passengers flocked back onto the buses*).
- "Elsewhere diesel carryings were up". (*That did not mean they would do so here*).
- "People would use the service, if it was as frequent as the bus". (*There was no evidence that they would walk past bus stops to catch a train, nor change from bus to train*).

The TUCC view was that bus services are on the door step. Stoke Council "felt that halts and stations could be placed in advantageous positions, and, in conjunction with diesels would reduce road congestion". We - the TUCC - are not convinced that circumstances had changed since 1956. The capital expenditure was not justified. The TUCC agreed to take no action.
*More halts would have reduced overall speed.*

190

## Proposed closure

Two months before Beeching's Reshaping Report was published, BR proposed withdrawal of all Loop services in January 1963, and closure of stations at Hanley, Cobridge, Burslem, Tunstall, Pittshill, Newchapel & Goldenhill and Kidsgrove (Liverpool Road).

Immediate savings were £21,220, of which £16,630 was staff costs. Renewals were £14,240 over five years, plus scrap recoveries worth £17,300 after allowing for the costs of recovery. There were 156 regular fare paying passengers, total journeys for all passengers, including reduced rate travel by staff, were 120,000 pa. A notice was placed in the Evening Sentinel on 26th June and 3rd July 1963. [PRO : AN155/236].

## TUCC Hearing

The TUCC issued a 36 page memo and map, setting out details of the proposed closure and alternative bus services which were available. A Notice was published by the TUCC calling for objections to be made within six weeks of 4th July, 1963. "If any objections are lodged the closure cannot proceed until the TUCC has reported to the MoT and he has given his consent": A Public Hearing was held at Stoke Town Hall on 15th October 1963.

*The Proposal* :-

- To withdraw and divert all regular passenger trains passing over the Loop,
- To close the line for passenger traffic at Hanley, Cobridge, Burslem, Tunstall, Pittshill, Newchapel & Goldenhill, Kidsgrove (Liverpool Road) stations,
- To maintain existing parcels facilities and parcels train services at Hanley, Burslem and Tunstall until a Parcels Concentration Depot is opened at Stoke on Trent.
- Estimated savings : Earnings : £12,376; Direct costs - movements : £20,383, - terminal : £12,650 - Total : £33,033. Expenditure on renewals in the next five years if the line remains open for passenger traffic would be £14,240. One fifth of the latter is £2,848. Total savings less *all* revenue would be £23,505 pa.

*Description of the Line & Traffic*

- The branch line was 7.25 miles long, and ran in a loop, varying from 0.25 to 1.25 miles east of the main line. It was double track from Etruria to Newchapel & Goldenhill : 5.25 miles, whilst the rest was single track to Kidsgrove.
- The number of trains in the Macclesfield direction was five - four on Saturdays - and in the Stoke direction was seven - ten on Saturdays. The interval between trains to Macclesfield was 185 minutes, and to Stoke was 128 minutes. The service was operated in the mornings and evenings only.
- The number of trains pa were passenger : 3,700, parcels : 1,000, freight : 2,900.
- Passengers - Hanley: 25,000, Cobridge: 16,900, Burslem: 27,900, Tunstall: 24,400, Pittshill: 16,200, Newchapel & Goldenhill: 7,900, Kidsgrove (Liverpool Rd): 2,600,
- Freight forwarded pa - Hanley: 400 tons, Cobridge: 4,600 tons, mainly scrap & clay products, Tunstall: 100 tons, Newchapel & Goldenhill: 16,500, mainly scrap.

The Loop was one of many branch lines constructed by the company. Of eight operating in 1908, four closed before the 1939-45 War, one soon afterwards, the others in

1956. Although, withdrawals were unpopular at the time, there was no hardship, bus services being adequate. The decline of Loop passenger services was attributable to similar causes, i.e. the greater convenience of buses for short journeys. Until World War 1, industry and housing was concentrated near to stations. Since 1920, there has been a gradual but progressive drift of population to new suburbs established by the enlarged Stoke on Trent. Industry has moved further from the town centre. These have been stimulated and fostered by growth of bus services direct to new housing estates and factories.

Local travel is negligible. Organised excursion and party travel and workpeople's trains to factories near the railway are the mainstay of bookings and receipts. An analysis of Hanley receipts showed : Bulk factory travel £5,000; holiday £2,200; Excursion £2,000; organised parties £2,000, local £300. This reveals that local travel is no longer significant.

| Annual passengers (thousands) | 1933 | 1938 | 1949 | 1955 |
|---|---|---|---|---|
| Hanley | 155 | 58 | 36 | 22 |
| Waterloo Road | 31 | 11 | * | * |
| Cobridge | 63 | 26 | 12 | 8 |
| Burslem | 311 | 91 | 32 | 28 |
| Tunstall | 327 | 102 | 16 | 21 |
| Pittshill | 132 | 65 | 11 | 10 |
| Newchapel & Goldenhill | 77 | 34 | 11 | 10 |
| Market Street Halt | 70 | 38 | 3 | * |
| Kidsgrove (Liverpool Road) | 87 | 37 | 5 | 4 |
| Totals | 1,253 | 462 | 126 | 103 |
| * Station previously closed | | | | |

BR said "A drastic reduction of railway passenger services in 1946/7 was imposed by Government directive to conserve coal".

This reduction coincided with an expansion in road transport which was allowed to obtain vehicles in huge uncontrolled numbers, leading to an increase in costly oil imports. [See "*Square Deal Denied*", Page 178].

| Passenger Train service | 1934 | 1939 | 1948 | 1956 |
|---|---|---|---|---|
| N° of trains - Except Saturdays | 46 | 45 | 17 | 12 |
| N° of trains - Saturdays only | 48 | 48 | 22 | 15 |
| First train | 5.50 am | 5.50 am | 5.44 am | 5.44 am |
| Last train | 11.10 pm | 11.10 pm | 10.33 pm | 7.30 pm |

BR pointed out that "the interval between bus services linking Potteries towns was six minutes - with two services giving a three minute frequency between Stoke and Tunstall. Comparative journey times showed bus less in all but one instance. There is a tendency of passengers to start and terminate journeys close to their home or place of work".

*There were very few Objectors* :-

1. A resident in Newchapel
2. Town Clerk, Stoke on Trent
3. National Society of Pottery Workers
4. G.Finsberg, of London
5. Midland Regional Board for Industry (their objection was later withdrawn).
6. Railway Development Association. (Their objection indicates a willingness to pursue the most impractical prospects).
7. Another passenger from Newchapel.

The TUCC Report summarised their objections (numbers refer to the objector above) :-

1. Would have to walk a mile to the nearest bus stop, and it will be inconvenient to people travelling to evening classes and entertainment (There was no rail service after 6.25 pm, hence existing rail travel for such purposes must have been nil)
2. A 15 minute interval diesel service from Kidsgrove through Hanley extended to Longton would relieve city streets. There should be a comprehensive enquiry into all forms of inland transport with a view to integration. They agreed that there is a first class bus service running parallel with train services and that there would be very little hardship to individual passengers, but any withdrawal of rail services will place a greater burden on an already overloaded road system. (See Bus company reply, page 194).   .
3. Employees of J. Wedgwood, Barlaston, will have difficulty travelling from the Burslem-Cobridge-Hanley area. Although the feeder service by bus is not greatly inferior to the present rail service, it does not take passengers to Stoke station, only to the nearest main road stop, quite a distance from the station, and a matter of great concern to pottery workers who work in heated workshops in winter. They did not propose to be at the Hearing. (Clearly, they were not that concerned).
4. Travels from London to Burslem once or twice each year, by sleeper to Manchester then by the 7.52 am Manchester-Burslem. Buses would be inconvenient. He would have to travel to Stoke, walk 200 yards to the bus, thence by bus to Longport, which takes eight minutes to Burslem.
5. } There should be a comprehensive enquiry into all
6. } forms of inland transport with a view to integration *
7. Lives near Newchapel & Goldenhill station, which he uses daily to get to work, there is a fifteen minute walk to a bus stop. The road was closed last winter for three days.

   * *Anyone who studied the area, would see that no one would change their travel from direct bus to travel bus-train-bus. and take longer in the process.*

*BR response* :-

- BR did not share the Council's view on the potential for diesels. Experience elsewhere indicates that the introduction of frequent diesel services makes little reduction in bus service frequency. Diesels may attract more, but it is highly improbable that it would be sufficient to justify the extra cost. Furthermore, no diesel units would become available for a long time ahead. Manufacturers are already fully engaged in fulfilling large orders for vehicles required for profitable operations elsewhere. There was a

marked decline in the number of passengers from 1933 to 1938. Outer suburban housing development has accelerated since then.
- When closed, the line will not be maintained to passenger standards, but may be used for excursion traffic as long as practicable but not indefinitely.

*Potteries Motor Traction (Bus company) response*
- There is a frequent bus service with a six minute interval from 5.0 am to midnight, which runs within sight of the Loop for almost its entire length.
- Displaced passengers will be conveyed without operating additional buses.

It is incredible, that the Council could believe that this line, with all its infrastructure costs, could be profitable now that it was bereft of coal, mineral and goods traffic. Industries had vanished, or by exploiting the inequitable terms enforced on railways by Government for 40 years, had transferred profitable traffic to road. Their revised proposal for a 15 minute service instead of one as frequently as buses required £175,000 for diesel units alone, plus other infrastructure and running costs. They made no revenue forecast to justify it. No profitable company, much less one in BR's position, would contemplate it.

Following discussion in Committee, the TUCC unanimously agreed on the following conclusion, after considering oral and written representations of the objectors :-
- In the event of closure, a minimal degree of hardship might arise to the small numbers of travellers using Newchapel & Goldenhill station.
- In view of the frequent alternative bus services, no great hardship is likely to be caused by the closure of the remaining railway stations on this line.

The TUCC Report to the MoT on 27th October set out these conclusions, full details of the Hearing and stated that all objectors had been invited, but only three appeared. The conclusions were given to the Press and others concerned on 28th October.

The MoT wrote to the BRB on 10th January 1964, that he had considered the TUCC Report and gave consent to the closure subject to the following conditions: -
- The BRB must inform the MoT of any change in bus services concerned.
- The BRB must inform the MoT of proposals substantially to reduce the frequency of passenger trains between Stoke on Trent and Kidsgrove.

On 16th January 1964, the TUCC wrote to all parties that the MoT has decided that there is not sufficient hardship to justify continuance of the Loop service. Under his powers in Sec.56 of the 1962 Act, he authorised closure subject to the condition that existing railway services between Stoke and Kidsgrove - main line services - and bus service at present being provided are to be maintained unless he decides to the contrary.

The line closed on 2nd March 1964.

### Postscript
TUCC minutes contain no report, at all, of any complaint regarding the adequacy of alternative services.

# Chapter 15                    Closures in the post-BTC Era

BR was told to submit details of future closures to the MoT before issuing public notices required by the 1962 Act. [BRB 1964 Report Para. 139]. "There are services which have little or no prospect of becoming directly remunerative - on the basis of revenue from users. Each proposal will go through normal procedures including consultation with Regional Economic Planning Councils", (which played no part before 1965). "BRB had refrained from proposing some commuter and cross country services for closure because of their social and economic importance". ["Transport Policy" 1966, Paras. 18, 21, 25]. Having been prevented from closing lines with strong cases, BR knew a dead horse when it saw one!

BRB cannot be expected to break even, if "accounts are burdened with losses on socially necessary lines for which they are refused permission to close". "The time has come to face this fact squarely: the services which require long term assistance will be identified and separately costed so that a conscious decision can be made whether the social benefit from maintenance of a service is sufficient to justify the cost of continuing it; the MoT not the BRB will decide". "The Ministry was making a start on the work". "Where the MoT decides against a grant, BR may submit an application to close". Payments to operators for bus services provided as a condition to withdrawal of rail services cost BR £0.5m in 1966. [MoT Railway Policy, 1967, Cmnd 3439, Paras. 4 & 8, & Page 21].

BR had not been free to decide for 20 years. They had been obliged to keep open lines without regard to losses. Until 1962, if the CTCC opposed closure the MoT usually overruled BR. Thereafter, TUCC's reported on hardship to the MoT who in some cases directed BR to keep open loss making lines. No case existed for inflating BR losses by delaying closures, keeping open loss making lines nor making payments to bus operators.

In 1967, Government stated "it is desirable in a few cases to provide services at some direct loss". [Cmd 3437, Para. 18]. The **Transport Act 1968** introduced the overdue change that losses caused by enforced retention of loss making services should be treated as a social cost, not a BR loss, and paid for by the State. Sec 39: If the Minister is satisfied that services are unremunerative, which are desirable for social or economic reasons, he may, with the Treasury consent ........ make grants to the Railways Board for provision of services for up to three years. Events proved that a Grant would not be made until closure was refused, after the usual TUCC inquiry, leaving BR carrying losses in the meantime. Some MP's who had tried to keep loss making lines open, voted against the 1968 Act.

BR managers had long pursued economies on main lines - every timetable change produced new opportunities. When Government began to fund branch lines, marginal branch line savings were pursued, because, for the first time they would reduce the taxpayers' bill. Hitherto, they paid nothing. Piecemeal economies before 1968 were not an alternative to the full economy of closure of loss making lines, (See pages 35-37). Some local authorities continued to oppose economies, which *they* would have advocated if the line in question was threatened by closure. There was strong opposition to modernising crossings, to recasting services to make more productive use of rolling stock and to destaffing stations. An example of our endeavours to cut costs was on the Cambrian line, which was opposed by local authorities. It involved modernising crossings, closing a small traincrew depot, reducing DMU requirements by ending the overlap between peak demand for school trains and peak summer services by shortening the latter as the hotel season had been cut by a decline in demand. It would have cut costs by an amount nearly equal to total revenue. Hence, there was no real risk of worsening the net finances.

Whilst pursuing savings to retain lines, I increased revenue by persuading councils, to support unremunerative lines by buying railcards to give, or sell at discount, to senior citizens. Of 22 councils contacted, all, except Llandudno, Stoke-on-Trent and Newcastle-under-Lyme agreed. They opposed rationalisation. [See "*Blueprints for Bankruptcy*", Page 153].

The **Railways Act 1974**, Sec. 3: Replaced route specific funds for losses on routes retained to meet Government demands for socially necessary services by an all embracing Public Service Obligation Grant - ("PSO"). Sec. 8: Provided Grants to companies to encourage transfer of freight from road to rail for environmental or other reasons.

Government reasons for the PSO - the so called "subsidy". [CTCC 1989/90 Report, Page 9] :-
> *To alleviate road congestion in the South East. (To contain and reduce road costs).*
> *To sustain loss making parts of the network, to maintain minimum levels of accessibility to areas where people have come to rely on rail for essential local journeys, and local communities are economically dependent on them.*

Government had an "eight year policy of reducing the PSO". [CTCC 1990/91 Report, Page 9]. Since road congestion was worsening, a reduction was illogical.

Despite all the noise made by local authorities that BR should get more traffic, some councils delayed schemes to transfer road freight to rail for which the 1974 Act had made special provision. [See Select Committee Report, 1977, Para 264].

BR was criticised for closing stations which have been reopened. Losses which fell for 20 years on BR, could not have continued in the uncertain hope that political opinion may change. In 1994, a Minister claimed: "We have opened or reopened 220 stations". According to local authority associations, apart from a few opened on BR initiative, most were due to funding by and initiative of Metropolitan, County and District Councils or Passenger Transport Authorities. This was facilitated by the Local Government Act, 1974, which introduced Transport Supplementary Grants, and led some Authorities to fund services or station improvements. Grants were used extensively for buses. Had they offered to underwrite original losses, many lines or stations would not have closed.

Many stations reopened under the "Speller" Act: **Transport Act 1962 (Amendment) Act 1981**, which permits stations to be opened or re-opened and later closed, without facing a formal TUCC inquiry, if they prove uneconomic. For this to apply, the Railways Board must have given notice that services were to be introduced on an experimental basis on a line or at stations which had no service immediately prior to the announcement.

### Preserved Branch Lines
Claims that lines could be run with fewer people are completely undermined by the examples of lines acquired by Preservation Groups - some with local authority financial

help - which require not tens, but hundreds of staff, most working for nothing. "A willingness of members to do a large part of the work can reduce the wages element in its cost - the whole financial position can be transformed". [Western Mail 11.6.63]. In addition to people working for nothing, they are usually charged a membership fee. Local Authorities were more willing to help amateurs, than to support professionals. In at least one instance, the Territorial Army assisted by laying track etc., as a training exercise.

The Borough of Charnwood helped by buying the track bed and leasing it to the Great Central Railway Association for 99 years. After a publicity campaign, sufficient was raised to buy the single line from Loughborough to Quorn, but Quorn to Rothley had to be paid for by January 1977, BR generously leaving the track in place. [Robotham, Page 111].

## Privatisation

In BR's last year, Inter City services and Network South East services had no subsidy. Under the new regime, all get one except the Gatwick service, which was profitable under BR. In the lead up to privatisation, Government, for the first time, increased the Grant or "subsidy", to provide an "Administrative Profit" of $18.8\%$. [OPRAF letter to me]. Hitherto, it had, effectively, been based on the forecast loss. Past Chancellors must have turned in their graves at the concept of giving BR more than the bare minimum to retain rural lines. It narrowed the gap to the subsidy paid to privatised operators and the subsidy of selling assets at, what some reports have claimed, was below their value. Government justified the new subsidies, by saying that over the period of the franchise: 7-15 years, the *average* annual payment would be less than that to BR in the last year of state ownership (after adding the "*Administrative Profit*").

- If a franchisee comes with a begging bowl pleading "circumstances beyond our control" (private sector's exclusive excuse), will Government dare to turn them down?
- If a franchisee says that a line cannot be maintained at existing subsidy levels - which were designed to cover their operation for the full term, and accepted as such by the franchisees - what will Government do, if the franchisee seeks authority for closures?
- If a franchisee decides to wind up, or is forced into receivership, will the Government seek recovery of a portion of the subsidy on the justifiable grounds that the contract was for seven years or so, and they were paid over the odds in the first few years, to enable them to learn to run railways and operate *all* lines within the franchise?
- There seems to be an unwarranted assumption that, when franchises are renewed, subsidies for the new franchises will start at, or below, the final year's figure for the first franchise period, and continue to fall thereafter, but no one may bid at that level.

Privatisation was forecast to preserve the *existing* network at less cost to the State. Some feared that when subsidies reach lower levels, questions would be asked as to why branch line losses should continue, and proposals would be made to close lines. The alternative options to closures include reducing services, transferring passengers to buses or re-negotiating franchises. There are already reports of the prospect of closures, and references to the replacement of trains by buses on "guided bus routes". These private sector practices were denied to BR, which could not own buses.

Branch lines should have been franchised first. That would have sorted the men from the boys. If closures are proposed, franchisees will be unimpressed by signatures on petitions - preferring signatures on cheques. Any back-of-the-envelope plan based on the empty promises made to BR, will get a pitying look and a blank refusal. As they are in the private sector, they are unlikely to face the vicious criticism which BR faced when seeking to close lines. *Their* statements that lines are irretrievable loss makers will be accepted.

A media article argued that franchisees will have great difficulty making profits from branch lines, despite Government subsidies, and exposed the unreality of the economics of rural lines. [Daily Telegraph, 30.1.99]. It has taken costly privatisation, with its huge legal and consultants' costs, to prove what BR management had been saying for over 40 years, but which critics refused to accept, professing belief instead, that losses on branch lines were due to incompetence. All it required in BR days, when *no subsidy was paid and fares trailed the RPI by 34 points*, [see *"Blueprints for Bankruptcy"*, Page 63], claimed the MoT in 1956, was *some enlightened private enterprise!* [Hansard vol. 555, col. 1320].

Much has been written about growth, which it may be hoped will avoid closures. An overdue clamping down on unsafe PSV's and HGV's will benefit rail. Some growth was a consequence of the end of recession - as had happened in the past. Unlike BR, franchisees have been free to vary fares *up* and down to maximise revenue, and have increasingly done so. The Regulator is a pale shadow of the courts of law and ministerial direction which BR faced. The new boys made staff cuts, but then found they had insufficient drivers and no one on stations to give information when information displays failed. They will learn, as we did, that pursuing economy is a never ending exercise.

The defensiveness of BR's critics who reject current allegations of higher fares, poorer performance and more complaints was predictable. Having blamed nationalised status rather than Government interference, excuses are produced to justify failures. No meaningful comparison is possible between BR's performance statistics and 25 sets. Worse still, current statistics make exclusions for "circumstances beyond their control", which were not accepted as beyond BR's control, in my day. Claims that "complaining is easier" has no foundation, [see *"Blueprints for Bankruptcy"*, Chapters 4 & 5], and are not borne out by my experience. Indeed, the new policy is to invite customers' *comments*, not complaints. The tendency to blame inherited assets for problems will backfire when they replace assets, as they find - have already found - that no one has yet managed to produce 100% reliable equipment. Finally, there are reports of scheduled station stops missed, trains cancelled and connections broken to maintain punctuality, thereby improving statistics.

Government's aspirations to effect a transfer from road to rail will lead to new criticism of past closures. Any transfer would not have made any economic impact on branch line traffic had they remained open, nor would it have reimbursed accumulated losses. Motorists willing to transfer to rail require a service frequency which no branch line can economically offer. The prospect is further diminished because some connections to branch lines are broken, which under BR were maintained. This will discourage transfer from road. Many will applaud the Government, if *other* motorists transfer to rail.

## Appendix A                    External Experts

BR managers in the period of the greatest criticism, over the Isle of Wight closures, had been running privately owned railways before and during the war, and warned that inequitable anti-rail legislation would cause bankruptcy. Ministers and civil servants foresaw that closures may be inevitable. Government wartime policy of freezing *only* rail charges from 1940 to 1946 was forecast by the Chancellor and the MoT to lead to bankruptcy. Government refused to release railways from 19th century legislation which enabled subsidised road hauliers to poach traffic. [See "*Square Deal Denied*"].

BR was judged to be wrong because closures did not correspond to pre-conceived notions of amateurs, who believed that they had all the answers and that pretty branch lines could be made to pay - even when they had struggled to compete with the horse.

Some objectors produced transport experts to support their views, (See pages 201-10 & 221). Other objectors proclaimed *themselves* as experts and claimed that BR could reduce costs and attract tourists to rural lines. The record of *their* professions is unimpressive. All pushed up inflation, whilst BR fares trailed behind. They came from many professions:-

- **Industry** - It has a remarkable record in complacency and often failed to resolve demarcation before being overtaken by insolvency, leaving a legacy of derelict premises. Some solved problems by transferring production abroad and increasing imports. Wages were uncontrolled until UK's manufacturing base had disappeared. Employees were blamed, when complacent and incompetent management was, at least, as much to blame. They managed to lose a world lead in virtually every field. [See "*Blueprints for Bankruptcy*", Page 167]. In shipbuilding, the ratio of tonnage built per employee, 1948-62 fell 12.5%, [CSO]. In the same period, BR's passenger/staff ratio rose by 30%, [BTC Accounts]. Today's fat cats are complacent. Cuts in *their* rewards would make more impression, than a policy of "Don't do as I do, do as I say". With that background in fields in which they, presumably, had expertise, whence came the assumption of ability to advise, as they did, on the conduct of a business in which they had no expertise. *They* had *no* experience of conducting a business in the face of the unique legislative strait jacket and political interference that dogged private and public sector railways. No other industry would allow customers or someone from another company to go round its premises, accompanied by the media, cross-examine managers, and be guilty until proven innocent. This is the analogy of BR's position in regard to closures and price control. The most delicious irony, is that industry had to be bribed by Government handouts to move production into the very areas in which railways could not survive without Government Grants, but were offered, at best, interest bearing loans, whilst unlike other industry, rail prices continued to be controlled. [See "*Square Deal Denied*" for evidence of pre-war subsidies].

- **Education** - Some criticised BR productivity and claimed that there were too many staff. In the period 1948-62, the pupil/teacher ratio fell by 10%, [CSO]. Some object to being judged on performance, which other professions including BR managers, accept is necessary and relevant to a fair reward. BR managers had to undertake unpaid activities out of hours and were subject to annual performance reviews. (See page 220).

- **Agriculture** - Had least cause to call on BR to cut costs, even before the Common Agricultural policy. They were subsidised before the war, and via a Government imposed rates system, by railway rates until 1957! In 1951, they told a Government Inquiry that passengers should pay more to keep freight rates down. [See *"Blueprints for Bankruptcy"*]. They were among the first to desert railways, precipitating closures.
- **Central Government** - Their railway legislation & policies - a court of law deciding charges, ministers directing wage increases & blocking closures - were completely illogical. [See *"Blueprints for Bankruptcy"*]. A former senior Civil Servant disclosed a failure to cut costs in areas which would not have cut essential services. [See Chapman]. Taxpayers' money is expended to finance more QUANGOS. [See Cook]. It is rare to hear of economies in administration. Ideas put forward by MP's to avoid closure were usually impractical, and similar advice would have been spurned in the private sector.
- **Local Authorities** - Until recently, it was unknown to hear them speak of economies. At each year end, there was a spurt of expenditure to use up allocations. They decided what would be spent and set the Rates accordingly, until capping was introduced. Rates rose without pause, and there was scant evidence of increased or improved service. Services, once covered by Rates, are now subject to extra charges. Since councils were convinced that there were tourists who could *profitably* be induced to travel by rail over closure threatened lines, it was open to them to charter trains. Under this system, BR would not risk losing more money by speculative excursions, whilst councils, assuming their claims were justified, stood to make a profit. The lack of action speaks volumes. It is noticeable that Tourist Offices often close at 5.30pm. Invariably, local authorities opposed modernising level crossings - until closure was threatened, when they became ardent advocates. Likewise, there was opposition to singling of lines until closure was announced. A typical example was Council opposition to singling the Wrexham-Bidston line, although DMU services would accommodate a **1600%** increase in passengers. Railways were seen as an insurance policy, but councils didn't want to pay the premium. Council costs were increasing, whilst they called on BR to further reduce railway costs. (See Appendix C).
- **Retail industry** - In 1958, critics argued that an uneconomic ferry service should not be withdrawn because BR ships, as a whole made a profit. If this *"enlightened private sector practice"* applied to the retail industry there would be few empty shops. Many have abandoned the principle *"The customer is always right"*, attempting to prove them *wrong* : "you must have misused it" (without a shred of proof); "no one else has complained" (as if that invalidates your complaint) and sincere apologies for defective products, with, if you are very lucky, a replacement, not always of equal quality - if you collect it. Shops closing at 5.30 pm in tourist areas are all too common.
- **Commerce** - If the *"enlightened private sector practice"* urged on BR in respect of ferries also applied to banks there would be no rural closures.
- **Hotels & Catering** Those who called on BR to attract tourists to branch lines, seemed to be oblivious that the British were going abroad where better, and less costly, service could be obtained in hotels and restaurants which did not close at 2.0 pm sharp. (See page 76).

**Appendix A.1**                          **Mr. S. W. Hill**

Hill was engaged as an expert witness by Isle of Wight County Council when the TUCC hearing, into closures on the Island, re-convened in London on 18th June 1953. His expertise has been enhanced by claims of BR's critics of his reputed role in the arbitration in the nationalisation of railways. (See page 64). There was no arbitration for railways. [See "*Square Deal Denied*"]. The transcript of the TUCC Hearing set his area of expertise. When it began, he was not present. He was "unable to attend as he is giving evidence before a Committee of the House of Lords". In his absence, the objectors' QC presented a paper headed 'Proof of Evidence of Mr. Stanley William Hill'. It began:-

*"I am a partner of Arthur Collins & Co., Financial Advisors, consultant accountants to local authorities, public utility undertakings, etc., with 18 years experience in this profession. I have appeared before Licensing Authorities appointed under the Road Traffic Act 1930, in connection with alterations of fares for stage carriages (i.e. buses, trams), made by (road) passenger undertakings. I have appeared as a witness before the Transport Tribunal in connection with the (BTC) Charges Schemes in 1950, 1951 and 1953. My firm was engaged with arbitration proceedings in connection with the acquisitions under the London Transport Act, 1930, and were for 17 years accountant advisors to the Railways Assessment Authority. The work involved a detailed and continuous acquaintance with the finances of the railway undertakings".* His firm was involved in *that* arbitration - not himself. The paper set out his views on the proposed closures, but made no mention of a role in railway nationalisation.

Arbitration proceedings in connection with the acquisitions under the London Transport Act 1930, took place between 1933 and 1935 and involved his firm not himself. Those proceedings appear to predate his experience - which being 18 years (see above), would be from 1935. This arbitration only involved road transport undertakings being taken over by the LPTB. The Underground Railways Group had accepted the terms for take-over in May 1931. [Blacker, Lunn & Westgate. Page 34]. The Metropolitan Railway, the only non-Underground Group railway company accepted terms in June 1932. [London Metropolitan Archives Acc 1297 MET/1/31]. The Arbitration Tribunal was not set up until 1933. So, there was no arbitration for London Transport *railways*. Moreover, the arbitration was not for all buses because the huge London & General Omnibus Company, with about 5,000 vehicles, was a wholly owned subsidiary of the Underground Railways Group, having been taken over in 1912 and were embraced within the terms accepted in 1931. The tramways were owned by municipalities, most of which also accepted Government terms before the Act was passed. The arbitration was confined to a few trams and a handful of small bus companies owning a few hundred vehicles. "Minor groups were not placated in the negotiations (with Government) - Thos Tilling, Tilling/BAT, and the independents, whose compensation had to be decided by the arbitration which came into existence in July 1933". [Barker & Robbins, Page 279].

The Railways Assessment Authority in the 1930's was the body which assessed the amount of municipal rates to be paid by the 'Big Four' privately owned railway companies. Its' role was set out in the Railway Rating & Valuation Act, 1930. Their assessments were judged, on appeal by the railways to the Court of Appeal, to be too high, and were subject to very substantial reduction. In five years, the railways had been overcharged 100% - £20m instead of £10m. (See *"Square Deal Denied"*, Page 91). This specialised field involved assessing the rateable value of property on a similar basis to shops & factories. It had no mandate on the operation of railways, its costs of operation nor its charges.

Mr. Hill's qualifications were included in evidence given at Transport Tribunal Hearings between 1950 and 1964. This was a Court of Law, where all witnesses were subject to cross examination by QC's and other barristers. In 1951, he said he was:-

> *Financial Advisor to Local Authorities and Public Utility Undertakings of all kinds, a Member of the Institute of Municipal Treasurers and an Associate Member of the Institute of Public Administration. He was well acquainted with railway accounting having acted as Accountant Advisor to the Railway Rates Assessment Authority. (See above). His firm was concerned with arbitration under the London Passenger Transport Act, 1933.*

Responding, in the 1951 Transport Tribunal Hearing, to questions by BTC's Counsel, he said that "he could not devise any method of making ends meet"; "a subsidy was the answer to balancing the books", [Q.5247-8]. Asked if the BTC was misleading the public, he replied "No". [Q.5322]. Asked if he was beginning to realise that we (BTC) are very different (compared to other nationalised industries, with whom comparisons had been made), he agreed. [Q.6597]. He said "passengers were being asked to suffer increases greater than would otherwise be the case so that BTC might be in a position to renew assets without raising as new capital the full cost of new assets". [Q.5143]. (New capital would incur interest which users would have to cover - it would not be covered by a generous benefactor). "Having provided for depreciation fully on all rolling stock, there is no need to provide for obsolescence". [Q.5147]. (That would only enable it to be replaced like for like, had there been no inflation). He forecast that "working expenses of the BTC would reach a peak next year and then decrease". [Q.7016]. (Events proved him wrong). In contrast he admitted that costs of 34 County Councils which he was representing, would increase. The BTC's QC remarked "everyone's costs will go up except ours". [Q.7036-7].

In the 1953 Tribunal Hearing, the objector's QC asked him "Your firm have been accountant advisors to various railway undertakings?" - "Not to railway undertakings. We were accountant advisors to the Railway Assessment Authority". [Q.4990]. (See above).

In the 1955 Tribunal Hearing, the BTC said that the introduction of TV had reduced leisure travel. Hill told the Tribunal: "I think that the TV factor has worn off - we hardly look at ours". BTC's QC stated that the BBC had said in 1952, that 23.4% of households had TV. [Q.3185, 3188].

In the 1958/9 Tribunal Hearing, the BTC stated that leisure travel had again been cut by the growth of television. The BTC's QC asked : "You said that TV is surely reaching saturation level, that three out of four households have TV. Where did you get that statistic?" Hill: "I'm not sure". [Q.4824]. QC: "It is unknown to the BBC who keep a close eye on it. They record 1958 as rising from 54.1% to 56.6%. 56.6% is still a long way from saturation?" Hill: "Yes". [Q.4825, 4829]. "If your 75% came from a more reliable source ....?" - Hill: "I don't think you can get a more reliable source than the BBC" [Q.4830]. "Saturation level" - 98% - was reached 30 years later. [OPCS Survey 1989].

He was asked "At no time since the BTC was set up has it been a good time to create reserves?" He replied : "Not since about 1950, there was good demand in 1946, 1947 and 1948. That was the time to put money aside". [Q. 5038]. 1946 & 1947 were *before* nationalisation. Fares and charges were even then held below inflation rates by the Government which insisted that only sufficient profit was to be allowed to pay the 'Rental' which they had imposed on privately owned railways in 1941. From 1941, unlike all other industry, they were not allowed to raise prices to cover increasing costs, and so were unable to create reserves. "You do know that the accounts of the BTC are formed in accordance with the Minister's directions?" - Hill: "Yes". [Q. 5080]. He was asked if he had ever managed a transport undertaking, and replied "No". [Q.4750].

In the 1961 Tribunal Hearing, he was asked what the Tribunal should take as the figure for a Net Revenue surplus for the BTC, he did not give an opinion. [Q.3645]. BTC's QC said that he had noticed that the LCC was increasing Municipal Rates by 6d (2.5p) in the £, and it would increase BTC expenses. Hill said it would not increase very much. The QC replied that Rates paid by the BTC had doubled since 1947 on properties in London. Hill said that he could believe that. [Q.3526/9]. Since 1947, fares had risen 29% and the RPI 57%, compared to LCC Rates 100%, and the LCC was objecting to a fares increase!

In the 1962 Hearing, he was asked: "If independent provincial bus companies are always granted increased fares to cover *replacement* depreciation?", and replied: "Yes". [Q. 1599]. When BR sought to close Isle of Wight lines, (see Chapter 5), they were criticised for including in costs, amounts which they forecast were required to replace rolling stock, on the grounds that the stock was presumed to be fully depreciated at *historical* cost.

In the 1964 Hearing on London fares, asked : "Is it any part of your case that BR is mismanaging affairs in other parts of the country?" he answered "Oh, no". [Q.2084].

At the 1953 hearing into the Isle of Wight closures, he tabled a paper which stated that, if the basis BR had used for assessing costs for the Isle of Wight lines had been applied to BR's 1951 accounts, "it would have produced a loss of £40.7m for BR instead of the working profit of £34.9m which had been made". Costs on the Island would be higher than the mainland, due to having to bring all materials across by ferry, and by taking rolling stock or parts to the mainland for major works repairs, which makes comparisons with national data difficult  Older stock maintenance tends to be high. His statement attracted much critical attention. He arrived at his conclusion by taking total receipts from BR's 1951 Accounts, and relating them to seven cost items apparently calculated by himself:-

> Vehicle movement costs: £202.3m; Terminal etc costs: £64.7m; Joint costs: £70.8m; Extra provision for depreciation on a replacement cost basis: £10.0m; Interest of 4% on replacement costs of £940m for rolling stock etc: £37.6m; Notional renewal funds for other assets: £24.0m; Interest on residual values, say: £4.0m; Total: £413.4m.

His paper does not indicate how he had arrived at these crucial cost figures, as one would expect in such a paper. He may have made assumptions, extrapolations or applied a formula with which others would disagree. Reading the paper enclosed with the TUCC Hearing transcript, I could not replicate his calculations.

# Appendix A.2          Professor  E. R. Hondelink

A surprise witness, Professor Hondelink, transport consultant to the UN, had made a very *close* study of the Isle of Wight railway and said it could be made to pay. [Burroughs, Page 18].

I found that he had written to the MoT in 1953 saying: "If BR ran regular fast services at the same fare as buses, people would use them and they would pay their way". [PRO: MT115/5]. There were no statistics, £ signs nor reference to market research in his letter. .

Inquiries of the IoW Record Office produced a letter to the County Council in **April 1964**, stating that he proposes to spend *one day* on the Island, before preparing a *detailed* schedule in support of his views on how the services could be run. (No insolvent industry would believe that a one day visit by a consultant would solve their problems).  He wrote that passenger services could be hauled by two industrial type diesel locos, coupled together and operated by one driver. These locos are usually limited to 15-20 mph, thus lengthening journey times, would provide no heat for trains, and are not usually designed to operate in pairs with one driver, as there would be little demand. He said that the Reshaping Plan [pages 16 & 17], shows an hourly service is profitable with traffic levels existing on the Island. The Plan related to a 2 car DMU on a rural line, not a line with a seasonal peak, discharging 2,000 passengers per hour from ship to train. It would take all day to clear them into an hourly DMU. That was the nub of the problem - a ferry peak within a seasonal peak. He said as an independent railway it could claim a bigger share of mainland receipts than the pro rata share allowed by BR. If they were independent, BR would have good reason to influence passengers to resorts which gave 100% of revenue - as any operator would do and pre-war railways sought to do. He could not understand why IoW lines were "under 10,000 per week" [Rehaping Plan Map N° 1], given the 2.8m passengers pa. The former is passengers per route mile, the latter is journeys.  If 2.8m passengers travelled 4.8 miles or 1.7m travelled 7.9 miles on the Island's 26 miles of line, it would be less than 10,000 passenger miles per week.  His evidence to the TUCC reiterated the letter written before visiting the Island.  (See references to 2.8m and 1.7m passengers on page 73).

"Traders and hoteliers have shown that they can operate their business under conditions that prevail on the Island and the railway authorities could have done the same". [Hondelink in Foreword to Burroughs]. Traders and hoteliers can - and do - increase prices at a stroke, charging outrageously higher prices in the summer and recruit temporary unskilled staff for seasonal work.  When a hotel is full, it is full, and they are not criticised and urged to buy extra accommodation, as BR was.  Some close for the winter - an option not open to BR. Restaurant are closed when many want to use them. He went on: "Flexibility is an economic characteristic of rail transport". This is an incredible statement from a transport expert. I would say that their main characteristic is *inflexibility* - to temporarily transfer costly *fixed* assets from one location to another is a non-runner. So too, is the transfer of rolling stock in the summer peak - when the whole of the UK has the same peak. To no other location in the UK would it be more difficult and costly to transfer railway assets.

Professor Hondelink criticised the insistence "that all equipment must be in use all the time". [Hondelink in Foreword to Burroughs].  There was no such insistence by British Railways which expected that most commuter stock would be idle 18 hours in 24, sleeping cars 12-14 hours in 24, other coaches 8 hours in 24, and that thousands of coal wagons would stand idle every summer due to reduced production and demand.

Hondelink claimed that [Henshaw, Pages 73, 136/137] :-
- "He had calculated a reduction in clerical staff, cessation of the standardisation programme and a few other sensible economies would improve finances by £10m pa".
- "Losses on branch lines were very small and could be virtually eliminated by a few economies".
- "There was no evidence that closures had saved or were likely to save a penny".

Unfortunately, the basis of his calculations does not appear to have been published. Ending standardisation would be costly. The sweeping claim that "closures had not saved or were likely to save a penny" should have alerted people to question his locus standi. Most critics admitted that lines under threat would still lose money, even if their unproven and uncosted remedies were implemented. Hence, closures must make some savings.

## International Consultant

Professor Hondelink had a "reputation in transport circles second to none. Before World War 2 he had an advisory capacity for railways throughout the globe with vital experience in China, Japan, New Zealand, Holland, Britain and many other countries". "After the war he became a senior transport and communications consultant to the UN and World Bank". [Henshaw, Page 54]. As a railway manager and a Member of the Chartered Institute of Transport, I was in "transport circles", but knew nothing of him, before I began researching into railway closures.

His remarks on branch line losses and closures raised questions as to his particular field of expertise. It may have been in any field of transport - references to him in books and reports which mentioned his role in the Isle of Wight closure gave no indication. Even on railways, there were fields of expertise which were not best qualified to give advice on branch line operations. He was not in "*Who was Who*", which contains the names of several leading UK railway figures. Obituary notices in the Railway Gazette and Chartered Institute of Transport Journal gave no details of his field of expertise nor wartime achievement, nor of his reputed eminence in transport circles. Inquiries of the UN, World Bank, and countries in which he had worked - to ascertain his area of expertise - were unfruitful. Research of the media eventually revealed that "He was with a Chinese railway 1921-26, when he returned to the UK, setting up as a Consulting Engineer in connection with 'communications generally', in which capacity he visited Australia, New Zealand, USA and Canada, Middle East and Far East". [Railway Gazette, 26.2.43, Page 220]. It did not mention any specific projects nor on what aspect of transport or communications he gave advice, nor could I trace any media report thereon. The "*Times*" carried a report that he had made a study of Scottish Transport. [Times, 4.3.65].

BR's critics emphasised his consultancy role, to underwrite his views on closures. BR provided hundreds of managers as consultants or on secondment to railway administrations and Governments across the world, including some for the World Bank.

## European Central Inland Transport Organisation (ECITO)

His reply to a question at the Isle of Wight hearing, (see page 71), gave an impression that the organisation was set up *to get Europe's railways moving after the war*. It appears to have led critics to believe that he was, almost single-handedly, responsible for getting railway services operational when Europe was invaded in 1944, and that he achieved that difficult task smoothly. As Allied armies had trained railway staff, the need for a civilian was unclear. The official history of military transport during the War, clearly shows that the Army's railway constructional, operating & maintenance units restored rolling stock, track, bridges, etc., opened through routes and gradually handed them over to European administrations. The US Army had a similar, but larger role in restoring railways in their zones. European railway staff, already in situ, were quickly involved in restoring services, before the war ended. The UK & USA supplied locos, rolling stock and other materials.

Little has been written of the organisation's work. The UN, UIC, ECMT, EEC had no information on it. The Public Record Office had no detailed record of its work.

Allied Governments set it up to plan and implement the transport of civilian relief supplies after liberation. ["*Railway Gazette*", 26.2.43]. This fell short of claims of "*restoring services behind allied lines*" and "*getting Europe's railways operational after the war*". It had no military purpose, nor an overall railway responsibility. It began work in October 1945, five months after the war, 18 months after the military began restoration. As it was not required to make a profit, its activities were irrelevant to the problems of loss making lines. It reported that almost all 3,200 bridges damaged in France had been repaired by the end of 1945. [Times, 28.1.46]. Clearly, that was due to military and civilian action before the ECITO began work. It seems to have been less successful than has been claimed:

- "ECITO recommends diverting coal from rail to waterways". [PRO: MT59/2398, 4.11.46].
- In January 1947, the British Control Commission in Germany informed the Foreign Office that the coal lift and German economy are suffering due to a lack of rail transport. [PRO: FO321/65599].
- The Polish Embassy wrote to the UK Government in January 1947, stating that the ECITO needed to be cheapened and simplified. They said that Hondelink and his Board were "always at loggerheads". [PRO: FO321/65599]. *The Board included transport experts.*
- Media reports in July 1947 stated German Railways were in a state of collapse. Of 240,000 wagons in service in January, only 180,000 remain. For months, only 50% of traffic is being lifted. There are warnings of a transport bottleneck. [PRO: MT59/2413].
- On 6th August 1947, about two years after the organisation was set up, an internal Memo from the DoT Permanent Secretary to Birtchnell stated: "We cannot reproach *ourselves* for the lack of success of this organisation". [PRO: MT59/2423].
- "Polish coal was being sent to France, and Ruhr coal to Germany & Czechoslovakia". They [E.C.I.T.O.] "tried to arrange the obvious and get Polish coal to Germany & Czechoslovakia and Ruhr coal to France, but had not succeeded". [Times, 5.9.47, 3e].
- "Its major task - the allocation of railway wagons - was hindered by Governments refusing to let their wagons out of their own country"; "it never overcame the problem of repatriating wagons over-painted by other countries" (i.e. sequestrated war booty); "often coal trains were unable to move due to lack of coal to move them". [Railway Gazette, 12.9.47]

The MoT wrote to the Foreign Office referring to the practice of Hondelink communicating direct with Governments, which was the role of the ECITO Executive Board. "It is one of the sources of trouble between him and the Board". [PRO: FO321/65599].

In reply to a question as to its achievement, the MoT said: "It is not possible to give an account of its work". [Railway Gazette, 7.2.47]. (That could not be for security reasons - the war was over). It was dissolved in September 1947 after only two years. Its functions were transferred to the UN, and Hondelink was not thereafter involved. [Railway Gazette, 12.9.47].

The Americans were sending food and aid to Europe. UK railways, desperately short of rolling stock, had to answer complaints and see traffic creamed off by road transport, because Government directed, against opposition by the railway companies and MP's, that 'Big Four' rolling stock, and newly built locos and wagons be sent to Europe, as their need was deemed to be greater than the UK's.

There are two papers by Hondelink: on commuter services and Scottish transport, which disputed contemporary policy and belief. Doubtless he must have been a good engineer, since he used skills around the world, but the papers reveal assumptions which undermine his standing on other railway matters, especially on costs and closures.

### Suburban Passenger Services - "Commuter Traffic"
In his undated paper, he claims that suburban services are profitable, and would be more profitable if run only in the peak. He attempts to prove it by taking a hypothetical 30 mile line operating *between 7.0am and 11.0pm*, using 8 car trains in the peak, and one car trains off peak. He said that "peak traffic periods come to 40-45 hours a week, exactly the hours of one shift. A commuter railway could operate for a few hours each day".

On a peak-only railway, equipment defects or track blockages arising from external causes occurring outside the peak would be unresolved when staff resumed duty. Short notice sickness of drivers of the first trains would be a problem. An accident at the end of the evening peak, could strand passengers for the night, as staff having been on duty at 7.0 am could not be detained for long. He did not address the problem of recruiting staff prepared to sign off at 10.00 and travel to or from home during off duty hours, nor specify what transport they would use to get to and from work when no trains were operated. "Every factory, shop or office works 42-48 hours per week". They don't work split shifts!

An off-peak service was costed. "All carriages would be used in rotation to equalise wear and life". Thus, the eight car train used in his peak required 16 cabs, not four. To use cars equally, the one required off peak would, on most occasions, not be the front car. He does not say whether unused vehicles would stand in platforms or be taken to sidings. No costs were allowed for station shunting, for taking cars away, nor for any sidings.

Peak travel would be at a discount whilst off peak would be at full fares - the reverse of any industrial or commercial practice. Air package tours cost more in peak season.

He seeks to prove his theory by "using statistics available in the Reshaping Plan". An examination shows that he made unwarranted assumptions, and that Reshaping figures used are inappropriate.

Assumptions made on his hypothetical 30 mile line were :-
- An average train load of 400 in the peak and 40 outside the peak.
- Passengers travelling an average distance of 25 miles.
- An average peak fare of 1.5d [0.6p] per mile, and 3d [1.25p] outside the peak.

The 1963 Reshaping Report figures he used were:-
- Cost per train mile of 6/- [30p] for peak, and 4/- [20p] per mile for off peak trains.
- Track cost of £235-665 per day, "which is covered by the profit over direct costs".

Relating his train miles to his passenger miles gives an average train load of 112. *BR's average, including long distance travel was 90.21*. The *average journey was 20.86 miles.* [BRB 1963 Accounts]. *His fares are not in the Report, nor BRB Accounts. The average season fare was 1.26d per mile and ordinary passengers 2.23d per mile.* [BRB 1963 Accounts]. It is a serious error to use 1963 costs, but fares for a later year.

Reducing his passenger miles to equate to a load of 90.21, reducing the average journey to 20.86 miles, and applying the above fares: average season fares in the peak and average ordinary fares outside the peak, cuts his revenue from £2,050 to £1,120 per day.

The Reshaping Report [Page 16] quotes 4/- to 6/- [20-30p] per train mile for an ***hourly service on*** a "lightly used branch line". These clearly relate to the workhorse on such lines - a *2 car* DMU. A few had railbuses, which cost 3/- per mile, [Report, Page 18]. *He uses 6/- as if it were the cost of an 8 car train.* These figures include train crew costs, fuel, *provision & depreciation.* Crew costs were 24% of total train working costs, [BRB 1963 Accounts, Table 4-A]. Increasing the remaining 76% by four to reflect an 8 car train, and then adding back crew costs brings the total to £1,126 per day, compared to his £342. His units requiring two cabs per car, instead of one, would be more costly to provide and maintain. Fuel costs for 8 cars would be quadruple that for 2 cars. Both increase costs further.

For his off peak service, he took 4/- per train mile - the cost for a two car *two* cab unit. Railbus technology would not suit his line. Costs for his one car train would be 3/- to 4/-, [15-20p]. Even reducing the figure he used by 50% to 2/- [20p], adds £138, bringing costs to £1,264 - a loss on ***direct costs*** of £144 per day, (instead of his postulated £1,432 profit).

Annual track costs for double lines were £3,500-8,250 per mile, [Report Page 9], equating to £288-678 per day. The lowest was for lines under 50 mph, which would be unacceptable for commuters. A 75 mph line would cost £596 per day, increasing daily losses to £740 or over £270,000 pa, before allowing for station & terminal costs, increased fuel used by eight cars instead of two, and higher provision costs of two cabs per car.

He stated that reduced formations avoid unnecessary cleaning. As all vehicles would be in daily use, it is unlikely that there would be any significant reduction in cleaning costs. Increased detachment of vehicle couplings means more wear. To achieve savings in depreciation which he envisaged, vehicle life would be extended beyond the 35 years typically included in Accounts. Older vehicles require more maintenance.

His one car off-peak train at half hourly intervals needed a single line, and each station, only one platform of single car length, not two of eight car lengths. Hence the peak must carry the full burden of track and stations.

Quite clearly, his hypothetical commuter line would have been unprofitable.

## "A Transport Plan for Scotland"

His 1965 23 page paper refers to railways "*being controlled and organised from London*". The Scottish Region planned and ran its own services. He later conceded that the region is "*now virtually organised as a complete administration in itself*". It had been for years. He said that timetables had been devised with "commendable skill". He claimed there would be no need for cross border liaison, but timing cross border trains required liaison. "*A priority would be to electrify Edinburgh to Berwick*". He did not say if trains to England would change locos at Berwick, nor if DMU's would run to Newcastle.

He criticises standardisation - but non standard stock would create problems if they broke down south of the border and would attract higher costs. He argued that separation from BR would end their contribution to central costs, but it included repayment of Government loans and interest thereon. Scottish Transport would have to pay its share. He would keep carriages which BR "were scrapping before the end of their useful life".

"Transfers of rolling stock across the border requires no complicated administration - there is the model of the working of a similar pool in the immediate post-war years across a hundred border points in Europe". It didn't seem to work well, (see page 206). In 1965, before computers, liaison, which he would end to produce savings, was unavoidable.

He envisaged that the "classification in the tariff structure for .... goods traffic should remain identical to avoid .... complications". There was no classification - it ended in 1957. There would have to be negotiations with BR on shares of through passenger and freight revenue, not in global terms, but in flow specific terms and individual items.

The "present day hankering after faster transit times keeps would-be travellers away from slow services". The "same route, whether single or double track will carry efficiently and economically all traffic, fast and slow, passenger and goods, through and local. Costs of stopping services will fall on earnings from overall working". Hence, freight customers and long distance passengers would pay more than sufficient to cover their own costs.

He said that closure of lines was decided in London. Each Region had a team reviewing branch lines and decided what to submit for closure. He claimed that lines "under threat of closure can be reprieved and closed lines re-opened when the true economic interplay between rail, road and water transport becomes known". He criticised the concentration of goods in zonal reception/delivery centres - but that is the essence of integration.

Most interesting in view of criticisms during the Isle of Wight closure, was his statement that "*railway ....... accounts are recorded to the last detail*".

On the last two pages of his paper, he sets out a "notional" forecast of the first year's finances, "derived from a combination of BTC Accounts and the Reshaping Plan". He does not show how he made each calculation, nor the source of any figure, including:-

- The number & value of rolling stock and assets which he allocated to the undertaking.
- £14m of current assets for Scottish railways comprising bank balance, traffic accounts and other outstandings.
- The net revenue which would accrue without knowing the share of revenue which would have to be paid for through movements beyond the border.

It was considered by the Highland Transport Board. [Times 4.3.65]. It was not implemented.

# Appendix A.3                                  Mr. R. French

Mr. French represented the Union of General & Municipal Workers, as an objector to the proposed closure of the Brightlingsea branch line in 1953, (see pages 82 & 85). As an ex-railwayman (of unspecified expertise), *"he affirmed that a modified service could be operated by one engine and two sets of men from Brightlingsea and one part-time crew from Colchester"*. He should have known that there was no such thing as a *part time* crew. What he presumably meant was an unproductively employed crew, for whom he *hoped* other work could conveniently be found. Like industry, BR employed part time office cleaners, but not part-time skilled staff. His modified service was as follows:-

|                  | B1   | C    | B1   | B1   | B1   | B2   | B2   | B2   | B2   | B2   | B2   |
|------------------|------|------|------|------|------|------|------|------|------|------|------|
| Brightlingsea    | 0640 | 0722 | 0819 | 1107 | 1315 | 1440 | 1645 | 1815 | 1900 | 1945 | 2115 |
| Wivenhoe arr     | 0652 | 0734 | 0831 | 1119 | 1327 | 1452 | 1657 | 1827 | 1912 | 1957 | 2128 |
| Wivenhoe dep     | 0707 | 0735 | 0832 | 1120 | 1328 | 1453 | 1658 |      |      |      |      |
| Hythe            | 0713 | 0740 | 0838 | 1126 | 1334 | 1459 | 1704 |      |      |      |      |
| St Botolphs arr  | 0717 | 0745 | 0842 | 1130 | 1338 | 1503 | 1708 |      |      |      |      |
| St Botolphs dep  |      | 0750 | 0848 | 1135 |      |      |      |      |      |      |      |
| Colchester Nth   |      | 0756 | 0854 | 1141 |      |      |      |      |      |      |      |

|                  | C    | B1   | B1   | B1   | B1   | B2   | B2   | B2   | B2   | B2   | B2   |
|------------------|------|------|------|------|------|------|------|------|------|------|------|
| Colchester Nth   | 0642 |      | 1022 | 1204 |      |      |      |      |      |      |      |
| St Botolphs arr  | 0648 |      | 1028 | 1210 |      |      |      |      |      |      |      |
| St Botolphs dep  | 0653 | 0745 | 1035 | 1216 | 1358 | 1612 | 1745 |      |      |      |      |
| Hythe            | 0657 | 0750 | 1039 | 1221 | 1402 | 1616 | 1750 |      |      |      |      |
| Wivenhoe arr     | 0702 | 0755 | 1044 | 1226 | 1408 | 1621 | 1755 |      |      |      |      |
| Wivenhoe dep     | 0703 | 0756 | 1045 | 1227 | 1409 | 1622 | 1756 | 1833 | 1922 | 2010 | 2209 |
| Brightlingsea    | 0715 | 0808 | 1057 | 1239 | 1421 | 1634 | 1808 | 1845 | 1934 | 2022 | 2221 |

B1 = Brightlingsea crew N° 1;  B2 = Brightlingsea crew N° 2;  C = Colchester crew

Based on train loadings supplied to the TUCC by BR, over half of the commuters from Brightlingsea each morning would depart up to 23 minutes earlier, and return home in the evening up to 30 minutes later. These numbered about 100. No reference was made to market research, hence, there was no real evidence that passengers would definitely increase. Some existing passengers may travel by other means to avoid a longer day.

Crew N° 1 departs at 06.40 and gets back at 14.21 = 7' 41", to which must be added time to sign on, check changes in safety notices, take over the engine, couple to a train, and at the end, put in defect reports and sign off. The roster would exceed 8 hours. Someone else would have to raise steam from cold. Crew N° 2 departs at 14.40 and gets back at 22.21 = 7' 41", to which must be added time to sign on, check changes in safety notices, and at the end, uncouple the train, put in defect reports and sign off. The roster would exceed 8 hours. Someone else would have to dispose of the engine, put out the fire and clean the firebox. Relief staff would be required to cover sickness, holidays, etc.

"The railway system was continuing to decay. In the Midlands, the situation had become so serious that, in June 1952, the Birmingham Junior Chamber of Commerce decided to set up an inquiry of its own. Its report published in February 1953, resulted in the West Midlands Railway Passenger Scheme - an ambitious project to re-open railways and stations throughout the Birmingham area". [Henshaw, Page 65].

Their Report was difficult to track down. Surprisingly, neither the Senior nor Junior Chambers could find a copy of this ambitious plan which has come nowhere near to fruition. One would have thought that it would be dusted off annually and Government and BR pressured to implement it in full.  Where it was published is unclear. Media reports in 1953 of a meeting between the Railway Development Association and the Chamber to discuss the need to modernise suburban services, make no reference to it. [Birmingham Post, 7.3.53 & 13.3.53]. The TUCC, a likely source, could not locate a copy, when approached in 1998. Birmingham Library located details in the Chamber's 1957 Journal. There are references, but no details in TUCC minutes at Birmingham:

- "A study had been made of transport needs. A TUCC member said that he would like people making representations to make full use of existing services before asking for increased facilities". [9.12.52]
- "The Railway Executive had been approached but the Report had been referred back for amplification, when completed it would come before the Senior Chamber, who would forward it to the BTC". [23.12.52]. *BR had to consider amateur plans, however impractical or unbusinesslike or face political criticism and pressure.*
- On 22nd September 1953, the secretary of the TUCC said "he had asked the Chamber of Commerce for copies of the Report, but they replied it was still under consideration and it would be tactically wrong to allow detailed information to get abroad". [22.9.53].
- "A copy of the Report had been sent to the BTC, and the local BR manager". [15.12.53].
- "A copy of the Report by the Junior Chamber had been received. They are not seeking TUCC support at this stage". [16.10.57].  This followed limited research into potential user of the proposed services, marking completion of the Report. (See page 212).

"The Chamber of Commerce had certainly done its research, for the report noted that the Railway Executive's ACV railcar was already undergoing trials between Marylebone and Princes Risborough. It was exactly the technology the Chamber wanted to see in Birmingham, but the Railway Executive although generally interested in the report, was unable to assist". [Henshaw, Page 65].  As the Report was incomplete, the Executive would be "*unable to assist*". The most important aspect had been left out. No criticism of the Executive is warranted. (See meeting of 23.12.52 and page 212). Moreover, the Junior Chamber's research was too narrow. (See page 214).

The Executive ceased to exist on 1st October 1953, less than two weeks after the Chamber declined to release copies to the TUCC - a potential ally. It is likely that the Report was held back, because they had not assessed the potential demand, and hence the plan's viability. The first public information mentioning a Report, which I could trace, was in the "*Birmingham Post*" in 1954. It said that a Report on services was being presented to the Chamber of Commerce, [27.7.54]. Fuller details were reported by that newspaper in 1957, which noted that BR intend to study the Report. [24.9.57]. Another media report on the same day, gave details and said that the Chamber "had *today* published a plan on which they had been working for four years". [Times, 24.9.57].

The TUCC meeting on 22nd September 1953 reported that "BR had experimented with diesel services from Birmingham to Solihull and to Cardiff". In April 1955, the TUCC recorded "more diesels were to be provided, but in 1956, expansion had been delayed by late deliveries of rolling stock". One of the main suppliers was in the West Midlands area.

Investigation into this Study reveals a different picture to that painted by its admirers. Their Report included no working timetable, but included a map of the area from which it can be seen that 54 stations were to be opened or reopened. Of these, one re-opened in 1978, one opened in 1978 and another opened in 1994. Of the 54 stations, 22 were to be re-openings of stations closed between 1873 and 1949, all, except for one, before nationalisation. A new station at the Civic Centre called for deep excavation to get down from street to track level. They envisaged a two level station at Moor Street, with one level being on the same route as New Street. Construction of these two stations would cause severe and costly disruption to services. The cost of the Moor Street station alone, *they* estimated at £2.5m, but this could not possibly take any account of costs arising from diversions and interruptions to services whilst this huge project was in hand.

"The total cost was set at £15m including Moor Street, Civic station, and 52 others, the cost of DMU's, signalling and track. Station costs were set at £50,000 each. They forecast £3m as the cost of signalling to provide a two minute headway". [Times, 24.9.57]. There was no reference to the source of signalling expertise. Moreover, a new signalling plan could not be produced nor costed without access to existing track layout plans. There was no reference to the forecast Return on Investment - a serious oversight for businessmen.

Having produced a Report specifying the new stations and new services, they *then* turned attention to ascertaining how people travelled to work and how many *may* turn to rail given the changes they envisaged. "A Questionnaire was prepared and a *number* of firms agreed to circulate them to employees". [Junior Chamber Journal, September 1954]. Clearly, not all firms were involved. It was not stated how many questionnaires were circulated.

The annual Report of the Junior Chamber for 1952 states that its Report had been sent to the senior Chamber and comments were awaited. A 1957 Report by the Junior Chamber stated that the questionnaire on travelling habits was issued in 1954 - *after* preparing an investment plan. This was putting the cart before the horse.

"1,400 completed questionnaires were analysed, 400 were compared with the method of travel which would be possible if the scheme were in operation. The Questionnaire did not constitute a random sample, figures derived therefrom must be treated with caution. **12%**

**of the 400** (i.e. *48*), whose travelling habits were examined would have benefited by changing to rail - an increase in traffic of 360%. More than half of this increase could be attributed to new stations or re-opened stations, and a quarter to the combined two level station at Moor Street. This station was the focal point of the entire plan. The estimated cost was £15m. *Assuming* an increase in traffic similar to that found in the sample, the scheme would be financially sound". [Junior Chamber's Journal, October 1957].

There was no estimate of increased revenue to justify this claim. How they arrived at a 360% increase from 12% of their non-random small sample transferring to rail was not explained. They did not explain why all 1,400 were not analysed - **48** beneficiaries of 1,400 would be **3%**. Their hoped for traffic increase would thereby be reduced by 75%, which may have made the scheme unsound - even in their view. If these figures were related to the total questionnaires circulated, it would have been even worse.

Unfortunately, the figures were not treated with caution, because critics and the media simply reported forecast increases of 300-360%. What they did not pause to consider, was to what base figure did that relate. Applied to 10 passengers per train it became an underwhelming 36, whom doubtless, critics expected would travel not at existing fares trailing the RPI, and certainly not at higher fares to fund new capital, but cheaper fares!

There had been no access to working timetables to determine what the effect would be on line capacity by introducing 54 new calling points, altered train movements across flat junctions and the effect on express passenger and freight services through the area. How they could judge the effect on train crew rosters, and hence labour costs, of hundreds of trains making additional stops at 54 stations and negotiating junctions is incomprehensible. No one could do so without drawing up new detailed schedules. They ignored the need for and cost of maintenance & fuelling depots. How did they determine how many DMU's were required without access to timetables, and without considering the location of depots? How they could assess the building cost of two stations in particular - Civic Centre and Moor Street - which would cause the most formidable disruption to existing services is impossible to speculate. Clearly, no-one outside BR would have any idea of the full costs (due to diversions and disruptions), over and above materials and constructional labour. The building of the other 52 stations would also involve disruption, speed restrictions and other measures which inflate day-to-day costs. The impact on train schedules, even given that the stations would not all be built at the same time, is something which could only be determined in the Train Planning Office after considerable study. These complex matters could not have been determined by such a study undertaken by unqualified people.

This plan was prepared before a survey was made of current travel patterns by existing modes. The forecast increase was based on assumptions by the Junior Chamber that some commuters would benefit from transfer to rail. No mention was made of the increase in fares which was bound to come to pay for improved facilities, not to mention trying to catch up on the rate of inflation being pushed up by UK industry, which was having a marked impact on BR's materials purchases. Any industry which planned to increase production first, as the Junior Chamber did, before conducting market research, would risk ruin. If it was common industrial practice, it may explain why so much UK industry went downhill. (See *"Blueprints for Bankruptcy"*, Page 164).

Endeavouring to track down the original plan, I was put into contact with a former President of the Junior Chamber, who remembered the project, but did not have a copy. He wrote that the group had no access to railway internal information, and over a period of months, travelled on local railway lines taking traffic figures. This was not a satisfactory method of establishing data. BR's more reliable method was a simultaneous record of passengers joining and alighting at every station, coupled with an analysis of tickets. He added that he *would not suggest that our report had any influence.*

That they "had done their research" (see page 211), must be disputed, otherwise they could not have failed to learn from Government White Papers and BTC Accounts, that BR was handicapped by a unique form of price control and inequitable application of Government controls on the allocation of raw materials. [See *"Square Deal Denied"*, Page 178]. Had they noticed this, would they have spoken out against the excessive amount of steel being allocated to Birmingham's motor industry to the detriment of railway modernisation?

There was another important direction in which they do not appear to have done their research. The 1947 Act, Sec. 88 shows that authority for investment lay with the BTC not the Executive, and even they needed the MoT's approval. Hence, sending a plan to the Executive, even had their abolition not been imminent, was pointless. The media reported in July 1952 - *five months before they approached the Executive* - that the Executive was to be abolished. It should have been sent to the BTC or even to the MoT. The retention of investment decisions at BTC level was essential, given that they were required to integrate transport. It would have been counter productive to give each subsidiary free rein on investment which might have contradictory purposes. In any industry, investment decisions were made at the top - by the Board. The BTC *was* the Board, so far as railways and other transport were concerned. The MoT was akin to a joint Chairman of the Board, but with an overriding vote, and was also the BTC's banker.

Rather than trying to run railways, they could have made an effective contribution to railway performance by addressing industrial shortcomings:-

- Escalating costs imposed on BR by suppliers, whilst BR fares were held up to 41 points below the RPI. "Rising costs outstripped financial provisions made by Government during the control period for maintenance. Shortages of steel and other materials. Able to do little more than continue works started pre-war such as Manchester-Sheffield-Wath electrification and deal with cases of war damage and extreme dilapidation - essentially make do and mend". [BTC 1953 Para 126].
- The failure of industry to supply essential materials, even in the reduced quantities which Government had imposed on BR. [See BTC Annual Reports 1948-53 inclusive, or a summary in *"Blueprints for Bankruptcy"*, Pages 64-67].
- The practice of blaming BR for delay in deliveries, when the cause was that delivery dates had been promised which could not be maintained and denying receipt of goods in order to delay payment. [See *"Blueprints for Bankruptcy"*, Page 162].

214

- Delays in delivery and unreliability of diesel locos and multiple units supplied by the private sector. [See *"Blueprints for Bankruptcy"*, Chapter 9].
- The failure of industry to control wages, so that "BR was short of labour in nearly all parts of the country, affecting manning of trains, shunting, permanent-way work, with alarming proportions in London and **Birmingham**. New factories attracted trained railway workers including tradesmen". Whereas industrial earnings had risen from 100 in 1938 to 380 in 1959, rail fares had risen only to 210. [BTC Reports, 1955, Para 12; 1959, Para 19 and Diagram 7; 1960, Para 20; 1962, Para 42].
- Industry passed on its cost increases, whilst BR was prevented from doing so. A Select Committee noted that "before the war, railway careers had the attraction of permanency. That is not important now, with full time employment. Standard wages on railways (imposed by Government) are a disadvantage where there are more jobs than people and local industry offer a higher rate". [BTC 1960 - Para 20]. An example came to my notice in 1961 when two men applied to be trainee Guards at Coventry. One, who could not read or write, was not recruited, the other was. A week later, he resigned because his illiterate friend had a job at a motor company at twice the wages!

Their Plan called for new diesel trains. Before 1955, BR was being repeatedly denied resources by Government, even to restore track to pre-war standards and replace the antiquated coal wagons which Government had forced them to buy for £43m. Entirely due to Government policy, war arrears were not cleared until the end of 1954. Government directed BR to give priority to coal and other freight. (See *"Blueprints for Bankruptcy"*, Pages 65-7). This information was publicly available.

When diesel services began in the Midlands, the Chairman of the Senior Chamber's Transport Committee wrote : "It is my opinion that the main credit for these developments is due to the impact on railway opinion of the Report of the Junior Chamber". [Junior Chamber Journal, June 1955]. This was two years before the Report was, even in their own eyes, "complete"! A former President of the Junior Chamber does not agree, (see page 214). Moreover, for his claim to have any validity, he must have assumed that BR had no intention of using them in the biggest conurbation outside London. Where did they think BR would use them? Certainly not on branches losing money hand over fist even when competing with the horse. Obviously, they would have been unaware that the Railway Executive submitted a modernisation plan early in 1953, before their Report was written - but not released - which envisaged, inter alia, the use of diesels. This formed the basis of the 1955 Modernisation Plan. They were miffed because trials in November 1952, began in Leeds: "*Birmingham should have been chosen first*". [PRO: MT124/65, Times 11.8.53].

What qualified the Junior Chamber to prepare a plan of this kind? One member of the committee was quoted as having "experience of the shortcomings of public transport". [Junior Chamber's Journal, January 1957]. Many of us had experienced the shortcomings of demarcation ridden UK industry, including poor quality, late delivery and high costs.

Among papers released by the Public Record Office in 1987, was a memorandum, written in 1951, by David Blee, then Railway Executive member for Commercial matters.

He had been invited as Guest of Honour at the luncheon of the Transport Committee of the Association of British Chambers of Commerce in May 1951, where, he later wrote: "The words of welcome by the Chairman turned out to be wholly critical". His revised address, developed on the spot, on a menu card - which was included with the papers - began by saying that he had resigned from one of their Councils because they did not support measures he took to increase membership, reduce its costs and make it more effective. He said that: "The BTC was not a monopoly, and was not in the same street as many trades and industries where price rings were abundantly apparent whenever we went out to tender. What BR bought from industry in 1939 per £100 now cost £259, whilst our charges at 90% of 1939 levels represented the efficiency and economy of the past three years. Everything I buy has gone up". Answering criticisms of delays, he said that with expanding demand for transport, BR had difficulty in expanding resources fast enough. He drew attention to the national manpower shortage by the example of the *Birmingham area* where 33,000 vacancies were chased by 6,000 unemployed, (to which UK industry responded by improving wages instead of productivity). Demonstrating that the private sector had not been able to meet expanding demand without delays, he added that "if I wanted to buy a car, I would put my name on a waiting list and hope to get it in two years time, whilst the wait for a refrigerator was only one year".

Little wonder that UK industry lost a world lead in so many fields and failed to meet BR needs for materials and reliable rolling stock. (*"Blueprints for Bankruptcy"*, Chapters 2, 9 & 10).

It was imprudent of Blee to speak of buying a car, as BR managers were subject to carping criticism for using cars. As trains were not allowed down Suburbia's "Acacia Avenues" - residents complain about trains on nearby lines which existed 100 years before their house was built - it seems reasonable for BR managers to use cars. Noticeably, bus managers were never criticised for using cars and their buses *did* run along the avenues.

A problem which needed resolvement was that of "Recalls": products recalled because "a small number have been discovered during ongoing quality assurance checks" that *may be* unsafe - even fatal. They are couched in similar language. They do not include items which may not last as long as expected, nor are giving less than 100% service. They do not explain why items were sold before discovering that "only a few" may be unsafe.

"Private Sector companies created a bad image by unsightly rubbish tips, piles of rusting cars and unsightly scrap on their side of BR's fence, giving passengers a bad visual impression. The Dickensian appearance of lineside industry emitting filthy, malodorous smoke, made rail travel unattractive, particularly as coaches were, thereby, made very dirty. When industry lost markets to foreign competition, and closed ancient premises, consequential dereliction created even greater eyesores. Industrial leakage of poisonous gases and fires on lineside premises, caused Fire Brigades to block lines creating delays and cancellations of trains". [See *"Blueprints for Bankruptcy"*, Page 168]. There has been no greater area of industrial decline than the West Midlands. The depressing sight of derelict factories did nothing to make rail travel more attractive.

# Appendix A.5                                 Mr. W. E. Sayer

W.E. Sayer, a haulier and quarry owner, wrote, in 1960, to "BR who declined to accept his proposal to take over the line or rent it and run it for a year. He stated that he could only conclude they were afraid to give him an opportunity. Without doubt, this line could be made a paying proposition. If I can make a profit with a 15 ton lorry taking limestone and returning empty, something is wrong if railways could not make a paying proposition with loads both ways". All wagons were *not* used loaded both ways, many were suitable for only one form of traffic. Hauliers did *not* pay as much as they should for the use of roads, and are not doing so today. He was free to determine his own rates, BR wasn't. [See *"Blueprints for Bankruptcy"* and *"Square Deal Denied"*]. He said that his traffic, over this route, from three stations, totalled 3,000 tons per week.

How could he say that he could make a profit without knowing the terms of a lease and how much BR would pay to have its traffic moved over "his" line? Noticeably, he never publicised financial details of his offer, not even after it was declined, when he had nothing to lose. How could he know what minimum number of staff the MoT's Inspector would deem necessary for safety? Research of MoT papers uncovered no letter on that subject, but uncovered a Report by his Chief Inspector of Railways, which said that track maintenance staffing was not excessive. (See page 147). Responsibility for monitoring the safety of many bridges and viaducts was vested in qualified bridge engineers, who covered a very wide area. Did he assume their services, and those for maintaining rolling stock and other off-line commitments - would come free of charge? Who would sign an annual certificate that the infrastructure was safe and properly maintained - not him - or it would be back by return of post - and not BR if he had "taken it over". BR stood to lose £36,000 pa, plus losses from further wear of assets which they planned to recover.

Media reports on his proposal make no mention of a willingness to reimburse the year's losses if he was wrong. It is surprising that a haulier was unable to understand the effect of gradient on load and running time. Reports do not mention the deposit which a lessee, would expect to provide against damage to or loss of millions of pounds worth of assets in his care. Such a condition is standard practice when leasing property, with the owner deducting an amount to cover damage or loss at the end of the tenancy. BTC policy was outright sale of unwanted lines - leasing ran the risk of a line reverting to the BTC with heavy liabilities in connection with deterioration of bridges etc. [PRO: AN111/52, 19.4.62].

No voice was raised in support of Sayer's takeover at public and private meetings of the two TUCC's and the CTCC or in Parliament. TUCC minutes for 16th January 1961 record that BR had declined his proposal. He did not spell out details of his plan, so that all could see if it was reasonable, as later admirers professed to believe. No one at TUCC meetings, which included other objectors took it as seriously as post-closure admirers have done.

Mr. Boyden, MP, wrote that "Mr. Sayer's re-organisation proposals show BR how they could *try* to make the line pay". [Cumberland & Westmoreland Herald, 20.8.60]. The "re-organisation" was to replace steam on freight trains with 2-3 diesels and by cutting staff. [Northern Echo, 13.8.60]. If diesels were drawn from another part of BR, it would revert to steam. On this line, diesels would work two shifts only, when BR, but not its critics, knew that the economical replacement of steam made three shift working *essential*. He did not propose to work three shifts - even his most devoted admirers would have seen the futility of that. He did not suggest buying diesels, at £100,000 each, to work this route, the economics would have been too plain to see, with freight charges having to be raised to cover interest and depreciation charges. His plan was based on "using some of your rolling stock, and you paying me a certain rate for traffic". [Cumberland & Westmoreland Herald 13.8.60]. He would use BR rolling stock - locos & wagons - and charge them for conveying his own - and other traffic. In 1960, and still in 1961, there were ten steam locos for every diesel (excluding shunt engines). The priority for allocation was express passenger and then express freight. In 1963, only one third of locos were diesel. It was years before there were enough to deploy on all freight. How would MP's and councils have reacted to reverting to steam hauled express passenger trains? Had it remained open, the line would have been a low priority because the economics were more favourable elsewhere. I suspect that the MP was playing for time, hoping that if closure was delayed, Government would pass legislation to pay for keeping socially necessary lines open, as advocated before the war.

Durham County Council wrote to the TUCC : "Sayer's offer is intriguing. It supports our view that, with re-organisation, the line could be made to pay". They did not say that he should take over the line. Neither did they address the question as to who would placate freight customers if their traffic was subsidising loss making passenger services. No one *ever* claimed that the passenger service could, throughout the year, cover its costs. Without exception, they spoke of "reducing the losses". These residual losses would not be borne by Government nor local authorities, but by other rail traffic - or by low wages.

Sayer never spoke of making *passenger trains* pay, but making the line pay with freight traffic on it. But BR said that freight was profitable in its own right, and could be made more profitable by re-routing. There can be no doubt, that if any freight customer, Sayer not excepted, became aware that freight traffic was supporting loss making passenger services, they would have demanded reductions to enable them to compete with suppliers elsewhere whose traffic was not being so used. Elected representatives, fearing industrial decline, would have vociferously supported such demands. No council having to make a choice would have put this line's retention in front of job losses in their own backyard.

The basis of rail charges since the 1957 Charges Scheme was to cost freight and passenger separately, allocating each a proportion of joint costs. This task was not left, until after 1962, (1968 in the London area) to BR's judgement - they had to spend months proving it in a court of law. The freight charges scheme which BR proposed to introduce in 1955, after being told to dump its first plan by Government in 1951, was delayed by court proceedings for over 18 months, and was finally approved for implementation in 1957. It had been significantly altered from the original by the court. It reduced existing rates on an appreciable volume of freight traffic. [PRO: MT132/32].

On 9th January 1961, BR wrote to the TUCC in response to a request for a reply to a letter from Sayer. He had referred to 1.5d per mile as the cost of moving freight. BR said this was the cost of fuel, ignoring costs of locos, wagons and other assets etc. It was not doubted that an additional passenger train would be of value, but there is small chance of the population of the area generating enough use to pay for an extra DMU.

## Appendix A.6          Enthusiasts Groups

These groups tended to be long on theory and short on practical knowledge.

### Vale of Rheidol Railway Supporters Association

In 1982, as BR's Divisional Manager, I presided at a publicity event at Aberystwyth to mark the return of its oldest loco to service on BR's only steam line, the narrow gauge Vale of Rheidol, after being painted by BR staff in original colours to mark its 80th birthday. The painting was funded by Davies & Metcalfe Ltd (builders of the loco) and Supporters at a cost of £500. Had it been by supporters alone, BR would have been grateful but not euphoric since the raison d'être for such groups was fund raising. Private sector funding was a different ball game, one company having given cash for BR's tourist railway, it seemed to me probable that others may do likewise. On the spot, I initiated, and announced, a project, to be externally funded, to paint coaches in pre-war GWR colours, repaint another loco, create "first class" and an observation car. I asked a guest, the manager of the Development Board for Rural Wales, if they would be sponsors. Within days they agreed to pay for the observation car conversion - the most expensive item. It was the first promise of funds. Knowing that the Wales Tourist Board had helped fund a Festiniog Railway extension, I asked Harold Naylor, Chief Executive of that Board for help for our "tourist railway". He agreed to match any private sector funds, £1 for £1. Within days, I contacted Shell, Westinghouse and Blundell Permaglaze who provided funds. Dyfed County and Ceredigion District Councils gave financial and other support. Within a year, the work was done and reported in "Railway World". I initiated this, whilst tackling, with my officers, many major issues in my Division - revenue generation, cost reduction and industrial relations. (This was the year of the Flexible Rostering dispute).

In a book on the Cambrian Railway, the Supporters Association claimed to have prompted BR to refurbish the trains. They also claimed to have urged repainting carriages in former GWR livery and to have paid for the first coach to be repainted. With main line trains and track crying out for investment, it would have been criminal to deploy scarce resources on this side show. BR couldn't get enough funds for things with a *guaranteed* return, much less for an unprofitable tourist attraction. BR paid *nothing* towards the work. Supporters did not initiate re-painting the stock. They offered £450 towards the total cost. It was not even the first offer of funds towards the project, and was not nearly enough to pay for one coach to be painted and represented 1.6% of the total sponsorship required, which I secured.

There were no letters from them, nor meetings with them advocating such action, nor time, since I put the plan in hand, on my *first* visit to Aberystwyth as Divisional Manager, within four weeks of my appointment. Prior to that, I had not even heard of the association. If they had been half as innovative as is claimed, they would have asked the Tourist Board to match the donations of Davies & Metcalfe and themselves for painting one loco. They lacked that vision - an opportunity missed.

Over the next two years, we marketed the line to increase revenue, but it remained unprofitable. Its biggest handicap was that we were unable to employ summer only traincrew and track staff. My officers produced a plan to re-organise the Cambrian line, to which it was geographically and historically linked. It involved rationalising traincrew depots, including Aberystwyth. The plan was opposed by local authorities and MP's. (See page 195). Summer only revenue did not support full time staff and all other costs. Consequently, I advocated that the Rheidol line should be sold, especially, as it now had a more attractive appearance, and traffic had risen. Sale took place a few years later.

## Cambrian Coast Line Action Group

Among the impractical, superfluous, uneconomic suggestions made by one of its members - who, I was told was a school teacher - in a letter to the media, not to BR, was:

- *BR should hold a loco at Machynlleth - on the Cambrian coast single line - on Summer Saturdays to cover possible failures.* (Even ignoring the heavy cost to this loss making line, and its limited value on a single line, BR had none spare to deploy in this way **anywhere**. *To be effective, it would also need a driver. To cover the whole day, would need two drivers*).

- *The line lacked publicity.* Councils had agreed to issue BR brochures. BR trained Tourist Board staff on railway travel and information and organised a competition for the best display of BR publicity. There was publicity in abundance. What the line lacked was usage. Some members of the Action Group and the Vale of Rheidol Supporters Association, had in the past, distributed leaflets in return for free travel. I decided it was not justified and directed that the practice must cease.

- *A lack of excursions was due to a shortage of locos.* It was not, they were invited to charter DMU excursions and pocket any profits, but did not do so.

- *Cheap Ranger tickets should be issued on Saturdays in July and August.* Trains were full! Income would fall and complaints rise.

- *BR had cash which could be unlocked by pressure from the local community.* A naive statement as independently audited BR Annual Accounts clearly showed.

He wrote, as if he had invented it: *BR should introduce Radio Signalling, which is being held up due to a lack of funds* BR developed it at Derby, where I went, two years before becoming aware he existed, to decide if it could be used in the London Midland Region. Its potential and limitations were evident to any railway operating manager. Of several possible locations, I decided that, if the system was approved by the MoT, we would try it on the Cambrian line, but asked for transferable equipment to be provided to avoid trains being tied to that line, since we ran through trains beyond Shrewsbury. There would be no problem with funds because we expected it to be self financing. It had been mentioned in BR's letter to the Cambrian News - *two months prior to his letter to that newspaper*.

His comments were neither constructive nor helpful and without financial justification, which BR has to establish. He advocated spending millions for an unknown return, leading to ruin and closure. We were trying to cut costs against external opposition. The line had been subject to several economy cuts. We had discussed new economies with staff on this line, which was costing £5 to operate for every £1 of revenue, the line having been subsidised by the taxpayer since 1968. It is a route which must have been unduly costly to operate in its heyday, and revenue in this rural area must have been very limited.

Often, objectors claiming that costs could be cut, quoted advice by *anonymous* experts or "consultants". It is puzzling why they were not named. The prospect of making a name for themselves, and securing business was a convincing case for free media publicity.

I tracked down one expert - quoted in Parliament. (See page 45). His plan was sent to the MoT by the MP who said that this document was the source of figures he quoted in Parliament, (see page 45). It would not have filled a page of this book. It envisaged:-

- A four wheeled vehicle, 30 feet in length, 8 foot in width, with capacity for 30 passengers seated, and 15 standing. It would be operated by an engine of 3 litre capacity, which would be suitable for severe gradients. (This engine would be twice the size of that used in a car to haul five people, compared to the 46 including the driver, this was supposed to carry!).
- Driving positions at each end, but no separate cabs. (*There are clear risks to safety in such a situation*).
- The Driver would collect fares from a ticket machine placed beside him.
- Driving, cleaning, ticket issuing & maintenance could be covered by not more than three men, and could well be covered by two.
- There would be provision for parcels. (*But no security. As he had dispensed with drivers' cabs, the only available space for parcels would seem to be between passengers' feet*).
- He quoted £8-9,000 for a prototype, at least one third less if ordered in batches of six.
- The costs of operation would be covered by fares of 2d per mile. (*The average fare then was 43% below that*).
- He quoted a precise cost of maintaining a vehicle which had yet to be designed.
- A ten mile line with a railbus costing £9,000, with six journeys each way per weekday covering depreciation, interest, wages and *allowing* £60 per mile pa for track maintenance would cost 15/- (75p) per journey.

Incredibly, the paper did not specify the weight of the vehicle, nor include working drawings. This was a double oversight, and doubtless the first such oversight, by an expert for a technical submission for any form of transport.

On 27th April 1956, The Chairman of the BTC replied to Archer Baldwin, MP, on the aspect of track maintenance: "You must believe me that he is a long way out. A ten mile line would cost between £3,000 & £5,000 pa, the higher figure includes renewals. Such a length of line would require four men". (That level of manpower was for ten track miles, on the basis that the hypothetical line was to be a single line to minimise costs).

The MoT wrote to an aide: "I would have hoped that he would mention some particular vehicle running in some part of the world where his estimates can be checked by practical experience". He hadn't, and neither had he quoted a source for his figures. MoT inquiries had revealed that this expert, Mr. F.T. Auld, had been manager of a coach station off Marylebone Road, which closed after four months operation following complaints from residents. After that, he was manager of Kings Cross coach station for a time.
[PRO: MT124/65].

Objectors or critics referred to Reports which, they claimed or inferred, undermined the validity of BR closure plans or challenged their basis. No details were given at all in three cases. In two cases, a brief reference to part of the text was made, but out of context.

### *Branch Line Re-Invigoration Society*
In 1962, after closure of the S&DR line was announced, it produced a report advocating:
- A new three mile section of railway, "whose cost would be high, but we believe that the operation would be profitable". (This rule of thumb conclusion defies belief, when objectors criticised BR figures and claimed BR did not apply business principles).
- Centralised signalling to replace 30 signal boxes on this 100 mile rural railway. (BR could not fund it on 100 miles of the West Coast main line north and south of Rugby! It was the most intensively used line in Europe. Centralised signalling at Swindon over 70 miles to replace 29 signal boxes cost £1.25m. [Shepton Mallet Journal 21.1.66]. The latter was busier, but items such as cable trunking & power supply would be as costly)
- Crossing gates replaced by automatic barriers or even only by cattle grids. (When local authorities and MP's were objecting to removal of traditional gates and keepers).
- In some cases, re-siting of stations was advocated, e.g. Glastonbury.
- Stations to be turned over to architects who can do a great deal through rationalisation, suitable use of paint and modern materials. (This displays a complete misunderstanding of the role and cost of architects, the consequences of diverting architects from main line modernisation, and totally ignores labour & material costs).
- Buses should be co-ordinated to bring people to stations. (Closures were opposed on grounds that, if a journey began by bus, they would not transfer to rail at a main line station, but now they argued that they would - at a branch and a main line station!).
- Seven daily trains should be run each way between Bournemouth/Poole and Bath, requiring four diesel multiple units.
- Station staff could work a 42 hour week on split shifts. (*If recruits could be found*).

There was no assessment of cost nor income. They "could not prove the existence of untapped revenue, but thought the commercial risk was worth taking".
- Traffic has not been sought by any method likely to produce it. (They did not itemise a *single* method which they believed would do so. BR was guilty till proved innocent).
- Within the "sales area", there were a million people. (10,000 per route mile. That was *three times* the ratio of population to route mileage for the rest of the country. A large proportion of the million, must have been well placed to use other routes).
- They listed "cities, towns and local authorities served by the S&DR". It totalled 807,900, of which over 50% was in Bristol. It required imagination to run wild to regard Bristol as being served by the S&DR, when it was on the former GWR and LMS main lines. To their million, they added those travelling from the Midlands to the South Coast. They had more than one route to the South coast, to which, in any case, they were not indefinitely wedded. If BR could influence passengers to other resorts which would produce more net income, it was their duty to do so.

- They conclude the potential is there. (but refrain from claiming potential for viability)
- They hazard a guess that the potential for parcels traffic is in six figures. (Whether this refers to *numbers* or *weight* or *money* was not clarified).
- "It may be that some freight traffic from Bristol for the south east could pass via the S&DR". (By definition, it was passing via other routes. This would denude other routes of traffic to prop up a line which was insolvent in the heyday of railways).

They urged locals to use the line or risk losing it. They "hoped to publish a supplement at a later date, when we shall examine the question of cost and finance generally".

Their 1963 Report, "*Unprofitable Railways? A financial study of certain railway passenger lines in Somerset, Dorset & Hampshire*", (which I found before that of 1962), made proposals for services on the "main line" and "branch line". The $73^3/_4$ mile "main line" was to be singled, with a weekday DMU service of 343,000 miles pa, giving 14.8 trains per day. *There was no timetable*. Anyone reading this Report, not having read the earlier one, would not realise that they envisaged seven trains each way. The viability of the "branch line" was dismissed by Ernie Cross (see page 175), who was praised by critics.

The capital cost of a DMU *vehicle* averaged £12,285 in 1961. [BTC 1961 Report, Tables V-8 & VII-5]. On that basis, a two car unit would be £24,570. Given 85% availability, (allowing for forecast time on maintenance), a spare was needed, requiring £122,850 capital, costing over £6,000 pa interest. Provision of facilities for fuelling & short notice repairs, a new three mile line, conversion of double to single, closing some signal boxes, conversion of stations to halts and re-location of Glastonbury station required capital, for which they allocated not a penny. They used track costs of £3,500 per mile from the Reshaping Report, [Page 9] - the minimum for a passenger line. They could not understand why BR track renewals would fall after year two. Clearly, *less were due after year two*! In any case, it made no difference, as forecast annual losses included *average* renewal costs.

They envisaged unstaffing 20 stations with one manager for the whole line. He would need a helicopter to enable him within reasonable time to institute special working in the event of a mishap or other problem. He would have no social life, given continuous on call requirement, which would not end when the service was not running. Who would cover him when sick, is not clear. Presumably someone from "*elsewhere*".

They said: "train working 'costs vary, but 4/- per train mile is a fair cost'". The reader would assume it was an average. It was the *minimum*. Costs were "4/- to 6/- per train mile, [20-30p], according to density of traffic on a lightly loaded branch with a single line". [Reshaping Report, Page 16]. They envisaged 5-10,000 passengers to cover costs. The Report shows costs of 5/- per train mile in that range. That increases *their* costs by 25%. Given a seasonal peak, it hardly counts as lightly loaded. A *fair* figure was above average.

Having calculated *their* working cost, but ignoring capital costs on which interest would arise, they proceed to reduce it. They postulate a total cost of £347,640 pa and deduct what they *assume* would be a *net* revenue contribution from parcels, mails and newspapers of £21,800 pa. They *assume* that freight will cover its own movement costs and contribute £25,900 to track and signalling. They advance no justification for these figures. This left a purely hypothetical £299,940 to be covered by passengers.

They stated that their net passenger train cost "could be covered by an average fare of 2d per passenger mile, equivalent to 8,040 passengers per week". That equates to 418,080 passenger journeys pa. At 2d per mile, that would produce £299,938 pa, *if* they travelled an average distance of 86.09 miles. The average fare per mile in 1963 was 1.97d, and the average journey was 20.86 miles. [BRB 1963 Annual Report, Table 5-A].

£299,940 at 2d per passenger mile represents 35,992,800 passenger miles. Their annual train mileage of 343,200 related to passenger miles, produces an average of 104.8 passenger miles per train mile, i.e. an average train load of almost 105, a figure that, like the average distance, was not mentioned. The average train load throughout BR in 1963 was 90.2 which included all urban commuter trains and inter city. [BRB 1963 Annual Report, Table 5-A]. In their report they note that BR loading figures for the line varied between 35 and 105 on a *summer weekday*. To achieve an average of 105 for *every* train mile on *every* weekday, means that some trains must be well above 105. During the holiday season, and in peak hours, some trains would have to carry substantially in excess of 105 to balance out trains which are, inevitably, lightly loaded. There would be standing in those peaks.

Perhaps realising this, they state there need only be "5,360 passengers per week at the standard 2nd class fare of 3d per mile, *or* an average train load of 64 passengers per train". Every adult & child would pay 3d per mile! The "standard fare" was the maximum adult fare. At 3d per mile and 5,360 pasengers, the average load would be 69.9. An average load of 64 gives £274,560. Either way, all would travel 86.09 miles. It was a day-dream to believe they would get passengers travelling four times the national average distance, at a fare 50% above the national average. Usually, BR was urged to *cut* fares by such groups. They try to justify their loads because the Reshaping Plan showed half the line was below 5,000, half above. Their lowest scenario is above 5,000 throughout.

At the average fare and average distance travelled on BR as a whole, passengers would need to be *four times* their lower figure even to cover the net costs, which they postulated after unproven deductions for other traffic. Moreover, *train costs should have been 25-50% higher*, (see page 223). No interest was included to cover capital works, (see page 222).

Their first Report was praised. (See page 176). Both were out of touch with reality. One is drawn to the oft repeated words "Accounts which would have been thrown out by a court of law". Having set out to prove the line could pay, they confirmed the reverse.

### Carrington

In the 1964 Hearings into the Isle of Wight closures, an objector mentioned "the Carrington formula, (see page 70). Sir William Carrington was a past President of the Institute of Chartered Accountants, asked by the MoT to study closure data on the advice of the current president of that Institute. The MoT said that "he had recommended minor alterations in the method of preparing the figures". [Hansard vol. 682, col. 253]. (See page 225).

He initiated no formula in his 1963 Report but stated: "*I personally chose a number of cases for examination, the non-profitability of which were abundantly clear beyond any possible doubt. I was very considerably impressed with the meticulous care with which the figures had been compiled. The Officers of the Board are exercising great care and diligence in order to arrive at the most accurate bases*". They were "*well founded and sound in principle". "Contributory revenue is a matter of subjective judgement".* He set out the information which the Board propose to give to TUCC's - annual receipts based on a sample count of passengers joining and alighting, direct costs, and renewals due over the next five years. He *did not recommend any change.* Critics who quoted him did not mention his complimentary comments nor his views on contributory revenue. (See page 33). (Critics believed that their *subjective judgement* should override that of professionals).

### Cohen

In the 1958 Hearings into the closure of the M&GN, reference was made to the "Cohen Report" by South Kesteven RDC. (see page 126). Their quote was taken from a lengthy paragraph. The *Council on Prices, Productivity & Incomes,* made its Second Report in August 1958. Its terms of reference were "to keep under review changes in prices & productivity and the level of incomes". Those who heard the remarks made in the M&GN Hearings would have assumed it to be a condemnation of railway closures. In fact in the 38 page report, only two of its 165 paragraphs mention railways - paragraphs 78 & 92 - and both relate to capital investment - the first to it being cut, and the second to it being relaxed to expand industrial production. The latter paragraph concerns the relaxation of restrictive measures imposed a year earlier on manufacturing industry to damp down inflation, and adds that industry was given a 50% increase in capital tax allowances.

The paragraph from which the objector made his selective quote was paragraph 114. It relates to wages increases "which should be met without a rise in the prices of their products". Contrary to popular opinion, BR was the last to be criticised for inflation - fare and freight rate increases, being subject to time consuming delays in the Court of the Transport Tribunal were trailing the inflation rate. (See *"Blueprints for Bankruptcy"*).

The RDC quoted from the second Report: "There has been a tendency in recent discussions to lump together economies obtained by producing services more efficiently and economies obtained by abolishing services as though they were the same thing ......... but from the point of view of the public, they are opposite things. Abolishing a service has the same effect as raising its price to a prohibitive level, with the convenient difference that no index number of the cost of living is affected". The paragraph does not mention BR at all. The RDC left out of the middle of the paragraph : *"on the grounds that they are means of paying higher wages without calling for a subsidy".* The paragraph goes on to say *"It by no means follows that greater harm is not done than by a rise in price. There is a presumption that the community is better off for having available to it any service which can be made to cover its costs at some price which it is willing to pay. A rigid rule against price increases could not be maintained in a sector where productivity grows slowly, without causing an unjustifiable elimination of wanted services".*

The comments applied to bus operators who reduced or withdrew rural services without an inquiry, and to industry which was ceasing to provide products which consumers needed. The comments applied to retailers squeezed out by supermarkets, and to local authorities. The public and the local authorities had made it quite clear, through objections to *any* increase in railway fares and charges, which were trailing the inflation rate, whilst BR had to pay inflated prices for its material purchases, that they were not prepared to cover branch line costs. Rural areas wanted inter city travellers, freight customers or underpaid BR staff to subsidise them. BR was not subsidised, only offered loans, hence there was no question of BR "calling for a subsidy". Indeed, the Chairman of the BTC was on record as being opposed to subsidies. [See "*Blueprints for Bankruptcy*", Page 49].

The RDC did not mention the paragraph which stated that "the excess of productive capacity consists of old and out-of-date plant, the expanded use of which would cause costs and prices to rise". The Cohen Report was referring to industrial capacity, but did not urge *them* to modernise, in contrast to branch lines, where critics never ceased to call for modernisation. The Report expressed concern that manufacturing prices which ought to be falling in response to reduced prices of imported materials were not doing so. They were also concerned that changes in the law on restrictive price agreements had strengthened the maintenance of resale prices! They defined a monopoly as a supplier controlling more than one third of the total supply. BR, which was merely one form of inland transport, moved about 25% in 1948, but its share had fallen since then.

### *Dartington Hall*
Objectors to the Stainmore line closure, (see page 143) referred to this Report, without tabling a copy. It was difficult to trace. It was a 28 page Report about rural buses & trains. Dartington Hall kindly supplied an extract, which included the following:-
- *If a line is retained for goods, running one passenger train for commuters and people joining main line trains may be justified.* (Lines retained for goods are down graded to reduce track & signalling costs. If passenger traffic is retained, there can be no down grading. One train per day could only be uneconomic).
- *More vigorous moves should have been made to overcome earlier the obligation to provide gatekeepers at public crossings. Experiments are being made with automatic barriers and these should prove valuable where little used lines cross little used roads.* (Relief was sought from the obligation even before the war, as costs were inflated by increased road traffic. Where little used lines cross little used roads, the typical provision was one resident keeper. Economy from their wages would not fund any form of modernisation. BR faced strong opposition to modern crossings, especially on lightly used lines : "Highway Authorities objected to control of level crossings by lights unless there were at least six trains per hour, 'as users of highways tended to disregard, when at red, such signals which were at green most of the time!'" [PRO: AN97/22, BTC minute 187]. Due to road user indiscipline, BR costs for crossing modernisation were substantially higher than was originally budgeted. See page 42).
- *Priority should have been given to building DMU's at the expense of main line diesel locos for a year or two.* (It would have caused losses of profitable main line business).
- *BR cannot afford to devote much of their limited capital to secondary lines while many main lines are in urgent need of attention.* (And even less so on branch lines).
- *Capital shortage for major works does not excuse BR for failing to make piecemeal economies.* (Such economies needed skilled labour & money to modify or remove equipment & assets, and/or train staff to undertake extra duties. *All* changes involved Consultation which cost time and money. Capital for minor works is from the same

source as main lines. No business would dilly dally making "piecemeal" economies over a period of years, to **reduce** losses, but would go for immediate total saving. To reduce, rather than **eliminate**, losses perpetuates insolvency.   See pages 35-37).

The Report forecast that *some subsidy for rural services will eventually be inevitable*. It was introduced for rail services, about eight years after the Report was written.

Had objectors tabled the Report, they may have been asked to fund it.

### Low Committee

The Select Committee on Nationalised Industries, published a report in March 1961. Its chairman was Sir Toby Low. It stated that the 1953 Act called for statements of Regional Accounts and Statistics as distinct from the Board's Annual Accounts. The Committee accept it is difficult to devise Regional Accounts. A firm of accountants had said it could not devise accounts within the meaning of consolidated accounts. Regional Accounts will not measure efficiency. They said that the existing system should be preserved. What the objector to the Barnard Castle-Penrith closure, who quoted this Report, (see page 144), failed to realise was, that the Committee was referring to audited Balance Sheets. Closures were based on an assessment of savings. The two are necessarily completely different. When a company believes that a part of their empire is losing money, they do not need to prepare a balance sheet for it, and have it endorsed by auditors - a task taking months - to conclude that they are throwing good money after bad.

The committee said "The BTC believe that a more compact system must be achieved quickly, and this Committee agrees with them. Branch line closures ..... are an essential part of the process of converting to a system suited to today's major needs".   "The consideration of profitability should be left to the BTC". "If Parliament specify that certain services should be undertaken, despite the fact that the BTC cannot profitably undertake them, the additional cost should be paid from public funds, and paid openly". [Paras 236, 239, 423-425]. Their comment on the unsuitability of railway statistics to compare each railway system related solely to the statistics which they listed, viz. : Wagon turnround, loads, train miles, punctuality.  They were not used in connection with closures. [Para 473 & Appendix].  Little wonder, the objectors did not table a copy of this Report.

### Reshaping Report

BRB's 1963 Plan, often referred to as the Beeching Plan.  It listed over 260 uneconomic passenger services to be withdrawn and nearly 2,000 stations which should be closed. They included withdrawals and closures already being progressed before the Report was prepared.  Some freight was identified as uneconomic. It was generally portrayed as dealing solely with closures, but it included proposals for the generation of new traffic.

### Serpell Report

The Serpell Committee produced a Report in 1982, setting out options for the future size of BR. The BRB published a response which castigated the committee's findings, many of which were not costed, whilst potential savings were inflated. The committee were too unsure of the basis to discuss it with BR. [See "Blueprints for Bankruptcy", Page 92].

*Society for the Re-Invigoration of Unremunerative Branch Lines in the U.K.*

On 10th November, 1956, they circulated a paper to all MP's, [PRO: MT113/5] calling for:-

- A list to be published of all loss making lines. (All closure submissions would be suspended for a year or so to examine every line. No other industry would have done so. The much maligned Beeching did so, but was criticised for delaying economies and creating uncertainty among freight customers. [See Pearson Pages 26 & 104]).

- An examination should be made of each one to see if there were prospects of improvement. (This *was* standard BR practice - see page 23. What seemed to escape the minds of amateurs, was that it was an easier and less frustrating course of action for managers to make a line pay, if it was feasible, than prepare a closure case and stand the hyper criticism and sarcasm which greeted almost every case).

- Where closure is recommended, suggestions should be invited, and trials conducted. A trial should last at least two years and embrace most of their ideas. (As all closures produced many suggestions - albeit impractical and ruinous - the task of considering ideas, which may be contradictory, from self appointed experts, unwilling to accept that *they* could possibly be wrong, would take years).

- Where trials fail to satisfy the BTC, the BTC to give long enough notice of intention to close and submit to a public inquiry. (It will be noted that there was an implicit belief that trials would *always* satisfy objectors. The period of notice was not defined).

- Before closing, an offer should be made to sell the line. (They made no offer to buy lines offered for sale in the Isle of Wight).

- In every closure, alternative transport to be provided.

- The BTC to be answerable to Parliament at every stage.

- Trains should have collapsible steps and run to the nearest large town to avoid having to change at junctions.

- Where stations are at a distance from the places they serve, light motor vehicles should meet trains. (The inference was that these would be "free". Their obsession with rural railways, where villages were some distance from a station, blinded them to the obvious - that most passengers using main line stations also live some distance from a station. They were equally entitled to be met by vehicles to take them home).

- Fares should be as cheap as buses. (They made a wrong assumption. This book contains evidence of bus fares which were higher than rail fares. On those routes, would they propose that rail fares be increased to match bus fares?).

- Freight services should be operated by light diesel locos. (For 2-3 wagons, the typical output from many lines. The cost would be prohibitive, and transits unacceptable).

- The growth of road transport has made awkwardly situated lines redundant, although "in some cases, a more enterprising attitude would have made road transport redundant". (To envisage the removal of *all* road transport in an area defies belief. In no closure case, did objectors suggest that road transport should be withdrawn instead of rail. It is an unrealistic scenario).

No £ sign appeared in their paper. This was surely not the way any other company conducts its business. They did not suggest who would pick up the tab for their social experiment. Despite its obvious weaknesses, some MP's gave support.

# Appendix C                    Local Authority "Productivity"

This table reveals *their* performance in cost control comparing 1948 with 1962, which mark the BTC era. Far from practising what they preached BR should do, they increased the Ratepayers' burden. [Source: Municipal Year Books except where all data not included in the 1948 Book: *from County & District Offices; #from 1950 Book as Local Authority records for 1948 are missing].

| Council | See Chapter | Rates per head of population £ 1948 | 1962 | Percentage increase |
|---|---|---|---|---|
| Alston RDC | 12 | 3.29 * | 9.11 | 277 |
| Barnard Castle UDC | 10 | 4.89 | 10.68 | 218 |
| Blandford Borough | 13 | 6.15 | 16.01 | 260 |
| Bourne UDC | 9 | 4.66 | 13.52 | 290 |
| Brightlingsea UDC | 6 | 4.79 | 9.81 | 205 |
| Cumberland | 4 & 12 | 3.84 | 9.31 | 242 |
| Darlington Borough | 10 | 7.84 | 15.08 | 192 |
| Denbighshire | 4 | 4.17 | 9.45 | 227 |
| Devon | 8 | 4.47 | 9.99 | 224 |
| Dorset | 4 & 13 | 5.07 | 10.52 | 207 |
| Durham County | 4 &10 | 3.04 | 7.82 | 257 |
| East Elloe RDC | 9 | 3.07 * | 6.50 | 211 |
| Erpingham RDC | 9 | 2.9 * | 7.84 | 257 |
| Essex | 4 & 6 | 5.45 | 11.22 | 206 |
| Haltwhistle RDC | 12 | 3.29 | 8.02 | 244 |
| Holland | 9 | 3.01 | 8.14 | 270 |
| Isle of Wight County | 4 & 5 | 5.13 | 13.81 | 269 |
| Isle of Wight RDC | 5 | 4.52 * | 15.32 | 339 |
| Kent | 4 & 11 | 5.60 | 12.37 | 221 |
| Norfolk | 4 & 9 | 3.15 | 7.81 | 248 |
| Northumberland | 12 | 2.97 | 8.38 | 282 |
| Penrith UDC | 10 | 6.79 | 13.73 | 202 |
| Sevenoaks UDC | 11 | 10.55 | 21.33 | 202 |
| Sevenoaks RDC | 11 | 5.96 | 13.51 | 227 |
| Somerset | 4 & 13 | 4.52 | 9.19 | 203 |
| South Kesteven RDC | 9 | 2.37 # | 7.77 | 329 |
| Spalding RDC | 9 | 2.30 * | 6.03 | 263 |
| Stoke on Trent | 14 | 5.90 | 13.65 | 231 |
| Sturminster RDC | 13 | 3.69 * | 8.88 | 240 |
| Ventnor UDC | 5 | 8.62 | 21.86 | 254 |
| Walsingham RDC | 5 | 4.10 | 8.80 | 215 |
| Westmoreland | 10 | 4.74 | 9.47 | 200 |

In contrast, in the same period, BR costs per passenger mile rose by only 33%, costs per route mile by 40% and fares by 40%, whilst the RPI rose by 61%. [BTC Annual Accounts]. None of the figures in this Appendix have been adjusted for inflation and, hence, are directly comparable.

# Sources

The greater part of the Chapters on individual closures is drawn from Closure papers and minutes of meetings of the CTCC and TUCC's. Where such information appears in Chapters 5 to 14 inclusive, without a source note, it is drawn from these papers.

The next major sources were from the Annual Reports of the BTC and BRB, Public Record Office files and Hansard (Commons). In the case of the BTC & BRB, the year of the Report and page or paragraph number is shown after the text. The Public Record Office file reference or the Hansard volume and column number are shown in each case after the text. Some data was found in the House of Lords Record Office and the National Railway Museum library, including the half yearly Accounts of the North Staffordshire Railway. Again the source is shown after the text.

Some material has been drawn from books by the same author, viz. : "*Blueprints for Bankruptcy*" (References are to the second edition), and "*Square Deal Denied*".

Information from the two documents prepared by Professor Hondelink, and referred to in Appendix A.2 :-
Suburban Passenger Services - Commuter traffic   [British Library, Shelf mark X515/22]
A Transport Plan for Scotland   [Scottish Record Office, DD17/1371].

Branch Line Re-Invigoration Society Reports referred to in Appendix B :-
Somerset & Dorset Railway   [British Library shelf mark 08236R29]
Unprofitable Railways?   [British Library shelf mark X510/224]

Information on the Westerham Railway Passengers Association meetings on page 161:-
[British Library shelf mark PP8002id]

Extracts from Proceedings of the Court of the Transport Tribunal on pages 202-203:
[Manchester Library PP380.1622.T1]

There are also various brief references to other books. The Author's name and page number are shown after the relevant text. The titles of their books and publications are shown with the authors' names and publishers on the following page.

In all other cases, sources are shown, after the text, thus, in [..........].

# Bibliography

Baker, A.C., : Potteries Loop Line. [Trent Valley Publications].

Barker, T.C. & Robbins M. : A History of London Transport. [George Allen & Unwin]

Blacker, Lunn & Westgate : London Buses, vol. 1. [H.J. Publications]

Brown, P. : Wivenhoe & Brightlingsea Railway. [Ian Henry Publications].

Burroughs, R.E. : The Great Isle of Wight Train Robbery. [Railway Invigoration Society]

Chapman, L. : Your Disobedient Servant. [Chatto & Windus]

Clark, M.J. : Railway World  (Ian Allan)

Cook, J. : The Sleaze File. [Bloomsbury Publishing]

Course, E.  : Railways - Then & Now.  [Batsford].

Deacon, T. : The Somerset & Dorset Railway -Aftermath of the Beeching axe. [Oxford Publishing]

Dow, G : Great Central, Vol. 3 (1900-1922). [Ian Allan].

Faith, N. : The World the Railways made. [Pimlico].

Fiennes, G.F. : I tried to run a railway.  [Ian Allan].

Freeman-Allen, G. : Modern Railways  (Ian Allan)

Grinling, C.H. : History of the Great Northern Railway. [Methuen].

Hawkins, M. : Somerset & Dorset Railway - Then and Now. [Patrick Stephens].

Henshaw, D. : The Great Railway Conspiracy.  [Leading Edge Press & Publishing]

Kingdom, A.R.: The Princetown Branch. [Oxford Publishing]. Republished as The Yelverton to
             Princetown Railway [Forest Publishing]

Kirby, M.W. : Origins of Railway Enterprise - Stockton & Darlington Railway. [1993, Cambridge
             University Press]

Newman, R. : Southern Vectis - The first 60 years. [Ensign]

Pearson, A.J. : The Railways and the Nation. [George Allen & Unwin]

Pratt, E. : British Railways & The Great War. [Selwyn & Blunt]

Rhodes, J. : Midland & Great Northern Joint Railway. [Ian Allan].

Rogers, H.C.B.:  Turnpike to Iron Road.  [Seeley, Service Co.]

Robotham, R. : The Last Years of the Great Central.  [Ian Allan].

Ruegg, L.H. : The History of a Railway. [The "Journal", Sherborne]

Sherrington, G.E.R. : Economics of Rail Transport in Great Britain, Vol. 2 [Edward Arnold].

Smiles, S. : The Life of George Stephenson. [Murray].

Walton, P. : The Stainmore & Eden Valley Lines. [Oxford Publishing]

Wood & Stamp : Railways. [Thornton Butterworth].

# INDEX

237

**The Author**

In 1946, Ted Gibbins joined the LMS as a junior, was a Station Master at 21, and ended as a Chief Officer with BR. His career took him to three Regions and Headquarters in London, serving in several Operating and General Management positions, before taking early retirement in 1987.

He has written two other books on railways :-

**"Blueprints for Bankruptcy", 2nd edition, 0-9521039-2-3, Published by Leisure Products**

How Government policies bankrupted BR. No industry in the private or public sector was subject to such interference & restriction. Ministers criticised BR for being unprofitable, when legislation required no more than "break-even". Worse, they enforced policies which ensured that BR could only make losses. In return Ministers offered interest bearing loans! No industry, however skilled its managers could have avoided bankruptcy. A Court of Law decided charges for 20 years, with interference by Ministers to make matters worse, and delayed increases for an aggregate 12 years! The Court reduced BR proposals on virtually every occasion. Fares trailed the RPI for 34 years. Despite this, BR was expected to modernise from revenue. The Watchdogs' role is highlighted, revealing 'U' turns, commercial unreality and some incomprehensible complaints statistics. Unreliable private sector equipment, industrial failures & public misconduct assisted BR's downfall.

*Railway Magazine - July 1996 :*
> An immensely thorough study of the industry, written by a professional railwayman.

*Chartered Institute of Transport - 1996, Proceedings Vol. 5, Nº 4 :*
> A healthy revision of the original, through access to more Government & BR papers, with some new and expanded chapters. The style is uncompromising and forthright. A remarkable collation of arguments which run contrary to conventional wisdom. Does not deserve to be neglected.

*Railway & Canal Historical Society Journal - July 1997 :*
> A store of missiles to hurl at Government policy. Reveals Government deliberately placed obstacles before railways & gave every opportunity to road haulage. Those opposed to privatisation will find useful material to support their case. A new aspect of British railway history. Comprehensive index. Paperback, well bound, does not fall apart with use.

**"Square Deal Denied" - 0-9521039-3-1, Published by Leisure Products**

Reveals the 18 year campaign which led to the 1938 demand by Britain's privately owned Railways for a "Square Deal", through three public inquiries, and to a final ineffective inquiry. Reveals facts held too long in the closed storerooms of the Public Record Office. Covers wartime sequestration and follows through to the date when Government eventually conceded equality to railways - regrettably too late to avoid the predictions of bankruptcy by Lord Stamp, President of the LMS.

*Railway World - June 1998 :*
> A myriad of convincing data. Many of his well thought-out arguments seriously question accepted concepts. A book for the serious student of transport politics, all must hope that scholarly works such as this will help to create a more level playing field in future.

*Chartered Institute of Transport "Proceedings" - 1998*
> The wealth of factual detail makes the arguments plausible and strong. The factual basis for Governmental bias is overwhelming. An excellent piece of factual research.

*Back Track - October 1998 :*
> Essential, not for just those with a narrow interest in railway history, but as an example of Government duplicity. A must (Rated Excellent by the magazine's reviewer)